Thomas Stearns Eliot
Poet

8

115

HOME
180   Ⓜ
181
186
212 *

Hogenson   75
129
147

4Q:
205
252

Virginia Woolf (Oliver and Boyd), 1963
Shakespeare: 'The Merchant of Venice' (Edward Arnold),
    1964
'The Waste Land' in Different Voices, ed. (Edward Arnold),
    1974
The Cambridge Companion to T.S. Eliot, ed. 1994

Thomas Stearns Eliot
Poet

A. DAVID MOODY
University of York

Second Edition

CAMBRIDGE
UNIVERSITY PRESS

Published by the Press Syndicate of the University of Cambridge
The Pitt Building, Trumpington Street, Cambridge CB2 IRP
40 West 20th Street, New York, NY 10011-4211, USA
10 Stamford Road, Oakleigh, Melbourne 3166, Australia

Printed in Great Britain at the University Press, Cambridge

A catalogue record for this book is available from the British Library

Library of Congress cataloguing in publication data

Moody, Anthony David.
Thomas Stearns Eliot / A.D. Moody. – 2nd ed.
p. cm.
Includes bibliographical references (p.) and index.
ISBN 0 521 46186 3 (hardback). – ISBN 0 521 46750 0 (paperback)
1. Eliot, T.S. (Thomas Stearns), 1888 – 1965 – Criticism and interpretation. I. Title.
PS3509. L43Z7874 1994
821'.912 – dc20 – 93 – 46172 CIP

ACKNOWLEDGEMENTS. The author and publisher would like to thank copyright owners for permission to reprint the following material:

T. S. ELIOT. The extracts from previously unpublished and uncollected sources, including material in The Hayward Collection, is reprinted by permission of Mrs Valerie Eliot and Faber and Faber Ltd., © Valerie Eliot. The pages from the *Syllabus of a course of Six Lectures* ... from the Hayward Bequest in King's College Library, are reproduced by permission of the Provost and Fellows of King's College, Cambridge.

The extract from *The Sacred Wood* is reprinted by permission of Faber and Faber Ltd.

Excerpts from *To Criticize the Critic* by T. S. Eliot, copyright © 1965 and copyright renewed © 1993 by Valerie Eliot; from *On Poetry and Poets* by T. S. Eliot, copyright © 1957 by T. S. Eliot and copyright renewed © 1985 by Valerie Eliot; from *Knowledge and Experience in the Philosophy of F. H. Bradley* by T. S. Eliot, copyright © 1965 by T. S. Eliot and copyright renewed © 1992 by Valerie Eliot; and from *The Elder Statesman* by T. S. Eliot, copyright © 1959 by Thomas Stearns Eliot and copyright renewed © 1987 by Valerie Eliot; all reprinted with the permission of Farrar, Straus and Giroux Inc. and Faber and Faber Ltd.

Excerpts from *Selected Essays* by T. S. Eliot, copyright 1950 by Harcourt Brace & Company and renewed 1978 by Esme Valerie Eliot; 'Song of Opherian' in *The Waste Land: A Facsimile and Transcript of Original Drafts including the Annotations of Ezra Pound*, copyright © 1971 by Valerie Eliot; from *The Idea of a Christian Society*, copyright 1939 by T. S. Eliot and renewed 1967 by Esme Valerie Eliot; from *Collected Poems, 1909–1962* by T. S. Eliot, copyright © 1963, 1964 by T. S. Eliot; and from *Collected Plays*, copyright © 1962 by T. S. Eliot and renewed 1990 by Esme Valerie Eliot; all reprinted with the permission of Harcourt Brace & Company and Faber and Faber Ltd.

The extract from *The Use of Poetry and the Use of Criticism* copyright © 1933 by the President and Fellows of Harvard College; © 1961 Thomas Stearns Eliot. Reprinted by permission of Harvard University Press and Faber and Faber Ltd.

RUDYARD KIPLING. 'The Appeal', copyright 1939 by Caroline Kipling, from *Rudyard Kipling's Verse: Definitive Edition*. Reprinted by permission of Doubleday and Company, Inc., Hodder and Stoughton and The National Trust.

ISBN 0 521 46186 3 hardback

ISBN 0 521 46750 0 paperback

TO MY PARENTS
EDWARD TABRUM MOODY
NORA (GORDON) MOODY

AND IN MEMORY
OF MY BROTHER
GORDON JOHN MOODY

Contents

Contents

Reproduced after chapter 2: Oxford University Extension Lectures, *Syllabus of a Course of Six Lectures on Modern French Literature* by T. Stearns Eliot, M.A. (Harvard), 1916

Acknowledgments

Many friends, teachers, colleagues and students have nourished and helped shape this work. They are its soil and climate. I recall in particular, with gratitude and affection, the more direct contributions of H. Winston Rhodes, Lawrence Baigent, Philippa Tristram, Ian Maxwell, Maggie Tomlinson, T. B. Tomlinson, Philip Brockbank, Owen Leeming, Faith Vernor-Miles, Jean Gooder, Richard Gooder, Adrian Adams, Nicole Ward, Anthony Ward, Elisabeth Grove, Robin Grove, Bernard Harris, Alan Charity, Brian Gibbons, and Helen Dennis. They enabled me to write my book.

Mrs T. S. Eliot, as Literary Executrix of her husband's estate, graciously permitted me to consult the unpublished material in the extensive collection of manuscripts, typescripts and printed editions of the writings of T. S. Eliot bequeathed by John Hayward to King's College, Cambridge; and also to consult the drafts of *Four Quartets* presented by Eliot to Magdalene College, Cambridge.

The late Dr A. N. L. Munby, as Librarian of King's College, did everything possible to advance my work there. His humane, wise and extraordinarily generous interest in it made him a most valued mentor. I am deeply appreciative also of the consistent helpfulness and kindness of his assistants, Dr John Saltmarsh, and Dr Penelope Bulloch, Archivist of the Twentieth Century Papers at King's.

The Librarians of Magdalene College very courteously showed me, at an inconvenient time for them, the drafts of *Four Quartets*; and the librarians in the Department of Western MSS of the Bodleian Library showed me the drafts of *Marina, Anabasis* and *The Rock*, and the Diaries of Vivien Eliot. From the Librarian of the University of York, Mr Harry Fairhurst, and from his librarians, I have received much indispensable assistance.

23 September 1977

Preface to the second edition

The first edition was published in 1979. In the 1980 paperback edition an essay on the drafts of *Four Quartets* was added as (Appendix D) and some errors and misprints were corrected. In this new edition a number of matters of fact have been revised in accordance with new information, and a few previously undetected misprints have been corrected. Appendix A, 'About the text of the poems', has been thoroughly revised, and has been expanded to take account of *The Complete Poems and Plays 1909–1950* (New York, 1952), and the most recent editions – the American as well as the English – of *Collected Poems 1909–1962*. There is a new appendix, on Eliot's dramatic verse, to supplement chapters 7 and 10.

I have not attempted to revise the substance of the book whether in the light of my own further reflections or that of more recent work by others. When one finishes a sustained piece of writing such as this, one is no longer the person who began it – one has been changed by the writing – and I have moved on further from it since 1979. There is a time for revising, and a time for letting well alone. I have continued to think and to write about Eliot, but from other angles and for other occasions, and these later essays and lectures form part of a separate project.

This book now belongs to anyone who reads it and makes it their own. My increasingly distant relation to it combines the caretaking of an editor with the vain care of the parent whose offspring is off on its own. Responsible for its existence but powerless to direct it, I can only follow its history with interest and detachment. It is gratifying to know that the book has found readers and recognition, and from people I respect. But how diverse readers are, and how different their readings! And how different, some of these, from what I thought I had written. It is fascinating, and very instructive, to observe what others can make of what one has done. The very first reactions made the point: the advisers to one university press were negative, even hostile; those advising another were wholly positive about the identical manuscript. The book was quite widely reviewed, in several countries and in various languages, and the reviews were nearly all generously favourable. Still, while it was said that 'Students of

Eliot are fortunate to have such a forceful and subtle account of a fine mind responding to the poetry of Eliot's verse' (*Year's Work in English Studies*), and that the book's 'major qualities are breadth of reference and meticulousness of analysis, carried out at a level which makes it essential reading for serious readers of Eliot's poetry' (*Critical Quarterly*), it was also said that 'as a poetry critic Moody is weak and usually dull; his research in this respect is questionable' (*Choice*). It was said that the book bullied Eliot, or that it bullied the reader; it was also said that it was too respectful of Eliot, and that it was urbane, sensitive and undogmatic. It was suggested that the experience of the poetry was missed in the analysis of the meaning; while another reader, a poet, wrote 'Never have I read anything on Eliot, nor in literary criticism in general, that so moved me as a poet both on the professional and personal level.' The range of judgments ran the full gamut from the first publisher's reader's outright rejection through to 'the best, the most far-reaching, the most perceptive, book on Eliot' (*THES*). In short, the book is whatever the reader can make of it. But it is probable that the equalising law of nature applies here as everywhere, and that those who get most out of the book are those who bring most to it.

One reviewer commented upon the 'orotund' title. I wonder how many readers have remarked that it is in fact a quotation – the source is given in full on p.2. It is hard to know what has been noticed and what not, nor indeed to what extent it matters. The 'Postlude' has been discussed, but I don't know if it has been noticed that it follows the inner form of Eliot's quartets. Doing it that way helped me immensely in making an end, but possibly it is of no significance beyond that. But the book's overall concern for form and structure is something that I would expect to receive more attention. Eliot composed in fragments, but he was always trying to make wholes out of his fragments, and his feeling for form was fundamental to his profound originality. To discover the forms of his poems – in the organisation of the two early collections, in *The Waste Land* and in *Four Quartets* – seemed to me as exciting and as rewarding as anything else in the book. I find that it is only when one arrives at an appreciation of the formal structure – what Eliot referred to often as 'the pattern' – that one can be confident of grasping the whole. The structure in question is of course a dynamic process, genetic rather than skeletal.

One aspect which a number of readers have found problematic is that of the relation of the private life to the published work. For some the book is too shy of using biographical information; while others have described it in all seriousness as 'biographical' or 'quasi-biographical' or 'biocritical'. I hope it is none of these latter, since I don't know enough about Eliot's private life to warrant featuring it in a study of his poetry, and since I did mean not to speculate about it. As for not making fuller use of biographical information, I am even more persuaded now than I was when writing the book that there are good reasons for reticence. Why did I not bring in Emily Hale? One reason is that we are not in possession of the relevant information, Eliot's letters to Emily Hale having been sealed until 2020, and her letters to him having been destroyed. We don't know what we don't know nor what a difference it might make. A second reason is that in any case Emily Hale cannot be certainly identified as a presence in his poetry. Those who would find her there are projecting a speculation upon its perfect and deliberate blankness in that respect.

There is an issue of principle here. If criticism is to be of any use it must know what it is talking about, and talk only of what it knows; and it must distinguish between different kinds of knowledge, and be careful about their relations. We have some knowledge of the facts of Eliot's life, and we have his poetry. The poetry is one thing, and the biography is something else; and any relations between them are invariably hidden from us and likely to be extremely complicated. The poetry does not give us the facts, having generally altered its facts out of all recognition. And for that reason the facts cannot account for or explain the poetry – the poetry is always going beyond the facts. If 'biocriticism' consists in reading the poetry as autobiography, and using biographical data to explicate poems, then it risks making chimerical findings.

Nevertheless the interest in the private life appears to be generally stronger than the interest in the poetry. What people really want to know about is the man behind the work. Even some critics who quite took the point of the Introduction and understood that the book is a work of literary criticism not literary biography, and that the life it is concerned with is the life of Eliot's poems, still homed in on the very few paragraphs which do touch upon his personal life. The nub of the problem would seem to be the difficulty of recognising that Eliot's *life* is most accessible to us, and in the most interesting respects only accessible to us, in the body of his poetry. It is of course a life transformed there into the medium of words, as Rembrandt in his self-portraits is transformed into paint – a profound transformation requiring a radical adjustment of our sense of the kind of life that is in question. I tried to clarify this in the Introduction, but even the clearest statement may leave the reader unaffected and still pursuing his or her own bent. I can only reiterate that I thought it both necessary and rewarding to restrict my study to Thomas Stearns Eliot *poet*.

In the course of writing the book I decided against registering my agreements and disagreements with other critics. There were various reasons for this, economy being the main one. Life is too short and the book was quite long enough without taking on Eliot's critics as well. But I also recognised that when one is intent on developing one's own line of argument one is not in a frame of mind to do justice to others', especially where they differ. Critics, in a more determined fashion than other readers, take from each others' books what serves their own immediate purposes; and what serves us best is to be able to differ. We pass over what does not bear upon our own line of interest, and what we agree with we take as confirmation of our own insight. But we are roused and stimulated by what is in our line of interest and deviates from it. There we find the error that calls for our correction, and the heresy that confirms our doctrine. Situating one's own work within the critical debate is the name of this game. But there is no real debate where one side is represented by the other and has not even a right of reply to defend itself against misrepresentation. What is really going on is a displacement of the other critics' work by one's own, or an enhancing of the power of one's work by associating it with that of others already established. Either way it has more to do with the politics of criticism than with the criticism of poetry.

These reflections are prompted by what seem to me to be misreadings or misrepresentations of this book in John Paul Riquelme's *A Harmony of Dissonances* (1991) and Jeffrey Perl's *Skepticism and Modern Enmity* (1989). Both have their own intellectually ambitious projects in hand, and it is not to be expected that they could give full and accurate accounts of the many books by others which they notice. But then what exactly is the value of their looking at them only through the apertures of their own preoccupations and with a view to justifying their own arguments? Perl cites my work because he needs an example of recent 'counter-humanism'. That is a label I don't wear, and which won't stick when the evidence consists of a few phrases torn from their contexts and jumbled together, and the attribution to me of a view I did not express and wouldn't hold. The feeling lingers that Mr Perl was too busy with his own argument to have time to attend properly to mine. John Paul Riquelme, having a different objective, labels the book rather differently as one of those which 'operate on implicit Romantic assumptions that lead at times in directions antithetical to Eliot's own'. But he fails to record that on the matter he is concerned with – the rejection of the Romantic idea of personality – the book closely follows Eliot's own thinking, and even his formulations; and that its explicit argument derives from tracing Eliot's anti-Romantic fashioning of another order of being 'in the realm of metaphysics and poetry'. He misses altogether the crucial distinction between an actual personality and an organisation sought after and fashioned in language. Had he noticed that he might not have made so much of our differences.

Over the years I have read a great amount of Eliot criticism, though far from the whole of it, and I have profited from it immensely: partly by having my mind opened to things I would not have seen for myself, partly by being provoked to work out my own ideas more coherently, and partly too from having the support of a micro-culture within which to work. I have absorbed more than I could begin to acknowledge, so much of the assimilation having been unconscious. Who can say where their own thinking ends and begins? (How much, for one instance, do I owe to Anne C. Bolgan's expert and undervalued *What The Thunder Really Said* (Montreal, 1973), which I came across when I was working out my own parallel but much less developed understanding of what Eliot had taken from F. H. Bradley?) What Eliot wrote in 'Tradition and the Individual Talent' applies at least as much to critics as to poets. If we have anything new or particularly worthwhile to say it is because we are the beneficiaries of what has been said already. One can only repay these debts by building on what one has borrowed. And when I come upon unacknowledged traces of this book in others' work I reflect, after the twinge of possessiveness, that in the realm of the mind just as in its realm of language, all things are held in common and property is indeed theft. The life of the mind depends upon the free circulation of thought, and upon the rapid absorption of others' ideas into our own. Thought is individual or it is dead – some one must always think it.

That applies *a fortiori* to poetry – its real existence is in the minds of its readers, and that is how it has a continuing life. Naturally therefore it will change as it passes from the mind of one time to another. This is where the recent work of some critics, Perl and Riquelme among them, is of particular interest as signalling the emergence of a new Eliot for the end of the century. In the 1920s there was the Eliot of *The Waste Land*, supposedly expressing the disillusionment of his generation, and being *poeta non grata* to the literary establishment. Later there was 'the literary dictator' of 'The Age of Eliot', supposedly confirming its critical and cultural anxieties and certitudes, and therefore requiring to be dethroned and debunked. Now, in the moment of indeterminacy and hermeneutics, we have a sceptical Eliot to nourish our faith in incertitude and non-closure, though with the unreconstructed Eliot still a target or fulcrum for the politically correct. The new Eliot is a necessary and welcome one, a genuine extension of our interpretation of his work, and so a continuation of its work of interpreting our world. Having tried in this book to clarify and define my own comprehension of his achievement, I would now attend more to what is not finally resolved in his poetry, to its irreducible contradictions, to its wisdom that opens the mind to what it does not grasp, to its mysteries that are only made the deeper by our elucidations.

The climate of literary studies has been somewhat destabilised in the fifteen years since this book was written. Now it is said, and by some professors of literature, that literature has no power and is of no value, though they will nonetheless denounce its power to reinforce the bourgeois structure of values which produced it. The death of the author has been proclaimed by authors who sign their proclamations with their own names, and the literary work has been displaced by their self-recycling discourse. From the site of the ivory tower of literature there rises a babel of warring jargons. I have no doubt that literature will survive, with or without the support of those who profess it. Eliot's poetry will survive. It has the focused and intensified mental power which only art can generate, a power to form and to focus the minds of those capable of experiencing it, and to develop in them a heightened sense of what it is to live and of what is worth living for.

Basic to this book are the twin convictions that that power is vital to us, vital to our ability to be intelligent about things, and that to draw upon it we need to commit ourselves to the experience of the poetry. There can be nothing passive about this commitment – and the effect is not to be had by being simply taken over by the poetry and letting our feeling and thinking be determined by Eliot's. We must actively perform the work in our own minds in order to be possessed by it, and we must be possessed by it in order to be restored to ourselves in a renewed and heightened state. A complete experience of a poem would be one in which we were the poem while the poem lasts, and simultaneously fully conscious critically of what it was doing, so that giving ourselves up to it and discovering our own point of view were but the two phases of a single activity. Criticism such as this book offers is an attempt to record the process by which the mind may be brought into a certain focus by the poetry, and so to bring the poetry into focus for other readers. But it cannot give the reader an experience of the poetry – every reader must experience the poetry at firsthand. Readers of this book will therefore find it helpful, even necessary, to keep Eliot's poems open alongside it. Its aim is to send them back to the poetry with an aroused sense of what they might find in it for themselves. In that way it may make a contribution to the survival of poetry and of its order of intelligence.

21 January 1994

Introduction

The 'Thomas Stearns Eliot' of my title is a collection of writings, and the 'Poet' is the author within his poems. For his readers Eliot now is an *oeuvre*, just as Shakespeare is. Of course we do know something of the man he was, and more is bound to come out; but the value of such knowledge is rather like that of knowing, when reading Homer, that Troy actually existed. Poetry, Aristotle said, is more philosophical than history – or than biography, we may add: seeking 'the universal' in the particular event, it tells the story differently, or it can tell another story altogether. Eliot's poetry is made up out of what the man lived through; but the *poet* we come to know in it is an elected self, a personality deliberately fashioned in the medium of language, and whose only real existence is in the poetry. This is not to say that the poet has no relation to life. On the contrary, being detached from the private and particular experience of one man, he becomes like the hero of a drama, one who outstandingly represents – and perhaps carries to excess – something characteristic of other lives and times beside his own.

There is a good introduction to Eliot's poetry in his 'Brief Introduction to the Method of Paul Valéry'. 'One is prepared for art', he wrote, 'when one has ceased to be interested in one's own emotions and experiences except as material'; then, he added, 'not our feelings, but the pattern which we make of our feelings is the centre of value.' In this process the ordinary personality is 'extended and transformed by the poet's superior organisation', which is 'impersonal in the sense that personal emotion, personal experience, is extended and completed in something impersonal – not in the sense of something divorced from personal experience and passion. No good poetry is the latter . . .'. [1] Another formulation of this view is of great interest for the glimpse it gives of the kind of personal experience and passion which Eliot himself was concerned to extend and complete in something impersonal:

What every poet starts from is his own emotions. And when we get down to these, there is not much to choose between Shakespeare and Dante. Dante's railings, his personal spleen – sometimes thinly disguised under Old Testamental prophetic denunciations – his nostalgia, his bitter regrets for past happiness – or for what seems happiness when it is past – and his brave attempts to fabricate something permanent and holy out of his personal animal feelings – as in the *Vita Nuova* – can all be matched out of Shakespeare. Shakespeare, too, was occupied with the struggle – which alone constitutes life for a poet – to transmute his personal and private agonies into something rich and strange, something universal and impersonal. The rage of Dante against Florence, or Pistoia, or what not, the deep surge of Shakespeare's general cynicism and disillusionment, are merely gigantic attempts to metamorphose private failures and disappointments.[2]

That is not true of all poetry – Ezra Pound's is one notable exception – and it smacks rather of the Romantic view of the artist which Eliot was struggling against. Yet it does tell us something true and important about his own art, and it is more deserving of attention than the over-publicised assertion of the separation in the artist of 'the man who suffers and the mind which creates'.[3] Eliot's poetry begins, like Yeats', 'In the foul rag-and-bone shop of the heart', and it seeks 'those masterful images' which grow 'in pure mind'. Its method is to observe himself and the whole world of his experience with passionate detachment, and to fashion out of his observations 'an individual and *new* organisation'.[4]

This ideal organisation is actually and immediately present to us in the poetry – it is precisely the business of poetry to make it so. When the Duke in *Measure for Measure* exhorts Claudio to 'Be absolute for death' he is merely practising the Friar's rhetorical skills. The voice of real conviction is heard in Claudio's protest to Isabella –

> Aye, but to die, and go we know not where,
> To lie in cold obstruction, and to rot,
> This sensible warm motion to become
> A kneaded clod, and the delighted spirit
> To bathe in fiery floods . . .[5]

Eliot's poetry attains that quality of conviction – but it is of the Duke's persuasion:

> The only hope, or else despair
>   Lies in the choice of pyre or pyre –
>   To be redeemed from fire by fire.

There is a world of difference between merely saying something, and really meaning it: and Eliot's poetry really means its meaning. His way of saying the things that matter to him is so resolved that they *are* him.

The things he has to say must be reckoned with therefore as in the realm of character, and not as ideas and beliefs merely. The ideas, to adapt a phrase of Pound's, have gone into action. For this reason the 'problem of poetry and belief', which haunts Eliot's criticism and that of some of his critics – and, indeed all attention to his thought and theory as something outside and apart from his poetry – seems to me a distraction from the serious business of coming to terms with a powerful and (for many of us) more or less alien mode of being. The poetry is a comprehensive and coherent articulation of sensibility, which would make us see the world and ourselves in a certain way, and which would have us live in the light of its vision. To treat it as if it were merely thinking about things is not only to mistake its nature, but to underestimate its potency in the minds of its readers.

I concur with the younger Eliot who was primarily a poet, against the older Eliot who, speaking rather as a prudent moralist, recommended that Christian readers 'scrutinize their reading with explicit ethical and theological standards'.[6] His earlier idea of the Perfect Critic was that he should look 'solely and stead-fastly at the object' – 'he must simply elucidate: the reader will form the correct judgment for himself'.[7] There is a useful statement of the principle in an unreprinted essay:

The work of the critic is almost wholly comprehended in the 'complementary activities' of comparison and analysis. The one activity implies the other; and together they provide the only way of asserting standards and of isolating a writer's peculiar merits. In the dogmatic, or lazy, mind, comparison is supplied by judgment, analysis replaced by appreciation. Judgment and appreciation are merely tolerable avocations, no part of the critic's serious business. If the critic has performed his laboratory work well, his understanding will be evidence of appreciation; but his work is by the intelligence not the emotions. The judgment also will take place in the reader's mind, not in the critic's explicit statement.[8]

Though it is rather austere – criticism does after all, naturally and necessarily, begin in experience and end in judgment – that account of the critic's business seems to me absolutely right in its emphasis. I would further enforce it with Pound's dictum that criticism can be substantive just so far as it is technical. In a poem everything is in the way the words work.

Yet shouldn't the critic have his axe to grind? Of course he should, as Eliot did, and Pound also.[9] And I have mine. But what is the critic's axe if it is not clearsightedness? To make good that saying we need to borrow Marvell's witty shift, in 'He . . . with his keener Eye/The Axes edge did try', from axe to *acies*, meaning sharpness of eye and insight: what the critic has to say is all in what he can see. It pays him to 'keep himself out of it'. The keener eye is dulled by seeing only what it likes and looks for; it is itself plucked out by a refusal to admit what offends it; but it achieves power over the things that vitally concern it by seeing them for what they are.

The first chapter of the study that follows is not criticism, but a version of Eliot's own introduction to his mind and art. Scattered among his writings are a surprising number of statements about his development and experience as a poet, and I have edited a representative selection of these into a kind of ghosted autobiography of the poet. The latter part of the final chapter is not strictly criticism either, but rather – taking off from Eliot's own retrospect in his late plays – the *hommage et tombeau* of the critic to the poet.

The rest of the book is a critical study of Eliot's life-work in poetry. The five parts mark the main stages in his development: the early originality; the years of personal crisis which found its fullest expression, and an initial resolution, in *The Waste Land*; the fashioning of a transcendent and increasingly assured poetic self in *The Hollow Men* and *Ash-Wednesday*; the perfection of that self in *Burnt Norton,* which in 1935 he thought was the end of his poetry; then, in the wartime Quartets, the final expansion of the poet into the protagonist of an ideal English and European culture. An account of Eliot's thinking about poetry is given in the course of the book, as the poetry calls for it and can be elucidated by it; overall this amounts to a fresh synthesis of his poetics, and leads to a clearer understanding of his quartet structure. His thinking about society assumes importance in chapters 7 and 9: the former dealing with his attempt in the plays of the 1930s to have 'some direct social utility';[10] the latter with his one effective political work, the three wartime Quartets. The appendix 'The Christian philosopher and politics between the wars' clarifies the sense in which he may be regarded as a political philosopher: the complete statement of his politics, I suggest, is to be found in his poetry.

A poet struggling to transcend himself – a poet of his time who was yet deeply opposed to it – such paradoxes are of the essence of the Eliot who emerges in this study. In the crises of his life he sought the solution of self-transcendence; and in the crisis of his society it was again to the way of self-transcendence that he bore witness. He wished to achieve what Yeats called 'Unity of Being'; and he knew, as Yeats did, that this was inseparable from 'Unity of Culture'. But because he was divided in himself, and because his culture was alien to his spirit, he was driven to devote much of his energy to what he termed the 'negative aspect of the impulse toward the pursuit of beauty' – that is, to the intensification of 'the death motive . . . the loathing and horror of life itself'. The sick side of this is most evident in some of the minor poems and rejected drafts. Yet in the best of the finished work the sickness is transformed by the positive aspect of the impulse towards the ideal. The difference this makes is the strange and shocking one of his insisting all the more upon sickness and death, only not as the ultimate reality, but as the necessary way to eternal health and life. His positive is not a turning away from the negative, but a passing through it. 'I should be very glad to be joyful,' he remarked when reviewing a book by G. K. Chesterton, 'but I should not care for any joy to be obtained at the price of surrendering my life's experience.'[11] An even more revealing statement occurs in the typescript of a speech given at Brussels in 1949: 'I think that the world – or that part of humanity which thinks, feels and reads – is now better prepared for literature which offers a hope so different from worldly optimism, a hope springing from renunciation of this world, a hope inseparable from a despair so different from that of the nihilists.' It is upon the hope born of negation that the struggle for personal integrity and cultural unity which is the life of his poetry was founded.

The poetry concerns us all, not because it is true or false, but because Eliot's mastery of our language makes his life-work a potent fact in the culture of the English-speaking world. His poetry has a power in our minds, through the authority of its diction and rhythms and images, to enforce certain meanings and feelings, and to suppress others. It has this power, of course, only because it is drawing upon meanings, and habits of feeling and perception already established in the language, and so in our mentality. Its potency is for animating a deep-rooted tradition of the common mind. We may like to think that Eliot's Mind of Europe is not ours; but very few of us can call our minds altogether our own. When Eliot writes of 'heaven and damnation/Which flesh cannot endure', we know immediately and inwardly what he is saying whether we share his beliefs or not. It is the same with his 'spirit' which he would have enter 'that refining fire/Where you must move in measure, like a dancer': we may prefer Yeats' (and Valéry's) vision of the unified being of the dancer; but I suspect that Eliot's lines impose themselves upon us with weightier authority. We can become free of him – free to accept his vision, or to seek another – only by seeing his poetry as in itself it really is.

I

The growth of the poet's mind

There is so much memory in imagination[1]

For Eliot being a poet meant to be always incorporating the past into a present self. And not merely his own past life, but that of his ancestors and of the race. The mind in his poetry is composed of all that memory could recover and imagination order: the mind of one man, but a man extraordinarily mindful of the whole reach of his history back to its remotest origins.

In 1668, shortly after the failure of the Puritan Commonwealth, and the restoration of the monarchy and the Anglican Church, a cordwainer named Andrew Eliot emigrated from the Somerset village of East Coker to the Massachusetts Bay Colony in New England, then and for some future time a Puritan theocracy.

About 1834, when the New England Calvinism was being tempered and transformed by Unitarianism, his descendant, the Reverend William Greenleaf Eliot D.D., went out from Boston to St Louis on the Mississippi River to found a Unitarian church there. His second son, Henry Ware Eliot (1841–1919), married in 1868 Charlotte Stearns (1843–1930), daughter of a Boston trader whose ancestor had been one of the original settlers of the Bay Colony. Their seventh and last child, born 26 September 1888, was Thomas Stearns Eliot.

He was to devote his life to the cultivation of 'a Catholic cast of mind', while acknowledging 'a Calvinistic heritage, and a Puritanical temperament'.[2] About the more primitive aspects of the heritage he could be wry. Where Ezra Pound had declared that none of William Carlos Williams' immediate forebears had burnt witches in Salem, Eliot appended a dry editorial note: 'We didn't burn them, we hanged them.'[3]

Other aspects of his origins concerned him more deeply. In arranging for his ashes to be buried in the west end of the Anglican parish church of East Coker, he was completing a pattern consciously given to his life. It is the pattern embodied in *The Dry Salvages*, which, he once said, 'begins where I began, with the Mississippi; and ends, where I and my wife expect to end, at the parish church of a tiny village in Somerset'.[4] A tablet on the wall there now reads:

> 'in my beginning is my end'
> Of your charity
> pray for the repose
> of the soul of
> Thomas Stearns Eliot
> Poet
> 26th September 1888 – 4th January 1965
> 'in my end is my beginning'

That puts it in the language of *Four Quartets* and the Catholic faith. On another level of feeling he found it expressed in Kipling's 'The Recall', a poem which went with a story about an American couple 'who settle in the village from which the wife's family had gone to America'[5]:

> I am the land of their fathers.
> In me the virtue stays.
> I will bring back my children,
> After certain days.
>
> Under their feet in the grasses
> My clinging magic runs.
> They shall return as strangers.
> They shall remain as sons.

There were many levels of emotion and idea in his becoming a naturalised British citizen, and being baptised, confirmed and buried in the Church of England. Nor was he renouncing his American background and upbringing. Rather, in returning to ancestral origins he was expanding his American into a European self. And the American child persisted in the older man.

Speaking as a sixty-five-year-old public man at the centennial of the university his grandfather had helped to found, he recalled how he had been brought up in the code of conduct which Dr Eliot had laid down, and particularly in the law of public service to 'Religion, the Community and Education'. He added that he thought it 'a very good beginning for any child, to be brought up to reverence such institutions, and to be taught that personal and selfish aims should be subordinated to the general good which they represent'.[6] One can glimpse that child in the schoolboy who instinctively preferred the *Aeneid* to the *Iliad:*

The obstacle to my enjoyment of the *Iliad,* at that age, was the behaviour of the people Homer wrote about. The gods were as irresponsible, as much a prey to their passions, as devoid of public spirit and the sense of fair play, as the heroes. This was shocking...
All this may seem to have been simply the caprice of a priggish little boy. I have modified my early opinions – the explanation I should now give is simply that I instinctively preferred the *world* of Virgil to the *world* of Homer – because it was a more civilized world of dignity, reason and order.[7]

At seven that little boy had concluded his brief life of George Washington: 'And then he died, of corse. He was never said to say *a lie*. He died at Mt Vernon.'[8] With hindsight we perceive there the indelible impress of the family code upon his individual temperament.[9]

However, it is not in this realm of conscious standards that poetic talent develops, so much as in the secret inner world of feeling nourished by spontaneous interests and immediate experiences. A child's reading is formative; and beyond that is 'the whole of his sensitive life'.[10]

'I was, I think, pretty well grown up before I began to appreciate Shakespeare,' Eliot told the students of Concord Academy. 'We start by being carried away by one particular poet: for me, at the age of fourteen, it was Fitzgerald's "Omar Khayyám" '.[11] He wrote then 'some very gloomy quatrains in the form of the *Rubáiyát*'.[12] Another 'first boyhood enthusiasm' was Byron, whose *Don Juan* he imitated in verses 'tinged with that disillusion and cynicism only possible at the age of sixteen'.[13] Other poets whom he had discovered for himself in childhood, and with whom he felt therefore a personal intimacy, included Shelley, Rossetti and Swinburne, 'and smaller men too, like Ernest Dowson'.[14] Kipling, he said in 1958, 'has accompanied me ever since boyhood, when I discovered the early verse – "Barrack Room Ballads" – and the early stories – "Plain Tales from the Hills" '.[15]

The mature Eliot was to speak of this as the first, adolescent phase in the development of taste and critical judgment; a time when 'I was swept with enthusiasm for one author after another, to whichever responded to the instinctive needs at my stage of development'.[16] And that was the right way to begin, for 'Taste begins and ends in feeling. . . [It] is an organisation of the immediate experiences obtained in literature, which is modified in its shape by the points of concentration of our strongest feelings, the authors who have affected us most strongly and deeply'.[17] Other greater poets were shortly to possess his imagination – Laforgue, read when he was twenty, the first really deep influence for his own poetry; and Dante, 'the most persistent and deepest influence', from 1910 to the end. His taste would become 'an ordered system of perception and feeling', informed by 'that critical ability, that power of self-criticism, without which the poet will do no more than repeat himself to the end of his life'.[18] But the consciousness of critical standards would have been a vanity without the passionate experience of the literature which set them.[19]

Before that there must be the passionate experience of life: 'a writer's art . . . must be based on the accumulated sensations of the first twenty-one years'.[20] In 1930 Eliot wrote this sketch of his childhood for a St Louis newspaper:

As I spent the first sixteen years of my life in St Louis, it is evident that St Louis affected me more deeply than any other environment has done. These sixteen years were spent in a house at 2635 Locust street, since demolished. This house stood on a large piece of land which had belonged to my grandfather, on which there had been negro quarters in his time; in my childhood my grandmother still lived at a house at 2660 Washington avenue, round the corner. The earliest personal influence I remember, besides that of my parents, was an Irish nursemaid named Annie Dunne, to whom I was greatly attached; she used to take me to my first school, a Mrs Lockwood's . . . The river also made a deep impression on me; and it was a great treat to be taken down to the Eads Bridge in flood time. . .

And I feel that there is something in having passed one's childhood beside the big river, which is incommunicable to those who have not. Of course my people were Northerners and New Englanders, and of course I have spent many years out of America altogether; but Missouri and the Mississippi have made a deeper impression on me than any other part of the world.[21]

The New England background was important too. The Eliot family had a vacation house at Eastern Point, East Gloucester, Massachusetts, near Cape Ann, and not far from Beverley and Salem where Andrew Eliot had settled. Eliot wrote in 1928:

The family guarded jealously its connections with New England; but it was not until years of maturity that I perceived that I myself had always been a New Englander in the South West, and a South Westerner in New England. . . In New England I missed the long dark river, the ailanthus trees, the flaming cardinal birds, the high limestone bluffs where we searched for fossil shell-fish; in Missouri I missed the fir trees, the bay and goldenrod, the song-sparrows, the red granite and the blue sea of Massachusetts.[22]

Looking back over the whole of his work Eliot remarked that 'in its sources, in its emotional springs, it comes from America'.[23] But as to specific images from these early experiences, it is remarkable how gradually they come to the surface in his poetry, and that it is in the later work that they are most fully realised. He himself observed (in his 1930 reminiscence quoted from above) that 'as one gets on in middle life the strength of early associations and the intensity of early impressions become more evident'. This is something other than the reversion of the aged mind to childhood memories. It is a case of experience having to undergo a long immersion in the unconscious mind to become metamorphosed into poetic material.

However, one area of his experience seems to have been more immediately available to the young poet. 'Preludes', 'Rhapsody on a Windy Night' and other early poems reflect a world he knew.

In St Louis, my grandmother . . . wanted to live on in the house that my grandfather had built; my father, from filial piety, did not wish to leave the house that he had built only a few steps away; and so it came to be that we lived on in a neighbourhood which had become shabby to a degree approaching slumminess, after all our friends and acquaintances had moved further west. And in my childhood, before the days of motor cars, people who lived in town stayed in town. So it was, that for nine months of the year my scenery was almost exclusively urban, and a good deal of it seedily, drably urban at that. My urban imagery was that of St Louis, upon which that of Paris and London have been superimposed.[24]

That superimposition was partly a matter of borrowing effects from Baudelaire and *Bubu of Montparnasse,* and from Dickens and Conrad. This makes it less of an exception to the generally slow process by which personal experience becomes charged with deeper significance.

In fact Eliot's earlier poetry can appear almost wholly dependent upon literary resources. His own feelings and experiences could find expression at first only through the medium of other poets. This brings us to a further aspect of his growth as a poet. When he was just beginning to write verse, as a young man at Harvard, 'there seemed to be no immediate great powers of poetry either to learn from or to rebel against' –

A very young man, who is himself stirred to write . . . is looking for masters who will elicit his consciousness of what he wants to say himself, of the kind of poetry that is in him to write. The taste of an adolescent writer is intense, but narrow: it is determined by personal needs. The kind of poetry that I needed, to teach me the use of my own voice, did not exist in English at all; it was only to be found in French.[25]

Specifically, 'the form in which I began to write, in 1908 or 1909, was directly drawn from the study of Laforgue'.[26] The later Elizabethan dramatists also helped – 'Marlowe and Webster and Tourneur and Middleton and Ford'.[27] But it was to Laforgue that he owed 'more than to any one poet in any language'.[28]

Although he was not writing about himself explicitly, nor of Laforgue, this account of how the dead may speak through the living voice must describe his own experience:

This relation is a feeling of profound kinship, or rather of a peculiar personal intimacy, with another, probably a dead author. It may overcome us suddenly, on first or after long acquaintance; it is certainly a crisis; and when a young writer is seized with his first passion of this sort he may be changed, metamorphosed almost, within a few weeks even, from a bundle of second-hand sentiments into a person. The imperative intimacy arouses for the first time a real, an unshakeable confidence. That you possess this secret knowledge, this intimacy, with the dead man . . . is a cause of development, like personal relations in life. . .

We do not imitate, we are changed; and our work is the work of the changed man; we have not borrowed, we have been quickened, and we become bearers of a tradition.[29]

The suddenness and completeness of Eliot's own transformation can be seen in the *Poems Written in Early Youth*. The five first printed in the *Harvard Advocate* between May 1907 and January 1909 are conventional late blooms of English romanticism. He discovered Laforgue in December 1908, and the poems written after that – 'Nocturne', 'Humouresque', 'Spleen', 'Conversation Galante' are all of 1909 – immediately assume the new tone of ironic detachment. In the following year he wrote the first two 'Preludes' and 'Portrait of a Lady'; and the year after that 'The Love Song of J. Alfred Prufrock'. The speed with which Eliot had modernised his poetry, as Ezra Pound understood when he saw these poems in 1914, remains quite astonishing. Within three years, between the ages of twenty and twenty-three, he had effected a poetic revolution equal to that of the *Lyrical Ballads*.

Then there was the lesson of Baudelaire:

From him, as from Laforgue, I learned that the sort of material that I had, the sort of experience that an adolescent had had, in an industrial city in America, could be the material for poetry; and that the source of new poetry might be found in what had been regarded hitherto as the impossible, the sterile, the intractably unpoetic. . .

Fourmillante Cité, cité pleine de rêves,
Où le spectre en plein jour raccroche le passant . . .

I knew what *that* meant because I had lived it before I knew that I wanted to turn it into verse on my own account.[30]

To these literary influences, Eliot added in 1910–11 the profoundly formative experience of 'a romantic year' in Paris. He went to read French literature and philosophy, and to be initiated by Alain-Fournier (then at work on *Le Grand Meaulnes*) into the intellectual life of Paris. But what most deeply drew him was that 'Depuis plusieurs années, la France représentait surtout, à mes yeux, la *poésie*'.[31] He even had 'at that time the idea of giving up English and trying to settle down and scrape along in Paris and gradually write French'.[32] He seems to have been aware already that it would be difficult for him to mature as a writer in America. Perhaps he sensed that for his puritan temperament, as for the earlier New England writers, that 'world was thin; it was not corrupt enough'.[33] Certainly the poems about New England in the *Prufrock* volume are among his thinnest. Henry James, however, had shown how an American sensibility could be nourished upon the corruptions of Europe; he 'had taken talents similar to Hawthorne's and made them yield far greater returns than poor Hawthorne could harvest from his granite soil'.[34] Eliot added to that, with Jamesian playfulness, 'It is the final perfection, the consummation of the American to become, not an Englishman, but a European – something which no born European, no person of any European nationality, can become.'

Though he did not transplant himself then, and was to become European by another process, Eliot felt an incalculable debt to Paris for the year he spent there. In his 'Commentary' in the *Criterion* of April 1934 he wrote:

Younger generations can hardly realise the intellectual desert of England and America during the first decade and more of this century. In the English desert, to be sure, flourished a few tall and handsome cactuses, as well as James and Conrad (for whom the climate, in contrast to their own, was relatively favourable); in America the desert extended, *à perte de vue*, without the least prospect of even desert vegetables. The predominance of Paris was incontestable. Poetry, it is true, was somewhat in eclipse; but there was a most exciting variety of ideas. Anatole France and Rémy de Gourmont still exhibited their learning, and provided types of scepticism for younger men to be attracted by and to repudiate; . . . the sociologists, Durkheim, Lévy-Bruhl, held new doctrines; . . . and over all swung the spider-like figure of Bergson. His metaphysic was said to throw some light upon the new ways of painting, and discussion of Bergson was apt to be involved with discussion of Matisse and Picasso.

I am willing to admit that my own retrospect is touched by a sentimental sunset, the memory of a friend coming across the Luxembourg Gardens in the late afternoon, waving a branch of lilac, a friend who was later (so far as I could find out) to be mixed with the mud of Gallipoli. . . But an atmosphere of diverse opinions seems to me on the whole favourable to the maturing of the individual.[35]

If that conclusion seems to be the reflection rather of the philosopher than the poet, at least it may recall that Eliot was both.

Indeed, in the years 1912 to 1914, he told Kristian Smidt, his philosophical studies *were* him. He devoted himself from the autumn of 1911 until June 1915, first in the Harvard Graduate School and for the final year at Merton College, Oxford, to preparing a doctoral thesis on 'Experience and the Objects of Knowledge in the Philosophy of F. H. Bradley'. He also studied Sanskrit – some of the Upanishads, the *Bhagavad-Gita* – and became involved 'in the mazes of Patanjali's metaphysics'. Some of his seminar papers which survive[36] show a wide acquaintance with philosophers from the pre-Socratics to Bradley; others criticise from an original point of view recent work in the fields of social anthropology and comparative religion, including Frazer's *The Dying God*.

What remained to him of these studies, he asked himself near the end of his life; and answered, 'The style of three philosophers: Bradley's English, Spinoza's Latin, and Plato's Greek.'[37] But the answer reveals that he was still the philosopher he had been. So also does his statement at about the same time that he could no longer understand his own doctoral thesis, though it had been received by his teachers as 'the work of an expert'. For in philosophy as he practised it the mind finds no objects of knowledge. Real knowledge is in immediate experience. Philosophy is but a training of the mind for the criticism of its experience. To put it another way, philosophy for Eliot was not a source of ideas, let alone of convictions and attitudes; he derived from it no 'philosophy of life'. It simply trained him to be the detached critic of his own sensuous and emotional life. As such it contributed to his development as a poet, first by confirming the primary value of immediate experience, and then by enabling him to be its conscious master. If it contributed most directly to the formation of his prose style, the instrument of his literary and social criticism, it contributed most deeply to the development of his powers towards their full expression in *Four Quartets,* a philosophical poem in which the philosophy serves only to order experience.

From his work on Bradley he gained something beyond the Ph.D., which he didn't in fact collect, and the chance of an academic career, which he didn't want. In an obituary tribute in 1924 he praised 'the consummate art of Bradley's style . . . in which acute intellect and passionate feeling preserve a classic balance'; and he added that upon the few who surrender patient years to the understanding of his meaning, 'his writings perform that mysterious and complete operation which transmutes not one department of thought only, but the whole intellectual and emotional tone of their being'.[38]

Wartime conditions prevented his return to Harvard to complete the formal requirements of his doctorate; but he had already decided, by the summer of 1915, to remain in England and devote himself to poetry. His mother tried without success to have him change his mind, having 'absolute faith in his Philosophy but not in the vers libre'.[38a] His decision to stay may have been influenced by his marriage at the end of June to Vivien Haigh-Wood, an English woman whom he had met in April at the start of the summer term; and it may have been influenced also by the fact that Ezra Pound, a vortex of the modern movement in literature and art, was then living in London. Whatever the accidental causes, he was to graft himself on to the stock of London and English life with a thoroughness that made it the one right place for his life's work. Pound left in 1920 for Paris, then Rapallo; but Eliot remained to become the most powerful and eminent man of letters in England, and to be celebrated as the great poet of his day.

However, 'poetry is not a career . . . the poet must find some other way of earning an income, and the less his way of earning a living has to do with poetry, the better'.[39] From the autumn of 1915 until the end of 1916 Eliot tried schoolmastering. He found that 'this most exacting and exhausting of professions leaves little time and energy over, for those who have the ability to teach, and whose conscience demands of them, for the benefit of their pupils, the best they have to give'.[40] After that he spent 'eight very satisfactory years working in a bank, dealing with sight drafts, acceptances, bills of lading, and such mysteries, and eventually writing articles on the movement of foreign exchanges for the bank magazine'.[41] 'I know from experience that working in a bank from 9.15 to 5.30, and once in four weeks the whole of Saturday, with two weeks holiday a year, was a rest cure compared to teaching in a school.'[42] The advantage of the bank was not that it allowed him rest, but that it left him energy to 'practise and perfect himself in writing', and to 'cultivate other interests as well'.[43] In fact he led a hard double life, doing a prodigious amount of work after banking hours as a poet and man of letters. Beside the labours of his verse, and the substantial essays in which he was establishing critical principles, he wrote reviews and gave courses of university extension lectures 'under the necessity of earning small sums quickly'. One can see why he urged in 1919 that the British Museum Reading Room should be opened 'in the evening and on Sunday'.[44] It was a relief when he could escape the work done merely for money; and his letters tell how glad he was to leave the bank in the end.[45] Yet he valued the discipline of reviewing, especially for Bruce Richmond's *Times Literary Supplement* and Middleton Murry's *Athenaeum*.

Moreover, he always found it positively useful to have other work than his poetry. For one thing, 'the difficulty of not having as much time as I would like has given me a greater pressure of concentration ... The danger, as a rule, of having nothing else to do is that one might write too much rather than concentrating and perfecting smaller amounts. That would be *my* danger.'[46] There was also the puritan conscience to be appeased:

What I have found desirable, to enable me to go on writing, is a life in which part of my time is spent on a definite paid job which I believe to be useful – in my case, concerning myself with the publication of other people's books – and only partly in writing those books which I write simply because I want to write them.[47]

He felt that while he could risk wasting some time on writing which might prove worthless, he needed the assurance and moral support of doing useful work which could be measured and recognised as such. So, from 1925, for nearly forty years, he was a busy working director of Faber & Faber, responsible primarily for their poetry list, but occasionally concerned also with writings on literature, religion and social questions. In this profession he was simply a practical publisher. Addressing younger colleagues in the trade about 'The Publishing of Poetry', he was prosaically sensible about building up the right number of reasonably recognised and successful poets, maintaining a good 'imprint' at a minimum loss, and so forth.[48] 'An artist needs to live a commonplace life,' he believed, 'if he is to get his work done'.[49]

For all this, the publishing, the reviewing, the literary and social criticism, and the founding and editing of the *Criterion* through 'the years of *l'entre deux guerres*', with the later public life as eminent man of letters and leading church-man, were an integral part of the poet's way of life. Eliot had a rare ability to make subservient to his poetry what to more romantic notions would seem preventive.

But the poetry demanded a more difficult inner discipline of courage and patience. About this Eliot made one of his most personal statements in 1947, when what was to remain his last great poem, *Little Gidding*, was behind him:

I have always been haunted by one or the other of two doubts. The first is, that nothing I have written is really of permanent value: and that makes it hard to believe in what one wants to do next. Neither one's inner feelings, nor public approval, is satisfactory assurance: for some men have been enthusiastic about their own poetry and nobody has agreed with them; and other men have been acclaimed as great poets, and ridiculed by a later generation. But the second doubt is still more distressing. I sometimes feel that some, at least, of what I have written, is very good, but that I shall never again write anything good. Some imp always whispers to me, as I am struggling to get down to any new piece of work, that this is going to be lamentably bad, and that I won't know it. At least three times during my life, and for periods of some duration, I have been convinced that I shall never again be able to write anything worth reading. And perhaps this time it is true. . .

[For] a poet humility is the most essential virtue. That means, not to be influenced by the desire for applause, not to be influenced by the desire to excel anybody else, not to be influenced by what your readers expect of you, not to write something merely because it is high time you wrote something, but to wait patiently, not caring how you compare with other poets, for the impulse which you cannot resist. . .

And in between the writing of poems one is not a *poet:* one is the author of certain *poems:* but . . . one is not sure that one will ever write another poem, and therefore has not the satisfaction of thinking of oneself as a 'poet'.[50]

In those barren times – as at the crisis of his twenty-fifth year; after *Marina*; after *Little Gidding* – 'the poet who wishes to continue to write poetry must keep in training': he must work consciously and persistently at the craft of verse, so that when he does have something to say he will have prepared an adequate technique.[51] Sometimes it happened that the real poetry was released by the experiments in technique, or in the plays written upon commission. The poems written in French about 1916 helped him to get started again when he thought he had dried up completely.[52] After *The Hollow Men* he thought his poetry was over, but his undertaking to contribute to the Faber Ariel Poems 'released the stream, and led directly to *Ash-Wednesday*'. *Burnt Norton* began as lines and fragments of 'pure, unapplied poetry' that came in the writing of *Murder in the Cathedral*.[53] But these were unlooked for gifts: the poetry was not directly the concern of the patient craftsman.

The real thing could not be willed or wished into being, nor constrained to serve any conscious purpose. It required a slow distillation of experience, by a process largely unconscious, subterranean and unpredictable. Eliot likened it to the gradual accumulation of a tantalus jar: 'it may be only once in five or ten years that experience accumulates to form a new whole and finds its appropriate expression.'[54] Then it is like a 'crystallisation' of the mind, or the sudden hatching of something that had been obstructed below the surface, undergoing 'a long incubation'.[55] Such poetry issues from, and speaks to, 'the deeper, unnamed feelings which form the substratum of our being, to which we rarely penetrate'.[56] But to penetrate to and express them is what 'alone constitutes life for a poet'.[57]

Eliot's deepest feelings were not, on the whole, pleasant. In speaking of Coleridge's inspiration – Coleridge being a poet, as he thought, of the same type as himself – he associated his Muse with the Eumenides, 'ghastly shadows at his back'; then he added, 'As André Gide's Prometheus said . . . *Il faut avoir un aigle*.'[58] He remarked that Coleridge remained in contact with his eagle, and he did the same himself: in 'Dans le Restaurant', *Ash-Wednesday*, *The Family Reunion* fairly transparently. What he had to express, as his deepest experience of life, was its vanity rather than any fulfilment, the burden of it more than the rare moments of release. Inevitably, the strain and deepening misery of his first marriage contributed: she was his Muse, as I. A. Richards said of Vivien Eliot, in the most illuminating comment that has been made upon it. Yet Eliot's basic attitudes towards life had been formed before he met her, and his best wisdom was of the sort he approved in Dante's *Vita Nuova*: 'There is also a practical sense of realities behind it, which is antiromantic: not to expect more from *life* than it can give or more from *human* beings than they can give; to look to *death* for what life cannot give.'[59] That was published in 1929, but it is only a more explicit statement of what he had written in 1919:

Beyle and Flaubert . . . suggest unmistakeably the awful separation between potential passion and any actualisation possible in life. They indicate also the indestructible barriers between one human being and another. This is a 'mysticism' not to be extracted from Balzac, or even from Miss Underhill. 'Ainsi tout leur a craqué dans la main'.[60]

That phrase reappeared in the 1921 essay on Marvell, where Eliot added that 'that hold on human values, that firm grasp of human experience . . . leads toward, and is only completed by, the religious comprehension'. An elucidation of these remarks can be found in a letter to Paul Elmer More, dated 'Shrove Tuesday, 1928', where he writes of

the void that I find in the middle of all human happiness and all human relations, and which there is only one thing to fill. I am one whom this sense of void tends to drive towards asceticism or sensuality, and only Christianity helps to reconcile me to life, which is otherwise disgusting.[61]

Eliot's formal conversion to Christianity in 1927 did not make for any radical change in his poetry, but enforced its natural development. Even in the matter of belief it amounted, at most, to a move from a heretical to an orthodox form of Christianity. He could say, 'I was brought up outside the Christian fold, in Unitarianism',[62] because in that Church belief in the Christian revelation, and specifically in the basic doctrine of Incarnation, was vague and faint. He became dissatisfied with its 'intellectual and puritanical rationalism', being convinced 'that the supernatural is the greatest reality here and now'. This belief he found most satisfyingly formulated in orthodox Christian doctrine. But the doctrine only confirmed and formulated his already developed convictions. Moreover, it did not take the place of his 'inspiration', or become what he had to express. It simply contributed to his poetry, to the articulation of his deepest feelings, a more conscious and definite understanding. But he considered the doctrine and discipline of Christianity essential to its perfection. As epigraph to his 1929 study of Dante he set this sentence: 'La sensibilité, *sauvée d'elle-même et conduite dans l'ordre*, est devenue un principe de perfection' (my italic). Thus Catholicism came to fill the role that philosophy had played in his earlier development:

Humanism has much to say of Discipline and Order and Control; and I have parroted these terms myself. I found no discipline in humanism; only a little intellectual discipline from a little study of philosophy. But the difficult discipline is the discipline and training of emotion; this the modern world has great need of; so great that it hardly understands what the word means; and this I have found is only attainable through dogmatic religion. . . It takes perhaps a lifetime merely to realise that men like the forest sages, and the desert sages, and finally the Victorines and John of the Cross and (in his fashion) Ignatius really *mean what they say*. Only those have the right to talk of discipline who have looked into the Abyss.[63]

Another way of putting it, and a key to much of the later poetry –

We had the experience but missed the meaning,
And approach to the meaning restores the experience
In a different form

Ash-Wednesday and *Four Quartets* carried through a profound revaluation of experience in the light of Christian belief and practice. But the experience remained primary and personal, so that the poetry is the expression, and in a sense the perfection, of Eliot's own 'spirit unappeased and peregrine'.

Apart from that he wished to be thought of as 'merely a man of letters' –

and men of letters should emulate those small marine creatures, the name of which is known only to biologists, whose small skeletons contribute to the formation of coral islands. Like these obscure little creatures, it is only what we leave behind us that matters.[64]

He should like to have been the author, he said once, of the poem which concludes Kipling's collected verse:

> If I have given you delight
>   By aught that I have done,
> Let me lie quiet in that night
>   Which shall be yours anon:
>
> And for the little, little, span
>   The dead are borne in mind,
> Seek not to question other than
>   The books I leave behind.[65]

To which should be added Ezra Pound's valediction: 'Let him rest in peace. I can only repeat, but with the urgency of 50 years ago: READ HIM.'[66]

Part One

1905–1912

An individual talent

1905	24 January	'If Time and Space, as Sages say'. ('The first poem I wrote to be shown to other eyes', Eliot later noted on the manuscript, which was marked 'A' by his English master.)
	February	'A Fable for Feasters'.
	June	'At Graduation 1905': Class Valedictory Poem.
1905–6		Preparation for Harvard at Milton Academy.
1906–7		Freshman year at Harvard.
1907	May	'When we came home across the hill'.
1908	November	'Before Morning', 'Circe's Palace'.
	December	Read Arthur Symons' *The Symbolist Movement in Literature*.
1909	January	'On a Portrait', 'The moonflower opens to the moth'.
	November	'Nocturne'. [Also written in November but published later: 'Humouresque', 'Conversation Galante'.]
1910	January	'Spleen'.
	February	['Portrait of a Lady' begun. Also 'Prufrock' ll. 111–19.]
	June	'Ode' for Graduating Class of 1910.
	October	['Preludes' I and II written in Cambridge, Mass. Probably also 'Portrait of a Lady' I – Eliot always placed it as composed in Cambridge, though in the notebook it is dated November, by which time he was in Paris.]
1910–11		A 'romantic year' in Paris, reading literature and philosophy at the Sorbonne.
1911	March	['Rhapsody on a Windy Night'.]
	July	['Prelude' III.]
	July–August	['The Love Song of J. Alfred Prufrock' – completed in Munich.]
1911–		Studying philosophy in Harvard Graduate School.
	November	['Portrait of a Lady' completed.]
		['Prelude' IV – possibly later, in 1912.]
1912		['La Figlia Che Piange' – possibly 1911.]

Where titles are given in square brackets the date is that of composition according to the evidence available. For other titles the dates are those of first publication.

2

Prufrock observed

the only cure for Romanticism is to analyse it.[1]

Since he was growing up in the 1890s and 1900s, Eliot's first verses were naturally in the late romantic vein. Yet even the 'poems written in early youth' – that is, from his last year at Smith Academy when he was sixteen, to the end of his undergraduate years at Harvard when he was twenty-one – reveal the individual talent that was soon to cure itself of romanticism.

The half-dozen lyrics written before he discovered Laforgue, with 'At Graduation 1905', faintly evoke the poetical effects of Gray, of Blake's *Poetical Sketches*, of Wordsworth, Shelley, Keats, of Tennyson, Arnold, Swinburne, and of Fitzgerald's Omar Khayyám. The diction is drawn from these poets, and is undisturbed by the young author's own direct sensations. This makes the verse not impersonal but remote and artificial, its images not original but reproductions. In spite of that there is some distinctive character. The many borrowed voices are composed into one voice; and that voice *thinks through* the conventional images with a rare cogency. If the flowers are forever withering, at least they do so to some definite effect.

The two versions of the earliest lyric, after Jonson, attempt a metaphysical variation upon the *carpe diem* theme: but the dissolution of what is transient into the timeless 'divine' is hardly effective. However, 'When we came home across the hill' does transform the apparently idyllic into the elegiac. The still living landscape is first seen in terms of the suspended, imminent, withering and falling; then the close asserts, as a positive statement and with the rhythm enforcing the climax,

> But the wild roses in your wreath
> Were faded, and the leaves were brown.

It is a surprising fulfilment. Should the wild roses not have been plucked? Yet the same fate is only suspended for the leaves and flowers that are ungathered. And though 'wreath' becomes funereal, it is first festive. This order of argument, with its assurance that a specific emotion is being formulated, and with such sensitive precision of rhythm, is most unusual in an adolescent's verse.

'Before Morning' further refines the poet's first sense of his world. The ordering of its images inextricably joins the blooming and the dying, so that the final 'dawn' opens as much upon death as a new day. This is quite minor verse; and yet it is individual, in the way it just stands apart from its images and feelings in a thoughtful inspection of them. Nor is it fanciful to hear Eliot's voice finding its authentic movement in the phrasing and the varying rhythm, just as in Blake's early poems the 'originality is in an occasional rhythm' [2] –

> This morning's flowers and flowers of yesterday
> Their fragrance drifts across the room at dawn . . .

These images will return, their values fully realised, in the sestina of *The Dry Salvages,* when this fashion of thinking lyrically has become the poet's trained habit of mind.

'On a Portrait' begins with the world-weariness of Tennyson's *In Memoriam* and *Maud,* and of Arnold's 'Scholar Gipsy'. The second quatrain might be related to Pater's vision of *La Gioconda.* However, the sestet – for this is a sonnet – resists all the romantic invitations. The irreducible otherness of the portrait puts a stop to the wearied yearning and self-satisfying fantasy. Pater imagined in the *Mona Lisa* 'a beauty wrought out from within upon the flesh, the deposit, little cell by cell, of strange thoughts and fantastic reveries and exquisite passions'. But this woman stands beyond the circle of such thoughts; and the poet attains the detachment of the parrot's 'patient curious eye'.

Eliot may have written that poem about the time he came upon Arthur Symons' *The Symbolist Movement in Literature,* which introduced him to Laforgue: that was in December 1908, and the poem appeared on 26 January 1909. Certainly he had not yet read Laforgue for himself. But his own instinct was already guiding him towards the Laforguian irony, which, as Symons put it, dried out the pathos of the passing world. In 'Circe's Palace', published in 1908, there was a movement in each of the two stanzas 'from highly coloured "decadent" statements to plain, terse statements'.[3] Eliot's natural impulse was to detach himself from feelings and experience, to be the coolly conscious observer, not the celebrant, of his sensibility.

The effect of his reading Laforgue[4] was that he was galvanised into being himself. Laforgue could rewrite *Hamlet,* which, for the romantic imagination, had been an irresistible invitation to self-dramatisation, with the ironic condescension of one who knows it all. His Hamlet reflects that at least he has saved Ophelia from a life worse than death; and then is himself saved from the banalities of a passionate elopement when Laertes stabs him. Eliot, in 'Nocturne', applied that treatment to *Romeo and Juliet,* another classic of tragic passion. Seen as if from behind the scenes, Romeo appears the lovelorn Pierrot, and the affair just the usual stale romance. It calls for a merciful release for all concerned, and finds it in a risqué pun. This is high tragedy in dead-pan burlesque, with the poet as puppet-master, beyond illusion. There is no romance in it for his eye, which has seen it all before and plotted all the moves. His only relief from the boredom of the inevitable is to send it up by some witty transformation.

Laforgue was Eliot's master in this art of cosmic detachment, an art which contrives to stand outside the inescapable. One of his masks is Pierrot, hopelessly in love with the moon and fixed in the usual dull world. Another is a Hamlet with his five senses tying him to life, but with a sixth sense for the infinite. Such longings for the Ideal are of the essence of Romanticism. However, Laforgue feels them with a difference. Instead of making them a means of escape from the ordinary world, he uses them to sharpen awareness of the props and pretences, the habits and vanities which pass there for life. And the increase of that awareness only intensifies the distance from the unattainable ideal. The drama, the play of feeling, is the conflict of a mind conscious of an unknown ideal yet having to live in the realm of the commonplace. It does not simply oscillate from the one to the other, as Keats does in his 'Ode to a Nightingale'. Somehow the poet must place himself simultaneously within and above his experience; must hold together, in the double vision of his irony, the unreconcilable points of view.

Yet in Laforgue this attitude remains a development of romanticism, not a liberation from it. Because his personae yearn for the moon they only confirm their fate as trapped victims of earth. Their sole freedom is in being conscious of their fate, which they cannot master. This is the predicament of Prufrock; and Eliot's criticism of Prufrock may be read as a criticism of Laforgue also. The latter had turned its own romantic illusions against a too solidly materialised world, and exposed its vanity by the light of the unattainable. But to do only that was to arrive at the last impasse of romanticism, and to be the trapped intelligence of its dead end. By making that predicament itself the object of detached analysis Eliot was soon to save himself from it.

A measure of dissociation from Laforgue is apparent even in the first poem to acknowledge his influence: 'Humouresque'. The direct debt is to a stanza from 'Locutions des Pierrots: XII' which Symons had quoted:

> Encore un de mes pierrots mort;
> Mort d'un chronique orphelinisme;
> C'était un coeur plein de dandysme
> Lunaire, en un drôle de corps.

However, Eliot's marionette has no heart: he is simply the jumping-jack of the moment. And his moon is pasteboard; his only world the one in fashion. 'Where would he belong?' if not there. The effect of the question, and of the observations which prompt it, is to assume a point of view quite detached from earth, marionette and moon. Yet there is no ideal stated: the mind is wholly engaged in contemplating the actuality. The feat of detachment is therefore all the more extraordinary, for somehow the poet has contrived to stand outside his world without placing himself in the realm of the merely imaginary. Laforgue is never so objective. This is verse that really is hard and dry, with all trace of subjective pathos squeezed out. At the same time it is not much more than an 'imitation' of his master's style, expressing an attitude to Laforgue rather than his own feelings.

It is with 'Spleen' that Eliot begins to deal with his own world and to find his own voice. The title is after Baudelaire's *Spleen et Idéal*. Though the word is no longer current in English, the French sense is derived from a usage found in Pope's *Rape of the Lock* and many other English writings of that time, signifying 'excessive dejection or depression of spirits' (*O.E.D.*). It comes from being got down by banalities, from being baffled and dulled by the appearances most people keep up. Eliot's poem is almost wholly out of Laforgue, and the last stanza is a brilliant distillation of Symons' characterisation of him. Yet it is also his most original poem so far. The speech is living; the perceptions are felt; and the verse, freely over-riding the octosyllabic line, achieves significant harmonies of rhythm and stress. The rhymes are not only telling but structural: as in the dejected effect of *alley/rally*, and the clinching of the stanza and the irony with *suit/Absolute*.

What is most remarkable is the method of mind. If the Sunday procession displaces a would-be superior self-possession; and if there is no stay for the inner self in simple familiar things; yet there remains the final resource of becoming the alienated observer. From that point of view the complacent Sunday world is magnified into its own Ideal, seen as Life got up fit to meet its Maker; and thus, 'on the doorstep of the Absolute', it is put in its place. The wit is satisfyingly effective. The eye has been fixed steadily upon its object, un-clouded by spleen; and by the end the spleen is purged.

'Conversation Galante' was probably Eliot's next poem.[5] Again there are direct debts to Laforgue, together with an increasing assurance in his own method and meaning. Its main interest, however, is in its adumbration of 'Prufrock' and 'Portrait of a Lady'. To personify the lover as Pierrot is some advance upon the puppet-master's detachment of 'Nocturne' and 'Humour-esque'; and to allow him the elegant raillery of one perfectly in control of his situation is greatly to increase his interest. At the least, his irony is an assurance of superiority, allowing him to patronise the lady's romantic taste. But then her imperviousness to it reduces him to a desperate explicitness, and forces him to concede to her viewpoint – 'it is I who am inane', 'our mad poetics'. Thus her indifference disarms his irony, and it is she who has the last word. So much for Pierrot as lover of the Absolute! This is a sketch of the predicament explored more fully, and with greater realism, in the two principal portraits of *Prufrock and Other Observations*. Its function, as an element in the composition of that collection, is simply to provide a contrast and setting for its conclusion, 'La Figlia Che Piange'; and to suggest the connection of that poem of strangely fulfilled love with the unsatisfactory *têtes-à-têtes* of the initial drawing-room and salon.

The transformation of Eliot's poetic personality under the influence of Laforgue can be seen in the development of his verse within the single year of 1909. In the difference between 'The moonflower opens to the moth', and 'Spleen' or 'Conversation Galante', there is all the difference between a romantic and a post-romantic state of sensibility. The development was confirmed in 'Portrait of a Lady' and 'Prufrock', the main works of 1910–11. In these the late romantic condition is made the object of a searching critique, from a point of view as much outside and above it as Joyce's in *A Portrait of the Artist as a Young Man*.

'Portrait of a Lady' is of course charged with romantic sentiment, yet the poem itself is not at all romantic. The sentiment is the lady's, and the portrait records it but does not necessarily share it. The *vers libre*, giving each thing said its own idiom and rhythm, creates the two characters and their worlds quite objectively; and it places the reader, with the poet, as the observer of the drama.

The young man, the narrator, begins a trifle heavily – with two lines of fourteen syllables each, in fact. Since each line has just five strong stresses, like sombre chords, the effect is of dragged-out pentameters. Is it through boredom, or gloom of spirits – spleen? The third line, though standard iambic, has the same time-value or felt weight: the lady's emphases are heavy with feeling. In the following lines it is her scene that is set, and her tone that comes through, in spite of the man's meaning to be ironic at the expense of the atmosphere and the preciousness. He is maliciously clever about the latest Pole; yet she counters effectively with 'soul', and flows on gracefully to a full rhyme. Her velleities may be transparent, but they persist insidiously in his very exposing of them. Indeed what else is there, while he and we are in her presence, but the appeal of those exquisitely caught hesitations and modulations?

However, they are so much hers that we are left free to observe rather than sympathise. Certainly the poem does not require us to make her subjectivity our own. In some of Arnold's poems – 'A Buried Life', 'A Summer Night', 'Dover Beach' – such nostalgias and vague longings are offered in a purely subjective form, and the only way to take the poems, if we can take them at all, is to enter into those feelings and to make them our own. Eliot is doing just the opposite of that: presenting a subjective state as an object for detached contemplation.

That, however, is more than the young man can do. The lady does oppress him, and his escape is unconvincing. His 'false note' is a sort of rude noise; his self-assertion a matter of clocks and bocks – banalities against her velleities. The drama is in fact very Jamesian: one in which the narrator, complacently assured of the adequacy of his point of view, turns out to be the spokesman merely for the commonplace and the conventional. His claims to superior strength of mind, and to the possession of a 'real world' to set against her over-refined one, are of course more defensive than assured. The trouble is that his world is no more proof against hers, than hers is against his.

While her sensibility is hypertrophied, his is atrophied. As she is at the mercy of gross things – for her world is not subject to her fine feelings – so he is at the mercy of unknown emotions: the street piano, and the smell of hyacinths recalling 'things that other people have desired'. Her end may be pathetic, but his is clownish or worse. Given his grotesque mimicry of the human arts, his feeling like a bear, a parrot, an ape, how should her 'dying fall' not prevail? Though she stands only for dying romanticism, he cannot conceive a better attitude to life or death. So he must capitulate at the last to her tone and terms. 'Afternoon grey and smoky, evening yellow and rose': it is a kind of tribute, in which his 'smoke and fog of a December afternoon' is resolved with her 'April sunsets'. Moreover, it was love-sickness that made Orsino remark 'This music is successful with a dying fall'. The final irony is that even as he acknowledges her advantage, he remains too self-possessed fully to comprehend it. He seems still unaware that, after all, there might be a virtue in romantic passion.

According to Conrad Aiken in *Ushant*, his fictional autobiography, Eliot had frequented the salon of just such a *précieuse* in his graduate year at Harvard, and had felt obscurely involved when he left for Paris in 1910. I do not know the truth of the matter, but the story is good for this at least, that it connects the poem with Eliot's own life.[6] Here he was not imitating Laforgue, but taking over what he needed to express his direct experience of decadent romanticism and dull realism.

At the same time the poem owes much to the English writers who were the moderns then, most notably to Browning and James. Their distinctive quality was to seek the soul in particulars, like the former's Fra Lippo Lippi; to cultivate the kind of mind which, as Eliot was to say of James, no Idea could violate.[7] Pater had called Browning 'the most modern, to modern people the most important of poets', because he took for his subject 'the individual, the personal, the concrete, as distinguished from, yet revealing in its fullness the general, the universal'.[8] Ezra Pound said much the same thing when placing the author of 'Portrait of a Lady' and 'Prufrock' as a successor to Browning:

For what the statement is worth, Mr Eliot's work interests me more than that of any other poet now [1917] writing in English. The most interesting poems in Victorian English are Browning's *Men and Women*, or, if that statement is too absolute, let me contend that the form of these poems is the most vital form of that period in English . . . Browning included a certain amount of ratiocination and of purely intellectual comment, and in just that proportion he lost intensity. Since Browning there have been very few good poems of this sort. Mr Eliot has made two notable additions to the list. . . Art does not avoid universals, it strikes at them all the harder in that it strikes through particulars.[9]

The significant relation of 'Portrait of a Lady' to the Browningesque dramatic monologue, and to the Jamesian novel, is in its following their method of 'expressive particularisation' – a phrase James used to distinguish Browning's incessantly discriminating intelligence from Tennyson's Bardic afflatus.[10]

In 'Preludes' Eliot applied the method in its essential form, stripped of the conventional interest in character and story. They exhibit the mind of the poet operating directly upon his experience, and making up a vision almost exclusively from the data of his sordid and unromantic world. It is as if he were deliberately practising the virtue which he admired in Charles-Louis Philippe, whose *Bubu of Montparnasse* he read in Paris in 1910 and drew on in 'Preludes' III and IV:

His great quality is not imagination: it is a sincerity which makes him a faithful recorder of things as they are, and of events as they happened, without irrelevant and disturbing comment. He had a gift which is rare enough: the ability not to think, not to generalise. To be able to select, out of personal experience, what is really significant, to be able not to corrupt it by afterthoughts, is as rare as imaginative invention.[11]

When he remarked that quality in James, 'the most intelligent man of his generation', Eliot significantly added that the really superior intelligence was the one able to maintain 'a point of view, a viewpoint untouched by the parasite idea' – which amounted, in James, to 'a merciless clairvoyance'.[12] That kind of vision, unclouded (as he said of Blake) by education or opinion or sentiment, is surely what he is after in 'Preludes'. The fidelity to things as they impinge upon the senses is not for him a way of immersing in experience: it is rather a way of mastering it in the mind.

It is remarkable that the poet does not declare: '*I* am experiencing these things; this is what I see, what I feel.' Yet the objectivity is an illusion. It is not a world in itself that we are being given, but his consciousness of it. His ordinary egotistical self is suspended, while he exists, it seems, simply as the consciousness of the scene. However, what he observes is charged with his feeling and understanding –

> The winter evening settles down
> With smell of steaks in passageways.
> Six o'clock.
> The burnt-out ends of smoky days.

There is a definite emotion in the shaping of each phrase, and in the rhythm of the sequence, as well as a sensitive wit in the perceptions. There is a sense of structure, too, in the way the fourth line rhymes with the second in its movement as well as in the terminal sound. By the end of this first 'Prelude' a state of mind has formed distinct enough to make the purely subjective leap:

> And at the corner of the street
> A lonely cab-horse steams and stamps.
>
> And then the lighting of the lamps.

The last line has no objective connection with the one before; yet it follows as a right conclusion, because it realises the feeling that has been growing through the sequence of observations.

The second 'Prelude' presents the development of consciousness beyond immediate sensation. It is the world that is already known which comes into the waking mind. It is 'out there' no doubt; but it is in the mind's eye that the street is 'sawdust-trampled', and in the inner ear that the feet beat in a rhyme that comes too soon. Then the mind withdraws into generalisation –

> One thinks of all the hands
> That are raising dingy shades
> In a thousand furnished rooms.

To understand one's world, said Santayana echoing Arnold, to form a reasoned idea of it, 'is the classic form of consolation'.[13] Or one might say that the oppressive spleen is eased when it is expressed as an 'objective' vision of all the world.

At the next stage, in 'Prelude' III, the poet's object is the mind itself, or at least that process of consciousness which has just been presented. Now he observes it from outside, and interprets the experience of the persona or alter ego –

> You . . . watched the night revealing
> The thousand sordid images
> Of which your soul was constituted;

and again,

> You had such a vision of the street
> As the street hardly understands.

This is to be the natural philosopher of the mind, studying how a soul is constituted, and how it expresses itself as a point of view. The 'vision of the street' is determined by experience, and yet is a criticism of it: so that the soul, which is a product of its world, may separate itself from it by the process of understanding. Nevertheless, it is only the mere observer who is detached from the contingent existence of

> Sitting along the bed's edge, where
> You curled the papers from your hair . . .

The soul of 'Prelude' IV appears not to have a vision of his world, but rather to suffer it – 'stretched tight against the skies', or (like the hero of *Maud* in his madness[14]) 'trampled by insistent feet/At four and five and six o'clock'. His 'conscience' goes beyond 'consciousness' into the realm of moral discrimination; and that presses 'Impatient to assume the world' towards religious overtones. While the philosopher would be thinking from the street to the world, from the particular to the universal, conscience might be taking the world upon itself, assuming responsibility for it. We seem to have progressed from the primary level of sensation, to an ultimate religious conviction.

At this point the poet speaks for the first time in his own person, and confesses to being more than the detached eye and mind:

> I am moved by fancies that are curled
> Around these images, and cling:
> The notion of some infinitely gentle
> Infinitely suffering thing.

This, I take it, is to *not* speak of Christ and the suffering which redeems. It intimates an ideal beyond the images afforded by experience, but places that as notional merely. For all that, the ideal moves him as nothing actual has done.

To the realist it is ridiculous. But then the real worlds, from the viewpoint of the ideal,

> revolve like ancient women
> Gathering fuel in vacant lots.

That of course is satire – the poet viewing the universe as if he were a god.

His strict fidelity to experience has been after all a way of approaching the Absolute; his objectivity terminates in a form of idealism. Life should reveal at least to reason, wrote Santayana, attacking Browning for remaining immersed in the flow of experience, 'the ideal which it fails to attain'.[15] For the poet that would mean being also a philosopher and epistemologist. But that is just what Eliot was studying to be. Like his Aristotle, but in the mode of poetry in which criticism of 'the objects of knowledge' is not separated out from immediate experience, he was looking 'solely and steadfastly at the object', and following the method 'of intelligence itself swiftly operating the analysis of sensation to the point of principle and definition'.[16]

The application of this method to Bergsonism, in 'Preludes' III and IV and 'Rhapsody on a Windy Night', was an important stage in his cure for romanticism. In the Paris of 1910–11 Bergson was 'the most noticed figure'.[17] From December to May he was lecturing at the Collège de France, on Personality on Fridays at 5.00, and on Spinoza on Saturdays at 4.15.[18] Eliot followed the Friday course at least, along with all the world it seemed. Later, if not at the time, he thought the enthusiasm of the audience excessive. The lectures presented ideas developed in *Les Données Immédiates de la Conscience* (1889), *Matière et Mémoire* (1896), and *L'Evolution Créatrice* (1907). Eliot once mentioned the second of these as a book which had deeply influenced his intellectual development, and he also said that he had closely studied the others.[19] What he took from Bergson, and used in his poetry right up to *Four Quartets*, was a way of thinking about certain problems of the mind in time, together with the conclusion that Bergson's answer to them would not do.

Bergson's *durée réelle* is 'simply not final', he wrote in a philosophy essay in 1911.[20] I should think that it was the exciting promise of immortality – as offered at the end of chapter III of *L'Evolution Créatrice* – that would least bear examination: a seductive appeal to the irrational, he called it in 1923.[21] In the Syllabus for the lectures he gave in 1916 – it is appended to this chapter – Bergson figured as a representative of the romantic tendency in France in 1910: that is, as one whose *vitalism* encouraged 'escape from the world of fact' and disbelief in Original Sin. Doubtless, Eliot's final fact would be Death, first fruit of Original Sin.

Eliot recalled in 1948 that he had undergone 'a temporary conversion to

Bergsonism';[22] but the disciple must have become the critic within a very few months. The third 'Prelude', dated July 1911 in the notebook now in the New York Public Library,[23] comes very near to certain of Bergson's conceptions. He too thought the soul constituted of its memory-images; he characterised the passive state of the mind as one in which life was like a ciné-film, a fixed sequence of flickering clichés; and he opposed to that the act of intuition, or the immediate consciousness of life-in-process which placed the mind within the absolute. However, Eliot's 'vision of the street' implies a point of view exactly opposite to Bergson's. And the vision with which the sequence closes presents the temporal world not as moving irresistibly towards its apotheosis, but as preparing for the final conflagration. So far as the poem bears upon Bergsonism, it would seem to be insisting upon the facts which Bergson wanted to transcend.

'Rhapsody on a Windy Night' gives an extended, and probably earlier, critique. Its draft is dated 3 March 1911, which places it before the fourth 'Prelude', and probably before the third also.[24] The month might account for the wind. But it is also possible that the title refers, not without rude irony, to the *élan vital*, which Bergson would have possess the mind otherwise fixed in the matter of memory. As it turns out, the rhapsody is not made up of divine inspiration; and the reason for this is that it keeps to the immediate data of consciousness.

Among the many passages in Bergson's writings with which the poem could be connected, there are three which are especially suggestive. This is from the conclusion to *Matter and Memory*:

Between the plane of action – the plane in which our body has condensed its past into motor habits – and the plane of pure memory, where our mind retains in all its details the picture of our past life, we believe that we can discover thousands of different planes of consciousness. . . To complete a recollection [consists] . . . in going away from action in the direction of dream. . . The interest of a living being lies in discovering in the present situation that which resembles a former situation, and then in placing alongside of that present situation what preceded and followed the previous one, in order to profit by past experience. . . But, in order to understand the mechanism of these associations and above all the apparently capricious selection which they make of memories, we must place ourselves alternately on the two extreme planes of consciousness which we have called the plane of action and the plane of dream. . . And this double movement of memory between its two extreme limits also sketches out, as we have shown, the first general ideas, – motor habits ascending to seek similar images in order to extract resemblances from them, and similar images coming down towards motor habits . . .[25]

About the kinds of general ideas Bergson had more to say elsewhere. He ended his *Introduction to Metaphysics* (1903) with this declaration:

But metaphysical intuition, although it can only be obtained through material knowledge, is quite other than the mere summary or synthesis of that knowledge. It is distinct from these . . . as the motor impulse is distinct from the path traversed by the moving body, as the tension of the spring is distinct from the visible movements of the pendulum. In this sense metaphysics has nothing in common with a generalisation of facts; and nevertheless it might be defined as *integral experience*.[26]

Eliot's 'broken spring in a factory yard,/Rust that clings to the form that the strength has left' might be his comment upon that. The third passage comes towards the end of chapter III of *Creative Evolution*:

Consciousness, in man, is pre-eminently intellect. It might have been, it ought, so it seems, to have been also intuition. Intuition and intellect represent two opposite directions of the work of consciousness: intuition goes in the direction of life, intellect goes in the inverse direction, and thus finds itself naturally in accordance with the movement of matter. . . Intuition is there, however, but vague and above all discontinuous. It is a lamp almost extinguished, which only lights up now and then, for a few moments at most. But it lights up wherever a vital interest is at stake. On our personality, on our liberty, on the place we occupy in the whole of nature, on our origin and perhaps also on our destiny, it throws a light feeble and vacillating, but which none the less pierces the darkness of the night in which the intellect leaves us.[27]

But *integral experience,* Eliot would seem to be retorting, can be only an immediate apprehension of what the intellect already knows.

'Rhapsody' consists of an introduction, three episodes (discreetly marked – by the 'half-pasts' – 'one', 'two', 'three'), and a finale ('four'). In each of the three episodes memory adds to the lamp's epiphanies associated images which complete and interpret the present situation. In Bergson's view, this is the intellect at work; but Eliot seems to arrive at universals in this way, at what Bergson would call intuitions of the absolute. Only the absolute which Eliot perceives is already near to 'that which is only living/Can only die'.

The hallucinatory or surrealistic vision of the first episode might be on 'the plane of dream'. Memory matches 'And you see the corner of her eye/Twists like a crooked pin' with

A twisted branch upon the beach
Eaten smooth, and polished
As if the world gave up
The secret of its skeleton,
Stiff and white.

Thus the particular is swiftly expanded into the universal, without loss of immediacy, and in a form that is both intellectually and musically final. The second episode might be on 'the plane of action'. Again the intelligent memory escapes the trap of materialism (or mere realism), by following the given image with a sequence of like images – ('So the hand of the child, automatic') – which produce an intuitive recognition of their general *likeness*. In the third episode it appears that a dream world is breaking down into automatic habit – or is it the habitual response which is seeking its dream? Specifically, the Rose-maiden of Laforgue's lunar idealism has become withered and lunatic – a variation upon 'Complainte de cette Bonne Lune', with its 'rosière enfarinée'. There is a glamour still haunting the decay, and an aura of fascination and pathos, after the manner of the Decadents' clinging to the corrupted forms of romanticism. Here memory's associations simply dispel illusion: in cold fact all that remains of romantic moments are such aftersmells as these –

> Smells of chestnuts in the streets,
> And female smells in shuttered rooms,
> And cigarettes in corridors
> And cocktail smells in bars.

The finale might be the moment of integral experience, the moment of truth; and this proves the least transcendental of all. The lamp shows what memory knows already, the ordinary everyday reality. In this immediate perception intellect and intuition coalesce, and discover the *durée réelle* to be the boredom and horror of banality. That is the absolute of merely living.

Bergson had said, of course, that this was just what the intellectual memory would make of life: that being fixed in what had been it would see death every-where in life, and miss the ever-moving *élan vital*. Eliot's poem accepts that; but maintains that to the best of our knowledge this really is a universe of dying matter, and that the final truth about it is that it is running down and getting nowhere. His use of memory is already a form, though only the critical and negative form, of what it will be in the Quartets. Not less of horror, is how one might put it, but expanding of horror beyond despair, and so liberation from 'the enchainment of past and future'; for to be conscious of 'the one end which is always present' is not to be in time. It is to be damned, so long as 'the one end' means only death – like Prufrock, whose clairvoyant consciousness knows, like Marlowe's Mephistopheles, that 'this is hell, nor am I out of it'.

Baudelaire, Eliot later wrote, was trying to express this, 'that damnation itself is an immediate form of salvation – of salvation from the ennui of modern life, because it at last gives some significance to living'.[28] In these poems of 1911, in which he is detaching himself from Bergson and romanticism, it is Baudelaire in particular whom he appears to be following. From him he learnt 'the poetical possibilities . . . of the more sordid aspects of the modern metro-polis, of the possibility of fusion between the sordidly realistic and the phantas-magoric, the possibility of the juxtaposition of the matter-of-fact and the fantastic.'[29] That is clearly one formula, and a post-Laforgue one, for this group of poems. But it is not merely in his use of such imagery that Eliot was following Baudelaire, but above all 'in the elevation of such imagery to the *first intensity* – presenting it as it is, and yet making it represent something much more than itself' – that is, 'something universal in modern life'.[30] This was already, in 1911, Eliot's way of seeking the Absolute: not by escaping from experience into anything else, but by so intensifying it that its particulars yielded its universal meaning. Thus:

> 'The bed is open; the tooth-brush hangs on the wall,
> Put your shoes at the door, sleep, prepare for life.'

'The Love Song of J. Alfred Prufrock' is the leading poem in the 1917 volume of *Observations* not just because it is the most substantial, but because it gathers up the others written about the same time into a more developed and more fully resolved vision. Prufrock's consciousness includes the same streets and drawing-rooms, and can rhapsodise their horrors. But then he more than knows them: he knows that he knows them. He exists on the plane of the universals, and is aware of the overwhelming question that looms behind all experience. There should be no need now to insist that Prufrock is not Eliot. Within the poem, the poet is simply an intelligence contemplating and analysing its object. To appreciate this, to attempt to see beyond the character to the point of view from which he is being seen, is to discover in the poem more than its hero would reveal.

'The very metric tells the tale', in Karl Shapiro's words.[31] Our first significant impression of the poem is likely to be of a voice distinctively musical in its rhythms and cadences. Then will come the sequence of perceptions and reflections with their various charges of feeling. The musical voice composes these into Prufrock's consciousness. Yet, on another level than his, the successfully sustained harmonies and progressions and variations seem to express a more profound impulse, as if Eliot's own art, behind Prufrock's love song, were aspiring to the condition of music. There seems to be some connection with the aesthetic idealism of Pater and other late romantics, but it is not a simple one. Henry James too, in a sense, was a late romantic – but never simple. And Eliot's affinity with James, in this stage of his work, was close and deep. The limitation of the simpler sort of aesthete is that his aspiration is self-satisfying, his love ends in its own music. Prufrock's song perhaps comes to that in the end. Yet his attempt to fit the elements of his world to his music creates a larger interest. His lyrical impulse, though it closes with the forlorn hope of hearing mermaids singing, has before that applied its implicit idealism as a measure of his world and of himself. The music of the poetry thus serves to operate a radical critique of experience. Instead of being a symptom of a persistent romanticism in Eliot himself, this music transforms its aesthetic idealism into an active force. Romanticism weakened when instead of criticising its world from the viewpoint of its ideal feelings, it sought to escape the world and indulge the feelings in mere dreams. But the feelings express something permanent and vital in human nature. By applying them to the actual world of experience Eliot was carrying romanticism through to conclusions that had been missed.

The technical basis of the music is the phrasing. Eliot had arrived at the *Imagistes'* basic principle before it was formulated, possibly with the aid of his *Symbolistes*: 'As regarding rhythm: to compose in the sequence of the musical phrase, not in sequence of a metronome'.[32] He has usually a metrical substructure, but the movement and feel of the verse are determined by the rhythmic shape of each phrase, and by the relation of one phrase to another in the musical sequence. The older prosody would scan

> Ín/the róom/the wóm/en cóme/and gó
> Tálking/of Mí/cheláng/eló.

However, that metre is overlaid by natural speech rhythms, which follow the phrasing, and in which the phrase is shaped by its pattern of stresses:

> Ín the róom/the wómen/cóme and gó
> Tálking/of Míchelángelò.

In the first line, the first and last phrases match, and the middle one is a variation. The second line, though apparently lighter in weight, is in fact precisely equivalent. The long phrase 'of Michelangelo' has the same duration and stress-pattern as the latter two phrases of the first line, which it accurately echoes. Thus we have a perfectly correct couplet, elegant, languidly drawled, and with the form in miniature of its social scene and ethos. One hardly notices the presumption of its being so much at ease with Michelangelo: rhythmically, in sensibility, he seems perfectly subdued to the drawing-room.

'The sequence of the musical phrase' is everywhere the best guide to the sense. One begins –

> Let us go then,/you and I,
> When the evening is spread out against the sky
> Like a patient/etherised/upon a table . . .

There is no distinct pause in the second line: it comes as a single extended phrase, a flight of feeling-in-perception. In the third line, however, sound, phrasing and sense together enforce slight but distinct pauses – which are also weightings – upon 'patient' and 'etherised'. Thus the flow of feeling associated with the evening sky is broken, and by more than the rhythm. There is the shock of 'patient . . . upon a table'. That is intensified into a wholly new idea by the immensity of the pun: for in this context *aethereal* may lie just beyond 'etherised'. We may be teased into seeking their relation. Are the ethereal emotions generated by the evening sky – as in 'These April sunsets', or 'It is a beauteous evening, calm and free', and (Wordsworth again) 'a sense sublime . . . Whose dwelling is the light of setting suns' – are these feelings merely other to the mind? Or are they a decadent form of something more remote and genuinely of heaven? Certainly the pathetic fallacy, the great resource of the romantic soul expanding itself into a cosmos, has been despatched with surgical sureness. Certainly, too, Prufrock's wit has found an image to express his own state. Yet against these reductive effects, which are dominant, there comes a subdued counter-suggestion that there may truly be, out there, a higher reality corresponding to his state as does *aethereal* to ether. The image, then, is a major chord, containing complex possibilities.

Whether Prufrock means them all is not clear, but he should not be underestimated. He surely knows what he is doing in deflecting the sentimentality of evening – and the invitation to the reader – into a pathetic fallacy to end them all. The wearily courteous cadences recall Laforgue's Pierrot, bored to devastating irony. Later in the poem the resources of his wit will include a crossing of Genesis with Hesiod (ll. 28–30), and very pertinent allusions to John the Baptist, Lazarus and Bunyan's Heavenly Footman. It might be best to assume that he is fully aware of what he is saying. That, after all, adds a further dimension of interest. If he knows all that is implied in being 'etherised', is he able to do anything about it, and does he mean us to take the point or to miss it? The epigraph, considered as an allusion to *Inferno* XXVI and XXVII, should perhaps put us on our guard. His name, moreover, might be a variant of Touchstone: how he rubs off on us is the vital question.

The poem develops as a dramatic monologue of an unusual kind. The love song which Prufrock is attempting seems to have something in common with Donne's more dramatic songs and sonets. Then there is the nearer likeness to the manner of Browning's personae. But where Browning's is an art of 'getting inside' his characters, Eliot's method is to remain wholly detached. Andrea del Sarto reveals all in a lucid light of regret and resignation, drawing the reader into sympathetic understanding. Within the poem, his tone determines ours, his consciousness circumscribes ours. Prufrock can be read in that way, but only by ignoring the perspectives and possibilities which open beyond those he submits to. 'The really fine rhetoric of Shakespeare', Eliot wrote in ' "Rhetoric" and Poetic Drama' (1919), 'occurs in situations where the character in the play *sees himself* in a dramatic light'. But, he went on, 'it is essential that we should preserve our position of spectators, and observe always from the outside though with complete understanding'; by this means we gain the 'necessary advantage of a new clue to the character, in noting the angle from which he views himself'. What must be avoided are the degraded forms of the dramatic sense, which appeal to our sentimentality, or at least invite us 'to accept the character's sentimental interpretation of himself'. Prufrock, I think, is doing that, with skill and effrontery: at once frankly revealing his private hell, and seducing us into it. He needs to be analysed.

After the urbane wit of the first lines, the 'certain half-deserted streets' impose their restless sordid impressions, insistent in rhythm and mean in detail. In just a few lines an alien world is given, as much apart, and oppressive, as the first 'Prelude'. Prufrock's attention shifts from what it is, to what it means to him –

<blockquote>
a tedious argument
Of insidious intent
To lead you to an overwhelming question . . .
</blockquote>

– which he does not care to face. His evasion breaks the pattern of the verse, for ll. 8–11 were shaping to parallel ll. 4–7. It then seems odd, that after thinking of the women to be visited, he should revert to a vision of the streets. This proves to be fantasy, however, in which the smoke and fog are domesticated, and the nightmarish and the seductive become confused. The cat is familiar, yet vaguely terrifying; the sordid images of the street are neutralised. Where is the intelligent memory? Prufrock, it appears, is putting to sleep those disturbing impressions, and gaining time from that other world in the drawing-room.

But the logic of time – and perhaps some imperative within the verse form to reach a full close – returns him to the inevitable room. He would use time to fend off tedium and its moral implication, would involve himself in mere flux of mind; but the couplet insists on the fixed facts he is approaching. In a reflex of self-consciousness he sees himself as he will be seen, and attempts self-defence in kind. But the rhymes are merciless; his pathetic correctness shrinks within the frame of what 'they will say'. Aware that he should disturb their little universe, he might well say with Hamlet, 'O cursed spite,/That ever I was born to set it right'.

By what though should he disturb them? Is it by a vision of their world such as they would hardly understand? But dare he speak out? As he enters the room, or as it enters his consciousness, Prufrock moves into a kind of lyric: three stanzas, rhyming and with a refrain. The refrain tellingly transposes 'Do I dare?' into the polite form which is already a defeat: not to dare will be to fail, unambiguously; but in the drawing-room distinctions are blurred, and one simply does not presume. In that way Prufrock's whole vision of the women's world is muted and made powerless. He sings what it really means as it presses upon him, but in a form which might be that of a drawing-room aria. Up to a point he does express its tedium, terror and charm, yet the dominant impression is of its subduing power. He is the victim of the music he would parody, and his song becomes a form of homage to the world which is too much for him. His wit defines his defeats – 'I have measured out my life with coffee-spoons', 'eyes that fix you in a formulated phrase'. And what a complex of feeling there is in 'But in the lamplight, downed with light brown hair!' He is not in love with these women – his passions, if declared, would be closer to boredom and terror – but he is, in the literal sense of a word the drawing-room aria might play with, its 'slave'.

Of course he keeps this vision to himself, sings it only in his head. Then, withdrawing further into himself, he begins to rehearse what he dare not say. The three lines of plain statement come near to fact and objectivity. There might be something there to oppose to the drawing-room, some release from self in observation. Yet the lines are tinged with his own mood; and is he perhaps watching himself watching the lonely men, self-dramatising still? The sudden self-revelation tells all –

> I should have been a pair of ragged claws
> Scuttling across the floors of silent seas.

In Laforgue's *Salomé* there is the Aquarium to match that wish:

> O monde de satisfaits, vous êtes dans la béatitude aveugle et silencieuse, et nous, nous desséchons de fringales supra-terrestres. Et pourquoi les antennes de nos sens, à nous, ne sont-elles pas bornées par l'Aveugle, et l'Opaque et le Silence, et flairent-elles au-delà de ce qui est de chez nous? Et que ne savons-nous aussi nous incruster dans notre petit coin pour y cuver l'ivre-mort de notre petit Moi?'[33]

It is as if a certain kind of idealism, Prufrock's kind, were exposed as merely recessive egoism, motivated by the inversion of love, the death-wish.

Having attained his instant of self-knowledge, Prufrock appears less oppressed, better able to observe his little drama with a wit equal to his predicament. Perhaps he has found *his* point of view in acknowledging defeat. From that, at any rate, follows a new access of consciousness, and a new tone that is self-mockingly comic. The levity is perhaps a form of emotional relief, as Eliot said of Hamlet's – better to send himself up than be taken seriously. At the same time this levity is contained and damped down within a stanzaic form. The verse paragraph which begins at 'And the afternoon, the evening' resumes a patterning rhyme; and the next two go with it, repeating the opening line and refrain, to compose something like a song of Donne's modified after Laforgue. This song is like a revision of the first one. It is for the speaking rather than the singing voice, and it effects an adjustment of the vision to a consciousness of failure.

The earlier stanzas had concentrated the impact of the room; these expand to contain more highly charged effects within soothing banalities. There are intimations of an order of things vaster than this world conceives – yet they do not disturb it. There has been a progression of such intimations from 'etherised', through 'all the works and days of hands', up to John the Baptist ('I am no prophet') and the 'eternal Footman'. That last neatly blends a bored phrase and petty fear with anguished suggestions of 'the doorstep of the Absolute'. Behind it could lie an uneasy recollection of the first sentence of Bunyan's work: 'Solomon saith that "The desire of the slothful killeth him". ' These intimations reach their climax in the allusion to Marvell and the association with Lazarus (Luke xvi, 19–31). Here is the overwhelming question at its most magnified. To squeeze his universe into oneness would be to conquer the tedium of time, and to put its life to the final test – to measure it by the annihilatingly objective vision of one who has passed beyond it. Laforgue's John the Baptist had initiated Salomé into that realm of the Absolute (*l'Inconscient*), and she has his head as the seal of the initiation and its meaning. Prufrock has undergone all that in parody, and remains the mere fool of banalities. His wit is so easily diminished by the mere reflection of what one might say, a woman's languid dismissal of some meaning which exceeds her interest. Her social phrase catches up the intensities of 'into a ball' and 'I shall tell you all', and dissipates them into nothing at all. As much had been done to Michelangelo, but Prufrock as good as asks for it. His wit is capable of that crescendo of great imaginative power – as Eliot said of Marvell's – yet his tone is perfectly in accord with the woman's. 'And would it have been worth it, after all' rhymes in every way with 'That is not it, at all.'

Moreover, he harmonises the very streets with the drawing room. There is no false note in

> After the sunsets and the dooryards and the sprinkled streets,
> After the novels, after the teacups, after the skirts that trail
>   along the floor . . .

It is almost a vignette of the period: a little distanced and generalised, catching the local flavour appreciatively, and with the observer quite subdued to these effects. However the tone is not quite certain, for the details come with a certain insistence, yet in falling cadences. It is as if they were fixed in his mind but he was no longer sure what to make of them. What has happened to the meaning they had for him at the start, to his immediate feelings in the half-deserted street? He had wished, in wanting to be 'a pair of ragged claws', to escape the imperatives of consciousness; and that wish is virtually realised. In Henry James' *The Jolly Corner* there is a character who in the midst of a 'dim secondary social success', projects himself beyond it 'into the other, the real, the waiting life'; and he thinks, 'It was all mere surface sound, this murmur of their welcome, this popping of their corks – just as his gestures of response were the extravagant shadows, emphatic in proportion as they meant little, of some game of *ombres chinoises*.' The difference with Prufrock is that he must fear there is no more to him now than the shadow of his nerves upon the social screen.

His final state is inward reverie – an expansion of ll. 70–4. In the mirror of self-consciousness he makes himself small and shuffles off responsibility. He has not played a hero's part, but if he has been merely the politic counsellor then he has played the fool indeed, a Hamlet being his own Polonius. Dreams and desires disturb him still. In the six lines from 'I grow old' he undergoes startling modulations of feeling and tone, as his romantic soul, defeated in its actual world, dreams of transformation. Yet the ministering sea-girls are simply the actuality reinterpreted according to feeble desires; and the actuality is stronger than the dream. In the last three lines the room, the women and his fate among them are all implicit; and the brief intensity of the illusion is lost – '*We* have lingered', not 'I have seen'. The human voices summon to the surface of existence where he fails.

The allusion to Arnold's 'The Forsaken Merman' is obvious, and ironic – a criticism of *his* elegiac defeatism as well as Prufrock's. For in the latter's defeat is implicated the general failure of nineteenth-century romanticism. To complete a remark of Santayana's which I quoted earlier, 'To understand oneself is the classic form of consolation; to elude oneself is the romantic.' That his love song should turn out an elegy for himself is very much in the spirit of the age of Arnold, and of Tennyson.[34] What was lacking was the ability to turn to account either the modern world or the unsatisfied longing for another. The one might be unreal and meaningless, yet it still oppresses; and while the finer feelings only go into escapist forms they confirm its power. 'To elude oneself' is not the way out. But Prufrock, like his historical antecedents, is incapable of drawing the conclusions Eliot was demonstrating in 'Preludes' and 'Rhapsody'.

In point of fact, he is the exact antitype of the poet himself. He resembles the speaker of the poem's epigraph, Guido da Montefeltro, a politic counsellor whose hell is to be enclosed in the flame of self-knowledge; and who believes, having abandoned hope himself, that hell has no way out. Thus he reveals himself to Dante, who is of course not of the damned, but an observer of them as his love of Beatrice and his art as a poet draw him towards his ultimate vision of Love. Eliot's relation to his character is like that of Dante's to his. Moreover, he did not mean to give way to the unreal world: 'La Figlia Che Piange' is the love song of one whose idealism is as anti-romantic as he thought Dante's.[35] Later he would choose to identify himself with another figure enclosed in flame, the poet Arnaut Daniel, whom Dante placed near the summit of Purgatory. But that connection was already somewhere in his mind when he was drafting 'Prufrock', as a cancelled epigraph shows.[36]

In spite of the significant relation to Dante, the achievement of the poem might most relevantly be measured by the relation to Henry James. James was probably the obvious living writer for Eliot to read and study – the literary master of America and Europe. To read his later fiction alongside Eliot's earlier poetry brings out the clear fact that Eliot read him not dutifully but passionately, and to immense effect. In particular, James had perfected his method of surrounding his protagonist, some more or less forceful man or woman of the world, by an observing consciousness, often someone so ineffectual as to appear the mere passive observer; and yet to have this observer become, on the moral plane, the really interesting protagonist – the one who discerns good and evil, and actively chooses between them. In *The Beast in the Jungle* he stated this as the structural principle:

He allowed for himself, but she, exactly, allowed still more; partly because, better placed for a sight of the matter, she traced his unhappy perversion through portions of its course into which he could scarcely follow. He knew how he felt, but, besides knowing that, she knew how he *looked* as well; he knew each of the things of importance he was insidiously kept from doing, but she could add up the amount they made, understand how much, with a lighter weight on his spirit, he might have done, and thereby establish how, clever as he was, he fell short.

That becomes a suggestive formula for 'Prufrock', where the poet, putting himself in the position of the observer, is the active moral protagonist.

Thus to follow James is to make the conscious imagination the principle of the moral life. Moreover, it is to make life, at its finest, a matter of ultimate discriminations and choices – of not only seeing all that should be seen, but of living by one's fullest perceptions. Now this involves, when the perceptions are those of a James or an Eliot, some renunciation of the usual hopes and fulfilments. Given that the actual falls far short of the ideal, then the moral effort becomes a matter of learning detachment from what life offers, and of striving to keep open communications (Arnold's phrase) with the as yet unborn ideal. However, this idealism, as Eliot said of James' 'romanticism',

> implied no defect in observation of the things that he wanted to observe; it was not the romanticism of those who dream because they are too lazy or too fearful to face the fact; it issues, rather, from the imperative insistence of an ideal which tormented him. He was possessed by the vision of an ideal society; he *saw* (not fancied) the relations between the members of such a society. And no one, in the end, has ever been more aware – or with more benignity, or less bitterness – of the disparity between possibility and fact.[37]

Again one may be reminded of Eliot's own achievement in 'Prufrock'. But then there is the important difference, that he was not possessed by the vision of an ideal society in the sense in which James was. He gave much thought to the question, early and late; but the vision which imperiously possessed him was of the poet's relation to God, his own soul's ideal. His ideal society, as it emerges in his later writings, would be the City of God or Dante's Christian Empire.

That 'La Figlia Che Piange' *completes* the poems of 1905–12 is somewhat obscured in the *Prufrock* volume by its being separated from them by the half-dozen written in Oxford in 1915. These relatively slight studies – etched rather than painted – of New England *moeurs* helped to fill out the slim collection, and added a drily detached sense of comedy to its range of tones. But to appreciate the deeper structure we need to look back from the last poem to the first, and see how the poet in it is opposing himself to Prufrock and all he represents.[38]

By a *dédoublement* of personality, of a kind practised by Laforgue and by James in some of his later tales, the poet assumes a double presence, being at once the actor and the consciousness of his action. Moreover, as his consciousness develops in the poem, it alters from detached observer to an active, directing will. Thus he does not yield to his fate, as Prufrock does, but deliberately orders his feelings according to his vision. This is a love song in which the love and the poetry become a form of the moral life.

The passion so directly expressed in image and rhythm, not inhibited nor guarded by ironies, is a quite new force in the poetry so far. After the loveless or passionless aridities of the preceding poems here at last is the felt power of love. But then, that he should prefer 'a gesture and a pose' to their being together, comes as a sharp challenge to human feeling. Nevertheless, this strange fulfilment appears prompted by a deep impulse or instinct – not by principle, nor yet by anything in the immediate situation. However, that instinctive response has been forming in the two poems placed before this one.

In 'Hysteria' we are exposed to raw experience and disturbing emotion without benefit of aesthetic distance. It may be that the lady is hysterical – what *is* she laughing at? or is it at him? But the speaker plainly gives himself away: he is reduced to a state of nerves by her sexuality. Lost in the struggle for mere self-possession, simply the prose 'I', he is far below the mastery of poetic consciousness. 'Conversation Galante' presents a situation opposite yet equal. Its Pierrot is master of aesthetic distances and ironic perspectives, yet he is no better able to keep his lady in her place. Just to be amorous of the Absolute leaves him, as much as the ordinary man, at the mercy of its 'eternal enemy'.

'La Figlia Che .Piange' finds a way out of these failures – and the related failures of Prufrock and the young man of 'Portrait'. It has taken the point also of the withering flowers of the poems of early youth. Accepting that ideal passion may not be satisfied in any actual world, nor yet in romantic dreams, the poet turns away from them. But he does not give up his passion. Indeed, that is in a way fulfilled in its immediate object; only it is not the girl in herself who satisfies it, but what she is *and* what she seems to stand for. But then things are so arranged, by fate or the poet, that he must lose the girl in the image. The verbs at once declare her actions and direct them; and this transforms them from mere reactions into responses, and establishes a kind of intimate relation. It is their very parting which unites them, and the images of that moment which remain to him become a satisfying expression of his love. The 'gesture and a pose' serve for that because they objectify the intense feelings in a form that is true both to the actual and to the ideal.

The poem finds support for its extraordinary ordering of its feelings in the examples of Dante, and of Virgil, Dante's guide. The epigraph is from Aeneas' meeting with Venus near Carthage: she appears disguised as a maid of the country, and only reveals her divinity as she leaves him. That meeting is echoed in his later encounter with Dido in Hades: his duty to found Rome has compelled him to leave her, renouncing her love; now she turns from him coldly, disdaining his regrets. The title may echo *Inferno* v, 126; and in any case the whole poem gains from a comparison with that most moving meeting with Francesca, who could not constrain desire, and is forever bound to her lover in the wind of Hell. Then there is a positive general relation with the visions and separations of the *Vita Nuova*, and the meetings with Matilda and Beatrice in the Earthly Paradise at the summit of Purgatory. The common meaning which the poem draws from these allusions is that a passion for the ideal can be fulfilled only by passing through and beyond the immediate occasions of love.

To affirm renunciation as a way of love for the poet was to be already following after Dante, though with help also from James and from Baudelaire. And to place the affirmation at the end of the volume which began with 'Prufrock' was surely to indicate a conscious direction. Though *The Waste Land* and *The Hollow Men* come between 'La Figlia Che Piange' and *Ash-Wednesday*, the later vision of the love which makes perfect has its seed in the earlier. Moreover, the poet–lover's visionary experience in the hyacinth garden is an essential stage in its germination. The 'cure for Romanticism' was a long one – and became before the end 'a lifetime's death in love'.

Syllabus

of a

Course of Six Lectures

on

Modern French Literature

by

T. Stearns Eliot, M.A. (Harvard)

Oxford

Frederick Hall, Printer to the University

Copies can be obtained from the Secretary, University Extension Office,
Examination Schools, Oxford

1916

No. 1325

BOOKS

Rousseau : *The Social Contract* (Everyman's Library, 1s. 3d. net); *Confessions* (3s. net, in French 2s. 10d. net); *De l'origine de l'inégalité* (in French, 2s. net).

Lemaître : *Jean-Jacques Rousseau* (Heinemann, 10s. net). 2/8

Barrès : Novels : For the first period. *Le Jardin de Bérénice* (3s. 3d. net). For the later period, *Colette Baudoche, La Colline inspirée* (each 3s 3d. net). Political writings : *Scènes et doctrines du nationalisme* (3s. 3d. net); *La Patrie française* (6d. net). *Pages choisies* (2s.).

Maurras : *L'Avenir de l'intelligence, La Politique religieuse* (each 3s. 3d. net).

Lasserre : *Le Romantisme français* (3s. 3d. net).

Péguy : *Œuvres choisies*, 1900–1910 (3s. 3d. net); *Le Mystère de la charité de Jeanne d'Arc* (3s. 3d. net); *Notre Patrie* (3s. net).

Sorel : *Reflections on Violence* (Allen and Unwin, 7s. 6d. net; French text, 4s. 6d. net).

Claudel : *Art poétique* (3s. 3d. net); *The Tidings brought to Mary* (Chatto and Windus, 6s. net ; French text, 3s. 3d. net); *The East I Know* (H. Milford, 5s. 6d. net ; French text, 3s. 3d. net).

Bergson : *Introduction to Metaphysics* (2s. net).

Maeterlinck : *Wisdom and Destiny, The Life of the Bee* (Allen and Unwin, 2s. 6d. net each).

P. Sabatier : *Modernism* (5s. net); *Disestablishment in France* (3s. 6d. net); *France To-day, its religious orientation* (6s. net).

Loisy : *The Gospel and the Church* (1s. 6d. net); *War and Religion* (1s. 6d. net).

Recommended for Special Subjects.

For Rousseau : Lord Morley, *Rousseau*, 2 vols. ; F. Macdonald, *Rousseau*. For the influence of Rousseau and the ideas of the Revolution outside of France, such books as Brailsford's *Shelley, Godwin and their Circle* (Home University Library, 1s. 3d. net) or Waterlow's *Shelley* (People's Books, 6d. net).

For the leading ideas of the nineteenth century : Renan, *Souvenirs d'enfance et de jeunesse* (Nelson, 1s. 3d. net); Taine, *Introduction à l'histoire de la littérature anglaise* (D. C. Heath & Co.); Babbitt, *Masters of Modern French Criticism* (Constable); Bourget, *Essais de psychologie contemporaine* (2 vols., 3s. 3d. net each).

For exposition and criticism of contemporary ideas (neo-classicism, neo-Catholicism, &c.): various works of F. Brunetière, E. Faguet, and J. Lemaître will be referred to in the course of the lectures, and especially A. France, *La Vie littéraire* (4 vols., 3s. 3d. each).

For contemporary literature : Amy Lowell, *Six French Poets* ; J. Rivière, *Études* (3s. 3d. net); H. Ghéon, *Nos directions* (3s. 3d. net); E. Pound, *The Approach to Paris*.

For Bergson : H. Wildon Carr, *Bergson* (People's Books, 6d. net).

For recent publications of French men of letters in connexion with the war : Loisy's *War and Religion* and Barrès' *Pages choisies*, mentioned above, and Romain-Rolland, *Above the Battle* (2s. 6d. net); A. Suarès, *Péguy, Nous et eux* (3s. each); Lasserre, *Le Germanisme et l'esprit humain* (1s. 3d.).

The best short history of French literature is G. L. Strachey's *Landmarks in French Literature* (Home University Library, 1s. 3d. net).

Inquiries are being made as to other translations than those given above.

LECTURE I

THE ORIGINS: WHAT IS ROMANTICISM?

Contemporary intellectual movements in France must be understood as in large measure a reaction against the 'romanticist' attitude of the nineteenth century. During the nineteenth century several conflicting tendencies were manifested, but they may all be traced to a common source. The germs of all these tendencies are found in Rousseau.

Short sketch of Rousseau's life.

His public career consisted in a struggle against
   (1) *Authority* in matters of religion.
   (2) *Aristocracy* and *privilege* in government.

His main tendencies were
   (1) Exaltation of the *personal* and *individual* above the *typical*.
   (2) Emphasis upon *feeling* rather than *thought*.
   (3) Humanitarianism: belief in the fundamental goodness of human nature.
   (4) Depreciation of *form* in art, and glorification of *spontaneity*.

His great faults were
   (1) Intense egotism.
   (2) Insincerity.

Romanticism stands for *excess* in any direction. It splits up into two directions: escape from the world of fact, and devotion to brute fact. The two great currents of the nineteenth century—vague emotionality and the apotheosis of science (realism) alike spring from Rousseau.

LECTURE II

THE REACTION AGAINST ROMANTICISM

The beginning of the twentieth century has witnessed a return to the ideals of classicism. These may roughly be characterized as *form* and *restraint* in art, *discipline* and *authority* in religion, *centralization* in government (either as socialism or monarchy). The classicist point of view has been defined as essentially a belief in Original Sin—the necessity for austere discipline.

It must be remembered that the French mind is highly theoretic—directed by theories—and that no theory ever remains merely a theory of art, or a theory of religion, or a theory of politics. Any theory which commences in one of these spheres inevitably extends to the others. It is therefore difficult to separate these various threads for purposes of exposition.

The present-day movement is partly a return to the ideals of the seventeenth century. A classicist in art and literature will therefore be likely to adhere to a monarchical form of government, and to the Catholic Church. But there are many cross-currents. Our best procedure is to sketch briefly the relation of politics, literature and religion, and then consider the work of a few representatives of these three interests.

A. Politics: General feeling of dissatisfaction with the Third Republic, crystallizing since the Dreyfus trial. Hence two currents: one toward syndicalism, more radical than nineteenth-century socialism, the other toward monarchy. Both currents express revolt against the same state of affairs, and consequently tend to meet.

Nationalism is an independent movement, but tends to associate itself with monarchism.

44

B. Religion : Neo-Catholicism is partly a political movement, associated with monarchism, and partly a reaction against the sceptical scientific view of the nineteenth century. It is very strongly marked in socialistic writers as well. It must not be confused with modernism, which is a purely intellectual movement.

C. Literature : Movement away from both realism and purely personal expression of emotion. Growing devotion to form, finding expression in new forms. Disapproval of dilettantism and aestheticism. Expression of the new political and religious attitudes in literature.

We shall consider men of letters only as they represent political, religious, or philosophical tendencies.

LECTURE III

MAURICE BARRÈS AND THE ROMANCE OF NATIONALISM

Barrès illustrates the transition between the nineteenth and the twentieth centuries.

His two phases:

(1) Begins as an exponent of egotistic aestheticism in the 'nineties', comparable to J. K. Huysmans and Oscar Wilde. His early novels. Novels of Italy. *Bérénice.*

(2) His entrance into politics as a deputy. In his later novels he returns to the scenes of his childhood—Lorraine. Becomes the champion of the irreconcilables of Alsace-Lorraine.

Barrès' later novels: *Les Bastions de l'Est: Colette Baudoche.*

These novels illustrate two features of nationalism: growing spirit of revenge against Germany, and the cult of the soil—the local, as contrasted with the Parisian spirit—which has been taken up by many modern writers.

While the gulf that separated France from Germany always widened, French writers turned more and more to England. Evidences of the Anglophile sentiment in French letters.

LECTURE IV

ROYALISM AND SOCIALISM

Besides the loyal band of traditional royalists there are several intellectuals who have been led to the royalist position largely as a protest against all the conditions in art and society which seemed to be due to the Revolution.

The two most noteworthy of these men are Pierre Lasserre and Charles Maurras.

Characteristics of their work:

Their reaction fundamentally sound, but

Marked by extreme violence and intolerance.

Contemporary socialism has much in common with royalism. Growth of proletariat, as contrasted with bourgeois socialism. Causes of this: conservative and compromise character of official socialism.

A peasant journalist: Charles Péguy.

Sketch of his life. Celebrity due to his death on the battle-field.

His relations with Jaurès. Foundation of the *Cahiers de la quinzaine.*

His writings and literary style.

Péguy illustrates nationalism and neo-Catholicism as well as socialism: and the fusion of nationalism and Catholicism in his *Jeanne d'Arc.*

A more violent reaction against bourgeois socialism is found in Georges Sorel, the initiator of syndicalism.

His philosophic creed.

His theory of the general strike.

His development toward royalism.

Both of these men—Péguy and Sorel—were strongly influenced by Bergson.

LECTURE V

THE RETURN TO THE CATHOLIC CHURCH

Reaction against the positivism of Taine and the scepticism of Renan, the two chief intellectual leaders of the nineteenth century. Tendency of the French intellectual to return to orthodox Christianity.

Modernism is merely a compromise between the point of view of historical criticism—inherited from Renan—and orthodoxy.

This return to the Church is illustrated in authors of all types. Among poets by—

Francis Jammès.   Sentimental Christianity, really romanticist. And especially by—

Paul Claudel.   Claudel is also nationalist.   His Christianity is that of mediaeval philosophy.   The national and the Christian sentiments are the mainspring of his poems and his poetical dramas. Claudel a writer of great force and great influence, but often falls into rhetoric and verbiage.

Contrast between the Catholicism of twentieth-century men of letters and that of the nineteenth century.   It is more social and political, less individualistic and ascetic.

LECTURE VI

BEFORE AND AFTER THE WAR: QUESTIONS FOR THE FUTURE

The philosophy of 1910.

Henri Bergson was then the most noticed figure in Paris. The leading idea of his philosophy. Comparison with Maeterlinck: the two men have in common

(1) The use of science against science.

(2) Mysticism.

(3) Optimism.

Influence of Bergson upon some of the men already mentioned. Is this influence good or bad? Whether it is likely to persist.

Summary of contemporary tendencies. Influence of the war.

Forecast of French thought after the war.

Part Two

1912–1922

'Shall I at least set my lands in order?'

The classicist point of view has been defined as essentially a belief in Original Sin.

It happens now and then that a poet by some strange accident expresses the mood of his generation, at the same time that he is expressing a mood of his own which is quite remote from that of his generation.

1911–14		Graduate student of philosophy at Harvard.
		The earliest of *The Waste Land* materials drafted.
1914		To Paris in the summer, then to Marburg and to London at the outbreak of war in August. In October commenced his year at Oxford on a Harvard Travelling Fellowship. Met Ezra Pound in September.
1915		At Oxford wrote 'Morning at the Window', 'The *Boston Evening Transcript*', 'Aunt Helen', 'Cousin Nancy', 'Mr Apollinax', 'Hysteria'. Thanks to Pound's efforts the poems of the *Prufrock* volume appeared in periodicals in England and USA.
	26 June	Married Vivien Haigh-Wood.
	September	Schoolmaster at High Wycombe Grammar School.
1916		Junior master at Highgate Junior School. Oxford University Extension Lecturer. Early criticism: by the end of 1920 he had contributed about ninety articles and reviews to a dozen journals.
	April	Completed doctoral thesis.
1917	March	'Reflections on *Vers Libre*'. Entered Lloyds Bank, Colonial and Foreign Department, in the City. Poems in French.
	May	'Eeldrop and Appleplex' I (II appeared in September).
	June	*Prufrock and Other Observations*. Assistant Editor of the *Egoist*.
	July	'The Hippopotamus'.
	November	*Ezra Pound: his metric and poetry*.
		[Eliot himself dated as of 1917 'Sweeney Erect', 'A Cooking Egg', 'Mr Eliot's Sunday Morning Service', 'Whispers of Immortality' – though this was not finished until May–June 1918 – and 'Gerontion' which was only 'half-finished' in June 1919.]
1918	September	'Sweeney among the Nightingales'.
		['Burbank with a Baedeker: Bleistein with a Cigar'.]
1919	December	*Ara Vos Prec* – collected the contents of the *Prufrock* volume with the poems later grouped as 'Poems – 1920', but omitted 'Hysteria' and included 'Ode' [1918].
1920	November	*The Sacred Wood* – 'the essays taken together are planned to form a whole and give a statement of principles of general application – a study of past poetry for the appraisement of the present' (dust-jacket).
1921	March	'Andrew Marvell'.
	June	'John Dryden'.
	September	'The Metaphysical Poets'.
		In September Eliot's health broke down and he took three months' leave from the bank; he went to Margate for a month, and then for another month to Lausanne; on his way back to England after Christmas he showed the completed draft of *The Waste Land* to Pound in Paris.
1922	October	*The Waste Land*.

3

Gerontion, and the historical sense

Those who do not remember the past are condemned to relive it. (Santayana)

> Do not let me hear
> Of the wisdom of old men ...

Eliot thought of 'Gerontion' as a possible prelude to *The Waste Land*;[1] and certainly this persona of 1919, the successor to Prufrock, is nearly related to Tiresias, his successor. Since the poetry of the period 1916 to 1921 is predominantly a study in the state of mind of which Tiresias is the most important representative it may be useful to bring him to mind at once.

Tiresias has a considerable history, of which this is only a brief abstract. In Homer he is the prophet 'who even dead hath yet his mind entire' – the phrase is from Pound's *Cantos* – whom Odysseus summons from Hades to tell whether he will reach Ithaca. In Sophocles, as the blind, withered prophet of Thebes, he is the seer of the sins of Oedipus, and of Creon, for which the city is cursed. Ovid tells how he became expert in the pleasures of both sexes, and was struck blind, and gifted with prophecy which no-one would heed. Dante placed him in Hell with the augurs and diviners, who because they wish to peer into the secret future have their faces turned so that they can only look back. Yet he takes his character from Ovid, recalling his change from male to female, and subsequent recovery of his manhood. Tennyson, in a striking variation based on Callimachus' fifth Hymn, partly assimilates him to Actaeon, giving as the cause of his blindness and prophetic sight a moment's overwhelming vision of the goddess Athene as she bathed. Tennyson's Tiresias is perhaps the nearest to Eliot's in feeling, yet clearly Eliot has been conscious of the whole of his story.

Moreover, his Tiresias is distinctively of *The Waste Land* –

> And I Tiresias have foresuffered all
> Enacted on this same divan or bed ...

Seeing these present events, he sees them in a long backward perspective as simply 'the present existence, the present significance, of the entire past'.[2] That makes him an expression of 'the historical sense', not a seer of the future. His is the point of view, regarding the living present in the light of the dead past, which characterises the second phase of Eliot's development.

However, just as the *Prufrock* volume concludes surprisingly with 'La Figlia Che Piange', so there are in this phase other feelings which will prove ultimately more vital. Pound dubbed the author of *The Waste Land* 'Vates cum fistula',[3] which could refer to Tiresias' troubles, but might allude also to the music he makes of them. A *fistula* is a pipelike ulcer; or a pipe to make music with; or, in the early Christian Church, a tube through which the sacramental wine was taken. It is a neat knot of associations; and these take us beyond Tiresias to Philomela and to Arnaut Daniel, two very important figures in the poem whom he cannot be seen to contain. He sees only what he has foresuffered, and identifies the living with the dead. But Philomela in her anguish is transformed into an 'inviolable voice'; and Arnaut in the *Purgatorio* weeps and goes singing, enclosed in the flame of his past follies, yet seeing with joy the dawn he hopes for. Arnaut is the type of a mind very different from Tiresias and Gerontion. It exists not in the contemplation of what is dead, but of what is desired; and it does not despair but lives and sings in the intensity of active suffering. The creation of a lyric mind of this type is the surprising achievement of *The Waste Land*.

It would surprise less if more of the work that went into it were on view. The verse Eliot published appears to lead naturally and inevitably from Prufrock through Gerontion to Tiresias. But the drafts of *The Waste Land* show that what he was really wanting to write was 'What the Thunder Said'. There is even a draft of 1914 or earlier, 'So through the evening, through the violet air', which looks like an attempt to carry 'Prufrock' through to that conclusion. In fact it took a long and painful labour to get there; and until it was achieved there was little in the poems in print to suggest the nature of his deepest feelings. In 'Poems – 1920', 'Dans le Restaurant' seems out of keeping with the rest, and the end of 'Sweeney among the Nightingales' is desperately obscure. Yet these are the significant revelations of the collection.

'Any poet, if he is to survive as a writer beyond his twenty-fifth year, must alter; he must seek new literary influences; he will have different emotions to express.' So Eliot wrote in 1917, in *Ezra Pound: his metric and poetry*; and again in 1919, in 'Tradition and the Individual Talent', 'the historical sense . . . we may call nearly indispensable to anyone who would continue to be a poet beyond his twenty-fifth year'. For Eliot, that was the year after he completed the 'Prufrock' group.

He had done nothing so good in the years immediately following. By mid-1915, when he decided to renounce philosophy and Harvard, the only new verses worth publishing were the slight observations of New England. In 1916 or 1917, feeling he had dried up completely and rather desperately seeking new influences, he tried writing in French, with a vocabulary largely drawn from Tristan Corbière. 'I did these things as a sort of tour de force to see what I could do.'[4] That enabled him to get started again in English, with 'Gerontion' and the poems in quatrains. For the latter the model was Gautier's *Emaux et Camées*. He found that concentrating his conscious mind on experiment in metric and language helped to release his imagination: 'the form gave impetus to the content'.[5] That could be said of much of his verse in this decade, of which the characteristic quality is a deliberate effort to find what needed to be said and done next.

The immediate influence behind this was Ezra Pound, grand instigator of the modern movement, and to Eliot in particular a powerful mentor and ally in his work up to *The Waste Land*. 'Il miglior fabbro', Eliot acknowledged; and Pound's annotations on Eliot's drafts show how he deserved that. It was Pound who put Eliot onto Gautier. He was able to show him the manuscript chapters of *Ulysses* at the moment when Eliot could profit most from them, in 1917 and 1918. Once, as an experiment, 'with the firm intuito that a poem wd result, and intention that it should', he introduced him to 'Grishkin'.[6] Above all, by his conversation, convictions and example, he stimulated in Eliot the search for new models and the cultivation of the historical sense. Much in Eliot's criticism of those years is the echo of Pound's ideas; indeed, the argument of 'Tradition and the Individual Talent' is a formula for *Homage to Sextus Propertius* and *Hugh Selwyn Mauberley*.

So far as Eliot's own work is concerned, that essay applies most directly to 'Poems – 1920' and the first three parts of *The Waste Land*. It also provides evidence of the different kind of poet that was struggling to be born. There is the betraying over-emphasis upon the need to suppress personality: 'The progress of an artist is a continual self-sacrifice, a continual extinction of personality.' That is far from Pound's tone. He was already the most conscious and impersonal of poets, but without any repression of personality. It seems that for Eliot at this time 'impersonality' involved some violence to self. 'Only those who have personality and emotions know what it means to want to escape from these things.' Beneath the veiling flicker of scorn there is the bitterness and weariness of his being, like his Hamlet, up against an emotion he could not elucidate. Later, in the three wartime Quartets, he would become a poet who could hold in the one vision his own experience and that of the nation, if not quite of the race. By then 'tradition' would have come to mean not the whole mind of Europe since Homer and the Magdalenian draughtsmen, but that element of it especially cultivated by Catholicism. This element, the 'orthodox' organisation of sensibility to be found in Dante, provided the form in which he could express his personality most directly. But the more comprehensive idea of tradition, as practised by Pound, was for Eliot between 1916 and 1921 rather a means of escape from his deepest problems. It enabled him to assume the role of the detached observer of his own most painful emotions; but his need was to be not a Tiresias, but an Arnaut.

'The historical sense compels a man to write not merely with his own generation in his bones, but with a feeling that the whole of the literature of Europe from Homer and within it the whole of the literature of his own country has a simultaneous existence and composes a simultaneous order.' In those terms, the author of *Prufrock and Other Observations* had written merely with 'his own generation in his bones'; but the author of 'Poems – 1920' was cultivating an awareness of the past in its simultaneity and its ideal order, so that he might command 'not merely the present, but the present moment of the past'.

The wit of the earlier poems is that of a mind intent on analysing its immediate world, and drawing on former meanings and values to help define it, but without bringing the past itself under scrutiny. Its use of the past is simply to create startling shifts of viewpoint, scale and perspective. In 'Prufrock', the references to Genesis and Hesiod, to John the Baptist and Lazarus, and to *Hamlet*, work in that way; they do not compose, with each other and with Prufrock, a simultaneous order. As in the wit of some of Eliot's masters, Donne and Webster and Marvell, things remote and unlike are 'yoked together' – 'The worlds revolve like ancient women' – in order to intensify some immediate emotion or perception. The effect depends upon there being no necessary connection between the elements: it is the wit alone which holds them together. It is nearly the reverse, therefore, of the wit which discovers the necessary connections of the past and the present, and sees beneath their seeming disparity to what is recurrent or permanent. This more searching wit identifies the contemporary soldier returning from war with Agamemnon and Odysseus; recognises in the hyacinth girl Dido, Cleopatra and other ill-fated *femmes fatales*; and in the voice of the nightingale it hears Cassandra and Philomela. Prufrock and Hamlet have a certain likeness: among other things, both succumb to a world beneath their finer consciousness. But the hyacinth girl is not just like her prototypes: for the moment she is Ophelia.

In the poems of 1915 the wit is still of the simpler sort. In nodding a distant goodbye to La Rochefoucauld the poet sets up a point of view from which to observe the readers of the *Boston Evening Transcript*. Rochefoucauld 'is hard', Eliot wrote in 1919, 'but there is not in him even the germ of cynicism: he is an implacable moralist . . . he persists in measuring men by an invisible standard, fundamentally a Christian standard'.[7] In 'Aunt Helen' the turn of wit opens a void beyond the solid ways of her world. The silence at her end of the street is hardly the apocalyptic 'silence in heaven' of Revelations viii, 1. 'Cousin Nancy' works by similar subtle shifts of perspective and viewpoint. Though a problem to her aunts she is the product of their ethics, based on 'Emerson's doctrine of self-reliance and . . . Arnold's individual culture'.[8] 'The army of unalterable law', which puts Meredith's insurgent Lucifer in his place, has come to this! The very syntax of 'Mr Apollinax' declares that he brings to mind many things which are not to be found 'In the palace of Mrs Phlaccus' – (from the Greek for 'to be broken or rent asunder with a noise'?) – or at Professor Channing-Cheetah's. Yet he is not quite the contemporary Fragilion or Priapus or centaur; and these allusions simply go to define his laughter and his 'dry and passionate talk'. All that matters is that the pallid banalities should be disposed of.[9]

The two slighter of the poems in French of 1916–17 show little advance on the work of 1915. 'Mélange Adultère de Tout',[10] on the surface a comic self-portrait, conceals in its final image a startling joke to disperse the adulterous mixture of existence. A cenotaph, strictly speaking, is 'an empty tomb; a sepulchral monument raised in honour of a deceased person whose body is elsewhere' (*O.E.D.*): the risen Christ, as it might be. The secretive wit is clever, but it is not yet that of the historical sense. In 'Le Directeur',[11] the clipped observation may include an awareness that Blake and Dickens in their times saw such things beside the Thames; but Tom-all-Alone's and the youthful harlot's curse are not present in the vision.

With 'Lune de Miel' the past does begin to enter into the poetry as something to be observed in itself and on a level with the actual. In this one poem their relation is very crudely perceived: a caricatured present set against an idealised past. The examples of Pound and Joyce may have saved Eliot from going on in that way. The poem is useful as an example of what the historical sense does not mean for his poetry in general. It sets up a series of easy and superficial contrasts: the flea-bitten legs and the crumbling columns of Sant'Apollinare in Classe; the love-feast of Leonardo's *Last Supper*, and the honeymoon which has become a matter of finding a cheap restaurant; a joyless and trivial 'doing Europe', and the disused works of God which holds Byzantium still in tumbled stone. Lines 257–65 of *The Waste Land* show how it can be done without crude simplification. This invocation of lost or neglected values appears merely arbitrary; and the Swiftian view of human relations and culture is here petty not powerful.

'Dans le Restaurant' is just the opposite in several respects. Indeed it stands quite apart from the rest of 'Poems – 1920', as part of Eliot's inner development – a link between 'La Figlia Che Piange' and *The Waste Land*. The quality to be remarked here is that it resists the superficial contrasts, and admits profound correspondences. The persona would reject the disgusting waiter, but has to recognise that he too has been awakened to love and regrets its loss, and is really his double. This recognition of their deep identity, though it is not strictly the historical sense, is yet a related form of discovery; and it is possibly the more vital as it is the more personal and inward.

The eight poems in quatrains of 1917 and 1918 are mostly – adapting Frank Kermode's neat title – puzzles without epiphanies. They are the work of the critic more than the poet, and exercise the critic's tools of analysis and comparison. These are applied, as in *The Sacred Wood* and *For Lancelot Andrewes*, to the morals and religion as well as the literature of European culture. But the poems are more cerebral, more allusive, elliptical and difficult even than the prose. To make out the meaning we must be alert for analogies and contradictions; for sameness beneath difference and difference beneath sameness; for complex contrasts and correspondences. Such puzzles are not everyone's idea of a good game; yet they can be, like other kinds of play, a form of discovery.

'Burbank with a Baedeker: Bleistein with a Cigar' gives in its composite epigraph a brief abstract of the poem's method. This is a collage of mainly Venetian associations: a snatch from Gautier's variation on an air of the 'Carnival of Venice'; an epigram, 'nothing stays if not divine; all else is smoke', to be seen there on a scroll attached to a burning candle in Mantegna's *St Sebastian*; some evocative phrases from Henry James' Venetian tale, *The Aspern Papers*; a bracketing of Othello's disillusioned disgust with his Venetian bride, and Galuppi's lament (in Browning's *Men and Women*) for dead Venetian women; finally a stage direction from an obscure masque by Marston, an improbable variation upon the legend of Niobe. All these allusions are too cryptic to mean much unless one knows the works they come from. But then that is true of the peom as a whole.

Nevertheless, in the poem all the resources of the verse are used to synthesise the complex of allusions. Within the sequence of simple quatrains there is a continuous varying of the syntax,[12] and continuously interesting variations of sound and rhythm. There is an uncommon use of initial and internal rhyming; and a trick of throwing the end and weight of a sentence beyond the line into the start of the next. It is a technique to make the reader catch at associations, seek mental connections, think on several historical levels at once.

The time-levels, roughly speaking, are the contemporary Venice, after Henry James; the older Venice of history and legend, as imagined by Shakespeare and others; then there is some allusion to the timeless divine. The synthesis seems to resolve this complexity into the suggestion that in Venice, now as ever, there is no divine presence but only the smoke of a wasting existence. Within that, certain discriminations are observed: lust for money goes with the lowest forms of life; an absence of passion, though its doom would be inevitable, is to be regretted.

Burbank has the air of one of James' cultivated consciousnesses, it hardly matters whether of England or New England. The Princess Volupine is also rather Jamesian, a serpent of Old Europe with a name that crosses Jonson's Volpone with the Voluptas of Jacobean tragedy. Their encounter is the old story, and without such moral retribution as Tennyson inserted in his 'The Sisters', from which l. 4 comes. But then the moral point is in the feeling that there is not much passion in this affair. The 'defunctive music' of Shakespeare's 'The Phoenix and Turtle' ('Love and Constancie is dead') therefore applies quite literally, not at all mystically. It modulates naturally into 'the passing bell', and from that to the music heard by Antony's men: a nexus of associations of love and death and the sea. The first stanza was simple, a terse narrative; the third gathers up the suggestions of the second into a powerfully charged, yet muted, apocalypse. The horses drawing up the chariot of the sun are those strikingly represented upon St Mark's in Venice; the beat of their 'even feet' is that of Horace's oncoming Death – 'Time's winged Chariot hurrying near' as Marvell rendered it. The large promise of the sun's rising and the extinction of its setting are nearly fused in a single action. The story of Antony and Cleopatra could be distilled in that effect. Yet the barge, Cleopatra's and the Princess Volupine's, burns on the water with a difference. Is she shutting herself up, as it were in her monument, until she can entertain her little Caesar? Has romantic passion declined into deception and self-interest?

Bleistein, heir to three civilisations – ancient, middle and modern, one might say – not only looks like an ape, but has an eye like the first slime before ever man or Venice were made. Yet, staring at a Canaletto, whose views of Venice imply a civilised beholder, he seems to be at the wrong end of its perspective, the burnt out extinction of time. Thus Bleistein, though his name means 'leadstone', is a parallel to Burbank: the bewitching moment of passion, and the end of the endless process of biological and cultural evolution, equated, are found equally wanting.

The two penultimate stanzas consider the wealth which may be made a substitute for passion both sexual and spiritual. Sir Ferdinand Klein seems to be a variation upon Bleistein: one in whom the Hebraic has undergone translation into, at a guess, an English merchant banker. 'On the Rialto once', Shylock's phrase in *The Merchant of Venice*, evokes the world of Christian traders financed by Jewish usurers. However, the equation of money interest with Jews, and Jews with rats eating away the foundations of Venice, is a brutal over-simplification – and one which Shakespeare's play exposes. Ruskin also, and dispassionate historians, have found the cause of its fall in itself, not in its scapegoat. What Eliot lapsed into here is not the best of the mind of Europe, but an infection in it. Henry Adams, as cultivated an heir of that mind as he could make himself, and a possible model for Burbank, wrote in a letter in 1896: 'Now no one doubts – and every Jew in London has acted on the belief – that America cannot maintain the gold standard. . . In the situation an investment is sheer gambling. We are in the hands of the Jews. They can do what they please with our values'.[13] There is matter for the historical sense in the parallel between Adams and Antonio. That the profit motive is at the heart of Europe's culture and ethics is a truth which we seem culpably unable to perceive. And Eliot was working in Lloyds Bank!

The call for 'Lights, lights' has been thought to allude to the waking of Brabantio to warn him of Othello's love for Desdemona. The same phrase occurs when Claudius, appalled at Hamlet's play, rushes from the scene. Either allusion serves for ironic comparison. Burbank, however, is more Hamlet than Iago, as he meditates like Byron's Childe Harold in Venice, 'a ruin amidst ruins'. He thinks, apparently, of Ruskin's thoughts on Venice, and wonders who was responsible for its decline. Does he realise that the lion of Venice is also the lion of Mark the Evangelist, and that Ruskin wrote not of the laws but of the spiritual life necessary for an architecture, and a culture?

There are many more allusions and further levels of irony; but this will do to suggest the kind of poem this is. Its many-mindedness does not arise directly from lived experience, but is forged, artificially, through the conscious exercise of wit. It is not a pattern of feeling, but an intellectual matrix.

For the other poems of this kind the notes can be briefer. Sweeney has some relation to Bleistein; as well as to Sweeney Todd the Soho Barber of fact and stage, notorious for cutting his victims' throats while shaving them. In 'Sweeney Erect' the epigraph and the two opening stanzas together evoke a scene in *The Maid's Tragedy* (II.II) as background to the modern drama. There is the

Greek tale of Theseus' desertion of Ariadne, the Roman tale of Aeneas' desertion of Dido, and the Jacobean version of the same story of passionate woman abandoned by heroic lover. The passing mention of Nausicaa and Polypheme just recalls two of Ulysses' morning encounters – ones charged with opposite feelings. Sweeney, whom Eliot thought of as perhaps a Boston pugilist, appears the end of this line of heroes called to set public duty before private passion. His morning rite is shaving; which causes the woman in the case to have hysterics, out of fright perhaps, yet an appropriate parody of grief. The final stanza may allude to a variant of Ariadne's tale, which has it that she did not die of a broken heart, but was loved by Bacchus. Perhaps this is what the ancient tragedy comes down to in its modern parallel. Yet bathos, without relation to any felt or intense vision, is a mean effect. 'A Game of Chess' is a much richer and more perceptive treatment of the matter.

If Sweeney can be associated with Bleistein, then the hero of 'A Cooking Egg' would go with Burbank. His case resembles the other's in the effect of its historical parallels and contrasts. In tracing these we should observe the rules of the game: our comparison and analysis must stick to the given facts and not introduce our own fancies and opinions.[14] In particular, speculations as to who Pipit was in Eliot's life are out of order. Besides, they obscure the one definite fact about her, that so far as the Cooking Egg is aware, she has no use.

A cooking egg is one that has not been used while fresh, and though not quite off is not what it might have been. Villon, on the other hand, as the epigraph recalls, was a thoroughly bad egg and knew it: in his thirtieth year he'd drunk the dregs of his disgrace. His *Grand Testament* is just the opposite of the Cooking Egg's meditations. Eliot mentioned it in *The Sacred Wood* as a touchstone for honesty and 'the right seriousness of great literary art'.[15] The question is whether the persona is serious enough to be completely honest with himself about what his life has come to. His testamentary dispositions, if that is what we have in the middle section, renounce the earthly goods which he expects to find in heaven in their ideal forms. But what of his present state? The *ubi sunt* echo, an elegant and eloquent variation upon Villon's 'Où sont les neiges d'antan', applies to his whole life, which collapses into the regretted world of childhood and its unfulfilled dreams of heroism. Meanwhile Pipit, whom he shall not want, sits in an aura of the past, preserving the mementos of his losses. But how, without facing *them*, can he begin to make his true testament? He is a very Jamesian character, and James' *Crapy Cornelia* is an illuminating background for the poem. That indicates a potential depth. When one adds the connections with *Animula*, 'Coriolan' and the first section of *The Dry Salvages*, there is some reason to feel that there may be more personal experience behind the poem than the wit would allow. Which is not to say that the biography would tell us anything the poem itself does not.

At about this point in the volume one might give a thought to the arrangement of the poems in it. There are links which suggest that there might be a certain coherence, even the ambition to have the poems combine in a comprehensive vision. 'Gerontion' attempts to sum up the meaning of history in a mind which knows it all. The next finds in Venice a particular centre and focus. The third considers Europe's founding heroes. And the Cooking Egg might be the last refinement of its civilisation – a passionless small soul, whose state is really no different from the common crowd's:

> Over buttered scones and crumpets
>   Weeping, weeping multitudes
> Droop in a hundred A.B.C.'s.

That echo of Blake and evocation of contemporary London leads into 'Le Directeur', a sardonic reflection upon the higher journalism, which might be supposed the superior consciousness of this culture. The poet then presents himself, mixed up to distraction in this adulterous world, yet secretly a spiritual Houdini, knowing a mysterious means of escape. With that dark hint, at exactly the mid-point in the volume, the attention turns from an analysis of the history and present state of the culture, towards its vital resources. It is ruined, but is there yet life? 'Lune de Miel' starkly contrasts the natural life of flesh in the world with the enduring forms of the divine. Against that is set a satire upon the natural life of the Church in the world. In 'Dans le Restaurant' the poet himself offers a rather different vision of life and another mode of salvation – one confirmed by other poets and by immediate experience in 'Whispers of Immortality'. The failure of the Church to preserve the knowledge of it incarnate in the Word is studied in 'Mr Eliot's Sunday Morning Service'. The sequence closes with an affirmation of a traditional wisdom answering to the contemporary predicament, but missed or lost by both the secular and the religious experts, as by the mere natural man. They have not heard the nightingales whose song only the poet now understands. This very summary sketch is of course more cryptic than conclusive, but it may serve to suggest that the individual puzzles may finally be answered in the organisation of the whole.

'The Hippopotamus' should be intoned in a solemn mode from the Christian hymnals – there are echoes of those of the Unitarian, Methodist and Anglican communions at least. The epigraph addresses it to the Laodiceans, to whom (in Revelation iii) God says:

I know thy works, that thou art neither cold nor hot: I would thou wert cold or hot. So then because thou art lukewarm, and neither cold nor hot, I will spue thee out of my mouth. Because thou sayest, I am rich, and increased with goods, and have need of nothing; and knowest not that thou art wretched, and miserable, and poor, and blind, and naked . . .

In that spirit, but satirically, the poem explodes the clichés upon which the established Church rests. However, the hippo of flesh and blood, while good for a smack at the Church, is also good for a laugh. The joke is against the Church, but it depends on the absurdity of such grossness entering into heaven. There is no redemption in this comic hymn for the unromantic honeymooners; nor is there any hint of the vision which Bottom, ass's head and all, was vouchsafed. The poet is aware rather of the absence of Christ's flesh and blood.

'Dans le Restaurant' (which will be considered at the end of this chapter) is a poet–lover's *memento mori*. 'Whispers of Immortality' expands its perceptions into a philosophical point of view. The main contrast is between the Jacobean vision of death in life, and an up-to-date dream of earth's bliss. But there is a third term of greater importance. Over and above the punning superimpositions of physical love and death, there is a questioning of 'thought'. Webster knew that thought has its own lusts and luxuries, and that knowledge of death may sharpen sensual desire, even clinging to dead limbs like Donne's 'bracelet of bright hair about the bone'. Each line in the two stanzas about Donne is a new move in the argument: he had only sense; and put nothing in the place of sense; when experience failed he became expert in the sensations of mortality, and knew the bone's fever to be freed of flesh. All this is to turn the sexual pun upon itself: to find a death-wish at the end of love and lust. The last stanza of the poem affirms in paradox that this is a metaphysical perception to be arrived at only by physical experience. The Abstract Entities, the bloodless categories of pure metaphysics, remain drawn to Grishkin's full fleshed charms. But wholly to derive one's knowledge from sensation is to know in the end the death of sense – and thus to rise above the merely physical. This, I suppose, is to carry carnal knowledge to its ultimate.

The one word which fills the whole first line of 'Mr Eliot's Sunday Morning Service', while it is opposed to the preceding message of mortality, is most strikingly not the Word. 'Polyphiloprogenitive' means to be busy about begetting, increasing and multiplying. It appears that it is the very Word of God which the sapient sutlers are breeding out of the One the many. Origen, having castrated himself 'for the kingdom of heaven's sake', brought forth 'an estimated 6,000 books', among them an elaborate exegesis of the first chapter of John's gospel which begins 'In the beginning was the Word'.[16] These begot in their turn proliferations of commentary and controversy, and so the Word became words, words, words. The painter, in contrast, makes a simple and enduring image of the incarnate Christ, and even of the Trinity. However, the modern Church, as in 'The Hippopotamus', seems to do without Christ's presence. It equates penance with expiatory pence, though Christ prayed and fasted in the wilderness; and its devotions are a burning of candles, while the true followers of Christ wish to be consumed in him.[17] The last two stanzas resume the whole. The bees recall the sapient sutlers and Origen, but in their case the office is natural. Sweeney, the natural man, takes his bath in a different sense from 'the Baptized God'. And 'the masters of the subtle schools', the cause of his knowing no better, are perhaps no better off than him. They are judged though, these ministers and theologians of the True Church, as 'religious caterpillars' in their treatment of the Incarnation.

Taken together these poems declare that what lives only in time, whether historical time or that of the individual person's physical existence, is only dying or already dead. Any lasting life must lie through or beyond a death like Christ's. 'Sweeney among the Nightingales' culminates in an anguished cry for that form of death, as the way to transcend the doomed state of mere endless existence and slaughter. This is a poem in which the allusions are especially dense, as well as nearly submerged in the contemporary detail; yet they can be seen to fit into a precise pattern, and to make the poem as a whole come clear in depth. The epigraph gives a bare hint of the degree to which it is saturated with awareness of the homecomings of Agamemnon and Odysseus from the Trojan War. The last books of the *Odyssey*, Aeschylus' *Oresteia* and Seneca's *Agamemnon* are relevant in general and in detail. There is reason then to suppose that 'the silent man in mocha brown' is a modern hero returning at the end of the 1914–18 war. Mocha brown could be a shade of khaki;[18] in *Sweeney Agonistes* Doris's and Dusty's visitors mention that they were all in the war together – and they might have called the girls 'nightingales', a slang term for the ladies of a house such as Mrs Turner's. There was also a popular soldier's song, more proper in its sentimentality –

> There's a long, long trail a-winding
> Into the land of my dreams,
> Where the nightingales are singing
> And a white moon beams . . .

All this suggests that the world of 1918 is being viewed as the present moment of what is perpetually recurrent; and that the past is being brought to bear upon the present, in order to clarify its meaning, and possibly to provide a solution to its predicament. The sense of doom generated in the early stanzas parallels that hanging over the House of Atreus. But it is how the curse may be resolved that matters most.

For that reason it is the final six lines that are most important. The nightingales' singing is dense with associations beyond the contemporary ones. To point to them Eliot added, in one printing, a second epigraph: 'Why should I speak of the nightingale?/The nightingale sings of adulterate wrong.' Çassandra was likened to a nightingale in the *Agamemnon,* as she uttered her vision of the bloody history of the line of Atreus about to culminate in the murder of Agamemnon; and she herself wished she could be, like Philomela, transformed and released from the horror. Penelope, telling the disguised Odysseus how the suitors were trying to make her break her vow to him, also thought of the nightingale. There could be a connection there with the nuns whose vows make them brides of Christ. That allusion brings in another realm. Devotion to the Sacred Heart stresses especially Christ's so loving the world that he died to save it – another kind of saviour and hero than the returning soldiers. Eliot said 'the wood I had in mind was the grove of the Furies at Colonus; I called it "bloody" because of the blood of Agamemnon in Argos'.[19] In Sophocles' drama the grove was filled with nightingales when Oedipus went lovingly to the death which would end his fateful existence. In its way it is a parallel with Christ's, only not miasmally misted over. The crescendo of feeling in these lines, so rare an event in the volume, establishes its major contrast: the difference between deaths which make for life, and those which only confirm a horror of life.

The volume concludes then with an epiphany, and one which is a sudden intense revelation of the feelings behind the whole series of dazzling puzzles. Those feelings, although mainly suppressed, or merely hinted at in such details as the cenotaph, the carved capitals, the Umbrian painting, must be what the satire exists for. Something Henry James said of his own work is to the point:

the strength of applied irony [is] surely in the sincerities, the lucidities, the utilities that stand behind it. When it's not a campaign of a sort, on behalf of the something better, (better than the obnoxious, the provoking object) that blessedly, as is assumed, *might* be, it's not worth speaking of. But this is exactly what we mean by operative irony. It implies and projects the possible other case, the case rich and edifying where the actuality is pretentious and vain.[20]

Eliot's satire is of that sort; except that his 'possible other case' is not a superior form of the actual, but involves transcending the actual altogether.

The poems read so far suggest that Eliot's historical sense was one to lead him beyond history. What he observes throughout time is the recurrence of futility and failure. The past is neither better nor worse than the present. And the only prospect at which the verse quickens is the prospect of release from an adulterous and bloody world. This suggests that when he stopped his account of the historical sense, in 'Tradition and the Individual Talent', 'at the frontier of metaphysics or mysticism', he was obscurely declaring that if it were fully followed out it would lead into those realms.

The peculiar difficulty of 'Gerontion' is that while it does not cross that frontier, it is fully intelligible only from a point of view on the other side. The character Gerontion is an expression of the historical sense, with a point of view within time. But as he carries his analysis through to its dead end, the poetry becomes an analysis of him. This analysis confirms his thought, but exposes its inadequacy. While he is summing up life in time, the poetry is attempting to place us outside time. Another way of putting this is that while there is much of Eliot's mind in the persona, he is finally no more Eliot than Prufrock was.

At the outset the versification establishes Gerontion as a contemporary with a tradition behind him. The first two lines are blank verse, close to the norms of Jacobean drama, and yet transformed by the natural stressing and phrasing of a modern voice. Or it might be that a modern voice is accommodating itself to the older verse. The lines are based on a passage in A. C. Benson's life of Edward Fitzgerald, the translator of Omar Khayyám: 'Here he sits, in a dry month, old and blind, being read to by a country boy, longing for rain'. Eliot's rhythm is latent in the phrasing there; but it needed an ear attuned to the early dramatic verse to realise it as a precise and solid form:

Here I am,/an old man/in a dry month
Being read to . by a boy,/waiting for rain.

The following sentence of four lines is as subtle and suggestive in its crossed rhythms as the choruses of *Samson Agonistes* (cf. ll.1268–307). The sequence of strong, rhythmically parallel phrases, vividly evoking heroic battles, is strangely modified by the emphatic negatives. Gerontion has missed the experience. Yet the images make real Thermopylae (literally 'hot gates') and later wars. 'Knee deep in the salt marsh' could be a universal particular distilled, say, from Pound's rendering of Sigismundo Malatesta's battles, together with his brilliant image of trench warfare, 'walked eye-deep in hell.'[21] The effect of the negatives on these powerful impressions is at first to suggest regret; then a deeper disillusionment. The second 'fought' is left hanging, doubtfully: would the missed heroic life have been worth while? Thus Gerontion defines what that history means to him.

The account of his decayed house telescopes another aspect of it. The owner is a descendant of the Chosen People become a low modern type: his genealogy is a truncated parody, bearing witness to the Diaspora, and to the flight of refugees from Belgium in 1914; instead of the Promised Land he has attained a rentable slum. A location in place and time, though as dislocated as in a Chagall painting, is given by 'The goat coughs at night in the field overhead'. Then its particular suggestions are expanded into a five-word summary, at once concrete and complete, of the course of evolution and history. The sudden accelerations in the sequence, from *stonecrop* to *iron*, from *iron* to *merds*, are a way of seeing the meaning: the line is even more devasting than the 'Dung and death' passage of *East Coker*.

While Gerontion is thus analysing his experience in its largest perspectives he still maintains a firm grasp on particulars. The diction alters appropriately with the shifts in time. 'Estaminet' was brought back from France by the troops in the 1914–18 war; 'The woman keeps the kitchen, makes tea' is bare current speech. Later there is the obsolete 'concitation' – stirring up, rousing – for what is not actual. More tellingly, this precise attention to words enables him to present in a few lines a concentrated critical history of the Incarnation, that is, of the spiritual or divine aspect of the culture. The quotation, 'We would see a sign!' recalls the Pharisees' failure to recognise the Messiah. The next line and a half, giving the opening words of John's gospel together with Lancelot Andrewes' expansion of them, in a sermon on Christmas Day 1618, is itself a palimpsest history of the Logos in time. Then the intelligence, as if demonstrating the nature of Incarnation, reveals (if that is quite the word for so hidden a sense) the word within a word: *juvescence*, derived from 'iuvare' (to help, aid), appearing in place of the expected 'juvenescence' of the youthful time of the year. Thus the pre-Christian word is made to yield a new, esoteric, meaning – one which would associate the rebirth of the year with the Redeemer rather than the natural seasons. But the apparently parallel phrase, 'In depraved May', reverses all that. The reflowering vegetation, in the ambiguously seductive reflections of Henry Adams, invites betrayal of the Word: 'No European spring had shown him the same intermixture of delicate grace and passionate depravity that marked the Maryland May. He loved it too much, as though it were Greek and half human.'[22] The evocation of that parody of the Incarnation introduces a sequence of communions, each a precise and suggestive image, in which the original divine substance and significance progressively disappears. 'Vacant shuttles/Weave the wind' There Gerontion echoes Job's 'My days are swifter than a weaver's shuttle, and are spent without hope' – Job being another whose life had become a vanity and a burden to him, and who could not depart out of it.

With the question 'After such knowledge, what forgiveness?', Gerontion sets himself to think through his observations to some saving conclusion; in doing so he brings himself into question. Now in the two paragraphs in which he is urging himself to thought, the quality of the verse undergoes a remarkable change. It is no longer giving new life to the form of blank verse, but imitating it even to pastiche. The imitation is impressive; and the densely compact, sinuously shifting verse does give a convincing illusion of dramatic experience wisely summed up. Yet is it not self-conscious? And aren't we made conscious of the performance more than the facts of experience? History had been brought to mind in its luminous particulars; here it becomes generalised, an abstraction personified in a theatrical mode. As for Gerontion himself, is he not looking at himself in the mirror of 'history', and assuming a self-dramatising role? He would have us see him as a character in a Revenge Tragedy.

The effect is to alienate us from him, at least to the extent that we find ourselves looking at him, rather than with him and through his eyes. His self-dramatising appears not only decadent, but very ironic. After all, the Revenger of the Jacobean stage did have his ghosts, the intensified presences of the evil to be purged. Indeed his vision of decay and corruption could be a nightmare 'loathing and disgust of humanity', as Eliot said of Tourneur's *The Revenger's Tragedy*; it could amount to 'the death motive, for it is the loathing and horror of life itself'. But that death motive is just what Gerontion lacks: with all his knowledge of corruption and decay he seems unable to put an end to it in any way. His echoing of *The Changeling* suggests a specific comparison. In his essay on Middleton (1927) Eliot wrote:

The tragedy of *The Changeling* is an eternal tragedy, as permanent as *Oedipus* or *Antony and Cleopatra*; it is the tragedy of the not naturally bad but irresponsible and undeveloped nature, caught in the consequences of its own action. In every age and every civilisation there are instances of the same thing: the unmoral nature, suddenly trapped in the inexorable toils of morality – of morality not made by man but by Nature – and forced to take the consequences of an act which it had planned lightheartedly. Beatrice is not a moral creature; she becomes moral only by becoming damned.[23]

She shows the self-awareness which makes Eliot take her fully seriously – as he could take seriously Baudelaire for being 'man enough for damnation' – in the speech Gerontion echoes:

I that am of your blood was taken from you
For your better health; look no more upon't,
But cast it to the ground regardlessly,
Let the common sewer take it from distinction.

Beneath the stars, upon yon meteor
Ever hung my fate, 'mongst things corruptible;
I ne'er could pluck it from him; my loathing
Was prophet to the rest, but ne'er believed.

Gerontion does not accept responsibility for his fate in that way, nor does he face it so directly:

I that was near your heart was removed therefrom
To lose beauty in terror, terror in inquisition.
I have lost my passion: why should I need to keep it
Since what is kept must be adulterated?
I have lost my sight, smell, hearing, taste and touch:
How should I use them for your closer contact?

Well, the retort might be, Dante did not lose his passion when he lost Beatrice; nor did Middleton's Beatrice adulterate hers. 'Whispers of Immortality' shows what short shrift Gerontion could expect from Mr Eliot.

Gerontion is not so much *suffering* his fate, as watching himself be its victim. His self-dramatisation has become a mode of resignation to Fate, of the kind Eliot diagnosed in 'Shakespeare and the Stoicism of Seneca': a way of abdicating responsibility for his own moral being. He is rather like Othello in his last speech, when he would have the onlookers 'Speak of me as I am'. Othello, Eliot wrote,

is *cheering himself up*. He is endeavouring to escape reality, he has ceased to think about Desdemona, and is thinking about himself. Humility is the most difficult of all virtues to achieve; nothing dies harder than the desire to think well of oneself. Othello succeeds in turning himself into a pathetic figure, by adopting an *aesthetic* rather than a moral attitude, dramatising himself against his environment.[24]

Gerontion does the same:

Gull against the wind, in the windy straits
Of Belle Isle, or running on the Horn.
White feathers in the snow, the Gulf claims,
And an old man driven by the Trades
To a sleepy corner.

In the lines immediately preceding these, he has been rather piling on the horrors. With the aid of Tourneur, Jonson, Webster, Chapman, Seneca – mostly lines quoted by Eliot in his essays – he evokes vividly the inevitable decay and dissolution of physical life. 'Whirled . . . /In fractured atoms' brings Lucretius and Seneca up to date with Rutherford. Yet it is all to no purpose, at least so far as his own response is concerned. Perhaps he is aware of moral cowardice – or is it Eliot accusing him? – in his seeing 'White feathers in the snow'. Instead of being saved, if only by damnation, he ends where he began: in his own 'dull head', as it were in a kind of Sargasso Sea.

The sexual innuendo which pervades the poem – and which is closely related to that of *Measure for Measure*, some Jacobean tragedies, and *The Waste Land* (especially in its draft state) – adds an important element to the diagnosis. What it suggests is that Gerontion's decay is essentially a decay of love, that he is as he is because he has attached his desire to no lasting object.

Gerontion's failings have been attributed by some critics to artistic failure on Eliot's part. This is surely to miss, or to mistake, what Eliot is doing. The truth he is seeking is not in the persona but in the point of view which can see him for what he is. The epigraph and title, in their shorthand and possibly short-circuiting fashion, suggest how far he is from wanting to make Gerontion's thoughts appear finally convincing. The epigraph is from the speech in *Measure for Measure* III.i in which the Duke, disguised as a friar, urges the condemned Claudio to wake from the sleep of a vain earthly life, and to reason himself into being 'absolute for death'. 'Gerontion' is the diminutive or disrespectful form of 'geron'. The latter would signify an elder deserving of respect, as in Newman's *Dream of Gerontius*, a poem tracing the passage of the soul from age through death and purgation into eternal life. Gerontion, because he is not absolute for death, is not that kind of elder. He is rather the Old Man of the theologians, the unredeemed soul. As Eliot said of Baudelaire, his *ennui* may be regarded as 'a true form of *acedia*, arising from the unsuccessful struggle towards the spiritual life'.[25] Even more to the point is what he thought of Shaw's *Back to Methuselah*:

the fact which makes Methuselah impressive is that the nature of the subject, the attempt to expose a panorama of human history 'as far as thought can reach' almost compels Mr Shaw to face ultimate questions. His creative evolution proceeds so far that the process ceases to be progress, and progress ceases to have any meaning. Even the author appears to be conscious of the question whether the beginning and the end are not the same, and whether, as Mr Bradley says, 'whatever you know, it is all one'. . . The pessimism of the conclusion . . . is pessimism only because he has not realised that at the end he has only approached a beginning, that his end is only the starting point towards the knowledge of life.[26]

That was written in 1921, twenty years before *East Coker*.

For a better understanding of the metaphysical or mystical point of view maintained in 'Gerontion' we may seek help in Eliot's prose of the period from 1916 to 1921. The main writings are the thesis on *Knowledge and Experience*, and the essays collected in *The Sacred Wood*, together with 'The

Metaphysical Poets' and 'Andrew Marvell'. In the criticism there is a set of apparent contradictions, which prove to be true paradoxes; and these, when resolved in a manner suggested by the thesis, reveal a more profound intent than one had suspected.

There is the matter of Impersonality. The individual talent must strip himself of his own personality; unless he does this he will not know what is to be done in the present moment of the past. But then we find this at the end of the essay on Massinger, one of the most important:

Had Massinger been a greater man, a man of more intellectual courage, the current of English literature immediately after him might have taken a different course. The defect is precisely a defect of personality. He is not, however, the only man of letters who, at the moment when a new view of life is wanted, has looked at life through the eyes of his predecessors, and only at manners through his own.

Moreover, the defect of personality is explicitly a defect of emotion: he took over the morals of his predecessors without having 'the personal and real emotions which this morality supported and into which it introduced a kind of order'. His characters do not live because they are not 'conceived from some emotional unity'. His verse suffers from 'cerebral anaemia', because it is over-laid with received ideas, and is not the instrument of a refined nervous system as it perceives, registers and digests impressions.

In the closely related matter of Tradition we find the same paradox. The poet must submit his own mind to 'the Mind of Europe' – 'a mind which he learns in time is much more important than his own private mind'. Yet Massinger is said to have failed precisely because he inherited traditions 'without either criticising or informing them from his own experience'. Indeed 'Tradition and the Individual Talent' itself implies that the poet must be the critic of the Mind of Europe: 'the difference between the present and the past is that the conscious present is an awareness of the past in a way and to an extent which the past's awareness of itself cannot show'. Thus the poet's mind, as the conscious present, must transcend that more important mind to which he submits.

That paradox involves a further one. The historical sense, the fullest possible consciousness of the past, is 'nearly indispensable' to the mature poet. But it should be 'a sense of the timeless as well as of the temporal'. Does that mean that the historical sense includes a sense also of what is outside history? Is it part of the poet's business in observing tradition, as it is part of the critic's, 'to see literature steadily and to see it whole; and this is eminently to see it *not* as consecrated by time, but to see it beyond time'?[27] The essay on Marvell appears to confirm these intimations when it carries the account of the historical sense just across the frontier of metaphysics or mysticism. There we find that the quality of mind which, implicitly, Massinger failed to develop – 'an educated mind, rich in generations of experience', a mind given to 'a constant inspection and criticism of experience' – 'leads toward, and is only completed by, the religious comprehension; it leads to the point of the *Ainsi tout leur a craqué dans la main* of Bouvard and Pécuchet'. After that we may wonder whether, in approving Cowley's definition of Wit, Eliot was going beyond strictly literary criticism:

> In a true piece of Wit all things must be
>   Yet all things there agree;
> As in the Ark . . .
> . . . that strange mirror of the Deity.

But in any case the 'religious comprehension', everything crumbling at their touch, gives a definite conclusion to which the historical sense should lead. That is, the wisdom to be derived from the study of history is that history is futile and meaningless. The purpose of being conscious of the past is to avoid repeating it. Eliot does not explicitly declare this position, nor even bring it into question. But that is because it is not really in question for him. When he approves the historical sense, as when he approves the Mind of Europe, he is regarding them not as ends but simply means to an end beyond time: an end which is their antithesis and in which they are annihilated; though it may be also, from a certain point of view, their fulfilment. 'History may be servitude, History may be freedom.'

While these paradoxes lead into metaphysics, there is yet another paradox to return the poet to the realm of actual experience. This is that the metaphysical impulse only intensifies, or is itself the intensified form of, sense-perception. That appears to be the argument of 'Whispers of Immortality'; and some of Eliot's best known formulations assert it. Massinger, once more, 'was not guided by direct communications through the nerves', so that 'with the end of Chapman, Middleton, Webster, Tourneur, Donne we end a period when the intellect was immediately at the tips of the senses. Sensation became word and word was sensation.' Then there is his diagnosis of immaturity in Henry Adams:

It is probable that men ripen best through experiences which are at once sensuous and intellectual; certainly many men will admit that their keenest ideas have come to them with the quality of a sense-perception; and that their keenest sense-experience has been 'as if the body thought'. There is nothing to indicate that Adams's senses either flowered or fruited: he remains little Paul Dombey asking questions.[28]

In that review James is offered as the example of an intelligence properly educated and nourished, with the remark 'it is the sensuous contributor to the intelligence that makes the difference'.

Even thought, or especially thought, requires sensuous realisation. 'Tennyson and Browning are poets, and they think; but they do not feel their thought as immediately as the odour of a rose. A thought to Donne was an experience; it modified his sensibility.' Again, there is the complex passage which opens that paragraph in 'The Metaphysical Poets', and which calls for the incorporation of erudition: 'their mode of feeling was directly and freshly altered by their reading and thought. In Chapman especially there is a direct sensuous apprehension of thought, or a recreation of thought into feeling . . .'. This is to move always from the notional to the real, from knowing about something, to having one's being informed and shaped by what has been known. So that thought, in its full realisation not merely *like* sense-experience, but itself a sense-experience, is digested in the sensibility and incorporated into personality. Thus we are returned from the impersonal – what has been thought and said – to the individual poet.

But we are returned with a difference in which the whole set of paradoxes may be dissolved. The personality of the poet, or the sensibility realised in the poetry, is not the same thing as his ordinary personality. What every poet *starts from* is his own emotions; but his life as a poet consists in transmuting 'his personal and private agonies into something rich and strange, something universal and impersonal'.[29] This new creation is essentially a new self, the man recreated in the making of the poem. Thus what is impersonal and objective becomes instrumental to the subjective life of the poet.

The basic preoccupation with a higher, a developed form of personal life, which underlies and explains so much in Eliot's thought and poetry, is fully established in the doctoral thesis he completed in April 1916: *Knowledge and Experience in the Philosophy of F. H. Bradley*, as it is now known.[30] From the point of view of philosophers, as by Eliot himself 'forty-six years after [his] academic philosophizing came to an end' (p. 10), this is regarded as a rather opaque and unrewarding work. Yet to the student of his poetry it can be genuinely illuminating. Perhaps it is best read as a covert *ars poetica*.

Bradley's philosophy, in Eliot's account of it, is concerned with the self that is composed in the mind as it experiences and knows. This self, in its beginnings, is not self-conscious; but simply experiences its world as an immediate reality; and exists simply in its immediate experience. With the advance to self-consciousness, its world breaks down into separated objects: 'By the failure of any experience to be merely immediate, by its lack of harmony and cohesion, we find ourselves as conscious souls in a world of objects' (p. 31). The life of the

73

conscious soul becomes a painful struggle to reintegrate its world: to unify what has been dissociated; and to enter a new form of immediate experience. Become aware of itself, in a world of jarring and incompatible experiences, it must seek to recover wholeness and unity of being, by a process of 'passing, when possible, from two or more discordant viewpoints to a higher which shall somehow include and transmute them' (pp. 147–8). The ideal end of this process would be 'an all-inclusive experience outside of which nothing shall fall': 'a timeless unity', a complete being, Bradley's Absolute (p. 31). Or, *Little Gidding*'s final 'condition of complete simplicity'.

While he makes it clear that he would affirm these 'opinions' (p. 31), Eliot is not satisfied by Bradley's Absolute:

Bradley's universe, actual only in finite centres, is only by an act of faith unified. Upon inspection, it falls away into the isolated finite experiences out of which it is put together. Like [Leibniz's] monads they aim at being one; each expanded to completion, to the full reality latent within it, would be identical with the whole universe. But in so doing it would lose the actuality, the here and now, which is essential to the small reality which it actually achieves. The Absolute responds only to an imaginary demand of thought, and satisfies only an imaginary demand of feeling. Pretending to be something which makes finite centres cohere, it turns out to be merely the assertion that they do. And this assertion is only true so far as we here and now find it to be so. (p. 202)

This is not the dismissal of the Absolute that it might seem, but rather a demand for it to be made actual and real. The objection is to its being merely asserted, to its being 'only by an act of faith unified'. This is the essential problem left unresolved in Bradley's philosophy, from Eliot's point of view; and it is the problem which, with his usual subtlety and indirection, he set himself to answer. That the answer lay quite outside the province of philosophy may have been the reason for the apparent indirection.

Philosophy, as the analysis and criticism of experience, belongs to the dissociated state; and cannot of itself lead beyond it. Yet, when itself subjected to analysis and criticism, so that its knowledge is found to be not absolute but relative and instrumental, then that very relativity and instrumentality 'is what impels us toward the Absolute' (p. 169). It impels toward – it does not reach to. It is instrumental in that it brings the objectified consciousness to a condition of clear definition and explicit meaning; it achieves an intelligible ordering in what was at first complicated and confusing. And this labour of intelligence prepares the objective world for a purely subjective contemplation, the end of which is the 'vision *amor intellectualis Dei*'[31] – which might be Richard of St Victor's way of suggesting the Absolute, as well as Spinoza's.

Now this realm of pure subjectivity, the realm of immediate experience, is the realm of metaphysics and poetry. For Eliot, from first to last, poetry is metaphysics, or it aspires toward metaphysics. Both, as they contemplate the objects of knowledge, effect 'the aesthetic expansion of the object':

The intense feeling, ecstatic or terrible, without an object or exceeding its object, is something which every person of sensibility has known . . . The ordinary person puts these feelings to sleep, or trims down his feeling to fit the business world; the artist keeps it alive by his ability to intensify the world to his emotions.[32]

This is frankly to assert the subjective over the objective: the meaning is not determined by what the object is, but by what the mind makes of it. The meaning of the object becomes then an expression of the mind's own feelings and point of view. With this Bradley would agree.

However, 'the aesthetic expansion of the object' implies, along with the realisation of subjectivity, the two things lacking from Bradley's account of the Absolute. It involves, as Eliot's literary criticism insists, a recovery of the condition of immediate experience. Thought itself, the knowledge derived from the analysis of experience, becomes in poetry something known immediately, not objectively. Then it involves the reintegration of experience: the putting together again, into felt wholes, what had been dissociated and analysed. These two qualities of poetry, immediacy and ordered wholeness, are virtually inseparable in Eliot's thought. 'The real is the organised', he affirmed in his thesis; adding, 'and this statement is metaphysics' (p. 82). Throughout *The Sacred Wood* and *Homage to John Dryden* the demand for direct feeling and sensation is accompanied always by the demand that they should be structured and unified. Massinger's plays are 'eloquent of emotional disorder'; his characters are not 'conceived from some emotional unity'; 'the debility of romantic drama . . . consists in an internal incoherence of feelings, a concatenation of emotions which signifies nothing'. Then in 'The Metaphysical Poets', as the positive side of the theory, there is the call for modern poetry to struggle toward a unification of sensibility.

In its context that call can be understood partially, as if it referred simply to a fusion of thought and feeling. But in the fuller context of Eliot's thought 'this statement is metaphysics'. Behind his concern with 'the problem of the integrity of poetry',[33] was always his concern with the problem of the integrity of sensibility. And behind that are such ideas as that the life of the soul consists in unifying its experience, in the struggle towards wholeness and the Absolute.

That is what made him a poet: a mind committed to making actual and immediate the whole of his experience. The ideal world was strictly for philosophers. 'In one's prose reflections', he said in *After Strange Gods*, 'one may be

75

legitimately occupied with ideals, whereas in the writing of verse one can only deal with actuality' – 'at the moment when one writes, one is what one is'.[34] He gave up philosophy, in 1916, because you cannot attain the Absolute simply by taking thought.

The theory which I have been sketching is distilled in 'Gerontion'. Yet only to a degree – there are no metaphysics within the poem. But then that would be the final criticism of Gerontion. He sees precisely how things have been and always will be in time; yet he undergoes no transformation in consequence of that. He fails to develop a mature personality of his own, as Massinger failed to; and as the Mind of Europe in English verse failed to, in Eliot's account given in the verse itself as well as in his prose. At the same time, the absence of metaphysics places the poem as a work of criticism and analysis: it is not yet the work of poetic self-realisation that the complete theory requires. It belongs rather to the kind of satire or criticism which Eliot described in his essay on Ben Jonson. The immediate appeal is to the conscious intelligence. Yet there is, in the design of the whole, a specific emotional tone; and the observations are unified by the essential emotion. The emotion, however, is expressed only as a point of view – a new point of view from which to inspect the actual world. That the point of view is new is evidence that it is the expression of an original and coherent poetic personality. But that its expression remains critical, in observations of the objective surface of experience, leaves it 'craving further expression'.

The poetic personality underlying 'Poems – 1920' is directly expressed – apart from the climactic evocation of Oedipus among the nightingales – only in 'Dans le Restaurant'. This is the one poem which transcends satire and criticism to attain the completeness of metaphysical poetry. The terms used in *Knowledge and Experience* to describe the development of the self or soul apply exactly:

we vary by passing from one point of view to another . . . or by occupying more than one point of view at the same time; . . . we vary by self-transcendence. . . For the life of a soul does not consist in the contemplation of one consistent world but in the painful task of unifying (to a greater or less extent) jarring and incompatible ones, and passing, when possible, from two or more discordant viewpoints to a higher which shall somehow include and transmute them. (pp. 147–8)

I should think that this process will be apparent in the poem. But since not everyone who reads Eliot knows French, I may be forgiven for offering a version in English.

He was a scarecrow waiter with nothing better to do
Than scratch his knuckles, and perch himself at my shoulder:
    'It will be rainy where I come from,
    Wind, and a burst of sun, then rain –
    They call it the tramps' washing day.'
(Stoop-backed, dribbling driveller
At least stop dribbling in my soup.)
    'Dripping willows, buds on the briars,
    You take cover there when there's a shower.
I was seven, she was littler.
    She got soaked, I picked primroses for her.'
I count up to thirty-eight spots on his waistcoat.
    'I tickled her, to make her laugh.
    I felt such power for a moment, such rapture.'

    At that age? come off it, you dirty old man . . .
'What happened was tough, sir.
    A big dog came up and pawed at us,
    And I was frightened – I left her half-way.
    It was such a pity.'
        What, you have your vulture as well!
Scratch the dirt from the wrinkles in your face,
Here, take my fork to your filthy skull.
What right have you to pay for it as I do?
Here's a penny for the Public Baths.

Phlebas the Phoenician, a fortnight drowned,
Forgot the cries of gulls and the Cornish surge,
The cargo of tin and the profit and the loss;
A current undersea carried him down
Through all the stages of his former life.
Think now: how hard his luck
Who used to be a fine tall fellow.

It seems that in this poem, writing in French and with French models, Eliot was able to tap his deeper feelings. Where his Elizabethan and Jacobean models confirm the negations of the historical sense, Corbière's sea poems, with Baudelaire's 'La Vie Antérieure' and Rimbaud's 'Les Poètes de Sept Ans', have here released an intense and disturbing experience analogous to Dante's first sight of Beatrice in the *Vita Nuova*. That Eliot had himself had such an experience is suggested in a paragraph in his introduction to Dante:

the type of sexual experience which Dante describes as occurring to him at the age of nine years is by no means impossible or unique. My only doubt (in which I found myself confirmed by a distinguished psychologist) is whether it could have taken place so *late* in life as the age of nine years. The psychologist agreed with me that it is more likely to occur at about five or six years of age. . . But I cannot find it incredible that what has happened to others should have happened to Dante with much greater intensity.[35]

The experience has not found in 'Dans le Restaurant' the sublime afterlife of the *Vita Nuova*. There is even a sense of bitter parody in the contrast. Yet the difference may be best understood as evidence of the different way which Eliot found himself compelled to follow towards the same end.

From one point of view the experience remains merely a cause of regret. But even that feeling, in the battered waiter, is to another point of view disgusting and alienating. However, there is the deeper recognition that the gnawing regret is a feeling they have in common; so that the persona must move to a further point of view which shall include them both. The image of the vulture serves to resolve the double identity: as the waiter has his vulture so he is being the persona's, who sees in him his own torment. This is to have moved to a deeper and more immediate experience of loss than in 'La Figlia Che Piange'. Now the unappeased torment becomes the cause of a further development. Eliot agreed with Gide that the poet, like Prometheus, must have his eagle;[36] or, as he represented it later in *The Family Reunion*, his Eumenides, Furies and Kindly Ones. Here it is the vulture which compels him towards the higher viewpoint which somehow includes and transmutes the rest.

The transmutation effected by Phlebas' watery death is not simply a matter of distancing the torment and releasing pathos and moral reflection. There is an analogy with Ophelia's death, even to a similar resolution of disturbingly irreconcilable feelings into a wholly different order of emotion and vision. Observation and analysis give way to a new experience in which the disturbing regret and anguish have been purged away. What remains is the feeling of what was deep and permanent in the event. The inevitable end, whether late or soon, is the loss and annihilation of such power and delight as life can offer. But this is to put as a moral abstraction what comes as a directly felt emotion. The end of 'Gerontion' invites moral reflection. But this, like the version in *The Waste Land*, has a visionary immediacy. The potential power of the images, for Eliot a power to resolve troubling experience into serene order, may be measured by their fuller development in *Ash-Wednesday* and *Marina* and *The Dry Salvages*.

4

Tiresias transformed

a disgust like Dante's is no hypertrophy of a single reaction: it is completed and explained only by the last canto of the *Paradiso*. The contemplation of the horrid or sordid or disgusting, by an artist, is the necessary and negative aspect of the impulse toward the pursuit of beauty. But . . . the negative is the more importunate.[1]

Its motive is truly the death motive, for it is the loathing and horror of life itself.[2]

The Waste Land is to 'Dans le Restaurant' as the oak-tree to the acorn. At its heart is likewise an intense moment of passion, 'ecstatic or terrible', now removed into memory; and it operates a similar process of conscious analysis and expansion, to the point at which the objective predicament is resolved into a new order of feeling. There are of course great differences, as between a minor and a major work. In *The Waste Land* the historical sense is fully developed, so that the poet is struggling to unify a vastly more inclusive and complex sensibility. Moreover, he reaches to a further stage in his development: Phlebas' death by water is no longer the end, but the transition to an order of poetry wholly new in Eliot's work.

To follow out that development, and to read the poem as an organic whole in which 'What the Thunder Said' follows from and fulfils the rest, we need to keep our attention upon the poet within the poem. We need to look through what is being said and seen, and at the point of view that is expressing itself. To read the poem only as a critique of its culture, as many have done in print at least, is to be rather simple-minded: it is to make out the mind of Europe perhaps, but to miss the poet's mind. It bears repeating that what alone constitutes life for a poet of Eliot's type, is 'to transmute his personal and private agonies into something rich and strange, something universal and impersonal'.[3] This is no invitation to probe his private life. We have the agony of the poet given us in the poem, at the heart of its matter and in all the process of its transmutation.

If, in that action, the poem becomes a critique of its culture, it does so in order to give the fullest possible expression to the poet's own mind and feelings. What we are given is not a world 'in itself', as the anthropologist or historian

79

would observe it, but the world as the poet sees it. And what he is seeing is primarily himself. He is completing the objectification and analysis of his experience by magnifying it into a vision of the world. If he presents a crisis or breakdown of civilisation, this has to be understood as first of all a crisis or breakdown in himself. If he achieves a cure it will be by reintegrating and transforming himself in poetry. Whether the poetic achievement will have any valid application to the state of civilisation is a very large question and one best left until we have the evidence of the poem quite clear in our minds.

At first reading *The Waste Land* is likely to appear a sequence of unrelated fragments. Gradually one learns to make some sense of the sequence, to see how one passage follows from another. But to read the poem straight through from start to finish still won't give a clear sense that it all coheres – that it all really 'works'. I suspect that the poem begins to work and be whole only when we perceive that it has a structure other than the sequential. Just because the separate passages are not obviously related, they become free to form a variety of connections among themselves. If instead of taking them in their simple sequence, one after another, one holds them simultaneously together before the mind's eye, then they may form an arrangement in space more complex than any possible in time alone. For an analogy, we might think of the solar system or of a compound molecule; or, indeed, of a painting. We should not think of the links in a chain.

A diagram of the structure of each of the first three parts would show at the centre a nucleus of more or less direct experience: the episode in the hyacinth garden; the bad nerves dialogue; the typist and her young man. The other passages would be found to arrange themselves fairly symmetrically about these. For example, consider part I. The memories of the hyacinth garden are enclosed in the fragments from *Tristan und Isolde*. Preceding that whole passage is the voice of the prophet in the desert; following it is Madame Sosostris, the modern Sybil. She leads into the Unreal City, which balances Marie's world of memories. Now we may wonder if Marie has a relation with the hyacinth girl; and if the man in the city was the one in the garden. Has his voice something in common with the prophet's? One might go further . . . But that should do to release the poem from a merely linear reading.

The nuclei of direct experience are of primary importance. In parts I and II especially they are the centres of subjective life; and in all three the other materials assume their full significance only in relation to them. The surrounding passages effect the objective analysis of the primary experience; they expand and elucidate its various aspects into impersonal generalisations. But the generalisations are not from a range of particulars: they are from this specific experience;

and they must lack particularity and precision if that relation is imperfectly appreciated. Moreover, their relation to each other, and the internal coherence of each part, follows from their being first related to the one centre. This is to say again, from a more practical point of view, that the poem's life is essentially the poet's life; that its complexities proceed from the complication of his consciousness; and that its ultimate coherence is a matter of the unifying of his sensibility.

The centre from which the entire poem radiates is this:

'You gave me hyacinths first a year ago;
They called me the hyacinth girl.'
– Yet when we came back, late, from the hyacinth garden,
Your arms full, and your hair wet, I could not
Speak, and my eyes failed, I was neither
Living nor dead, and I knew nothing,
Looking into the heart of light, the silence.

That was, one might say, 'the mere experience at the beginning': intense, immediate, purely subjective. Yet the complications of consciousness have already set in. The verbs are retrospective. For the girl the event has faded to a fact no longer directly felt: she remembers it as others saw her. Although the man's recall is vivid and detailed, for him the event has become charged with irreconcilable contradictions. In the passionate moment all consciousness was suspended; now this is perceived as a kind of annihilation; so that against the remembered rapture there comes a sense of fear or terror. This painful ambiguity, with the girl's apathy, and the clear fact that the state of pure feeling is passed, all compel the poet to become the conscious analyst of his experience.

The particular episode is at once associated with the appropriate myth, so that it becomes an intimate instance of the universal experience of romantic passion. The quotations from Wagner's operatic rendering of the medieval romance of Tristan and Iseult – which itself gave a classic form to other and older tales of the garden of love laid waste – make the hyacinthine memories a distillation of its whole action. The first quotation is from the opera's opening, before the love potion is drunk; the second is from the start of the last act, when Tristan is dying and the watchman can see no sail on the sea bringing Isolde.

One effect of this empty sea is to make absolute the desolation which is the end of passion: it confirms 'I will show you fear'. Yet in Wagner's music and in the myth the lovers' end is as ambivalent as 'the heart of light, the silence'; or rather, it seems a recovery of the ecstasy and a perfecting of what had been unfulfilled in life. The music scarcely heeds the physical death, but soars with intimations of transcendence. The passion that was kept, not simply in spite of, but all the more intensely for being unsatisfied in life, seems to be released at death into pure lyricism. By the very failure of their lives the fated and true lovers are exalted. This idea of romantic passion is one of the permanent responses to love – or of love in a world that does not live by love. Besides the Tristan myth and the *Vita Nuova* one might think of the myth of Orpheus with its revealing emphasis upon the life of song, and its origins in early religious rituals.

But the experience must be immediate and wholly possessing. To be conscious of it is to be conscious of being outside it. What one must be aware of, then, is the loss of the experience; and the memory of it, together with the ideal of ultimate transcendence, must become a torment to the conscious soul, making its actual life appear a desolate waste. The hyacinth garden, full of flowers, wet after rain, turns to dust.

Of course other reactions are possible; as the experience of dispossession is itself full of confused contradictions. These painful contradictions of actual life are expressed in the first choric lines of the poem. 'April' is echoed and altered in 'cruellest'; the lilacs hurt. Resurgent natural process is insistent in the verbs, but the rhythm of perception is heavy, resistant. The dead land renews itself, but this life is unwanted. Memory checks desire. However, at 'Winter kept us warm' the rhythm eases, as the mind slips into the past where the contradictions are reversed: there is warmth, shelter, food, in the dead time of the year. 'Summer surprised us' continues the regression from present anguish into memories emptied of all urgent desires or terrors. The vignette of how one lived in former summers is a faded daguerrotype, beyond reach of what the line in German might mean. That could be something said in conversation; or it could recall the violent breaking up of Europe latent beneath the surface of those pre-war summers.[4] As if in unconscious recoil from those associations the mind goes further back to a childhood scene. We may remark that only then does it assume a conscious identity. But that intense feeling is faded too: 'And down we went' is almost a sigh. The paragraph closes with the mature voice, nostalgic, sentimental, which has forgotten what it was really like. 'To feel free' has come to mean something close to freedom from feelings, or from any which would be painful. In part v, however, the mountains will be a place of suffering, and the suffering will confer freedom of another order.

Those dry mountains are foreseen in the next passage, but not yet as a place of lyrical suffering. The prophet's vision is first of all another way of regarding Marie's life and world, one which dissolves its forgetful reverie into definite dust. In a paradoxical effect, directly the opposite of the opening lines, the verse becomes strong and intense as it creates this negation of natural life. There is a positive energy here, where there was none in the preceding account of an existence. Yet this energy affirms death and intensifies fear. Moreover, so far as he is the presenter of the story of romantic passion, this voice would resolve its ambivalence into a simple negative: it appears to see only its inevitable natural end.

'The negative is the more importunate': because that is what the conscious mind knows as actual and immediate, and what it has to express, analyse and intensify. Put out from ecstasy and longing to escape its actual state, it must operate in the realm of the imperfect, the confused and contradictory, the failed or the unfulfilled. Contemplating this actuality, it must feel it as the negative of what it would be. To develop and intensify these feelings may be the only form in which the poet can maintain his passional life. The negation is a way of maintaining, in a dissociated and contradictory existence, the impulse toward the pursuit of beauty. It is, one might say, a sick form of life. Yet it is, at least from the poet's own point of view, a form of life, and so better than the death of feeling. Then again, we should note that the prophetic voice is but one voice in the poem, and one that will be transformed or superseded.

The significance of Madame Sosostris, 'Famous clairvoyante', at least from the poet's viewpoint, is surely that she does not see clearly into the meaning of things, nor create any definite fear. Her knowledge of the mysteries is a debased parody, a mixture of brazenness and credulousness. If we do connect the patter with ancient rituals, then it should strike us that she is far from being in touch with any serious practice or direct experience of them. There is no sense of the realities of life and death. The interpretations that could be put upon her cards are a miasma of will-o'-the-wisps. To take this seriously would be to mock ourselves with the fossils of dead meanings – or to go on a wild goose chase, as Eliot put it, regretting his mock-solemn note on the Tarot.[5] To think of the comedy of The Dry Salvages v should disperse any hush of awe. Of course Madame Sosostris does introduce certain of the characters and events of the poem. Only she does so in a way which would conceal or distract us from what is to be experienced.

For the poet who would keep his passion and live it to the absolute, the worst thing about her empty revelations is that they have been emptied of precisely what he most needs. They have been emptied so completely that critics still miss the fact. The rituals of which they are remains were concerned to effect something more and something other than a fertile planting and abundant harvest. It was simply Frazer's rationalist interpretation to regard them as fertility cults, as Eliot observed in 1913–14.[6] But even Frazer admitted, what Jessie Weston firmly stated, that the inner purpose of the rites was to initiate the soul, through a process of trial and purgation, into a higher state of existence. As much as the cult of Christ, the cults of the hanged, buried or drowned gods contained, within any overt wish for fulfilment in this life, a deeper desire to pass beyond it. But such a *rite de passage* is just what the poet is seeking.

His wild and whirling words to Stetson – the wit is after the fashion of Hieronymo's madness or Hamlet's – perfectly express his desperate dismay at the confusions of life and death in the Unreal City. It is because they have lost their passion that these workers in the City of London are seen as the dead in Dante's Limbo: they have lost the feelings which might have impelled them to a more complete existence. And the city is 'unreal' not only because it lacks the real life of passion, but because it does not even realise that it lacks it. Upon Stetson whom he meets near the Bank the poet projects his baffled horror. Whatever he might be, a *News of the World* murderer or simply a suburban gardener, Stetson appears to be practising some grotesque parody of ancient rituals, and therefore of the way in which the poet would get away from the Unreal City. If it is a crime meriting damnation in hell, it has been covered up from recognition as such.[7] If it is a sacrificing of the god, he has stupidly missed the point: you buried an effigy with the crops, but to pass into the world of the divine you must yourself undergo the death. As gardening this is not the way to restore the garden of love; it only returns us to the weary recurrences of the opening lines. That is, it would confirm the *Ennui* of which Baudelaire accuses his reader and himself, in a poem which is as much the model for this last paragraph as Dante's Limbo. Baudelaire offers the reader a vision of himself possessed by every sin and devil, and at the last simply inert with boredom or apathy: the reader as Gerontion.

Yet the poet has avoided that state. This end to 'The Burial of the Dead' has an intensity of wit and feeling which is just the reverse of Marie's living in the past. He has not escaped his actual world in any way. But he has seen it for what it is to him, and felt it as an appalling nightmare. He has attained something like the vision implicit in the last words of Kurtz in Conrad's *Heart of Darkness* – the words which Eliot told Pound were the most appropriate epigraph he could find 'and somewhat elucidative':[8]

"Did he live his life again in every detail of desire, temptation, and surrender during that supreme moment of complete knowledge? He cried in a whisper at some image, at some vision, – he cried out twice, a cry that was no more than a breath –

'The horror! the horror!' "

It is as if the poet had been striving to create, out of the consciousness of the experience in the hyacinth garden, *an oasis of horror in a desert of Ennui.*[9]

That image fits not only the sense but the dramatic pattern of 'A Game of Chess'. At the centre a couple now utterly removed from the ecstasy of the hyacinth garden suffer being terribly alone together – a state far removed also from that of Ferdinand and Miranda discovered 'playing at Chesse' in the last act of *The Tempest*.[10] The scene has the immediacy of real life, and is charged with pain and terror and horror. The pub scene which follows is real life in another sense: the unrealised and unrealising lower life of the Unreal City. The initial description of the woman and the room corresponds to that present world in its unreality, and fills in the background of its past. As a whole this part expands the one preoccupation, already stated in 'The Burial of the Dead': the ends of romantic passion. It does so with an ambitious inclusiveness, since it seeks not only to bring a historical sense to bear upon the immediately disturbing experience, but then to generalise its observations into a contemporary commonplace. There is an informing conviction that the mind of the present, together with its historical causes, is like Baudelaire's desert of *Ennui*. Then there is the paradoxical creation of an oasis of intensified negative feelings.

The close parallel with 'Gerontion' will be apparent. However, the failure of sensibility defined in that persona is here not only observed but virtually overcome. The first twenty lines give a brilliantly synthesised palimpsest of the literary tradition of fatal passion. Cleopatra and Dido, Marlowe's Hero, Keats' Lamia, Belinda in *The Rape of The Lock*, Imogen 'violated' by Iachimo in *Cymbeline*, and Milton's Satan spying his way to seduce Eve – these at least can be discerned behind Philomela and the modern neurasthenic. Yet the effect of this densely layered history is not to intensify perception: nearly the reverse. The diction and the images remain literary, antique. *Cupidon* and *laquearia* are hardly living speech. 'Glowed on the marble' is a *nature morte* version of 'burnt on the water'; 'a carvèd dolphin' is the same for 'His delights/Were Dolphin-like, they shew'd his backe above/The Element they liv'd in'. Moreover, the artful syntax involves the mind in needless complication, until all the carefully piled detail blurs – can one tell at once what precisely is doing what? With all this the accentuation and rhythm are strained from the natural and direct. The sensibility in this language is in the state which Eliot observed in the verse of Massinger and Milton, where models for the passage might be found. These carefully constructed periods are not a mode of the living intelligence.

Precisely that is their meaning to the critical mind. The literary tradition implicated in this style the kind of sensibility which descends, in Eliot's account, from Massinger and Milton – has failed to realise the experience of romantic passion. Neither seeing directly nor feeling intensely, it operates at second hand, and is cloyed and clogged with the mere glamour of passion. Applied to interior décor it would be a style for a Late Empire brothel. That is, the style is the appropriate expression of a state of sensibility – of the specific sensibility handed down to the present since the seventeenth century.

In the monologue of Lil and Albert and I there is something like the last consequence of that deliquescence. It runs on in a continuous present, with scarcely any shaping syntax of feeling or thought. This mind is simply a flux of incident and emotion, all on the surface, and living pretty much in and for the present moment. A mind whose past is indeed only the withered stumps of time. If we hear behind 'HURRY UP PLEASE ITS TIME' some echo of 'Time's winged Chariot hurrying near', are we not dragging in what she would be unconscious of and insensible to? Similarly, the shift from the shallow 'Goonights' to Ophelia's 'Good night, ladies', must get its point from passing beyond their comprehension. (This touches a problem to be taken up shortly: does the poet's superior attitude suggest that the whole pub scene may be rather factitious?)

What is not felt in the commonplace mind, and was unfelt in the associated literary tradition, does find surprising expression in the painted nightingale. She could be as inertly decorative as the other unfortunate women. Yet just here the rhythm quickens and perception clears. We are no longer observing the lifeless sensibility, but made directly and freshly aware of

> The change of Philomel, by the barbarous king
> So rudely forced; yet there the nightingale
> Filled all the desert with inviolable voice
> And still she cries. . .

This is what has been missed: a natural music, expressing the reality of evil and suffering, the compelling need for a release from it, and a possible mode of transformation.

But that mode of pure lyrical being is out of this world. If the woman's nervous suffering associates her with Philomela, it is still far from a final transformation. She is beside herself with irrational fears; and could be moving towards complete dissociation or madness – the antithesis of the nightingale, though not unlike Dido running wildly through Carthage, or Cassandra before the palace in Argos where Agamemnon is being killed. The man's responses, which see in her state or in their state together the reason for terror and despair, make him the woman's opposite and yet even less like the nightingale. He sees the horror, but feels nothing; while she feels it without knowing why. As she is going out of her mind, his, with its blank basilisk stare, is fixing their desolation into a waking nightmare. These are only the negative elements from the Philomela myth, and they imply no saving change or song.

In fact the man and the woman in their separation express the negation of romantic passion in a manner which is just the other side of the unconsciousness and insensibility of the pub monologue, and which is just as much an end product of the dissociation of sensibility which set in with the seventeenth century and from which we have never recovered.[11] At least the scene is a dramatic exemplification of that theory; and the theory can help us understand how it relates to other parts of the poem. There are two aspects or levels in the scene. First, the desolation of the man and woman when their love ceases to be immediately felt. Then the predicament of the sensibility which cannot cope with that state: the way it breaks down, and no longer *knows* what it feels, nor *feels* what it knows. Thus the analysis of the initial loss of ecstasy has become an analysis also of the sensibility undergoing that experience. But this involves the recognition that the sensibility is more than individual, that it is the product and expression of a common culture. That is, the failure of this couple to transcend their alienation is a common plight. In setting their particular drama in relation to past and present states of the mind of Europe, the poet is trying to diagnose its cause and seek a cure.

For him, as poet and lover, this amounts to undergoing the negation of himself. His mind, that would be whole and entire in love, becomes intensely aware of being out of love, dissociated, and unable to achieve the mysterious sea-change. Yet to feel this state and to know what he feels, as he does in entering fully into both sides of the drama, is to maintain his own point of view and the wholeness of his own mind. It is to express himself in the negative. But to experience this state as negation is a healthy response.

So far as it is a common state, the normal response to it should be terror and horror. In expressing his own feelings the poet is expressing what he has shown to be unrealised in the mind of the past, and unfelt in the commonplace contemporary mind. Thus he may be releasing anxiety and anguish generally repressed in the subconscious: feelings which, so long as they are not brought up into the sunlight and made intelligible, will remain to poison life and obstruct action.[12] In freeing himself from a failure of the common mind, he may be freeing that mind with his own. This can be put in the terms of 'Tradition and the Individual Talent'. The poem that expresses the inherited and shared mind of its culture from an original point of view may alter that larger mind. By freshly experiencing a common human predicament the poet modifies the ways in which others experience it. He changes the common perceptions, and releases unrealised feelings and motives. However, to achieve this he must observe two conditions. He must make the common experience immediately his own. And the new feelings, the new self which he realises, must be a renewal of the common humanity. Upon these conditions, in writing himself he may redeem his time.

Whatever is to be said of the poem as a whole, the monologue of Lil and Albert and I won't do when measured by these standards. The mimicking of their speech is exactly the opposite of voicing their life: it is a way of standing off and being superior. The speech is placed as 'theirs' not 'ours' – not the language of those who read and write. It holds them up to be looked at as other than us, certainly not 'mon semblable – mon frère'. The Thames-daughters, in their song, are not seen in this way. The style of Massinger and Milton is felt as something that has happened to the poet's own language and powers of expression. Then there is the telling effect of the closing allusion to Ophelia. With these 'common' people the relation is simply a blank; whereas there is a felt relation between Ophelia, the woman whose nerves are bad, and Philomela. Those perceptions come from the poet's being wholly engaged in their experience, and they effect a release from it. His not entering into and making his own the experience of these other people is a kind of damnation. Hell is other people, said Sartre, meaning that it is to have an alien and inauthentic view imposed on us. But to maintain such an alienated viewpoint is to be in a hell of one's own making. For the poet it is to be like the man who blankly observes the woman's hysteria. What makes the passage so bad is that there is not even the saving awareness that this is the case. In the earlier scene we do not see only what the man sees: we see him seeing it, and become aware of the predicament of one who sees the world in his way. But now the point of view appears to be adopted uncritically by the poet himself. That means that here it is he who is 'unreal'.[13]

This brings us to consider Tiresias, and the question of the poet's relation to him. Doesn't he, as it were 'pressing lidless eyes', fix the typist and her young man in a stare of loathing and disgust? Moreover, doesn't Eliot's note prompt us to take him for the all-embracing mind of the poem? 'Tiresias, although a mere spectator and not indeed a "character", is yet the most important personage in the poem, uniting all the rest. . . What Tiresias *sees*, in fact, is the substance of the poem.' But what *we* see beyond that – what is presented as an object for our contemplation – is his way of seeing it. That can make all the difference between having his point of view imposed on us, and being liberated from it. We need not be trapped spectators, any more than in Henry James' stories, if we will but enlarge our vision to include the observer. At the least, we may keep our minds open to the possibility that the world which he sees is precisely not the vision the poet is after.

88

The first dozen lines of 'The Fire Sermon' are antiphonal, as if expressing a state of divided feeling. From 'The river's tent/is broken' the Spenserian note alternates with a harsh realism. It is as if the 'melodious lay' had been broken into by the brute fact of Ophelia's 'muddy death'. In the Prothalamion the rutty bank is overlaid with floweriness, and *pain* goes easily into *painted;* the brides are swan-nymphs sailing in pure poesy down river to marry their City knights. Here the music of associations, linking 'the last fingers of leaf/Clutch and sink' back to the final line of part II, might call to mind how Ophelia drowned, who was to have been Hamlet's bride. In any case, the nymphs, whether Spenser's or of a later day, with all the litter of sensual summer must always depart. Against the nostalgic music of the bridal day sounds the more powerful image, out of Marvell and Horace, of perpetual death: a stark couplet closing the sonnet in a manner nearer to Shakespeare than to Spenser.

Yet Spenser's music does register its appeal before the negative becomes dominant. The satiric contrasts must dismiss any sentimental feelings for his sweet Thames and 'lovely daughters of the flood'; but only to transform the bridal song into elegy. There is a kind of love, some positive feeling for the too simple mortal beauty. And this feeling is intensified in the echo of the exile's lament in Psalm cxxxvii:

By the rivers of Babylon, there we sat down, yea, we wept, when we remembered Zion.
We hanged our harps upon the willows in the midst thereof . . .
How shall we sing the Lord's song in a strange land?

Just as that is lyrical though in exile, so the opening lines of 'The Fire Sermon' express a feeling for some musical fulfilment beyond what is actual in them. Indeed, they recover something of the ambivalent responsiveness of the hyacinth garden itself.

But that is abruptly dismissed again. Ferdinand, an expansion of the man from the hyacinth garden and the Unreal City and 'the room enclosed', is fixed in a consciousness of death and of the loss of what would mean life to him. Instead of hearing Ariel's song in which the lost father is miraculously sea-changed, he sees murdered bodies and bones. Instead of Miranda discovered in all her innocence, he finds a burlesque Diana welcoming her Actaeon, not transforming him to be hunted and killed.[14] He reacts, in the desperate manner of 'O O O O that Shakespeherian rag' and 'That corpse you planted', with a remove by wit to what he is cut off from. There is a washing of feet also, as in the Maundy Thursday ritual, when Parsifal the chaste hero of the Grail has passed untouched through the trials and temptations of the flesh. In that mysterious spring the children's singing is like the ecstasy of his passing from natural to immortal life. Heard here, however, it is ironic and lacerating. Like the broken fragments of swallow and nightingale it only intensifies the failure to experience the rites of transformation, and emphasises the actuality of untransmuted nature. In his meeting with Mr Eugenides in the Unreal City there is again a lacerating sense of parody. The sodomite Smyrna merchant is not a carrier of the ancient mysteries – a function noted in *From Ritual to Romance* – but only of dried currants. Moreover, his love seems not to be of the quality approved in Plato's *Symposium,* which leads up from the lower to the ideal.

What Tiresias then sees is a more developed episode in the same Unreal City. He sees it with greater objectivity, with a more complete detachment, than Ferdinand. But then he is not troubled by Ferdinand's sense of what has been lost. The typist and young man carbuncular, as he presents them, are a pair of lovers in every way the opposite of the hyacinth garden couple. Here is no passion: neither ecstasy nor anguish. The spectacle of the forms of love used as a relief for lovelessness is depressing, possibly disgusting. It is seen dispassionately, without pity or sympathy. But the detachment is that of a *voyeur,* outside the window. That means that these lovers exist only in the eye of their Seer; and he beholds only what he already knows and has foresuffered. We are in the enclosed world of a dead mind, alienated from the immediacy of feeling and passion, and hence merely objective about it.

While his view is thus uncomplicated by memory or desire, Tiresias goes beyond Ferdinand in his criticism of the unlovely actuality. He completes the application to present experience of the cultural critique worked out in *The Sacred Wood* and *Homage to John Dryden.* There is a sustained allusion in the verse to the eighteenth-century followers of Milton: the half-buried quatrains, after Gray's *Elegy* and innumerable other invocations of Melancholy and the Evening Star and Nightingales; the typical evening setting, as in Collins' *Ode* as well as the *Elegy*; certain effects in the diction ('Which still are unreproved if undesired'); and of course the explicit allusion to Goldsmith's 'When lovely woman stoops to folly'. In Eliot's account of the literary tradition, these were the poets of an age which 'had lost that hold on human values, that firm grasp of human experience, which is a formidable achievement of the Elizabethan and Jacobean poets'.[15] That achievement has been drawn upon earlier. Marvell's 'To his Coy Mistress' informs 'But at my back in a cold blast I hear/The rattle of the bones and chuckle spread from ear to ear.' Those lines also have behind them the dramatic verse of Shakespeare and other Jacobeans, who are a powerful presence in the fourteen which follow them. Behind the typist's evening hour lies Gray. Musing at evening in his country churchyard, he hardly saw the skull beneath the skin, and rather blurred life and death into each other.

The curfew tolls the knell of parting day,
    The lowing herd wind slowly o'er the lea,
The plowman homeward plods his weary way,
    And leaves the world to darkness and to me.

Gray's wanting to be at rest rather than to die perhaps finds a latterday echo
in R. L. Stevenson's 'Requiem', 'Home is the sailor, home from the sea'. What
is lacking is a final sense of mortality, of the sort just given in Ferdinand's
musing upon death, or to come in 'Death by Water'. That sense is lucidly given
in Sappho's image of the evening star herding homeward all that dawn sent
abroad.

With the Goldsmith allusion the critique cuts deeper. What that song in
The Vicar of Wakefield misses is not simply that death and guilt may be real
experiences, but that death may purge guilt and redeem love.

When lovely woman stoops to folly,
    And finds too late that men betray,
What charm can soothe her melancholy,
    What art can wash her guilt away?

The only art her guilt to cover,
    To hide her shame from every eye,
To give repentance to her lover,
    And wring his bosom – is to die.

This 'little melancholy air' is sung at her mother's request by the 'ruined'
daughter as she sits on the bank where she met her seducer – and of course it is
not meant, as the softness of the verse shows.

To get free of the limitations of this sentimentality and its contemporary
consequences, Tiresias makes use of Dryden – whose *Annus Mirabilis*, a poem
in quatrains dedicated to the City of London, gives a description of the Great
Fire – according to the prescription in the 1921 essay. Dryden's value, we are
told, is his ability to magnify the ridiculous and the trivial, and to create the
object which his satire contemplates.

He, the young man carbuncular, arrives,
A small house agent's clerk, with one bold stare,
One of the low on whom assurance sits
As a silk hat on a Bradford millionaire.

There Dryden may be seen helping to objectify the importunate negative,
and to kill off any sentimental feelings the scene might be expected to afford.
Tiresias thus becomes the realist of Eliot's essay on Dante, irritated to denounce
the sentiment spilt 'especially in the eighteenth and nineteenth centuries, upon
idealising the reciprocal feelings of man and woman towards each other' – 'this

sentiment ignoring the fact that the love of man and woman (or for that matter of man and man) is only explained and made reasonable by the higher love, or else is simply the coupling of animals'.[16]

Tiresias, however, is merely the realist: there is nothing of the higher love in what he sees. In his essay Eliot added – what is perhaps implicit in the mention of Magnus Martyr, as it was in 'Lune de Miel' – that a practical anti-romanticism looks to '*death* for what life cannot give'. Tiresias looks for nothing but death. He might be said to have Dryden's limitation with his virtue: he does not go deep enough to discover the soul. His seeing is soulless throughout. But we may catch at the end something of what he is missing. In the last quatrain what is *seen* is the reduction of 'lovely woman' to 'automatic hand'; while any pathos in 'alone' is mocked by the mechanical 'gramophone'. Over and apart from this though we may *hear* in the verse a movement of feeling which is closer to sympathy than to satire. As it were in counterpoint to the witty dismissal of the typist, the music gives another and inward account of her, and we sense what she might feel and suffer. That is, the verse moves us beyond Tiresias' cold study towards a felt and immediate experience of her state.

That suggestion of direct response – a power which becomes dominant once Tiresias' spectacle is passed – defines his limits. His is the mind in the poem that sees but does not feel; or which criticises, but does not live its experience. More specifically, he is the consciousness of how sexual passion ends and of how life ends, completely objectified, and dissociated from the soul suffering that experience. In this way he may be said to unite all the personages in the poem for whom life is only a desert of *Ennui*. At the same time he becomes the final expression of the poet's anti-self. From the point of view of poetic life, which is in immediate feeling, Tiresias means death. His seeing, without love, passion or pathos, is the dead heart of *The Waste Land*: what the poet must pass beyond or perish. This difference between the poet and Tiresias is in a way 'given' in the latter's background. In the Greek and Latin sources he is never the main protagonist, but the one who knows what others have done and must suffer. What he sees and says is a crucial turning-point for Odysseus, for Oedipus; but the action, the *agon*, is theirs. Even as a Seer he does not suffer what he sees, as Cassandra does; and whereas she is possessed by Apollo, he is always self-possessed. This is underscored by an oblique irony in Ovid's third book of metamorphoses: he is the exceptional figure who undergoes no profound transformation. Thus his 'throbbing between two lives' may remind us of Arnold's image, 'between two worlds, one dead,/The other powerless to be born'.[17]

From about the point at which the typist is heard directly in her own voice (l.252), the action of the poem – that is, the creative effort of the poet – becomes all that Tiresias is not. There is a striking development in the music of the verse, which is a development of feeling; and with that a process of profound trans- formation, or animation begins.

The lines following 'This music crept by me upon the waters' are very dif- ferent from Ariel's song; yet the difference is not lacerating. Indeed there is a music in them answering to and allaying Ferdinand's anguish. 'O City, City' brings us to the same London as in part I, but it is no longer 'Unreal'; and the fishmen of Lower Thames Street, which is not far from the Cannon Street Hotel, live in another world from that of Mr Eugenides. If we reflect that ancient Ionia was where Smyrna is, we should notice also that there is no backward looking satire here. The earlier passage is somehow transmuted within this quite differently felt scene; and what might be discordant within it is resolved into a harmony of feeling. The mandoline and the fishmen's chatter go with the inexplicable splendour, in a rhythm which is sensitive to both, and able to accommodate a feeling for both. Instead of an antiphony of contradictory elements, as at the start of part III, the lines create a new whole of feeling.

With the Thames-daughters' song the change is complete. These forty lines give something like the lyrical and purely subjective vision answering to the objective world of Ferdinand and Tiresias. The verse of those two is the ex- pression of the mind consciously criticising what it sees. Many of the sentences, especially in Ferdinand's part, are as near to the prose of Conrad or Joyce as to any earlier verse models. From 'The river sweats' that consciousness is dis- solved, and reconstituted in direct visual impressions related musically rather than syntactically. That is, sensation and idea become feeling without the interpreting consciousness intervening. The Thames at London, river, bank and city, both modern and Elizabethan, are recreated with the intense partic- ularity of inward vision. The rhythm is that of a mind following the images without reflecting upon them; its structure is in the beat, and the emphases of rhyme. That the images be felt is all the meaning here.

A measure of how far this is from conscious interpretation is provided by the echo of the description of the Thames at the start of *Heart of Darkness*. There the red-sailed barges drifting up with the tide make Marlow comment: 'this also has been one of the dark places of the earth.' But here there is no detached narrator and no explicit comment. However, Marlow's experience in the Congo, of the dark heart of Europe's civilisation, may be directly felt in the sequence of images. The echoes, the intellectual associations, work below consciousness. 'Drifting logs . . . Past the Isle of Dogs'. Marlow's Congo and his Thames could flow together there. Other echoes join them. There was 'the

Dog . . . that's friend to men' – man's best friend? – not gods, but dogs – and 'rolls dead dogs to Thames' (Pope's line). But all the associations of this sort are subdued to the images and the music which sustains them in the inward eye and ear.

Now at this level, below or before thought, there is no analytic wit or irony to divide the mind, and no sense of parody to alienate it. The association of the historical Elizabeth with the legendary Cleopatra – or with Mrs Porter, the modern Diana or Virgin Queen – goes deeper than criticism and its negations. The mind is now in a different state, caught up in immediate perception –

> Southwest wind
> Carried down stream
> The peal of bells
> White towers
> > Weialala leia

Spenser's London, Wren's after the Great Fire, the modern Unreal City, perhaps the Rhine's towers, all that would have complicated the mind in the first half of the poem, is here recreated as a simple and whole experience. No 'meaning' has been lost: rather it is more completely expressed. But if we would recover it in conscious paraphrase, we must analyse what has been synthesised, and interpret the past tense and the broken syntax. That would be to undo the poem's work, and to regress into the state which it is outgrowing.

The process of resolving the complex experience of the poem into a full simplicity is carried still further in the three strophes from 'Trams and dusty trees'. All the dead ends of passion are here distilled into what is essential and permanent. The words have that finality of fact which characterises the souls who declare themselves to Dante – Francesca da Rimini, Brunetto Latini, Ugolino, La Pia. There is no illusion or evasion; no rationalising and no sentimentalising. The speakers express their state fully and lucidly in the bare essentials. And this honesty, this articulate integrity, is the rarely heard voice of self-knowledge, giving a direct vision of the life that is being lived.

A critic has seen the Thames-daughters as 'these three whom lust has defiled'. That is to be as blind as Tiresias, to go by preconception and miss the actual experience. To observe and judge is precisely not the appropriate response to their song. The song expresses a state of being as it is actually and immediately known. The moral judgment misses this important fact: that the Thames-daughters are really suffering the failure and breakdown of sensual passion, and that the poet has placed himself (and his readers) inside their suffering. Judgment is consumed in a sympathy such as Dante feels for certain souls in Hell and Purgatory: a recognition that one is or might be as the other is. The Thames-daughters sing a common predicament, a permanent human state.

Their song realises this common condition as a new order of sensibility in the common speech. The language is utterly simple and idiomatic, what anyone might say. ('Supine' is the one word at all out of the way.) Yet it is charged with felt life, and expresses ordinary experience in a way that ordinary speech rarely does. Thus it is the opposite to the pub monologue: not hollow mimicry; but the commonplace made to yield its own poetry, its own vision of life.

Moreover the appropriate new form is found for this new order of feeling. The two quatrains put immediate life into the traditional verse form. They are as simple and natural as speech can be, an inevitably right order of words bearing the common stress and emphasis. Thus Gray's form is made new with the meaning he missed. The addition of the third strophe completes a sonnet. This is to renew the Elizabethan form which can be seen breaking up in the opening fourteen lines. What was there dissociated is here unified; the broken music is fulfilled in the finally right song.

Thus the new sensibility forming in the poem is a development in the common speech and literary tradition. It is a modification of the existing culture by an original talent, just because it is the 'perfection of a common language'.[18] That quality Eliot found in Dante; and he achieved it in this song by making Dante his master. The echo of La Pia, to which the notes draw attention, is like an acknowledgment. Now Dante wrote sonnets, in the *Vita Nuova,* which might give a pattern for this one. Certainly the lucid simplicity, and the sense for the musical form of feeling, is like a return from the Elizabethan conventions to his *dolce stil nuovo.* We may recall that *The Sacred Wood* concluded with an essay on Dante – not the 1929 one in *Selected Essays* – implicitly declaring him the master of *metaphysical* vision, which had been lost in English poetry since the time of Massinger and Milton. The recourse to Dante at the moment of vital development in the poem is an application of that remedy for 'the dissociation of sensibility'.

In Dante may be found, what Eliot missed in Blake and what the secular metaphysical poets hardly afford, the art to transform suffering into purgation, and death into a passage to the new life. The English poets who were 'much possessed by death' serve to confirm the fear and horror of mortality. Dante assists in the simple acceptance of it as a state of being, and in making a whole and immediate experience of suffering and dying. That is what *The Waste Land* has been working towards: the absolute of its predicament. The advance can be marked in the difference between the alienated blankness of 'Nothing again nothing' (l. 120), and the plain statement 'I can connect/Nothing with nothing'.

Or there is the fact that the Thames-daughters are really undergoing what Ferdinand can conceive only in ideal or nightmare terms – Ariel's song and Parsifal, or a rattle of bones. The complete acceptance of frustration, failure, desolation, mortality: that is the meaning of this new development of the common sensibility. It needs to be said firmly because it is a hard saying and often missed. 'The restoration of fertility to the waste land' – 'the recovery of potent life for a barren civilisation': these are the critical commonplaces, but they are not what the poem sings.

The fragments at the close of 'The Fire Sermon' are a direct expansion of the song. In Wagner's *Götterdämmerung* Brünnhilde joins Siegfried on his funeral pyre. (From its ashes the Rhine-maidens recover their gold.) Augustine's 'To Carthage then I came, where a cauldron of unholy loves sang all about mine ears', reinforced by the Buddha's denunciation of man's sensual life as a burning of fires,[19] could confirm Tiresias' view of the Unreal City. But 'O Lord thou pluckest me out' is a cry to connect the cauldron with Arnaut Daniel in purgatory, and to transform the consuming fire of mortal love to a refining flame. It requires a further development, from the passive state of the Thames-daughters, to an active and creative suffering.

Those fragments are like a bridge-passage to lead directly into 'What the Thunder Said'. 'Death by Water' effects a gentler transition, preparing the emotions for the next stage. (Given the earlier allusions to Ophelia, there is a parallel with Gertrude's elegiac account of her drowning.) At the same time it is the coda to all the previous associations of water with mortality. 'The Fire Sermon', apart from Tiresias' spectacle and the closing lines, has been implicitly unified by an image of the river of sensual life flowing through the City and out to sea. Part IV marks its end. What is drowned and fixed in the whirlpool – the climactic word – could be said to be all the personages of the poem who meet in Phlebas the Phoenician. His Carthage was perhaps the one Augustine found; which was also in its time the heart of a commercial empire, another heart of darkness or 'unreal city'. Stetson, Mr Eugenides, Ferdinand and Tiresias might all melt into him. Critics who have been reading *From Ritual to Romance* and *The Golden Bough* identify him with the drowned god of what Eliot called 'vegetation ceremonies'. In short, all of natural life that in its flowing flowering and drowning may be associated with water is implicated.

But to what effect – what is the tone and point of view? The closing admonition would make a *memento mori* of it. But that simplifies the subtlety of the rhythm, the strangely cool sensitivity with which the facts are felt. 'Picked his bones in whispers' is not the nightmare death of the Unreal City. It is nearer to the curious matter-of-fact-ness of Alonso's 'O thou mine heir/Of

Naples and of Milan, what strange fish/Hath made his meal on thee?' (*Tempest* ii.i). Yet there is an unappalled feeling into this death which is almost a feeling for it. What the critical mind might sum up and judge to be just the inevitable end of a merely material existence, is felt as if it were a release and relief. There is the whirlpool to check an easy death-wish; and yet there is a calmness of acceptance as if the Sybil had had her wish. The unwanted life is being dissolved away, done with. At the same time this is being experienced from a point of view which passes through that death or transcends it; so that the death of what lives and dies by water is not the end but a catharsis – a purging away of untransmuted mortal life, and of the disturbing negative feelings connected with it. For all that, it is a death to be suffered, accepted. Thus the passage at once warns and reconciles; ends and initiates.

'We who were living are now dying/With a little patience' – that sums up the state of being resolved out of parts I–IV. The key word for 'What the Thunder Said' is *patience*. It signifies suffering, suffering that is resigned, possibly expectant. Not 'like a patient etherised'; rather nearer to the idea that 'the souls in purgatory suffer because they *wish to suffer*, for purgation'.[20] A word to connect, in this context, with *passion*, so far as that means a suffering, redemptive love. What follows might be 'a little passion',[21] after Christ's. It anticipates, then, the glimpse of Arnaut Daniel at the end of the poem, sheathing himself in refining flame.

The 'We', at once personal and inclusive, is a new voice, a new subject. The earlier parts of the poem call for a reading in different voices – perhaps four or five for the several distinct states of mind and feeling. But here, in a dramatised reading, the lines can no longer be distributed according to those characters or personae. One voice alone will not do either. All the voices are present; but changed out of themselves into an intensified common voice, as individual speaking voices can become one in song or incantation. Whether the lines are spoken in unison or in alternation this single lyrical voice is the one that will be heard. Deeply personal, but without individuality: the expression of many persons merged in a common action, a shared state of suffering, and united by the intensity and depth of feeling.

This is now the voice of the poet in the poem. The lyricism is as direct as if he were simply speaking to himself. But the self voiced is the 'impersonal' poet created in the common speech and the common experience. In expressing this self the poet is also genuinely speaking for others. There are no longer the objectifying, dissociated personae; simply the poet *in propria persona*. Become whole in pure lyric expression, he has become a voice of the human being. To speak or sing so inclusively means to go beyond our ordinary awareness, beyond what for practical purposes we agree to call reality. It is to enter the realm of what we are usually not quite conscious of: but know in dreams or visions. The conscious mind calls it the subconscious; but it can be an intensified or more developed form of consciousness, drawing upon forgotten knowledge.

The relation of the poetry of dream or vision to 'realistic' prose is not a simple contrast. Swinburne's word-music is the mere opposite of prose; and Eliot found it for that reason less useful than the prose of Joyce or Conrad. His exemplary sensibility is one struggling to digest and unify a full range of interests and experience, leaving nothing out, and resolving complexity into completeness. The poetry of vision differs from prose, as from dramatic or satiric poetry, only in being a further development from it: a refinement and recreation of the objective substance (what Tiresias sees) in image and music. It can be just as intellectual; but the intellectual 'content' will have been digested and incorporated into the mode of feeling.[22]

Such a fusion of many ideas into a single state of feeling occurs in the introduction to the direct experience of patient dying. There are images which call to mind Christ's passion and death, and then also Kurtz's in *Heart of Darkness*. The 'torchlight red on sweaty faces', and 'the shouting and the crying', clearly evoke the former, especially as painted by Breughel and other Flemish masters. They could equally well evoke Kurtz's last rites. Again, while 'the frosty silence in the gardens' will suggest Gethsemane, it might recall also Stetson's gardening, and the hyacinth garden. The 'agony in stony places' is of course Christ's, whether Golgotha, Gethsemane, or the forty days of fast in the desert; it might be also the desert the prophetic voice shows in part I. The 'thunder of spring' must become charged, amid these associations, with other than natural force: its effect might be something like 'In the juvescence of the year/Came Christ the tiger'. Thus analysed these half-dozen lines appear a dense complex of allusions. But as we read them the images are simple and straightforward; the doubling allusions are fused into direct impressions which need no explanation; and the meaning is settled in the closes of the rhythm – the chord-like weighting of the sequence *dead, dying, patience*.

Eliot wrote, in a review of Pound's versions of the Noh, 'the less "realistic" literature is, the more visual it must be. In reading *Pride and Prejudice* or *The Wings of the Dove* we hardly need to visualise at all; in reading Dante we need to visualise all the time. Dreams to be real, must be seen'.[23] This is the principle of Eliot's own 'dream songs' or vision poetry: *The Hollow Men, Ash-Wednesday* and *Marina*. And these begin within *The Waste Land*, in the 'Thames-daughters' song' and the 'water-dripping song' (ll.331–58). It needs to be added, obviously, that the natural medium of vision poetry is song. The dreams, to be fully realised, must be both seen in image and heard in music. The quality of 'dream song' is brought out by the difference between the prophet's seeing of the desert and the immediate experience.

> What are the roots that clutch, what branches grow
> Out of this stony rubbish? Son of man,
> You cannot say, or guess, for you know only
> A heap of broken images, where the sun beats,
> And the dead tree gives no shelter, the cricket no relief,
> And the dry stone no sound of water.

That is a voice speaking at others, seeing their condition, not suffering it. This is the condition itself, urgent and intense in the here and now:

> Here is no water but only rock
> Rock and no water and the sandy road
> The road winding above among the mountains
> Which are mountains of rock without water
> If there were water we should stop and drink
> Amongst the rock one cannot stop or think . . .

The repeating words; the rhythm that will not stop and yet winds back upon itself; the images insistent but without context: it is frustration and desolation intensified to feverishness or hallucination. The anguish is made real to a further degree than in the Thames-daughters' song. It is felt now not by sympathy, but immediately and inescapably in oneself.

Equally felt is the modulation at l.346, 'If there were water', into a deeper more trance-like state. The next dozen or so lines are virtually a passing through to what is longed for. The water, not there to sense, is so realised in imagination that there is the sensation of refreshment. After that the closing 'But there is no water' is almost peaceful, accepting patiently what was at first desperate, deranging. As it may do in dreams, the mind has imaged what it desires in a form which remains true to the actual deprivation. This is not to satisfy desire with delusions. But it does sustain patience.

The questioning passage which follows marks a further modulation of the mind. Its continuous movement, and the repeated phrase, relate it to ll.331ff. But it is a new development of that music. The unbroken rhythm is that of a partly tranced state, beyond the previous desperation. And the repetition is structural, finding a formal order. The questioning thus becomes wondering, not wandering; and it is not rhetorical, but really being asked, needing an answer and confident there will be one. The unknown other, sensed not seen, not to be counted, grows definite 'wrapt in a brown mantle, hooded'. It is a presence somehow corresponding to the water only heard in the bird's song; yet more distinct, more real as this is a more fully realised experience. Moreover this is better able to stand conscious inspection. The water-dripping is only dreamt. The sense of another presence might be delusion, as the Antarctic explorers sanely supposed; but there are precedents – the disciples meeting Christ on the road to Emmaus after his death, and Dante's vision of Love dressed as a traveller (*Vita Nuova* sect. ix). Such associations give the critical mind something to hang on to. But they do not explain the feeling, nor are they exactly the cause of it. They are rather the way of consciously accepting a development of feeling which has taken place at a deeper level, musically. To emphasise the assured expectancy there is the difference from the hysterical questioning in 'A Game of Chess' ('What is that noise?'). There may be fear and awe at this unknown third, but he (or she) is really there.

What follows are not so much questions as ways of exploring what is echoed and already known: 'What is that sound . . . Who are those hooded hordes'. Madame Sosostris saw 'crowds of people walking round in a ring'; they might have been the crowd that flowed over London Bridge, blindly passing Magnus Martyr. These hordes are the same, yet perceived with a difference. They are hooded, like the unknown other; and their plight resembles that suffered in the water-dripping song. Refugees, they might be pilgrims also. These recognitions discover in 'the present decay of Eastern Europe', which is a repetition of the building and breaking of civilisations throughout history, the universal form of the poet's suffering. The invading hordes and displaced peoples, the forever falling towers of great cities, these are the permanent facts of human history, as the anguish of dying is the ultimate fact of the individual's life. Now there is a sympathetic insight in this, which would make the universal suffering a purgatory like the poet's own. Thus the reaching toward the hoped for Other, is followed by a recognition of fellowship with others throughout time and space. That alters the feeling in 'Unreal'. It is no longer denunciatory, but comes as a simple statement and acceptance of fact. What it dismisses is only the illusion that any human city endures or offers an abiding home.

'Unreal' leads into a recapitulation of the horrors of parts I–III. This is in the past tense, except for the present participles in ll.383–4; up to here we have been in the simple present, and will return to it. There is a rather formal rhyme scheme; whereas the verse throughout the rest of this part is formed from within and is directly responsive to the movement of feeling. Then the images exaggerate to the point of grotesquerie. Altogether, it is a passage of 'the horrors', or a nighmare seen in retrospect by the awakened mind. It is hardly real as what we have just seen and heard is real. Nor has it much power over the poet: the last two lines easily alter to another feeling. After the insistent stressing and assonance and alliteration, the movement lengthens out and lightens at 'Tolling reminiscent bells', and the rhyme with 'wells' is a gentler, freer chime. Moreover, voices *are* heard 'singing out of empty cisterns and exhausted wells' – such aerial voices, recalling the *voix d'enfants* and Ariel's, as might become audible after the water of sensual life had been dried up in the burning desert air. Within its eight lines the passage thus gives both a retrospect of the poem's horrors, and the confirmation that they have been passed through.

Now the half-dozen lines of horrors are at the centre of part v, as if corresponding to the place of Tiresias in III and the nerves passage in II. The transformation of sexual feelings in the symbolism strengthens that connection. Beyond that, they are the final state of the Unreal City. But in keeping with that having become simply unreal, the structure, while outwardly following that of the earlier parts, is inwardly profoundly altered. Parts I and II were closed about the centres which they expanded and intensified. Part III appears to follow the same plan, until a surprising music displaces Tiresias; then the end answers the beginning not by confirming its dissonances, but with a profound resolution. In part v the music is dominant, and the objective horror is a brief retrospect set off in a superseded style. Certainly it is no nucleus, for the surrounding passages neither take their meaning from it nor give it meaning. If it is their centre, it is not their source. Our analysis, looking for the pattern established at the outset, finds it, but finds it incorporated into another. There is a symmetrical arrangement still: an introduction matched by a coda; the water-dripping song balanced by the responses to the thunder; 'Who is the third' matched more or less by the cock and the introduction of the thunder; 'What is that sound' might go with ll.382–90. But the diagram doesn't give the structure of feeling here. Just as the feeling flows unbroken through the midpassage of horrors, proving them unreal then changing them to a new sense, so the entire movement is a continuous progression of feeling. The initial analytical structure, which was a critical arrangement of the poem's elements, has been caught up into a wholly inward unfolding. The poetry has developed to a state beyond conscious control, and is a direct expression of the poet's being shaping itself in the music of words.

This musical expression, without ceasing to be musical, increasingly assumes the plainness and simplicity of prose. From 'In this decayed hole among the mountains' the verse is quite factual and realistic. What was beyond ordinary reality has become the ordinary; the visionary state is now a calm and complete consciousness. And this is the reverse of the objective consciousness: it is unified, not dissociated – simply a fully lucid state of being.

The mind sees the dry bones without the horror of 'rattled by the rat's foot only'; and it hears without anguish the dry grass singing. Decay, emptiness, death, these states are natural now. At the same time, in this moonlight consciousness, the images stir expectancy. We might have arrived at Kurtz's station, that decayed hole where there is dry grass and bones and faint moonlight. The empty chapel could be part of the decay of civilisation. Yet the simple and complete acceptance allows other intimations. The Chapel Perilous was meant to be empty: the Grail was not there. Like Kurtz's station, like ll.377–84, it was a place of horrors, where those in quest of the Grail underwent trial by terror to purge fear of death. Again, the empty chapel is like Christ's tomb when the disciples sought him there and were told 'He is risen and gone before you'. The cock on the roof-tree is like a confirmation of these ideas. It might be the bird of dawning, as in *Hamlet,* dispersing the terrors of the night; it might be the token of resurrection. Or it might be the warning to Peter against cowardly betrayal. The sum of these images is courage: courage to face the lightning and rain, to reply to the thunder.

This rain, coming with the 'thunder of spring', is not the April shower of the opening lines. It might be rather the tropical downpour lashing Conrad's outcast of the islands as he stands exposed in lacerating shame. The poet, attending to the thunder, might be preparing himself for such a purgation.[24]

What the thunder says is merely 'DA'. In the Upanishad each group thus addressed by the creator has to apply it to themselves and find their own meaning. It is the interpretation of the sacred book that he meant, 'Control yourselves; give alms; be compassionate'. The poet adapts that, but his meaning is wholly his own. His responses are a final formulation of the primal love-experience, in the hyacinth garden and the enclosed room, which the whole poem has been working out. They are his confession corresponding to the Thames-daughters', and strive for the same ultimate honesty. But he is not fixed *in* the experience, so much as moving into the freedom of understanding its necessity and submitting to it. In the terms of 'Hamlet and His Problems', this is the ordered and impersonal form of what his art has been dragging to light, and rendering 'intelligible, self-complete, in the sunlight'. Or one might say that he is now at last able to face and accept, in calm wisdom, what was at first annihilating, and then an agony.

The moment of surrender in the hyacinth garden is now affirmed in its most positive aspect: 'By this, and this only, we have existed'. The response to *'Datta'* is like a refutation of Gerontion's dozen or so lines from 'I would meet you upon this honestly'. And the few lines in the same literary mode as his, after Webster as it might be, are a final placing of its inadequacy. This passion transcends mortality. It exceeds the scope also of Bradley's philosophy, alluded to in the reply to '*Dayadhvam*'. That, in spite of his affirmation of self-transcendence and the Absolute, could only confirm the 'indestructible barriers between one human being and another'.[25] But the poem has shown how even from such passion as its personages have suffered may be won transformation and renewal, validating such 'aethereal rumours' as Pericles hears when Marina is restored to him. That phrase suggests a Coriolanus placed in the more hopeful perspective of the later play. Yet any hope depends upon his being first broken. Eliot saw profound significance in the scene where Roman Duty, by breaking Coriolanus, sets him free to understand the love which it has repressed, and releases him from the shell of the public, the traditionally educated self. That might mean, when connected with Bradley's prison, and with Dante's, that the soul formed in love, if it follow love far enough, may be freed both from its isolation and from the unreal.[26]

The final response, to '*Damyata*', has the quality of an uneasy acknowledgment of how things have worked out between two lovers. The voice might be that of the man who recalled the hyacinth garden in the first episode; and he appears to be looking back to such a love experience from the new state to which he has won through. The images bring back the opening of *Tristan und Isolde* – but also an echo of the Thames-nymphs. The change of mood in the verbs is touching and troubling, revealing something unresolved:

> The boat responded
> Gaily, to the hand expert with sail and oar
> The sea was calm, your heart would have responded
> Gaily, when invited, beating obedient
> To controlling hands

The form of the verse implies a parallel, but '*would have* responded' makes the second statement nearly the opposite of the first. We have a vivid sense of the fulfilment missed. But why or how is not clear. Eliot's note, translating *Damyata* as 'control', makes it apply like 'give' and 'sympathise' to relations with another: so the hands might have controlled 'your heart'. However the interpretation of the sacred book is 'control *yourselves*'. If we apply this we find a further and deeper meaning. The poet has been changing his mortal passion into an ascetic purgatory, and this is to practise self-control of a profound order. But it must leave the other's heart unfulfilled, wishing to respond and vainly waiting. This is what the passage may be confessing, with compassion and guilt: that the poet's new way of suffering love may mean only frustration to his beloved.

This comes as a simple human recognition. The situation is not transposed into veiling myth nor viewed transcendentally. It is a real difficulty, and to recognise it is a new development of feeling and insight, both for the poem, and for the system of feeling which the poem follows. Beatrice being dead, Dante could pursue her into the New Life. But what if the woman is alive? Other poets before Dante and since have tended to idealise the lady in the process of idealising their own feelings, without paying much attention to hers. *The Waste Land* has done that in the negative, by identifying the woman with what the poet would transcend, from the hyacinth girl to the woman who draws her long black hair out tight. Yet she reappears now, in the poet's acknowledging her feelings and his responsibility to her, as a person whose humanity is after all to be respected.

This is to arrive, not at a conclusion, but at a new emotion which is as complex, unresolved and disturbing as the original hyacinth garden experience. The effort to perfect love after Dante's fashion grows complicated when the woman would love as naturally as a boat moves on the sea. Not every woman would choose to be cast in the role of Beatrice or Isolde or Brünnhilde; nor is the natural life of love only frustration and death. To resolve the living woman with his own dying in love becomes the deep motive of the poems that grow from and beyond *The Waste Land* – *The Hollow Men, Ash-Wednesday* and *Marina* – and it is in them that we must look for the progressive resolution of the complex of feelings in these lines.

As if in recognition of that new work to be begun the poem breaks off, and concludes inconclusively with a coda of fragments. These indicate where the poet has got to in his poetry, and mark its reach and limits in a way which show this to be far short of his real end. He presents himself now as mortal and therefore maimed. Eliot's note suggests an association with the impotent Fisher King and his infertile land. We may think also of Ferdinand 'fishing in the dull canal'. The arid plain could be continuous with the 'endless plains' of l.369. And London Bridge, in the Unreal City, is falling with the falling towers. There could be a mocking glance through the nursery rhyme at the builders of bridges, entered in Frazer's records along with Stetson's putative antecedents, who buried a living person in the foundations to appease the river god and keep the bridge from falling.[27] Finally, the poet's own tower is down with that of de Nerval's El Desdichado: an image signifying, cabalistically, that he is driven out from the earthly paradise.

Thus it is lands inevitably waste that he must set in order. As that phrase

echoes 'Set this love in order, o thou who lovest me' – the words of Jacopone da
Todi prefixed to the *Purgatorio* in the Temple Classics edition (the one Eliot
used) – so the ordering of these fragments is a diagram of Dante's pattern of love.
The confirmation of ruin is followed by three lines which might transfigure it.[28]
There is the example of Arnaut Daniel placed by Dante among those who did
not order their love on earth, but who now gladly refines his soul in the flame:
an example to Dante himself, and to Eliot, of how love will be a refining fire
whether in life or after it. That process has been linked throughout the poem
with motifs of transformation and song, and is again here. The *Pervigilium
Veneris* is a May morning invocation to Venus, with the refrain 'Let whoever
never loved, love tomorrow,/Let whoever has loved, love tomorrow.'[29] The
phrase quoted in l.428 comes in the surprising turn at the end:

Now the raucous swan song sounds on the lake: the girl of Tereus pours forth her
music from the poplar shade, as if moved to tell of love, not to lament her sister and
the barbarous husband. . .
Hers is the song, and we are silent: when will my spring come? When shall I
become as the swallow that I may cease to be silent?

'O swallow swallow' translates the Latin phrase into pure longing; and utters
the aspiration, felt throughout *The Waste Land,* for the condition of music in
which anguish is at once felt and transformed.

The line from de Nerval could be a fusion of many of the preceding associations. 'Aquitaine' was the ancient name of the region in which the troubador
poets flourished, until the culture of which they were a part was destroyed by
the Albigensian Crusade. By that destruction de Nerval's persona was disinherited, as Eliot in his own post-Christian situation felt disinherited, of a
living cult of love. Yet in the mystique of Amor, the laying waste of the earthly
paradise may prefigure the perfecting of passion. In Dante's reworking of the
troubador love-ethic, the paradise of nature is restored at the summit of
Purgatory. Thus the line might reveal cryptically the poet's deeper intent: the
ruin of his earthly love should be – if a cult, a *praxis* could be recovered – the
foundation of a new life.

Line 431, as I understand it, has a quite different bearing. It is as if the poet
were declaring his relation to the world or to his readers – as Hamlet might
his to rotten Denmark. To present himself as Hieronymo providing an entertainment for his murderous masters must mean also that he is meditating an
inspired revenge. Hieronymo, the prototype of Hamlet, differed from him in
that he did carry through a bloody revenge with resource and resolution. So
the poet, in the guise of an antic wit, would have us know that he is the genuine
Revenger: that he has not been putting on an empty show, like Gerontion, and

that he has not failed like Prufrock. His claim is good, for has he not disposed of what meant death to him? In Tiresias, and through Tiresias, and in and through Gerontion, he has brought to its natural end the cultural tradition which would prevent the perfecting of his love. 'Mistah Kurtz – he dead': that, as epigraph to *The Hollow Men,* is another way of putting it. Moreover, having seen how the poetry applies to actual experience the cultural critique of *The Sacred Wood,* we may recall the meaning of that title. On the first pages of *The Golden Bough* Frazer evoked the sacred grove at Nemi, and how the man who would succeed to the priesthood must slay the reigning priest. In Eliot's introduction to his programme for the modern literary revolution, the first name we meet is that of Matthew Arnold, the high priest of culture in the nineteenth century. By 1920 Eliot had effectively displaced him. That achievement, incorporated into *The Waste Land,* does justify its hidden claim to have ended a dead era.

The two closing lines resume the positive and more profound action. An Upanishad is a 'speculative and mystical treatise', consisting of Vedic hymns and precepts to be meditated upon (as 'give, sympathise, control').[30] To end 'What the Thunder Said' with the Sanskrit invocation is to imply that it has been a form of Upanishad; and to imply also that it has been aspiring to the state of final blessedness in which the individual being is consumed within the All. Less mystically, it may have meant for Eliot himself, as he completed the work, 'a moment of exhaustion, of appeasement, of absolution, and of something very near annihilation, which is in itself indescribable'.[31] That feeling is the perfect opposite of Kurtz's 'the horror, the horror'; and the positive fulfilment of the Sybil's 'I would die'.

A CURE FOR A CRISIS OF CIVILISATION?

'Shantih' thrice repeated is a strange ending to a poem so ambitious to reform the mind in its own language. Whatever might be 'our equivalent', those words to most of us must be quite meaningless. If we recall that Hieronymo used strange tongues to mask his true intent, we may suspect that the Sanskrit is meant not to be readily understood. Its plain meaning may be just that it does pass beyond what we are likely to think and say. Its deeper meaning may be set dead against our likely turn of mind. In fact the ready way so many readers have taken to the poem makes me wonder if it has been seen for what it is. To most of us, in our customary minds and ways of life, it must be radically subversive. If it appears to confirm some of our ideas and emotions, it probably does so in a way we never meant.

This may become clear if we consider how *The Waste Land* is at once the fulfilment and the contradiction of the romantic tradition in English poetry. The wanting to cease to suffer, and to be at peace, pensive peace, is a main characteristic of the line of poetry which descends from Milton down to Arnold, to go no further. *Il Penseroso* and *Lycidas* are the obvious beginnings, but it is as much a motive in the major poems. Milton's paradise is on the verge of eighteenth-century pastoral, and shades as easily towards the tranquil evening scene. The closing departure from Eden, resolving loss into sad harmony, completes the transposition of the epic 'tale of the tribe' into terms and feelings near to those of Gray's *Elegy*. At the end of *Samson Agonistes* we find the key terms for an age of poetry:

> His servants he with new acquist
> Of true experience from this great event
> With peace and consolation hath dismist,
> And calm of mind all passion spent.

The endings of *Hamlet* and *Lear* leave us lucidly facing what is beyond ordinary endurance. But in this later form of catharsis there is not that gathering up of agonising reality into an intelligible whole, nor the deepening of our capacity for experience. Rather there is a dissolving of the burden of existence in the comfort of ceasing to suffer. Submission, consolation, calm, and above all freedom from troubling passion, these are the states cultivated by all but the greatest poetry in the eighteenth century.

Gray's melancholy musings upon mortality are a way of reconciling his sensitive soul to its failure to cope with the world; and his attitude in death – 'Here rests his head upon the lap of earth' – is the one he had taken up in life. Even Johnson, who mocked the illusions of pastoral paradises, and for whom melancholy was a black dog to be fought off, could end *The Vanity of Human Wishes* with a prayer in the manner of the minor verse of the time

> for a healthful mind,
> Obedient passions, and a will resign'd;
> For love, which scarce collective man can fill;
> For patience sov'reign o'er transmuted ill . . .

The last line can be connected with 'What the Thunder Said'; yet the quality of feeling is nearer to Cowper, 'a stricken deer that left the herd . . . To seek a tranquil death in distant shades'. That this form of mind was not abnormal, but was the dominant one, is demonstrated by Richardson's *Clarissa*. Surely the most representative literary work of its age, and the one with the best claim to be regarded as its epic, it is at once the complete expression of the Christian–

romantic sensibility founded upon Milton, and itself the determining form for the emotional and moral structure of the English novel down to James' *The Wings of the Dove* and Conrad's *Victory*.

Wordsworth gave a new strength and substance to the sensibility in poetry which he inherited, by developing the interest in the self and world which were to be harmonised. He did not want simply to escape the world that is too much with us, but to recompose a universe of being within the imagination. His tranquil mood is one

> In which the burthen of the mystery,
> In which the heavy and the weary weight
> Of all this unintelligible world,
> Is lightened; – that serene and blessed mood,
> In which the affections gently lead us on, –
> Until, the breath of this corporeal frame
> And even the motion of our human blood
> Almost suspended, we are laid asleep
> In body, and become a living soul:
> While with an eye made quiet by the power
> Of harmony, and the deep power of joy,
> We see into the life of things.

'For it is ultimately the function of art, in imposing a credible order upon ordinary reality, and thereby eliciting some perception of an order *in* reality, to bring us to a condition of serenity, stillness and reconciliation . . .'.[32] That is Eliot, of course, and it suggests the profound correspondence, which goes with the profound difference, between his use of poetry and Wordsworth's.

Arnold, at the moment when English romanticism was about to fall into decadence, has the special interest of being both an example of its weakness, and its diagnostician. His poetry, saturated with unresolved longing to be at peace within himself and with his world, resumes much of the elegiac verse of the preceding two hundred years. His Scholar Gipsy is in a direct line of descent from Milton through Gray and Keats. But Arnold felt how near the consolations of 'Sad Patience' could be to despair. He accepted with Wordsworth that the poet's work was to master his oppressive world in vision; and he saw that the melancholy which haunted his own and so much romantic poetry came from a failure to see modern life clearly and to see it whole. When Eliot called Tennyson the great master of melancholia, and associated him with Virgil as Dante saw him, 'among the Great in Limbo', he could have been applying 'On the Modern Element in Literature' to the representative poet of Arnold's own time. Tennyson's doubt and despair made him 'the most instinctive rebel against [his] society', in Eliot's view; but he 'turned aside from the journey through the dark night', and became 'the most perfect conformist' – 'Tennyson seems to have reached the end of his spiritual development with *In Memoriam*; there followed no reconciliation, no resolution.'[33] That, I should think, places him with Gerontion.

The romantic poets did not know enough, according to Arnold. To Eliot the graver defect was that they did not feel enough. Tennyson should have felt the anguish of spirit in his busy world 'as immediately as the odour of a rose'. Arnold, thinking it 'an advantage to a poet to deal with a beautiful world', did not penetrate beneath both beauty and ugliness to 'the vision of the horror and the glory'. He did not comprehend that the new conditions of life required 'a new discipline of suffering'.[34] Eliot might have thought the same of Wordsworth's always connecting wisdom with gentleness, serenity, tranquillity. It was because he had 'no ghastly shadows at his back, no Eumenides to pursue him, that he went droning on the still sad music of infirmity'.[35] In general, from his point of view, the romantic poets had consoled themselves with melancholy ruminations, when only keen and intense suffering could have saved them. They were at once weary of the world and resigned to it; if they could not master it spiritually, they would have been better broken or ruined. They should have suffered more, instead of wishing not to suffer.

The Waste Land put an end to English romanticism by taking absolutely seriously the feelings it had soothed. Poets had listened to nightingales and been sad, or 'half in love with easeful death': he meant to live the reality behind the myth. Arnold had found in Dante's *la sua volontade è nostra pace* a touchstone of peace and consolation: Eliot set himself to practise the stern discipline of feeling which might bring him to that condition. What he found in the *Vita Nuova* was a *practical* sense of realities; and his anti-romanticism consisted in putting romantic feelings into practice. The oppression of the alien world, the withdrawal into the wilderness, the ecstasy of love sharpening the grief of loss: these were afflictions to be cultivated, once they were perceived to be not the opposites of perfect peace, but the very way to attain it. This was to fulfil the romantic tradition, but critically, as Christ's death fulfilled the hopes of the Old Testament.

Yet its readers received the poem as if it were expressing the old weariness with the world and the old hopes for its renewal. Civilisation was breaking down but might be restored to its former glory; the sterile would become fertile; the sexually exhausted might be mystically revitalised. Eliot reflected in wry understatement: 'I may have expressed for them their own illusion of being disillusioned, but that did not form part of my intention.'[36] What had happened appears to have struck him as oddly like the reception of *In Memoriam* -

whatever the prevailing beliefs and illusions there is always the same wish to have them confirmed:

Apparently Tennyson's contemporaries, once they had accepted *In Memoriam*, regarded it as a message of hope and reassurance to their rather fading Christian faith. It happens now and then that a poet by some strange accident expresses the mood of his generation, at the same time that he is expressing a mood of his own which is quite remote from that of his generation.[37]

Beyond question he had his own similar experience in mind. The rest of that essay expresses his conviction that the poet must not submit to the mood or mind of his generation. When his poetry and criticism after *The Waste Land* made explicit how remote in feeling he was from most of his readers, there was a defensive tendency to find that he had betrayed his own real convictions as well as theirs. It is hard to accept that the poet who is using our language greatly is using it for purposes alien to us. Yet the simple truth of the matter is that Eliot had been working from the start for another world than the one men and women make up together.

The cause of the general misapprehension could be that modern readers, like romantic poets, do not *feel* enough. Certainly we hear the music of feeling – it is what most of us first respond to. But when we come to think and talk about the poem we put the music in the background, and ask 'what does the poem mean?' When we would be serious we grow rational, and regard feelings as less real than ideas and opinions. Yet the profound and original life of the poetry, which is the life of feeling, is all in its music. To neglect that is to miss the essential action, the patient dying in order to pass beyond death.

He was so conscious of what, for him, poetry was *for*, that he could not altogether see it for what it is. And I am not sure that he was highly sensitive to the musical qualities of verse. His own occasional bad lapses arouse the suspicion; and so far as I can recollect he never emphasises this virtue of poetic style, this fundamental, in his criticism. What I call the 'auditory imagination' is the feeling for syllable and rhythm, penetrating far below the conscious levels of thought and feeling, invigorating every word; sinking to the most primitive and forgotten, returning to the origin and bringing something back, seeking the beginning and the end. It works through meanings, certainly, or not without meanings in the ordinary sense, and fuses the old and the obliterated and the trite, the current and the new and surprising, the most ancient and the most civilised mentality. Arnold's notion of 'life', in his account of poetry, does not perhaps go deep enough.[38]

The last remark should make us realise, if we had not already been aware, that throughout the passage Eliot is talking of poetry and life as one thing. What he would remind us of is what Aristotle noted about the rites at Eleusis, that 'the initiated do not learn anything, so much as feel certain emotions, and are put into a certain frame of mind'. In spite of that, if published criticism is fair evidence of our more advanced reading habits, we mainly strive to be dull heads and dry brains. A superfetation of commentary and interpretation prevents the direct experience of the word in the ear. The critiques of the myth and the studies of the sources have perhaps seen as far as Tiresias, but no further. All our information and interpretation is vain unless it is caught up into the immediate, musical experience which carries us quite beyond it.

Eliot's interest in myth, old story and ancient ritual, was not for the sake of pure learning. It was intelligently practical: he wanted a *rite de passage* that would work. The ancient forms, as dug up and pieced together by scholarship, could not be revived. For the modern world a new form had to be found; and Eliot, in his poetry, did what he could. If *From Ritual to Romance* does elucidate the poem, it is less by glossing allusions, than by reminding us what kind of poem it would be: a way of passing through death to a new life.

But is it a valid rite, will it work, for the civilisation of Europe in our time? It is a rite, I think, for the dying and the dead. There are other rites for the living, as that of Eleusis, which enacted the love that sustains the vital universe. The discerning reader of Lévi-Strauss and of Ezra Pound will know that that is neither 'primitive' nor superseded. The rite of *The Waste Land* is one to save the self alone from an alien world. The poet's negative relations, with his fellows and with his beloved, are improved only by being made nearly absolute, so that whatever is other (and therefore unreal) may be annihilated in the supreme I AM. There is no impulse towards a renewal of human love, and no energy is generated for that. Even less is there a movement toward a human city or civilisation. In short, this is the rite of Eliot's Saint Narcissus.[39] Thus to act out love's negatives may be indeed a necessary and inescapable phase, especially in a world that does not live by love. In such a world as ours to save even oneself takes courage, even heroism, and Eliot's poetry shows him to have had enough for that. But the heroism of *The Waste Land* is of the kind which would end the human world, not give new life to it.

Part Three

1922–1930

'Ordina quest'amore, o tu che m'ami'

La sensibilité, sauvée d'elle-même et conduite dans l'ordre, est devenue un principe de perfection.
(epigraph to *Dante* (1929))

1922–1930

1922	October	First number of *Criterion* (contained *The Waste Land*).
1923		[*Sweeney Agonistes* (pub. 1926–7) in draft by April.]
1924		*Homage to John Dryden.*
	November	'Doris's Dream Songs', 'We are the hollow men'.
1925		Left Lloyds Bank to join Faber & Gwyer, publishers.
	November	*Poems 1909–1925* (with *The Hollow Men* in its final form).
1926	February–March	Clark Lectures at Cambridge, 'On the Metaphysical Poetry of the Seventeenth Century' (not published).
	September	'Lancelot Andrewes'.
	November	Introduction to *Savonarola: a dramatic poem* by Charlotte Eliot (his mother).
1927	March	'Shakespeare and the Stoicism of Seneca' (an address).
	29 June	Baptised and confirmed in the Church of England – 'I believe . . . that the chief distinction of man is to glorify God and enjoy him for ever' (*Dial* (March 1927)).
	August	*Journey of the Magi* (Ariel Poems no. 8).
	September	Introduction to *Seneca: His Tenne Tragedies* (Tudor Translations series).
	November	British citizen by naturalisation.
	December	'Salutation' (= *Ash-Wednesday* II).
1928	(Spring)	'Perch'io non spero' (= *Ash-Wednesday* I).
	May	'A Dialogue on Dramatic Poetry' (written to precede Dryden's 'Of Dramatick Poesie; an Essay').
	September	*A Song for Simeon* (Ariel Poems no. 16).
	October	[Draft of *Ash-Wednesday* shown to L. and V. Woolf: I–III near to final form; IV some way from that; the last poem at this date contained the beginning of V with the basis of VI (and also a hint for *Marina*).]
	November	*For Lancelot Andrewes: essays on style and order.*
1929	September	*Dante* (The Poets on the Poets no. 2).
	October	*Animula* (Ariel Poems no. 23).
1930	24 April	*Ash-Wednesday* – 'a new sequence of six poems with certain recurrent themes' – dedicated 'To My Wife'.
	May	Translation of *Anabasis*, a poem by St-J. Perse.
	September	*Marina* (Ariel Poems no. 29). 'Baudelaire'.

5

The poet saved from himself

the difficult discipline is the discipline and training of emotion

'As for *The Waste Land*, that is a thing of the past so far as I am concerned' –
this was in November 1922, just a month after its first appearance in print –
'and I am now feeling toward a new form and style'.[1] The difference between
that poem and the work of the next decade is obvious at a glance; and the
thicket of notes separates them past question. Yet *The Waste Land* had not
completed what began in the hyacinth garden; nor is the form and style of *The
Hollow Men* wholly new. This, with *Ash-Wednesday*, completes the preceding
work; and they do it by carrying further the new style of the Thames-daughters'
song and the water-dripping song. They are a further development, not a new
start.

Through *The Waste Land* the poet liberates himself from the 'unreal'. But
at the end the love by which alone he exists is not yet redeemed from unreality.
The response to '*Damyata*' leaves the relationship broken off, unresolved.
Moreover, his absolution in the desert is that of a solitary, a sanctified Narcissus,
or the more ambiguous self-immolating soul of 'Exequy'.[2] Of course, the poet's
recovery of his vital powers in 'What the Thunder Said' is so positive that we
scarcely attend to this limitation. Yet how is this 'desert in the garden' to become
'the garden in the desert' – 'the Garden/Where all loves end'? That change
requires the transmutation of human love, however anguished, not its abandon-
ment.

Eliot's account of how the last part of *The Waste Land* was suddenly given
to him, after a long period in which it just would not come, is most deeply
interesting because it recognises that the burden of anguish was lifted only for
a moment, not resolved:

To me it seems that at these moments, which are characterised by the sudden lifting
of the burden of anxiety and fear which presses upon our daily life so steadily that we
are unaware of it, what happens is something *negative:* that is to say, not 'inspiration'
as we commonly think of it, but the breaking down of strong habitual barriers –
which tend to reform very quickly. Some obstruction is momentarily whisked away.

The accompanying feeling is less like what we know as positive pleasure, than a sudden relief from an intolerable burden.[3]

The intolerable burden that remained to be dealt with, on the evidence of *The Waste Land,* were those unresolved feelings of the poet towards his beloved. Where the final version breaks off abruptly, we find in the draft –

> The sea was calm, your heart would have responded
> Gaily, when invited, beating obedient
>   You over on the shore
> To controlling hands. I left without you
>   There I leave you
> Clasping empty hands[4]

That uncertainty is painful enough; but the inability to face what is happening connects the passage with still more painful and imperfect drafts: 'The Death of the Duchess', 'Elegy' and 'Song for the Opherion'. In these we find the defeated lover confessing his own part in the failed relationship, with helpless or horrified remorse. In 'Elegy' the feeling of having wronged 'the injured bride' is expressed, 'as in a tale by Poe', in a nightmare vision of her returning from the dead to haunt him:

> That hand, prophetical and slow
> (Once warm, once lovely, often kissed)
> Tore the disordered cerements,
> Around that head the scorpions hissed!
>
> Remorse unbounded, grief intense
> Had striven to expiate the fault –
> But poison not my present bliss!
> And keep within thy charnel vault!
>
> God, in a rolling ball of fire
> Pursues by day my errant feet:
> His flames of anger and desire
> Approach me with consuming heat.[5]

The attempt to exorcise the Fury anticipates *The Family Reunion* – and that connection indicates how deep and lasting a preoccupation this was to be.

The idea is present in Eliot's 'Eeldrop and Appleplex', a prose sketch published in 1917. There is a mention of 'young Bistwick, who three months ago married his mother's housemaid and now is aware of the fact' – the fact being, not that he is to be 'classed among the unhappily married', but 'the awful importance of the ruin of a life'. As if by a natural transition the speaker explains this in terms which make one think of Dostoyevsky, and of *Sweeney Agonistes*:

In Gopsum Street a man murders his mistress. The important fact is that for the man the act is eternal, and that for the brief space he has to live, he is already dead. He is already in a different world from ours. He has crossed the frontier. The important fact is that something is done which cannot be undone – a possibility which none of us realise until we face it ourselves. For the man's neighbours the important fact is what the man killed her with? And at precisely what time? And who found the body? . . . But the medieval world, insisting on the eternity of punishment, expressed something nearer the truth.[6]

Presumably that is why 'Any man has to, needs to, wants to/Once in a lifetime, do a girl in' – in order to cross the frontier to where 'Death is life and life is death.'[7] And presumably the point of 'Sweeney Erect' is that the girl is not done in and so the frontier is not crossed.

That point of view is so ideal as to be pathological: any feelings associated with murder are perfectly controlled by conscious thought or wit or comic style. But in 'Elegy' strong feelings are dominant. It is the other side of the situation, for now Aspatia is fatally abandoned, and the speaker is already in eternity. Yet the manner in which the feelings are expressed is forced and falsifying. Instead of some direct method of presentation, there is an imitation (if it is not a parody) of Hawthorne's and Poe's Puritan variants of Gothic romance. The macabre tone is riskily near to burlesque melodrama. If we are to take the poem at all seriously, then we must take it as symptomatic of a diseased state of sensibility. The feelings are powerful but unreal: unreal because there is no-one experiencing them. The mental correlative of the theatricality is a merely contrived order. The rhyming stanzas, the reasonable syntax, the narrative explanation and the logic of the conclusion, all these pretend to make sense of what remains obscure and unintelligible.

In taking that poem as symptomatic of a poetic disorder, and indeed in my approach to all of Eliot's mature work, I am of course assuming that there is a single poetic personality seeking expression in it. This is not the case with many poets. But it is the special distinction of Eliot's achievement, and the source of its deepest interest, that the development of his poetry has this extra dimension of being also the development of a consistent personality. This is what makes even his minor and unsuccessful verse worth looking at. Now most of the aborted drafts behind *The Waste Land* and *The Hollow Men* reveal the state from which the poet needed to be saved. They show the mess he was in, in this matter of his relationship to a woman. To see that is to appreciate his need for some saving order, and to be brought to a deeper understanding of his writings in the 1920s.

The work of the poems which follow *The Waste Land* is to resolve the anguish of separation from a beloved person into 'something permanent and holy'[8] – to transform a love relationship which had become either negative or blank into a positive way of life. What had to be done can be put as a problem of style. He had found the right style for realising the predicament of the Thames-daughters, and of himself alone in the desert. Now he needed to express with the same immediacy and honesty this confused complex of love and guilt. He had to move from the dead forms of the nightmare vision, into the waking reality.

The first step was to face the negative aspect, in particular the feelings of guilt that went deeper than frustration, and which had not found an adequate expression in *The Waste Land*. Eliot had attempted this in 'Song for the Opherion', which he wanted to find a place for in that work right up to the last revision, although it was clear to Pound that it could not be used in the body of the poem.

T.S.E. Would you advise working sweats with tears etc. into nerves monologue; only place where it can go?
E.P. I dare say the sweats with tears will wait.[9]

In fact it was from it that *The Hollow Men* gradually evolved. Here is the 'Song', as it was in the typescript draft before revision.

> The golden foot I may not kiss or clutch
> Glowed in the shadow of the bed
> Perhaps it does not come to very much
> This thought this ghost this pendulum in the head
> Swinging from life to death
> Bleeding between two lives
> > Waiting that touch
> The wind sprang up and broke the bells
> Is it a dream or something else
> When the surface of the blackened river
> Is a face that sweats with tears?
> I saw across the sullen river
> The campfire shake the spears
> > Waiting that touch
> After thirty years.[10]

The connections in image and cadence with 'A Game of Chess' and with Tiresias are fairly obvious. But apart from making explicit the identity of the Ferdinand and Tiresias figures, this would have added only a false note of self-regarding pity to those passages. The last half-line – which Eliot firmly cancelled in the typescript – would have been still more damaging, by making us think of the man behind the poet thinking about himself. There was no poetic progress there; rather regression

However the main part of the second stanza is quite another matter. Certainly it is closely connected with the Thames-daughters' song, by the wind, the bells and the sweating river, and by the association of the Thames with the Congo of *Heart of Darkness*. Yet it has its own distinct cadence and feeling. These derive from some wholly new elements, the urgency of statement and question, and the deeply troubling interrogation of the 'face that sweats with tears'. By 1924 the 'Song' had been revised, developing this stanza and dropping the rest, and appeared as 'The wind sprang up at four o'clock', the second of 'Doris's Dream Songs' (see diagram on p. 120: 'Versions of *The Hollow Men*'). Now the dream is placed in 'death's dream kingdom', which in the other two songs is distinguished from 'death's other kingdom' – that is where 'death's other river' appears to belong. Thus we move as with 'so many,/I had not thought death had undone so many', from the Unreal City to the Underworld; and make out, beyond the blackened Thames and the Congo, what might be Phlegethon, the river of boiling blood where the violent suffer, in Dante's *Inferno* XII, guarded by Centaurs armed with bows and javelins. Then again, the Tartar horsemen might be the scourge of the endless plains of decaying Eastern Europe.

On a relatively miniature scale, 'The wind sprang up at four o'clock' appears to be doing something similar to *The Waste Land* itself. Its images and their associations are freed from the usual conditions of prose sense, and are held together in the mind rather by a musical syntax. But they find their centre in that dominant image of 'a face that sweats with tears', and arrange themselves about it in a form of explication. The face is not one but several: perhaps a woman's, Ophelia's as it might be; perhaps Christ's as depicted in his passion; perhaps that of a lost violent soul, the dreamer's double, in Phlegethon. The feelings are correspondingly complex, guilty, horrified, remorseful, certainly anguished. Yet they are composed into a coherent order: the music makes sense. One could interpret the poem according to the argument of 'Elegy'; but its distinction is not to offer any argument. It communicates its feelings before they have been interpreted, and in a way which seeks an ordering past the reach of conscious thought. The nature of the ordering can best be stated through the contrast with 'Elegy': what was there histrionic nightmare and rationalisation, is here an instant and complete apprehension of the reality of crime and its aftermath.

Why is this poem not part of the final *Hollow Men* sequence? There we find another point of view, to which all this is unimportant:

Those who have crossed
With direct eyes, to death's other Kingdom

Versions of *The Hollow Men*

(1) in *Tyro* (1921), signed 'Gus Krutzsch'	(2) in *Commerce* III, 'Poème' dated 'November 1924'	(3) 'Doris's Dream Songs', *Chapbook* 39 (November 1924)	(4) 'Three Poems' by Thomas Eliot in *Criterion* (January 1925)	(5) 'The Hollow Men' in *Dial* (March 1925)	(6) *The Hollow Men* in *Poems 1909–1925*[4]
	'We are the hollow men'[1]			I 'We are the hollow men'	I 'We are the hollow men'
		I 'Eyes that last I saw'	I 'Eyes I dare not meet'	II 'Eyes I dare not meet'	II 'Eyes I dare not meet'
		II 'The wind sprang up'[2]	II 'Eyes that last I saw'[2]		
		III 'This is the dead land'[3]	III 'The eyes are not here'	III 'The eyes are not here'	III 'This is the dead land'
					IV 'The eyes are not here'
					V 'Here we go round'

'Song to the Opherian'

---

[1] Draft now in Humanities Research Center, University of Texas, bears the note 't/s given by Eliot to Ottoline Morrell before 1922'.

[2] Reprinted in *Collected Poems* as 'Minor Poems'.

[3] First draft now in Hayward Collection suggests 1923/24 as date of composition; it is in pencil on verso of the final typed version of I and II, as if composed when they were being prepared for publication.

[4] First appearance of the epigraphs on the title-page and following the title in the text.

Remember us – if at all – not as lost
Violent souls, but only
As the hollow men
The stuffed men.

These voices have lost all self-importance, and seem to yield even the sense of self-loss to this other's vision. (There is much force in the line-break which isolates 'not as lost' as a distinct phrase, so that it goes as much against 'Violent' as with it.) In the first ten lines, from 'We are the hollow men', the nerveless rhythms and the soft rain of rhymes renounce all claims to significant existence; and the images, like the related ones in 'What the Thunder Said', arouse no ordinary feelings. There is neither hope nor despair: merely a vacancy. Now this is to start the new sequence from the furthest point attained in *The Waste Land*, where alienation gave way to humility, and the importunate negative was resolved into simplicity; for this is a patient dying that has let go pretty well everything human that resists death. Whereas in 'The wind sprang up' there was a kind of pride, an assertion of the self feeling those things, which belongs to the still living and to Dante's damned.

The first poem of the sequence does something beyond that putting off of self-assertion. The apprehension of another point of view from another Kingdom stirs the syntax and rhythm into a more definite statement, so that an end is affirmed beyond this end. This is an effect more definite than 'aethereal rumours/Revive for a moment a broken Coriolanus', since it brings the hollow men into an actual relation with those 'direct eyes'. This is like Arnaut's sight of the dawn before him. Now it is by this relation that the poet is saved from himself, and his love given a positive direction.

The eyes appear first in 'Eyes that last I saw in tears', which may be regarded as a wholly new formulation of the emotion in the first two lines of 'Song for the Opherion'. Instead of 'the golden foot', it has 'the eyes' and 'the golden vision'; and from that change of object there comes not just a refinement but a clarification of feeling.

For all that this is a 'dream song', it is as much a poetry of thought as any to be found in Eliot's work. The intellect is not now at the tips of the senses, but is active in analysing feeling, and thinking it into lucid form. With the *eyes* as the key term, there is a taut set of distinctions: what they were (in tears); their appearance in dream (the golden vision); their present state (eyes of decision). These distinctions hinge upon the more abstract terms of a parallel sequence: 'my affliction', 'decision', 'derision'. The first and second of these are structural ambiguities: the tears were seen through division, and the division is the cause of the states which follow; again, the affliction is to have lost the eyes as they were in life, and it is also what they are become in death. These are the ambivalences and uncertainties of 'death's dream kingdom'. In 'death's other kingdom' there are definite attitudes to life and death, decision and derision.

In the finished sequence this intellectual structure is more clearly worked out, and carries larger implications. We move through five kingdoms: the lost kingdoms of broken men; the dream kingdom; the twilight kingdom of transition; death's other kingdom; and finally, in prayer only, 'For Thine is the Kingdom'. In parallel there are the *eyes*: lost; in dream transformed; known to be not there – unless they reappear in the form beyond death of the multifoliate rose of Dante's Paradise. Thus the afflicted sensibility is brought into order.

The full life of the poetry is in the modulations of feeling through the musical development of image and rhythm. In 'Eyes I dare not meet in dreams' there is not the negative sense of affliction and derision. In the dream state the loss is suffered joyfully. 'Sunlight on a broken column' is like an aethereal rumour 'reviving' a broken empire. Then the following images are light and lyrical, a further refinement of the singing heard around the empty chapel in 'What the Thunder Said'. There is little sense of decay now: even 'a fading star' contributes to awakening wonder. While this state is like and yet so different from the hollow men's dry voices, so the death is more absolute and yet only 'a deliberate disguise'. The hollow men are stuffed like scarecrow or guy, and paralysed. This voice is an emptied dried skin, moving in the wind, and glad to be so. Its only negative attitude is toward the daunting 'final meeting'. Yet the attention is directed toward that, not backward. At the same time this lyricism is almost too light and easy: what it so freely gives away seems to cost nothing in sacrifice or suffering. It is like a comforting dream in an interval of the process of trial and transformation.

'This is the dead land' puts off that dream and directly feels the bitterness of loss. It might be the waste land suffered in the water-dripping song, but felt with cool lucidity. What matters in that first stanza is that it evokes a world of feeling which is suddenly internalised, and realised as an acute personal agony. The rhythmic development in the second stanza is powerful and profound. The other four sections unfold directly in musical forms that are simple and right; they satisfy rather than surprise expectation. But from 'Waking alone' this verse throbs with urgent and unsatisfied passion. It is barely controlled by the rhyme on 'broken stone', and remains unappeased, repeating itself in the mind. The conclusion is a 'naked vision' (the phrase Eliot applied to Blake) of what had been seen as if by Tiresias in 'Song for the Opherion'. 'The golden foot I may not kiss or clutch', with the afflicted self, are felt now with a clear intensity –

Waking alone
At the hour when we are
Trembling with tenderness
Lips that would kiss
Form prayers to broken stone.

'The eyes are not here/There are no eyes here' is a flat recognition, placing the poet in a state beyond the dream of section II. It has something of the effect of 'But there is no water' (*The Waste Land* l.358) – only it is more final. The lines following it are at once a distillation of *The Waste Land* ll.359ff. and an expansion of them, through associations with apocalyptic and archeological visions of the world in its beginnings and its endings; and then by the merging of the world of time and place into the underworld of Homer and Virgil and Dante. At the same time the poet's self and state has merged with the hollow men and theirs: the 'We' includes both the 'I' and the implicit 'those others' of the first two poems. This movement from alienation to humility and humanity is again a recapitulation and confirmation of the earlier poem's achievement. There is a new development, however, in the absolute disposition towards death. In the progress to the empty chapel the poet showed himself unafraid; and in 'Eyes I dare not meet' he is wholly at home in death's images. But now he is bringing himself into 'the twilight kingdom', towards the final meeting.

'Sightless, unless' is a complex assonance: lack of sight is balanced by hope of meeting the eyes perfected beyond experience; but this is a hope only. The rhythms at this point modulate from definite statement to a tentative reaching out for the ideal values attributed to the sensory images: 'the *perpetual* star/*Multifoliate* rose'. Moreover, what is invoked is actual only in Dante's achievement, *his* Beatrice and Paradise. That the poetry has entered a new realm, one not known but only hoped for, is then clearly signed: 'The hope only/Of empty men'. All that has been known in experience, the life of 'lips that would kiss' and of the lost kingdoms, all that makes up the stuffing of the hollow men, must be emptied out for this hope to grow real.

We have been brought, by a transition so effective we scarcely notice, into a quite new poetic region. From the vision of the world as the antechamber to the underworld, our gaze has been fixed for an instant upon an ideal vision possible only beyond sense, and requiring the death of sense. One might have thought that this would mean passing beyond the reach of poetry, which must deal with what is actual, into the realm of faith and hope. Yet the passionate desire is fully actual. And it is not dependent upon belief. The intellectual structure is an ordering of the feeling, but not a cause nor an explanation. To speak of a 'problem of belief' would be to mistake the genuine and much deeper difficulty, presented by what has really occurred at the level of feeling. We have found the poetry reaching down to express the most intensely personal experience. It is not abandoning that now, but developing those feelings, extending them towards their ideal object. And it is at the level of our own feelings that we may find this hard to follow. Perhaps only 'empty men' could feel it as a passing *through* the human to a fuller love – Dante's *transumanar*. To most of us it is likely to feel like a dehumanising idealisation.

The love had seemed attached at first to human eyes. It might have been, if we may connect one poem with another, love of the hyacinth girl, whose heart would have responded gaily; it might have been stirred by *la figlia che piange;* or there might have been, back before the poetry, an experience like Dante's first sight of Beatrice.[11] But now there is no human presence whatsoever – the woman has become a pure symbol. In order that the love, of which she was the natural object, may be directed towards an ideal object, she has been transformed from 'the golden foot' to 'the eyes', and finally to 'the perpetual star'. Thus the complex of feelings left unresolved at the end of *The Waste Land* is resolved in *The Hollow Men*. The method is not to enter more fully into the human relationship; but to transmute it just as the rest of experience has been transmuted. The poet has harmonised his deepest personal experience with his ideal needs.[12] Having made his life a state of living for a life beyond this, he has transferred the object of his love to a form beyond life. He has not ceased to love; possibly he has intensified his passion. But it is no longer love for a woman.

If this is sublimation, then it is sublimation of an unusual kind. What the term commonly means is evoked by the line from James Thomson which Eliot quoted at the end of *The Use of Poetry* – 'lips only sing when they cannot kiss'. That is echoed in 'Lips that would kiss/Form prayers to broken stone.' But what is hoped and prayed for is not a substitute, nor simply a release for frustrated feelings. It is felt as the ultimate and proper object of the love. The sublimation then is a development of love towards a more complete fulfilment.[13]

In his Clark Lectures in 1926 Eliot described the classic form of love poetry, to be found in Mallarmé and Baudelaire as well as Dante, as one which passes the frontiers of ordinary experience and extends reality. The lectures are unpublished, but an extract published in French includes the idea: 'leur oeuvre était une expansion de leur sensibilité au-delà des limites du monde normal, une découverte de nouveaux objets propres à susciter de nouvelles émotions... C'est le monde réel qui est par eux agrandi et continué.'[14] But to do this, and to do it to the extent achieved by Dante, the poet, in Eliot's view, needs an orderly system of thought to give structure and definition to his feelings. The thought enables the feeling to complete its development, to grow beyond the actual towards the ideal. Now we may observe that Eliot has been following 'the system of Dante's organisation of sensibility – the contrast between higher and lower carnal love, the transition from Beatrice living to Beatrice dead, rising to the cult of the Virgin'.[15] The sequence of transpositions in these dream songs corresponds precisely with that: golden foot–eyes; eyes–perpetual star; and then the multifoliate rose. We may observe, too, that he has been following the very modes of Dante's sensibility, from the 'simple, direct and even austere manner of speech', to the phantasmagoric and the visionary. That is to say, he has taken over not a system of thought, but an organisation of feeling.[16] It is apparent from the quality of the poetry that he has made this the organisation of his own sensibility: the images out of Dante are informed with his own feelings, and offer them a symbolic fulfilment. It is then a genuine expansion of his sensibility, in its deepest and most personal feelings, beyond the normal limits.

We may gather what this conformity with Dante meant to Eliot from the way he presented his 1929 essay in its book form. In the preface he said his purpose was 'to persuade the reader first of the importance of Dante as a master – I may even say, *the* master – for a poet writing today in any language'. One epigraph affirmed that sensibility, saved from itself and brought into order, is a principle of perfection; another, on the title page, capitalised Dante's *INCIPIT VITA NUOVA*. Then this, in effect the closing sentence: 'We have to learn to accept these forms [of Dante's mind]: and this *acceptance* is more important than anything that can be called belief. There is almost a definite moment of acceptance at which the New Life begins.'

Yet 'it must not be forgotten that a poet in a romantic age cannot be a "classical" poet except in tendency' – there will be 'discrepancies between head and heart, means and end, material and ideals.'[17]

> Between the idea
> And the reality . . .
> Falls the Shadow.

Section v is mainly concerned with the unfolding of that thought, through something like an ascending scale of being up to the divine. The Shadow is, of course, indefinable. But it belongs with 'death's twilight kingdom'; and it may have some association with Plato's image of the shadows cast on the back wall of the cave, meant to suggest that the material world we see is merely the shadow of the real. Again, Eliot wrote of Baudelaire's 'looking into the Shadow';[18] he also said that Baudelaire's significance for him was summed up in the lines

Fourmillante Cité, cité pleine de rêves,
Où le spectre en plein jour raccroche le passant . . .[19]

There is just such a fusion of the region of the shades and the Unreal City in *The Waste Land*; and 'the Shadow' could be a refining into symbol of that scene. But then it could as well be the annunciation of the dark night of the soul – at least it becomes that in *Burnt Norton* III. We have to bear in mind that our natural response is likely to catch only the outside of Eliot's meaning.

If that set of propositions can be taken as the expression of 'the order of mind', then the other two elements may be defined by the other terms in this sentence concerning Pascal: 'Capital, for instance, is his analysis of the *three orders:* the order of nature, the order of mind, and the order of charity. These three are *discontinuous*; the higher is not implicit in the lower as in an evolutionary doctrine it would be.'[20] The order of nature is present in the parody of nursery rhymes, as at the end of *The Waste Land* ('London Bridge is falling down'). This is a placing of the world, as if it were properly to be dealt with only in the form of children's songs. At the same time rounds may be runes and have a hid sense. A mulberry bush in fruit can be an overwhelming image of fertility; and both the mulberry bush and the 'Nuts in May' rhymes probably go back to 'vegetation ceremonies'. The prickly pear, too, can be prolific: a species of cactus which flourishes in desert land, in fertile soil it becomes a raging pest – a kind of death's head of fertility. In itself this world of nature is a round endlessly repeating itself . . . And the sort of bang a Guy Fawkes might have produced would no more have brought it to an end than a childish firecracker.

It ends with a 'whimper', which I take to belong to 'the order of charity': by patience, not violence. 'This *is the way the world ends*' –

> For Thine is
> Life is
> For Thine is the

– if love is directed beyond nature to the ultimate kingdom symbolised in the multifoliate rose, and becomes love of God, which is called 'charity'. But this is something to be prayed for, and scarcely prayable – to be whimpered rather, as the agony of experience brings home the necessity. 'Life is very long' is an observation offered to a broken man in Conrad's *An Outcast of the Islands*, as a kind of induction into his purgatory – the one which appears to have been in Eliot's mind as he prepared to respond to the thunder. The whimper, we might say, is the cry of one beginning the New Life.[21]

This fifth section is fragmentary and elliptical; also a composition of notes which are the ungerminated seeds of Eliot's further growth in poetry up to the end of *Little Gidding*. The essential motive of all this later work is to reach an end, in response to the drawing of Love, which shall be a condition of un-Shadowed simplicity, costing not less than everything that belongs to human nature.

The fragmentariness is somewhat like the end of *The Waste Land*. But while *The Hollow Men* is in part made up of the distilled essences of that work, it has gone much further. Its final whimper is far from being a moment of appeasement: it is humble, suffering, helpless. Yet it is a more *ordered* conclusion: there is a more intelligible structure, and a more definite sense of direction. It is not even a moment of arrest, but has the forward set of one become whole in purpose.

From this point of view the epigraphs are signposts to what has been left behind. The final version of the sequence was first published as the concluding work in *Poems 1909–1925*, and thus set in relation to *The Waste Land* and to the 'Gerontion' and 'Prufrock' collections. '*Mistah Kurtz – he dead*', the African 'boy's' contemptuous announcement of the end of this white god of the Congo, might be the poet's claim to have done finally with the unreal world. 'A penny for the Old Guy' goes with that, with its obvious reference to the burning of the stuffed effigies of hollow men; and doubtless with a theological pun intended, upon the Old Man, or fallen human nature not regenerated by divine grace. Of all the allusions to lost violent souls that may be caught here,[22] the most interesting remains the primary one. This is because Guy Fawkes somehow became for England the representative figure in what survives of the November festival of the dead. (The penny tribute is a relic of offerings to the dead, perhaps to pay Charon for passage over Acheron.) Now in most European religions, if not all, November ends the annual cycle of seasons. In the Christian calendar the new year which begins with the birth of Christ is prepared for in Advent, the four weeks leading up to Christmas. Nearly all of Eliot's verse in the decade 1926–35 – the Ariel Poems, *Ash-Wednesday*, the choruses in *The Rock, Murder in the Cathedral* – is placed within this new season of the Incarnation, from Advent to Easter.

The theory of Eliot's 'new form and style', his special theory of metaphysical poetry, can be extracted from certain of his prose writings of the 1920s and 1930s, some of which have proved helpful already in this chapter.[23] The brief account of the theory which follows may serve to define the kind of poetry Eliot was now writing, to distinguish it more precisely from the style of

'Gerontion' and *The Waste Land,* and to distinguish it also from other kinds of writing with which it has been confused. *Ash-Wednesday* especially has been subject to confused approaches, and taken to be exclusively Anglo-Catholic, or exclusively *symboliste,* or exclusively private. It is in fact all of these, Anglo-Catholic, *symboliste* and private, but all of them at once, and so none alone. If those aspects can be separated out, it is only as phases of a single process: the poet *starts from* his personal emotion; he applies to it an intellectual organisation of experience, that of Catholic theology; the result is, or aspires to be, pure poetry, an immediate experience or vision.

Eliot's 1926 Clark Lectures, 'On the Metaphysical Poetry of the Seventeenth Century', were actually a study of three forms of metaphysical poetry: that of Dante and his contemporaries; that of Donne and his contemporaries, in the time of transition from the medieval to the modern mind; and that of the French *symboliste* poets. The argument turned upon an interpretation of the *Vita Nuova* and of the childhood of Dante: taking that work to be 'a record of actual experiences reshaped into a particular form' – a form given by Catholic thought. For passion must fade out, 'unless it be sustained by a high philosophy which interprets it into something else'. Laforgue, in an age which lacked intellectual order, presents the converse of that. With an 'innate craving for order', and feelings 'such as required intellectual completion, a *beatitude*', he could have saved himself from self-destructive irony only in a world such as Dante's: he needed 'a *Vita Nuova* to justify, dignify and integrate his sentiments towards the jeune fille in a system of the universe'.

In the poetry of Dante, and even of Guido Cavalcanti, there is always the assumption of an ideal unity in experience, the faith in an ultimate rationalisation and harmonisation of experience, the subsumption of the lower under the higher, an ordering of the world more or less Aristotelian . . . There was a unity in existence, a relation of real to ideal, which was not beyond the mind of man to trace in its outlines.[24]

To make that connection required a conscious effort of intelligence. In order to emphasise this Eliot preferred to speak of 'metaphysical' rather than 'mystical' poetry.

There is a type of religious mysticism which found expression in the XII century, and which is taken up into the system of Aquinas. Its origin is in the Metaphysics of Aristotle 1072b and elsewhere, and in the Nichomachean Ethics, and it is the opposite of Bergsonism. You know how the Absolute of Bergson is arrived at: by a turning back on the path of thought, by divesting one's mind of the apparatus of distinction and analysis, by plunging into the flow of immediate experience. For the XII century, the divine vision or enjoyment of God could only be attained by a process in which the analytic intellect took part; it was through and by and beyond discursive thought that man could arrive at beatitude. This was the form of mysticism consummated in Dante's time.

It was taught most notably by Richard of St Victor, whom Dante described as more than man in contemplation,[25] and whose passage of prose dissociating *cogitatio, meditatio, contemplatio*, Eliot gives as an example of classic mysticism. The first is thinking about experience, about things that have happened; the second is thinking upon God or upon the divine order of things; the third beholds this order as in a vision.[26] These are successive stages, in which emotion and feeling are subsumed through intellect into the vision of God. The intellectual operation is the part that a man can and must perform for himself in order to become more than man. Maritain wrote, in an essay which Eliot translated and published in the *Criterion*:

Alas! to neglect the intelligence costs dear. A reign of the heart, which is not first of all a reign of truth, a Christian revival, which is not first of all theological, would but hide suicide under the guise of love. The age swarms with fools who look down on reason. One must first earn the right to traduce her. Love goes beyond reason; what remains on the hither side of it is folly. Dazzled by ecstasy and ready to die, Saint Thomas could say of the *Summa*: 'it seems to me but straw'. He had written it.[27]

It will be apparent that Richard of St Victor's three categories correspond to Pascal's three orders: Nature, Mind, Grace. But it comes as something of a surprise to find that both may be correlated with the three stages of Eliot's earlier poetic method, as outlined in chapter 3 above (pp. 70–6). That too was a way of progressing from the painful confusion of experience, by means of conscious criticism, towards the vision of the Absolute. Upon consideration, however, a radical difference appears: the 'historical sense', which in the earlier form of the theory governed the criticism of experience, is now subsumed into the point of view of Catholic theology.

What is to be thought out is not experience alone, but the ideas of the divine order; and the experience is to be brought into conformity with that order. The poet is to master the point of view of theology, and then inspect experience from there. This is to assume a new object of thought, and to give his thought an object in a new sense: instead of the importunate negative, which must be transcended, theology posits an absolute Love. From this follows a quite different line of poetic development. *The Waste Land* is a poem of passive suffering, an Orphic passage through the dead world leading to a recovery of the poet's inward self. But in the later poetry there is a strong element of active will, consciously seeking its end, and that an end beyond the self. It aspires not to the state of lyricism but to vision, and the poet seeks to be united with the

ideal Other. Eliot declared this aspiration as early as 1920 on the last pages of
The Sacred Wood:

Dante helps us to provide a criticism of M. Valéry's 'modern poet' who attempts 'to
produce in us a *state*'. A state, in itself, is nothing whatever. . . The mystical experience
is supposed to be valuable because it is a pleasant state of unique intensity. But the
true mystic is not satisfied merely by feeling, he must pretend at least that he *sees*, and
the absorption into the divine is only the necessary, if paradoxical, limit of this
contemplation.

The later poetry, following this line, is more nearly related to prayer, where the
earlier was near to criticism. But this is not to say that it is prayer, any more
than one would call 'Gerontion' criticism. It is only to observe that the element
of criticism which was within or behind the poetry is replaced by meditation.
The poetry, in *The Hollow Men* or *Marina*, is as purely poetry as that of Mallarmé or Valéry.

However it is not *symboliste* in the strict sense. The *symboliste* poem aspires
to be itself the ideal other. With Mallarmé especially, the poem intends nothing
but itself, is its own end, and would end in itself. Valéry goes further only to
make the poetic process the object of his contemplation. For both, poetry
creates a self-consistent world to be looked at, not through. But Eliot could
come to say 'the poetry does not matter', because in the end it is not the end,
but only a means towards another reality. In an unpublished lecture given in
America in 1933 he spoke of what he had long aimed at in writing poetry:

to write poetry which should be essentially poetry, with nothing poetic about it,
poetry standing naked in its bare bones, or poetry so transparent that we should not
see the poetry, but that which we are meant to see through the poetry, poetry so
transparent that in reading it we are intent on what the poem *points at*, and not on the
poetry, this seems to me the thing to try for. To get *beyond poetry*, as Beethoven, in
his later works, strove to get *beyond music*.[28]

Eliot's great respect and admiration for Valéry – 'it is he who will remain for
posterity the representative poet, the symbol of the poet, of the first half of the
twentieth century – not Yeats, not Rilke, not anyone else'[29] – has to be understood in the light of his lifelong judgment upon the modern mind. To him it
was a mind which had lost faith in any reality outside itself; and Valéry perfectly
expressed its state: 'In *La Pythie* I find, not a philosophy, but a poetic statement
of a definite and unique state of the soul dispossessed.'[30] He realised that state
in a supremely lucid and civilised intelligence. 'There is only one higher stage
possible for civilised man: that is to unite the profoundest scepticism with the
deepest faith. But Valéry was not Pascal.'[31] He was Narcissus rather:

It would almost seem that the one object of his curiosity was – himself. He reminds us of Narcissus gazing into the pool, and partakes of the attraction and the mystery of Narcissus, the aloofness and frigidity of that spiritual celibate.[32]

Eliot took over from *symboliste* poetics their highly refined consciousness of what a poem is. He departed from them in caring that the poem mean as well as be. It must be poetry in order to do its work; and for him its work is to compose the soul into an order not poetic but divine. The *Symbolistes* transcended ordinary experience by a supreme development of self-awareness. Eliot chose to follow Richard of St Victor's contemplative: 'he transcends the mode of human intelligence by what he knows through divine revelation'.[33] He varies from him only in his use of the modern form of poetry. What he said of Valéry was surely what he hoped to achieve himself: to rejoin the long curve of romanticism to the classic.[34] Valéry's work is marked by the perfect absence of that authority and order transcending the individual which became the formal principle of his own. The difference can be stated very precisely in the case of his relation to Mallarmé, whose poetics he studied passionately in the 1920s and 1930s. Mallarmé's ideal was to create the ultimate Word and Book; but Eliot's book remained the Bible, and his ideal was that his words should conform totally to the Word of God.

6

Love through the looking-glass

One ought, indeed, to study the development of the art of love from the Provençal poets onwards. . . But such study is vain unless we have first made the conscious attempt, as difficult and hard as rebirth, to pass through the looking-glass into a world which is just as reasonable as our own. . . When we repeat *Tutti li miei penser parlan d'Amore* we must stop to think what *amore* means. . .[1]

In Eliot's mind the Christmas tree becomes one with Christ's cross. His Thomas Becket preaches to this effect in the Christmas sermon which is the preface to his martyrdom in *Murder in the Cathedral*:

It was in this same night that has just passed, that a multitude of the heavenly host appeared before the shepherds at Bethlehem, saying 'Glory to God in the highest, and on earth peace to men of good will'; at this same time of all the year that we celebrate at once the Birth of Our Lord and His Passion and Death upon the Cross.

That sermon is very helpful for an understanding of Eliot's view of the Incarnation, which became the governing idea of all his poetry after 1925. Thomas strives to make one event of the birth and death of Christ; to identify Christmas Day and Good Friday; and to associate the good tidings of great joy with the deaths of Christian martyrs. The emphasis is all upon Christ's entering the world to bring its life to an end. In the poems it is the same. To Gerontion, to the Magus, to Simeon, to the poet himself, Christ's birth means their death. As in *Ash-Wednesday* v, the Word made flesh becomes the antonym of the world. Thus the classic statement of the Incarnation, at the beginning of the Gospel according to John, is carried through to a poetics of decarnation – the non-sense of through the looking-glass.

The significant development in the phase following upon *The Hollow Men* occurs in *Ash-Wednesday* and *Marina*: it is in them that the poet most effectively sets his love in order. The three earlier Ariel Poems[2] are rather 'applied poetry'; and taken simply as that they serve as an introduction to the style and the preoccupations of the major sequence. They do of course have their own lyric force, which arises from the same need to conform love to the Word. The lyricism is the quality which every reader discovers at once; but what is less remarked is the formal order which the poet is imposing upon his feelings. Until we have grasped this order we can hardly understand the true nature of the lyricism. We must stop to think what it means, as Eliot advised the readers of his *Dante*. To that end the first part of this chapter is concerned with what the poems mean, and is not intended as a complete account of what they are.

Coming to *The Journey of the Magi* after the last section of *The Hollow Men*, one may be struck by a certain correspondence between its three divisions and the orders of nature, charity (here somewhat occultly revealed), and mind. But then that reflection leads on to the perception that here the mind is predominant – the mind intent upon meaning. It seems to find little of significance in the order of nature; but struggles to apprehend something beyond the natural.

The first paragraph presents the detail of the journey in a manner which arrives at no vision of experience. The present participles and the paratactic syntax, presenting one thing after another in a simple narrative, hold us to the banalities of romantic travellers. The voice recounting them is tired as if repeating the too well known. Only at the beginning and the end of the paragraph is there something to catch the attention of the modern reader, so far as he knows what the Magi did not know. Their 'cold coming' might suggest the cold coming Christ himself had, as the carols now tell it. Again, 'That this was all folly' becomes a commonplace Christian paradox when we know that they were seeking Christ. We are under some pressure to supply the meaning they missed.

In the rest of the poem that pressure increases. Are the images of the middle paragraph really charged with mysterious significance, some 'Symbolic value, but of what we cannot tell, for they come to represent the depths of feeling into which we cannot peer'?[3] They do have a dream-like clarity. At the same time they seem to offer themselves rather readily for allegorical exegesis: the valley of life; the three crosses of Calvary; the White Horse of the Second Coming; the Judas-like world. The immediate mystery of the images evaporates under such interpretation, to be replaced by 'the Christian mystery'. The primary sensory associations give way to an idea, and we find we are involved in a meaning beyond the Magi's actual experience. It is the same in the final paragraph, except that here we are confronted directly with the abstract idea. The Magus is baffled by the apparent contradictions of Birth and Death, and is left simply wanting to die. Yet at the level of ideas and meanings the paradox is easily resolved.

The mind of the poem exceeds that of the Magus simply because it is able to interpret the event from a Christian viewpoint. And the action of the poem is a reaching forward from the natural experience to the supernatural understanding of it. There is not much interest in the experience for its own sake; nor is there a significant consequence, unless it be the realisation that the old dispensation is alien and empty of meaning. This is an 'approach to the meaning', but no arrival. Yet it is charged with feelings: a felt weariness, a sensed mystery, a longing for the release of clear understanding, or for any release.

A Song for Simeon treats the next stage of spiritual advance: the effort to live one's life in the different form required by 'the meaning'. Simeon knows what the Magi could not know, that Christ is the long-awaited Messiah. Moreover, he knows that the fulfilment of the Old Law is to be its end; and that the fulfilment of Israel's history is to be followed by the destruction of Jerusalem and the Diaspora. For the Chosen People it is to be a ruinous salvation. Simeon rejoices in the coming of the Lord, yet he cannot make the move into the contradictory new order. His 'Let thy servant depart' differs from 'I should be glad of another death' only in its having an understanding of the Incarnation. It will be for others after him actually to live in Christ's way –

> Not for me the martyrdom, the ecstasy of thought and prayer,
> Not for me the ultimate vision.

The poem works by developing that double perspective, of the human response falling short of the spiritual understanding. Simeon does not follow the necessary rhyming of 'Israel's consolation', and 'thy salvation', with 'lamentation' and 'desolation'; and of 'thy peace' with 'decease'. He would rhyme 'peace' with 'ease'; and have the swords to be foreign, not what Christ came to bring. The word he would hold God to is not the Word, which is expressed in the destruction, the suffering, the martyrdom he would escape. Consequently he is one who is only dying, and aware only of death, not of the life to come. With each stanza he enters upon a further reach of death: his own, his city's, that of Israel's Messiah, that of his saints. Yet to the Christian soul this could mean a progression from the fallen, mortal world, to the Beatific Vision.

To compare the poem with the gospel passage upon which it is based – Luke ii, 25–35 – is to appreciate how much Eliot has filled it out with human and historical substance. His Simeon has a definite individual existence, and at the same time expresses the crisis of his people. The verse too has a rich texture, from the way their culture is directly felt and imaged. But then all of this goes to serve the irony against Simeon. For the more fully he becomes the conscious voice of his people in their time of crisis, the greater is the disparity between his life and the new life which Christ has come to initiate. He is made a human

and historic figure only so that those orders of experience may be judged by
this –

> They shall praise Thee and suffer in every generation
> With glory and derision,
> Light upon light, mounting the saints' stair.

This is the only time 'Thee' is capitalised in the poem, as if to mark the difference between the saints' and Simeon's senses of Christ. It is like an imprint
of the poet's own mind on the poem, showing where he stands. In any case he is
clearly not to be identified with Simeon, who remains in the order of nature.
The poet seems rather to be in the position of one who would accept what
Simeon cannot, and whose feelings are with those who will mount through
suffering to the ultimate vision of the Word.

Animula is the diminutive or pejorative form of 'anima', as 'gerontion' is
of 'geron'. I take it that the poem belongs in this series of approaches to the
Word – the series in which *Ash-Wednesday* is the poet's personal approach to
the Word – as a negative variation. In the context of these other poems the
absence of the Incarnation is significant. Nor is there any passion or power of
love. This is the natural history of a soul not drawn back to God. But it is
observed from the point of view, as it might be, of Dante's (and Eliot's) mentors
in cantos XVI and XVII of the *Purgatorio*.[4] Another significant presence is
Baudelaire. Yet another is the Wordsworth of *The Prelude,* and 'Ode: Intimations of Immortality from Recollections of Early Childhood'.

The main quality of the style is its detachment, amounting to alienation,
from the actual experience of growing up. 'To a flat world of changing lights
and noise,/To light, dark, dry or damp, chilly or warm' – that is not how a
child perceives or recalls its first world, but how a textbook of child psychology
might put it. 'Chilly', moreover, is an adult talking down; and the later *'grasping
at kisses and toys'* is the adult's bad conscience imposing itself. I wonder if the
pleasure taken 'In the fragrant brilliance of the Christmas tree' is meant to be
measured against the unapprehended meaning of Christ's birth and death.
Other images, at least, will reappear in later poems radically revalued. The
'running stags around a silver tray' prefigure 'the boarhound and the boar' of
Burnt Norton II; but lack the later understanding of the pattern and of how the
circular chase may be resolved 'at the still point'. Again, 'Pleasure in the wind,
the sunlight and the sea' will become something else in *The Dry Salvages* when
its ultimate meaning has been grasped. It must be because it lacks these mature
perceptions that the soul fails to grow up. That, and perhaps also that its desire
is simply checked, not directed towards its final object. Unable to live because it

does not understand the meaning of life and what it should live for, the small soul curls up 'Behind the *Encyclopaedia Britannica*' in a perfect parody of its proper absolute.

If one grasps the point of view which sees natural life in this way, as a deprived state inevitably resulting in spiritual rickets, then it will appear consistent that the soul should start to live 'in the silence after the viaticum' – the *viaticum* being the Eucharist as administered to the dying, a supply for the journey into the next world of the supernatural grace which this soul had lacked in life. Similarly, in the closing lines, one will accept that those others for whom that grace is invoked are equally in need of it. One will have accepted, that is, that the human soul does not develop in its natural existence, but only in the supernatural life of divine grace. These are the special and rarefied terms of Christian theology, and I am not sure that I know what they are referring to. But to recognise that is to know what Eliot is doing. He is viewing the world we grow up in from a standpoint not to be found in our experience. He is doing more, however, than expressing the theological idea. He is seeing, and making us see, our world as it would appear from that alien standpoint; and he would make us feel our growing up as a somewhat bleak and alienated state. We may not follow him past that, to regard death as 'the hour of our birth'; but his poem will allow us no other consolation or hope.

The saving quality is that Eliot really meant this, and that the poem is his way of taking it to heart. Its more particular images feel as if they were drawn from his own collection of childhood memories and photographs,[5] so that it is an aspect of his own growing up that he is discarding. His sincerity in this can be measured in the technique. The verse is English blank verse crossed with Dante's *terza rima*. The effect of the rhymes is to enforce a structure of thought, marking its divisions, weighting its conclusion. Thus a mode commonly applied to the feeling out of subjective experience, as by Wordsworth and his eighteenth-century precursors, is turned towards the philosophical analysis of the growing self. Moreover, the feelings that usually arise with memories of childhood are studiously excluded. No movement of sympathetic feeling is generated in the rhythm. And where precisely is the subject of the verbs? Instead of some form of egotism, sublime or petty, there is nearly a vacuum. But then the poem is not organised from within the self, as a romantic poem would be, and as *The Waste Land* was; it is ordered according to the godly viewpoint declared in the opening quotation and the closing prayer. Altogether, its technique amounts to a poetics of self-negation. The poet has been dissociating his spiritual aspiration from his natural life: that is, he has done for himself, as a product of the post-Christian world, what he had done with the

Magi and with Simeon. Animula is a fairly minor persona beside Prufrock, Gerontion, and Ferdinand–Tiresias – he is on the scale rather of the Cooking Egg – but he is in their line; and he is a more direct probing and cauterising of the poet's maimed self.

The opening lines of *Ash-Wednesday* announce a re-ordering of human love according to God's will. 'Because I do not hope to turn again' is a variation upon Guido Cavalcanti's

> Perch'io non spero di tornar già mai,
> Ballatetta, in Toscana,
> Va tu leggiere e piana
> Dritta a la donna mia . . .

But it is a variation also, and in his very manner, upon Lancelot Andrewes' 1619 Ash-Wednesday sermon on the text: 'Therefore also, now (saith the Lord); Turne you unto Me, with all your heart . . .' Now Cavalcanti was one of the poets to whom Dante sent the first sonnet of his New Life; but no more than the rest did he perceive the true meaning of that vision. And when Cavalcanti's father asks Dante, in the *Inferno*, why his son is not with him on his poetic journey, the reply suggests that Guido had disdained the higher love by which Dante is drawn. Eliot was of course aware of how Dante had thus placed himself against Cavalcanti; so that he appears to be consciously setting himself to follow Dante where he went beyond the love poetry of his Tuscan contemporaries and Provençal precursors. It is the difference of his poem from the *ballata* that defines the relation. Cavalcanti, writing from exile, separated from his lady, and feeling death upon him, conveys his soul with the poem to the lady whom he will forever adore. Eliot's reaction in his own predicament is, with the help of Lancelot Andrewes and of Dante, to turn to God.[6]

That crossing of Cavalcanti with 'the Right Reverend Father in God, Lancelot Bishop of Winchester', as Eliot called him in his 1926 essay, is followed by a correlative correction of Shakespeare – the Shakespeare of the sonnets, a mode descended from Tuscan love poetry. 'Desiring this man's gift and that man's scope' is adapted from sonnet 29, which begins in a state of feeling not unlike that of 'Perch'io non spero': 'When in disgrace with fortune and men's eyes . . .'. It also comes near in spirit to some of the sonnets in the *Vita Nuova*. But then it turns grief to joy in a sense renounced by 'the new intelligence born of grieving love'. When Dante remembers Beatrice in the last sonnet of his book, she is no longer the object of his desire, but an image mediating the great light of divine love by which his pilgrim spirit is abashed. Shakespeare might seem to have inherited the language but lost the meaning of that vision:

137

Haply I think on thee, and then my state,
(Like to the lark at break of day arising)
From sullen earth sings hymns at heaven's gate;
  For thy sweet love remember'd such wealth brings
  That then I scorn to change my state with kings.

In place of the lark Eliot has '(Why should the agèd eagle stretch its wings?)', a biblical commonplace, and one used by Augustine in a relevant passage of his *Confessions*.[7] Thus to resign hope of a renewal of youth's joy and strength, after invoking Shakespeare's celebration of such a renewal, is to re-order in ideogram the literary sensibility of the English Renaissance. More ambitiously, given T. E. Hulme's remark that 'the whole of the romantic attitude seems to crystallise in verse round metaphors of flight' – and given Eliot's persistent opposition to the romantic attitude – there might be an intent to revise English love poetry, with the aid of Christian imagery, in a spirit that would be counter- and anti-romantic.

Eliot's critical consciousness of the literary tradition is not prominent in the rest of the sequence, yet it is a shaping force. The sensual images of the sixth poem may involve an awareness of Whitman. More tellingly, the third stanza of the third poem parodies the sort of visionary sensuality to be found in Tennyson ('The Lady of Shalott') and the pre-Raphaelites ('The Blessed Damozel' and the paintings). Even the dissociated sexuality – 'a slotted window bellied like the fig's fruit', with the rhyming 'antique flute' – could be mocking the revenges of imperfectly sublimated sexual feelings in the works of the pre-Raphaelites. Eliot said that 'Rossetti's *Blessed Damozel*, first by my rapture and next by my revolt, held up my appreciation of Beatrice by many years.'[8] His four lines might be confessing and purging that lapse of taste, in imitation of Dante's confession at the summit of Purgatory that 'present things with their false pleasure' had lured him from devotion to Beatrice. Not all readers will follow me in these associations. Yet it is generally the case in *Ash-Wednesday* and the Ariel Poems, as in *Four Quartets*, that the more significant literary relations pass beyond criticism of the imperfect tradition, and become acts of conformity to the forms of orthodox order. In *Ash-Wednesday* the dominant forms are derived from Dante, from the Catholic liturgy, and probably also from the modes of Lancelot Andrewes' sermons and private prayers.

From Eliot's essay on Andrewes we can discover to what purpose he had studied his style. The important point to notice is that Eliot's following his style went with the acceptance of the order and discipline of the English Church: 'The intellectual achievement and the prose style of Hooker and Andrewes came to complete the structure of the English Church as the philosophy of the thirteenth century crowns the Catholic Church.'⁹ It seems that Eliot had sought in his own Church, as it was formed under Elizabeth, some equivalent to the intellectual order which Dante had found in Aquinas, and upon which, in his view, Dante's style was founded. In Andrewes he discovered someone who was classical in humane letters, royalist in politics, and Anglo-Catholic in religion; someone, moreover, in whom 'intellect and sensibility were in harmony'. His private prayers, in their style, show a unified sensibility; and as a churchman he did much to create the conditions requisite for a unified culture. To take him for a master of style based upon classical order was at once a way of bringing the poetic sensibility into conformity with 'the principle of unquestioned spiritual authority outside the individual', and of re-opening communications with the age before Milton and the chattering of the Inner Voice.¹⁰

But it is Dante above all who provides the forms for Eliot's feelings in *Ash-Wednesday*. His presence is all pervasive, and operates at all levels. He is behind the opening allusion to Cavalcanti, as the implicit master of love poetry. There are everywhere specific images, phrases and effects borrowed from him; at certain moments a feeling of the *terza rima* informs the verse; and the separate poems appear to be modelled more nearly upon the sonnets and canzone of the *Vita Nuova* than upon the Catholic liturgy or anything else I can think of. Most important of all, the inner form or pattern is after Dante's. The relation to the *Vita Nuova* is so deep as to make that a kind of sub-text. Then there are the titles in the 1928 typescript draft which give a scheme based on Dante's transition from Purgatory to Paradise – say from Arnaut Daniel at the end of canto XXVI up to 'la sua volontade è nostra pace' in *Paradiso* III. In this transition the most important event is the meeting with Beatrice perfected, which is the fulfilment of the *Vita Nuova*.¹¹ Eliot's second poem had the title 'Jausen lo Jorn', as if associating the poet with Arnaut rejoicing in his hope of seeing the dawn of divine love. At the same time there is much in that poem which corresponds to Beatrice's first appearing veiled and silent in the pageant of divine revelation. This may remind us that the effective relation is not a matter of details, but is a relation between Eliot's poem as a whole and a whole aspect of Dante's work. The third poem was titled 'Som de l'Escalina', implying arrival at the summit of Purgatory's three terraces. However, the more particular correspondence is with the effect upon Dante's conscience of Beatrice's radiant presence: he feels the flame of his former passion, and is rebuked; he confesses his sinful memories, and, being purged, sees Beatrice unveiled in a splendour of living light, so that his soul tastes its consummation. Dante's commentators speculate, with reason, that Beatrice is here identified with the Eucharist:

Eliot's poem ends with the prayer said by the priest in preparation for Communion. The title of the fourth poem was the line which gives its central image: 'Vestita di color di fiamma', from *Vita Nuova* section iii and *Purgatorio* xxx. Quoting the latter passage, Eliot observed 'how skilfully Dante expresses the recrudescence of an ancient passion in a new emotion, in a new situation, which comprehends, enlarges, and gives a meaning to it'.[12] By that he meant that the first love is now understood in its *final cause,* that is, as 'the attraction towards God'.[13] The last phrase of this poem, spoken as 'And after this our exile', from a prayer to the Virgin said after the Catholic Mass to ensure the soul sight of her Son, might be the seal upon the poet's transference of his love from the woman to the Word.

The whole sequence's pattern of renunciation and transformation – renunciation of human desire, and the turning of love towards God – is taken from that part of the *Divine Comedy* which Eliot felt to be 'of the greatest personal intensity'. It is the appropriate pattern for a work which is itself deeply and urgently personal. Even without the hint given in the original dedication 'To My Wife', we are likely to feel that a private anguish is not so much behind the poetry as its very substance. In the fourth poem in particular, it is always part of my response to wonder who is the indistinct and compelling presence who walked, as it might be, in an asylum garden, a patient among patients. But then again at other moments, in certain images, it seems that some childhood experience of irrecoverable intensity, corresponding to Dante's first sight of Beatrice Portinari, may be a vital part of what has to be worked out.[14] The ecstatic and terrible natural feelings are mainly focused upon one figure, but they seem to belong to the whole of the poet's sensual life. The essential impulse of the poem is a need to renounce human love which is a torment; to idealise the beloved; and to achieve a transcendent harmony and wholeness 'in His will'. This involves the whole of the poet's life and being, through the medium of the particular relationship which has failed in its promise of complete fulfilment. The specific private anguish is thus expanded into the poet's whole state of life. This is seen, moreover, only through Dante's vision, so that while the private situation is a felt presence, we are more distinctly in the situation of the Earthly Paradise. We are involved then not in the poet's own life, but in his escaping from it into the New Life.

So far this chapter has been a stopping to think what *amore* meant to Eliot. But *Ash-Wednesday* is not simply a thinking about setting love in order. It is an attempt actually to pass through the looking-glass.

The seed of the sequence seems to be these two lines in a draft version of 'We are the hollow men' –

> Waters of tenderness
> Sealed springs of devotion[15]

There is a hint there of the specific images in which the intense personal feelings are to be expressed; and also of the process by which they are to be transformed. The heart of the first poem is in these lines:

> Because I cannot drink
> There, where trees flower, and springs flow, for there is nothing again . . .

> I rejoice that things are as they are and
> I renounce the blessèd face
> And renounce the voice

Those images return, transfigured, in the fourth and sixth poems:

> Blessèd sister, holy mother, spirit of the fountain, spirit of the garden . . .
> Sister, mother
> And spirit of the river, spirit of the sea,
> Suffer me not to be separated

While that anticipates *The Dry Salvages,* the emotion can be traced back through *The Hollow Men* and *The Waste Land* to 'La Figlia Che Piange', and to the perennial fading of the flowers of love in the earliest verse.

With the sameness comes a deep difference. How removed from the complex immediacy of actual experience are the images of *Ash-Wednesday* – from 'Lips that would kiss/Form prayers to broken stone'; from 'your heart would have responded/Gaily'; from the hyacinth garden, and its desolation. Now the images merely refer to such experiences, without making them present reality. The 'blessed face' is neither actual nor distinctly human; and the trees and springs are more symbolic than sensual. The diction is mostly removed from direct sensation towards the ideas or ideals of things. For example, in the opening lines there is no equivalent to Cavalcanti's definite Tuscany; in 'The vanished power of the usual reign' there is no specific content; and the close is simply prayer. Anything that might revive sensual feeling has been refined out of the language, leaving only what will serve a mind and spirit intent on renunciation. The rhythm is similarly determined, placing the stress surely upon the negative, and leading the mind through reasoning to acceptance. The verse is a setting of controls upon love: as with 'I cannot drink' and 'there is nothing again'; and in the way the entire musical structure is built around the climactic word *renounce.* So the poem is hardly at all an *expression* of the love-experience. Instead it is perfectly organised to control, distance and transform the feelings which persist beyond the experience.

That set of thought and intention is so apparent from the start that one might take the poetry to be merely formulating the given attitude. At one level this is indeed the case. In these lines, for example, there is no originality or depth of feeling – they are simply the clear and precise expression of a commonplace:

> Because I knów that tíme is álways tíme
> And pláce is álways and ónly pláce
> And what is áctual is actual ónly for óne tíme
> And ónly for óne pláce
> I rejóice that things are as they are and . . .

However, the care over the formulation of the given idea becomes a way of modifying the language and disposing the sensibility. The exactness of emphasis, after it has clarified the understanding, quite naturally terminates in the required rejoicing to renounce. Even in this first poem there is the music which Karl Shapiro praised perceptively –

> in a hundred years no poem
> Has sung itself so exquisitely well.
> The frightened beauty of *The Hound of Heaven*
> Is not the sister of this psalm that sings
> In the ascendant voice of sad desire; but hear
> How every step enjoins the heart to follow
> Whether it will or not, or start or stop
> Or turn again or kneel and genuflect.[16]

Just the same, the first poem, while it may be from the heart, works rather in the realm of thought and prayer. What is felt is the idea of the right feeling, and the desire for it. At this level of submission and invocation the penultimate stanza ('Because these wings') attains a provisional harmony of sensibility. Here the feeling for the thought, and through the thought, which had been tentative and patient, is resolved in a stanza which is musically formed and complete. It finishes the *preparation* of the mind and feelings for the main work.

'Lady' is how a Provençal or Tuscan love poem might begin. But what lady is addressed in II, the Virgin just prayed to, or the blessed face? Is the juniper tree the one Elijah sat under (1 Kings xix, 4) asking that he might die? And what kind of love could be declared in the terms and form that follow? Let the music answer. The first passage is densely textured and complex, yet subtle and clear – a composition for trio or quartet. The punctuation, as in all the verse since the lyrical completion of *The Waste Land,* is a form of musical more than syntactical marking; and each sentence has its specific musical character. The first is emblematic and narrative: a line like a medieval tapestry, modulating towards actuality; but with the stress upon *cool* the scene is distanced; and the itemising of 'my legs my heart my liver' is strangely unconcerned; then the fullness in the sound and shaping of the phrase 'In the hollow round of my skull' is rich and satisfying. 'And God said' introduces another voice, in which each word is stressed evenly and emphatically. Do we recall that it was in the cool of the day that God walked in the garden of Eden calling Adam and Eve after their fall? Here his voice, repeating *bones*, gives the key word and sound for the whole passage – the image and tone in relation to which the rest is organised. Next the narrative voice, with its tendency to stretch out the line, introduces the bones' chirping: a kind of inset, in which the line is lightened to three stresses, while a sure onward movement is generated. The 'because' is not reasoning, as in 'Because I do not hope', but simply affirmative and connective: it makes a felt whole of the sequence 'goodness', 'loveliness', 'brightness', and of the movement from 'Lady' to 'Virgin' to 'We shine'. The line lengthens again into plainer statement, and what is said, with just four firm stresses to the line, is wholly clear and convinced:

> And I who am here dissembled
> Proffer my deeds to oblivion, and my love
> To the posterity of the desert and the fruit of the gourd.

(The 'fruit of the gourd' is said in Jonah iv to come up in a night and perish in a night.)

The relation between the lyrical sense of the Lady and the determined state of the bones now emerges clearly:

> The Lady is withdrawn
> In a white gown, to contemplation, in a white gown.
> Let the whiteness of bones atone to forgetfulness.
> There is no life in them. . .

From that follows a quite plain statement of thoughtful intention, more deliberate and resolved than 'And I pray that I may forget' – the stressing is precise:

> As I *am* forgotten
> And would *be* forgotten, so I *would* forget

That is a progression from the fact (he is forgotten by the Lady?), towards 'Thus devoted, concentrated in purpose'. This is the conscious conclusion of the passage: a resolved turning from the Lady toward God.

As a love poem it is extraordinary. The Lady is idealised, so that the human person is lost in images out of the *Vita Nuova* and *Purgatorio*; while the poet presents himself not as her lover, so much as dry bones under the burning eye of God. Moreover, the language in which he contemplates his own state is dense with Old Testament associations – but see especially Ezekiel xxxvii – as if he were a prophet in the wilderness, or a desert-father. The Lady comes in only because she turns from him to the Virgin, and so turns him to bones which may hear God and sing. This makes the passage an expansion of the heart of the first poem – negation, rejoicing to renounce, prayer – towards the kind of spiritualised love-vision which Eliot called *high dream*. Yet the texture is dense and complex in a way Dante rarely is, from the fusion of the language and feelings of Old Testament asceticism with those of the Dantescan love-vision. The bringing into harmony of those very different realms, the ascetic desert and the paradise of love, is an astonishing act of sensibility.

The serene harmonies of a state of final simplicity are heard in the first sentence of the closing passage; and the intervening litany is the mode of transition or ascent to them. Its two-stress line is at once a mode of purposeful paradox and a form of chant, as if the conscious meaning were spelt out of or into a deeper mind. Moreover, the paradoxes follow a logic at once given and willed. In each there is a negative or lower term, and a higher or positive; and the resolution requires a shift of viewpoint from the negative to the higher sense – as from 'torn' to 'most whole', and 'exhausted' to 'life-giving'. These are exercises in moving from a human to another understanding, a mental mode of transformation and transcendence. Their specific work is to translate the Lady and all that is painful about her into 'the Mother', who is associated with 'the Garden/Where all loves end'. That is, they complete the process of idealising the human person by applying to her the paradoxes of asceticism, and so fading her image into that of the woman who brought the Word into the world. *La donna* becomes the Madonna. Then she, in her turn, blends into her Son: as the rose which stands for the beloved becomes the mystical Rose of the Virgin, which becomes the Garden of the *Paradiso*.

By virtue of that meditation the poet, in the closing passage, rejoices in the ruin of his love: for through the looking-glass of its paradoxes, the waste land is resolved into a promise of the Garden, and the frustration of love is accepted as a mercy of divine Love. (These feelings are made definite in the music.) The title and epigraph given to this poem in one printing might stand as its formula: SALUTATION. 'The Hand of the Lord was upon me: – e vo significando.' The salutation which awakens to Love and salvation is not, as Dante's was, directly from his lady's eyes: it is from her being withdrawn and silent. The apparent contradiction is resolved when that is accepted as the Hand of the Lord touching the poet as he touched his prophets (cf. Ezekiel passim). The same spirit of Love then inspires and speaks through him as that to which Dante in *Purgatorio* XXIV attributed his sweet new style. The frustration of love has become the revelation of another order of love. The state of feeling is consequently hopeful, even joyful, 'jausen lo jorn'. The last two and a half lines identify the poet's situation with that of the Israelites arrived, after the years of wandering and exile, at the Promised Land, where the coming of the Lord was to be expected. (The fifth poem will resume the treatment of the theme in those historical terms, after the Word is come into the world.)

The third poem is a relatively simple 'bridge' between II and IV. It is confessional, not visionary and hieratic, and offers to deal directly with personal experience. Yet its emotional substance is thinner as well as less intense. It is a necessary stage in the ritual, but not one in which the poet is urgently engaged.

The first two stanzas are composed of discreetly modernised Christian commonplaces. The most obvious is the spiritual staircase or ladder of perfection. But the other images are no less controlled by specific religious associations. For example, we find in Lancelot Andrewes' 1619 sermon, in a passage exhorting to conversion with the whole heart and not some part only, 'The divell, to hinder us from true *turning*, turnes himselfe (like Proteus) into all shapes'. The limitation of the images is that they connect with nothing in particular. There was more substance in the early form of line 3, which had 'my own shape' instead of 'the same shape'. As they stand, these two stanzas are not much more than an allegory of devout patience getting above the Devil and the decaying World.

In the third stanza, which treats the Flesh, there is one passionate moment when a memory becomes suddenly actual –

> Blown hair is sweet, brown hair over the mouth blown,
> Lilac and brown hair.

Nothing so sensual has yet been admitted in *Ash-Wednesday*, though such experiences must be at its source. These might be images of the *antica fiamma*, which must be displaced by the new vision of the Lady *vestita di color di fiamma viva*. In contrast to the immediately preceding scene of rather decadent sensuality, they are simple and fresh in feeling. They might come from the first stirrings of romantic love; and they might be, therefore, what aroused the desire for the Ideal.[17] While the other images in the poem are dismissed as unreal, it may be that these are dismissed as the shadows of a higher reality. For a communion with Love itself is being prepared for, as the closing prayer intimates.

Because it is a very simple account of love that is given the poem is somewhat facile. Just a shift of rhythm and viewpoint will give the parodic treatment of the sensual life in the First Tempter's speeches in *Murder in the Cathedral*: a treatment which is the correlative to its having no meaning for Thomas. What is missing is the full power of human love, whether it be felt in splendour or in terror – or in agony, as we should expect after *The Waste Land* and *The Hollow Men*. But perhaps we must remember that this is a confession, and that what figures in it is only what would distract the poet from perfection. If his adult love for a woman does not appear here, it may be because it has been no distraction but a direct way to Love: his purgatory, or Lenten mortification of the flesh. That after all is what we have been given in I and II.

What II willed, and approached in meditation, in IV is seen and felt with visionary immediacy. Its thematic preoccupations and music go on directly from the litany. But it expands the two-stress chant into the flowing and checking but always onward driving movement of a dance. Moroever, in place of the contradictions to be resolved, the mind now ascends from like to like, by the consonances of the lower with the higher sense: 'the violet and the violet', 'in white and blue, in Mary's colour'. In this way the human sufferer is identified with Mary; so that, as Mary served for the divine recovery of Paradise, the Lady mystically restores the garden of love that had become desert.[18] This is the 'higher dream': a poetry which by expressing actual experience in symbol, and then transvaluing the symbols, creates the ideal world that is longed for.

'Sovegna vos', the musical close of the first passage, seems to place the poet with Arnaut, contemplating a vision beyond his actual state. That recalls him to his situation in time. Yet the next passage of verse, down to 'the gilded hearse', is like an intensifying mirror to the first. It faces it as a mirror image. And its exalted statement seems the voice of one rapt in the vision. The resolved certainty overflows the lines, sustained upon the key words *restoring* and *redeem*. 'This is not merely "music" ', as Eliot said of a verse of Swinburne, 'it is effective because it appears to be a tremendous statement, like statements made in our dreams.'[19] The centre of the passage, with the richest effect of image and music, is the vision of the woman transmuted into pure light. Then, as if quickened by that, the dance moves into a climax of affirmation and strengthened purpose. This is the moment of maximum intensity and attainment in the sequence, the fulfilment of its conscious striving in a movement that is all at once dance, incantation, vision and statement.

Yet, as is the way with visions and dreams, we miss the substance of sensory knowledge, and look to interpretation to make up for it. To say that it is a mystical state is not especially illuminating. When Beatrice has appeared to Dante clothed in the colour of living flame the meaning is very fully explicated. Or when Cavalcanti says of his beloved that she 'makes the air all tremulous with light', as Rossetti rendered 'Che fe di claritate l'aer tremare', he is directly celebrating the power of beauty to move love. But with Eliot's lines neither the direct effect nor the meaning are immediately intelligible. One must ask, what does it mean to redeem the time, to redeem the unread vision in the higher dream? And what is the meaning of that line of allegorical pageant which so effectively, and yet so strangely, makes a close in the music?

I imagine the gilded hearse to be conveying away the fiddles and the flutes, the dead years and the dry bones, all of the old life that is dust and ashes. The jewelled unicorns might be from the medieval bestiaries. With that symbolic horn, they yet flee all sensual contact, but may be tamed by a virgin. The line might be an allegory of the poet's 'brave attempt to fabricate something permanent and holy out of his personal animal feelings'.[20] But our one definite impression may be that, like Dante's Divine Pageant, it is a vividly visual expression of a meaning beyond sense.

That line of pure allegory is an extreme manifestation of the mode of mind which the poet has been cultivating. For he has been systematically revaluing experience according to a higher meaning. Now it is this, as I understand it, which will 'redeem the time, redeem the dream'. To see the woman as afflicted and *therefore* as Beatrice is to redeem her condition. And to perceive her, thus idealised, as a token of the Word – which is what Beatrice becomes for Dante – is to read the vision. For the theological idea of redemption means, not restoring things to their original state, but bringing them to their final cause, the end which is their beginning. It must be in this sense that the poet is urging himself to redemption.

Only by holding to that clue can I follow the development of the sequence beyond this point. There is a logical progression from the last eight lines of IV into V and through to the end of VI: the life of the world, and the poet's own life in the flesh, are now perceived in the light of the Word, and made sense of according to its meaning rather than their own life. Yet this revaluation is difficult if not impossible to follow through as a progression of feeling.

The difficulties begin, for me, with the altered sense of the woman immediately after the moment of vision. She has just been sheathed in light, as one consumed by and so revealing the divine Light. Now, without transition or explanation, she is simply 'the silent sister'.[21] Moreover, the syntax appears to dissociate her from what the vision meant: she spoke no word *but* the fountain sprang up. The implication is shocking after what has gone before, and it is offered with a calmness which compounds the baffling lack of feeling. Yet the dissociation is the product of deliberate revision, for the draft of the poem ended in this way:

White light folded, sheathed about her, folding the flame and green
Clothes that now clothe her, while the flowers rejoice
In the blessed face
And the blessed voice
Of one who has heard the unheard, seen the unseen.
Desire chills, and the hidden thoughts outrace
The way of penance to the means of grace.

Poi s'ascose nel foco and
After this our exile.

Perhaps the statement 'one who has heard the unheard, seen the unseen' was suppressed because it implied a continuity between the natural and the divine: whereas to Eliot's mind the lower and the higher are not continuous, though human feeling would have them be so, the unregenerate desire and hidden thoughts. It would seem that *any* attention paid to the woman in herself is now a distraction from what has been revealed through her. The proper way forward from the vision, a way which the drafts show the poet himself following with some difficulty, is that of penance – the Lenten way of mortifying human sense and feeling. Yet this is to return to or to reaffirm the *données* of the work. The value of the woman has been all along that she does not fulfil desire. It is just by being withdrawn and silent that she lets the desert become the garden, and becomes herself a vision of light. Shortly her 'word unheard, unspoken' will be received as the Word – in her negation is her supreme value. Thus feeling, which registers the denial of what is desired, is contradicted by an understanding which is beyond sense.

However, that may be a way of putting my own very real difficulties as a reader, rather than an accurate account of the poem. For what disturbs me is perhaps the disparity between my sense of the tortured and tortuous process of these transformations, and the ease and simplicity with which they are presented. There is no longer even the constrained effort to renounce the blessed face and voice; but just that simple remove to 'the silent sister', with the verse rejoicing in a fountain made to spring up in dispossession. The music of the poetry is disconcertingly in accord with the meaning. That means that the feelings of the poet have followed the meditation and vision so completely that they are no longer natural human feelings, but those of one who has passed through the looking-glass. For him, now, natural life is simply death, and its negation is the way to Life. This attitude he maintains with every appearance of naturalness and positiveness. To most readers the lyrical energy and beauty of the poetry are immediately convincing. It is not within the poetry as poetry then that our difficulties lie; but in reconciling our understanding of what the feelings in the poetry are *for* with our normal feelings towards deprivation and death. For the poetry really does celebrate, and would make us enter into, a world which is in every way the opposite of our ordinary one.

Some readers will resent having the lyrical simplicity complicated by this understanding. But I have found that it is only by way of the understanding that I can fully follow and appreciate the extraordinary achievement. If a consequence is to become aware that the poetry does not invite the usual flow of romantic feelings, but is set to redirect those feelings to an unromantic end, then that too is an integral part of the experience. This poem is not in sympathy with humanity: it is profoundly and necessarily opposed. Unless we really do share its alien point of view, it must greatly complicate our consciousness by its inversion of our normal attitudes. To miss that is to miss not just the meaning, but the experience too.

What would be the normal reading of the last two lines of IV? That the long-lived yew tree is associated with graveyards and remembrance, as in *In Memoriam* whispering perpetually of the dead about whom their roots are twined? Tennyson derives a kind of consolation from facing the fact of death in that way. Yet none of these feelings quite attaches to the image in *Ash-Wednesday*. They would appear to have been superseded by another sense, one which looks forward to the end of the world by making a millennium of particular anniversaries. Again, 'And after this our exile' might seem to imply exile from the visionary garden, and to be charged with regret. But in fact the prayer looks forward to what follows life on earth, and it is this life which is regarded as exile: 'And after this our exile show unto us the blessed fruit of thy womb, Jesus' would be the last line in full. Thus the inner feeling of both these lines is precisely not regret, but an esoteric hope.

The fifth poem singlemindedly adopts the viewpoint of the Word against that of the world, as at the beginning of the Gospel according to John which is read at the end of the Catholic Mass. It starts from a syllogism which is like a kicking away of the ladders of paradox and analogy. Now the higher viewpoint is established by insisting that the negative be only negative, so that the only good shall be God.

> *If* the *lost* word *is* lost, *if* the *spent* word *is* spent
> If the *un*heard, *un*spoken
> Wórd is *un*spoken, *un*heard . . .

With that line the marking of stress and sense becomes problematical: the weight thrown upon *Word* crosses one rhythm with another and opens a double sense. Is the capital typographical convention, or theological? It hardly matters once the question has opened the mind to the second possibility, and so prepared the way for the declaration that 'the unspoken word' *is* 'the Word unheard'. This of course is to make a plain statement of what the run of the verse and syntax partly veils. The second phrase appears to be in apposition to the first, as if 'word' and 'Word' were like terms. But it is the un-word that is the Word. The higher sense is not implicit in the lower, but is arrived at by the negation of the lower. The logic is that of *Burnt Norton*, where the argument adumbrated here will be more fully developed: what is required is 'World not world, but that which is not world'. The present application is to 'the blessed voice' – and, by implication, 'the blessed face'. If it be really silent and not heard at all, then what will be heard in the absolute silence will be the voice of God. And if the blessed face be wholly renounced, then in the void may be seen a vision of divine light. This is precisely what the preceding poems have been working for.

Upon that basis the poet proceeds to inveigh against the world for being neither the Word nor pure void, but simply itself. Its existence is mocked in cacophonous sound and monotonous rhythm, and by the iteration of words merely the same –

> Those who are torn on the horn between season and season, time and time, between
> Hour and hour, word and word, power and power . . .

These flattening distinctions without difference are as much as to say 'the world is the world is the world'. No range of associations is admitted, such as made possible a significant distinction between 'the violet and the violet'. And there is not the subtle discriminating of like sounds which composed the complex statement

> Against the Word the unstilled world still whirled
> About the centre of the silent Word.

The life of the world is being put down – as it will be again in *Burnt Norton* III and V. The trouble with it is not anything that could be put right by progress or enlightenment: it is just that it is not annihilated in God. It prefers its noise to the voice of silence; it avoids the absent face; it denies Original Sin, and will not be redeemed.

All of this is summed up in the very evocative image, 'in the desert/Of drouth, spitting from the mouth the withered apple-seed'. This is readily glossed as meaning Original Sin – see Genesis iii. But what does 'original sin' mean? There are some relevant though not wholly enlightening pages at the end of the 1930 essay on Baudelaire,[22] leading up to a citation of T. E. Hulme: 'In the light of these absolute values, man himself is judged to be essentially limited and imperfect. He is endowed with Original Sin. While he can occasionally accomplish acts which partake of perfection, he can never himself *be* perfect.' That assumes a desire or need to be 'perfect'; and asserts that man cannot be perfect in and of himself, being *in essence* imperfect. The same is to be said of the human world in general, in Eliot's view:

The Universal Church is today, it seems to me, more definitely set against the World than at any time since pagan Rome. I do not mean that our times are particularly corrupt; all times are corrupt. I mean that Christianity, in spite of certain local appearances, is not, and cannot be within measurable time, 'official'. The World is trying the experiment of attempting to form a civilized but non-Christian mentality. The experiment will fail; but we must be very patient in awaiting its collapse; meanwhile redeeming the time: so that the Faith may be preserved alive through the dark ages before us; to renew and rebuild civilization, and save the World from suicide.[23]

That is to be read in the looking-glass where meanings are inverted. The suicide from which the world is to be saved is that of persisting in its own life; the civilisation to which the Faith would give rise would order the life of the world towards death. For natural life is a life cut off from God, in Original Sin; and to be united with God means the end of nature, the end of the world. According to Christian legend, it was from the seed of the fruit plucked from the Tree of the Knowledge of Good and Evil that grew the tree upon which Christ was crucified. That is the one tree which can make 'the garden in the desert'.

The judgment of the world, if it is to be acceptable at all, requires the poet's own death within the death of nature. The contemplation of death in II hardly gives us that, since it is rather the vision or dream of one who is out of nature, a disembodied spirit. It is the death of the body, of the human being, that is called for. There may be an approach to this in v. The rage or spleen of the invective may be the projection of the poet's baffled need to make an end of his own life.[24] Then we may feel a quality of humility tempering the satire as it modulates towards prayer in the third and fourth stanzas: the poet could be implicating himself among those 'who chose and oppose' and 'are terrified and cannot surrender'. However it is in VI that he clearly confesses and seeks to mortify his own natural life as it persists in spite of his Christian will.

The action of VI is a progression from 'The dreamcrossed twilight between birth and dying', to 'the time of tension between dying and birth/The place of solitude where three dreams cross'. There is first an unresolved mingling of memory, desire, and knowledge of what must be –

From the wide window towards the granite shore
The white sails still fly seaward, seaward flying
Unbroken wings

Then what has been and what might have been are made to point to the one end which is always present – these being, it would appear, the three levels of dream which are to be dissociated.

The superimposition of 'Unbroken wings' upon 'the white sails' is a feat of imagination answering to desire and hope, and suppressing the menace of granite, the fear of being broken. In the following paragraph there is a conscious criticism of what is remembered and desired, with painful tension between the feelings which follow the sensual images, and the insistent judgment that they are *lost, weak, empty, sandy earth*. What is known to be lost is yet felt as actual; so that the stress upon 'lost' is countered by an equal stress upon 'lilac' and 'sea voices'. Perhaps the sensual music threatens to be dominant, actually becomes dominant at 'Quickens to recover/The cry of quail and the whirling plover'. But that is put down by 'the blind eye' and its underworld of dreams. Then the sequence of images reaches a natural close with the falling rhythm of 'The empty forms between the ivory gates' – in precise contrast to the rising movement of the preceding lines – and in the dragging of the last line to a stop at 'earth'. Now one discovers that the passage has composed a brief life or natural history of the poet – a miniature or sketch for *The Dry Salvages*. The source of most of the images could be those childhood summers on the New England coast, plus a recollection of Virgil. At another level the images carry sexual associations, and might correspond to an unfolding of love, from adolescent romance through a sense of its powers to an aftermath of loss and regret. There is too an implicit recognition of the succession of seasons, from the spring of life through full summer to the death of winter.

Thus the confession of his continuing in the state of sinful life has become an ordering of his natural existence according to the conviction that its end is death. The naturally romantic sensibility, which those images would express and to which they appeal, is being recomposed by an anti-romantic sense of realities. This is not a new thing, of course; but the confessional quality marks a significant advance in the sequence 'La Figlia Che Piange', 'Dans le Restaurant', *The Waste Land* and *The Hollow Men* – and upon the earlier poems of *Ash-Wednesday* itself. It is a move back from symbol towards reality, from the purely mental reflection towards a direct treatment of experience. Yet, paradoxically, this is a move forward for Eliot, from a poetry which expresses what has been actually known and felt, to one which reconstitutes experience 'in a different form', the form of new attitudes and emotions. To say that this is more personal than the poetry that led up to it is a way of registering that it cuts nearer to the quick of self. One has to add that it does this not for the sake of self-expression, but in order to question and radically to alter the personal life – to impose or to create an elected self.

The achievement of *Ash-Wednesday* is a deliberate and effective entering upon 'the way of penance' which means dying into the New Life. There is no sense of reaching any conclusion, but only of faring forward. With our hind-sight, we can see that the end of the sequence requires the fuller development of *The Dry Salvages* and of *Four Quartets* as a whole. But there is already a disposition toward that work in the prayers and invocations of the closing lines. At the end of the first poem it was his own will which rhymed with 'teach us to sit still': now it is 'Our peace in His will'. This is confirmed by 'Suffer me not to be separated from Thee', from a prayer to be said after Mass in the *Saint Swithun's Prayer Book,* which Eliot may well have used; and then by the last line, from a prayer to be said before Mass:

V. Wilt thou not turn again and quicken us, O Lord?
R. That Thy people may rejoice in Thee.
V. O Lord, show Thy mercy upon us.
R. And grant us Thy salvation.
V. Lord, hear my prayer.
R. And let my cry come unto Thee.[25]

That answers, albeit privately, the first line of this poem and of the sequence. That it comes from the beginning of the Mass might imply, again privately, that the poet is moving from one following through of its action into the next.

The recourse to prayer is itself a form of imperfection, an implicit recognition that what is willed is still to be realised. It is not poetry so much as a statement of intent for a future poetry. Of course the forms and formulations of Catholic practice are an inseparable element in the whole poem. But they are neither the poetry nor the cause of the poetry. They simply mediate between the poet's emotions and the effective realisation of them. As Eliot wrote to Paul Elmer More on Shrove Tuesday 1928 – the day for shriving or confession before Ash-Wednesday – he could not escape feeling a void 'in the middle of all human happiness and all human relations', and to turn from them to God was the only way he could fill it.[26] His acceptance of Christian belief and practice followed from and served his way of feeling, not the other way round. It was not a substitute for the practice of poetry; and it would be shallow of us to let either our acceptance or our rejection of Christianity get in the way of the poetry.

We have to guard against its distracting us from the real achievement and challenge of *Ash-Wednesday*. For this is a work which, being just as life-denying as it can be, is nevertheless the expression of human feelings and a human attitude. The revulsion from life is a phase of life itself, going naturally with failure, defeat, and impotency in situations we cannot cope with. The demand that art be only life-enhancing is simply a refusal to face this fact of life. But the deeper difficulty with *Ash-Wednesday* is that it denies life with purposeful energy and positive feeling. The vitality and beauty of its music is undeniable, and that is an actual and human experience. Somehow it achieves what should be humanly impossible, the celebration of death as a form of life. For myself, I can't say that I like it for that; but that is what it is and does, whether we like it or not.

Marina is a development of certain of the materials and preoccupations of *Ash-Wednesday*, and also a further development in the Ariel sequence. The implicit persona, following on in the historical succession of the Magus, Simeon, Animula, might represent the state of being actually achieved in *Ash-Wednesday*: what is there realised as poetry, as distinguished from what is merely invoked in thought and prayer. As that state was one of not finally resolved tensions, a crossing of dreams, so *Marina* is the expression of a mind just waking from dream into consciousness.

The first paragraph, an introduction, is a wondering questioning of images that are distinct yet mysterious. Are the images of the first line seen, or only sensed through the fog? The line moves fluidly, indefinitely; yet the adjective and extra stress give a presence to 'grey rocks'. 'Water lapping the bow' is more immediate though, and the scent and song: these certainly give a world of sensuous 'grace dissolved in place', and with the freshness of experience refined in dream-vision.

The next passage, or musical movement, runs to 'where all the waters meet', and has four distinct sections. The first, 'meaning/Death', is based upon a Highland charm or exorcism, and seems to require interpretation as a commination or denouncing of anger and judgments against those who live in the seven deadly sins.[27] Its function, as a line in the first draft put it, is to make 'the world in chase diminished from place'; and it does this with a certainty which stands in total contrast to the first wondering lines.

Those first images are then confirmed, in an assured, no longer questioning rhythm; from which the mind moves on to a more searching question –

What is this face less clear and clearer
The pulse in the arm, less strong and stronger –
Given or lent? more distant than stars and nearer than the eye

The allusion to Pericles' doubting recognition of Marina[28] gives to these cryptic images a definite and suggestive context. The recovered daughter is the very image of his lost wife. He asks

> But are you flesh and blood?
> Have you a working pulse? and are no fairy?

Being truly his daughter and alive, she begets him that did her beget, and will be to him 'another life'. Wild with joy, he hears

> Most heavenly music!
> It nips me unto listening, and thick slumber
> Hangs upon mine eyes: let me rest.

The two lines which close this passage – with the first full rhyme: up to now the rhymes have been all inward echoes – seem to be not so much part of the vision as a placing of it. The movement falls away from buoyant wonder into a swaying suspension. The tone is altered, and not easy to assess. I find myself seeking help from seemingly related contexts: the children singing or laughing in the orchards of 'Ode' (in *Ara Vos Prec*) and 'New Hampshire', and in *Burnt Norton*; the hurrying feet in the latter also, and in *The Family Reunion*;[29] and these lines in the draft of that play, spoken by Harry to Mary near the end of their 'duet':

> news
> You have given me a word
> Of a new world, ~~under sleep~~, in the deep, in the abyss of light, a <u>new</u> world,
> ~~Mary~~ . . .
> Stop!
> What was that? Did you feel it?[30]

What he feels, cutting across the glimpse of happiness, is of course the presence of the Eumenides. They enforce what Thomas had reflected when dismissing the First Tempter:

> The impossible is still temptation.
> The impossible, the undesirable,
> Voices under sleep, waking a dead world,
> So that the mind may not be whole in the present.[31]

Now, having called up these associated contexts, I have to recognise that their more definite meanings are not present in *Marina*, though they may be latent. Here the images might be merely dream echoes of a lost world; or they might be intimations of its recovery, as at the end of *Little Gidding*. All we can be sure of is that their meaning remains elusive. As with the rest of the vision, they have not yet been subjected to conscious analysis.

They do have the effect, however, of closing the visionary questing. The following section – the first of the second movement, which goes down to 'the new ships' – opposes to that a statement of facts. 'Cracked with heat' counters the dreamy 'where all the waters meet'. The repeated *cracked* is the most strongly stressed word in its line; then *forgotten* rhymes with *rotten,* and *remember* with *September.* In its objectivity and its being somewhat allegorical, this corresponds to the exorcism. The difference is that it is the persona's own making and living that are in question now, not others nor the world; and that instead of a surge of denunciation, this moves in stopped sentences, as if compelled to acknowledge what he would have forgotten. It is a reaching through recovered images very different from the first ones, and to a reality the opposite of their promise. The unknown to be accepted as 'my own' is not what was lost, but the fact that life is loss.

Through those seven lines one musical phrase has been matched by another, giving a rocking, pausing effect. The progression has been in consciousness rather than feeling, which has been checked, suspended. But with a sudden alteration at 'This form, this face, this life', the feeling for the visionary world is released in invocation and commitment. The long beautifully shaped phrases resolve the old world and life into an assurance of the new:

> Living to live in a world of time beyond me, let me
> Resign my life for this life . . .

Then the emphatically confident

> The awákened, líps párted, the hópe, the néw shíps.

The feeling is very powerful, and set right against the facts just acknowledged. It is as if the recognition of the facts had generated this reaction, which would make the ideal more real than the actual.

The last three lines make a conclusion by repeating the first lines with a difference. Instead of the hopeful moving forward into new images, the rhythm here is held closer to firm statement, and feeling is again suspended. The contraction of the opening two lines into 'What seas what shores what granite islands towards my timbers' discovers a sense of menace; so that the woodthrush *calling* through the fog might be now luring to shipwreck. Yet shipwrecks may be fortunate landfalls, as they are in *Pericles* and *The Tempest.* One hardly knows what tone to give to the final 'My daughter', no longer an invocation. So far as it sounds in apposition to the woodthrush it might be a new and unexpected recognition: that hers is a 'calamitous annunciation', as *The Dry Salvages* will put it.

But we can scarcely hope to say what the poem means, only what it is. A state of mind and feeling has been expressed in musical form; its elements have been dissociated, related, organised; and while that conclusion seems necessary and right, it remains inexplicable.

That it does not bring experience to the proof of meaning makes *Marina* an exception among the Ariel Poems and *Ash-Wednesday*. There can be no doubt that it belongs with them. Though it says nothing of the Incarnation, it is as much concerned as the three previous Ariel Poems with the revelation of a new life and the awakening from a dead world. It is most nearly related to *Ash-Wednesday*, though it has not the explicitly Christian element. They have in common a recovery in vision of what had been lost; the denunciation of the world; and the doubtful questioning of the dream of sensual renewal. Some lines near the end of the draft version of *Ash-Wednesday* might be a first sketch for *Marina*:

> If the lost eye creates
> The quickening form between the ivory gates
>   O my people what have I done unto thee
> In this pool all the waves are silent
> In this pool all the seas are still
> All the waves die against this island
> Our life is in the world's decease

But those are opaque images, and depend for their force upon the interpretation in the last line. *Marina* gives us simply the poetic fact.

However, appreciation of the poem can properly be advanced by an awareness of its place in Eliot's *oeuvre*. Beyond the connections already suggested, it would be illuminating and instructive to consider it as the reworking in a new form of the feelings of 'Dans le Restaurant', and of the shipwreck narrative – a New England adaptation of Tennyson's 'Ulysses' and Dante's – which in the draft *Waste Land* led up to the death by water of Phlebas the Phoenician. Now the quality in the poem upon which these and most of the other connections bear, is its romanticism. In all the poems of this period there are distinctive elements of romantic feeling: the regrets for past happiness and longings for an ideal world, poignant evocations of personal anguish and ecstasy. In *Marina* these appear to find their purest expression, and to be freed from critical reflection. That very freedom, however, when the poem is placed in its relevant contexts, may prompt a criticism. It may be that the poem presents for our inspection the effort of the romantic temperament to clarify its idealism without the aid of Christian revelation.

If that suggestion seems worth considering, then it may be strengthened by referring again to the 1930 Baudelaire essay. A quality which particularly interested Eliot in Baudelaire was that he 'is not always certain in his notion of the Good. The romantic idea of Love is never quite exorcised, but never quite surrendered to.' Out of this combination of the romantic idea with the reaching out toward something more than can be had in human relations, he invented a new kind of romantic nostalgia: *une poésie des départs*. In its origin in 'a beautiful paragraph' of *Mon coeur mis à nu* – 'he imagines the vessels lying in harbour as saying: "Quand partons-nous vers le bonheur?"' – this poetry of flight is 'a dim recognition of the direction of beatitude'. It is dim because Baudelaire while essentially Christian, had to rediscover Christianity for himself in a post-Christian age.

Inevitably the offspring of romanticism, and by his nature the first counter-romantic in poetry, he could, like anyone else, only work with the materials which were there. It must not be forgotten that a poet in a romantic age cannot be a 'classical' poet except in tendency.

Consequently, 'Baudelaire's notion of beatitude certainly tended to be wishy-washy': 'The complement, and the correction to the *Journaux Intimes,* so far as they deal with the relations of man and woman, is the *Vita Nuova,* and the *Divine Comedy.*' Looked at in the light of that essay, *Marina* might be an 'Invitation au Voyage' at the limit of the tendency toward classicism of a romanticism uncorrected by Dante. That would make its persona 'a fragmentary Dante'.[32]

The epigraph from Seneca's *Hercules Furens* might imply the Dantescan correction, while coming from a non-Christian source appropriate both to the romantic modern world and to the ancient Greece of Shakespeare's romance.[33] Strangely enough, there is a striking correspondence between Seneca's two Hercules plays – one begins, the other ends the *Tenne Tragedies* – and certain essential features of Eliot's own Christianity. (There is a similar sense of Christian parallels in *Pericles,* but that, given its date, is not so surprising.) Hercules, having unknowingly sacrificed his own wife and children, wakes to know what he has done; what he recognises, in the end, is his guilt; and this acceptance of responsibility entails exile. The parallel with Orestes and his Eumenides would not have escaped the author of *Sweeney Agonistes* and *The Family Reunion.* Moreover, he might well have reflected of Hercules as he did of Baudelaire, that 'the recognition of the reality of Sin is a New Life'.[34] Seneca's later play could be read as the fulfilment of that idea. Hercules, caught in the 'intolerable shirt of flame', builds his own funeral pyre. In a vision which allows a brief respite from the agony, he imagines himself received into heaven, and wonders:

'What heavenly harmony is this that soundeth in myne eare?' That is a link with Pericles' 'Most heavenly music'; but it is followed by the opposite development. His life is not renewed by the restoration of what he had loved, but is ended in the fire, and in a manner which brings to mind Dante's Arnaut. The play ends with him among the spheres, looking back to what Dante called 'this little threshing floor'[35] below, and saying:

> vertue opened hath
> To me the passage to the Starres, and set me in the path
> That guides to everlasting Lyfe[36]

Now of course none of this is actually in *Marina* – it is simply what the epigraph can lead us to. But it must have been in Eliot's mind, as a dimension of his conscious understanding of the poem. And the epigraph, giving Hercules' first words on waking and before he attains full consciousness of his dreadful deed, seems a declaration that such romantic moments of vision as the poem offers have to be understood as 'requiring, pointing to the agony/Of death and birth'.

Marina, taken as following on from *Ash-Wednesday* VI, establishes the sea with its rocky shore and islands as the finally dominant setting, after a series of poems mainly placed in the desert. Behind Eliot's use of it, from the drafts of 'Death by Water' to *The Dry Salvages,* there are two constant points of reference, both from Dante. There is the Ulysses narrative, in *Inferno* XXVI, of how he sailed beyond the western limits of the world in his quest for new experience, until (in sight of the mount of Purgatory) his ship was wrecked 'as pleased Another'. Then there is the image which follows 'la sua volontade è nostra pace' in *Paradiso* III: 'his will is our peace: it is that sea to which all moves that it createth and that nature maketh'.

Part Four

1931–1939

The Word in the desert

The voice of him that crieth in the wilderness, Prepare ye the way of the Lord, make straight in the desert a highway for our God. . .

The voice said, Cry. And he said, What shall I cry? All flesh is grass, and all the goodliness thereof is as the flower of the field:

The grass withereth, the flower fadeth: because the spirit of the Lord bloweth upon it: surely the people is grass.

The grass withereth, the flower fadeth: but the word of our God shall stand for ever.

(Isaiah xl, 3–8)

What faith in life may be I know not . . . for the Christian, faith in death is what matters.

(T. S. Eliot, *Criterion* XII. 47 (January 1933), p.248)

1931–1939

1931	March	'Thoughts after Lambeth'.
	September	Introduction to *The 'Pensées' of Pascal.*
	October	*Triumphal March* (Ariel Poems no.35).
		'Difficulties of a Statesman'.
1932	September	*Selected Essays 1917–1932.*
1933	January	'Five-finger Exercises'.

In the academic year 1932–3 TSE was Charles Eliot Norton Professor of Poetry at Harvard – the lectures were published as *The Use of Poetry and the Use of Criticism* (1933). In the spring of 1933 he delivered at the University of Virginia the lectures published as *After Strange Gods* (1934). Before his return to England in June he obtained a legal separation from Vivien Eliot.

1934	April	*Words for Music* ('New Hampshire', 'Virginia').
	May	*The Rock: A Pageant Play.*
	July	'John Marston'.

In the autumn Eliot visited Burnt Norton with Emily Hale.

1935	May	*Murder in the Cathedral.*
	October	'Rannoch, by Glencoe'; *Two Poems* ('Cape Ann', 'Usk').
	November	'Words for an Old Man' (= 'Lines for an Old Man').
1936	March	*Essays Ancient and Modern.*
	April	*Collected Poems 1909–1935* (first appearance of *Burnt Norton*).
	May	Introduction to *Poems of Tennyson.* Visit to Little Gidding.
	July	'A Note on the Verse of John Milton'.
1937		'The Development of Shakespeare's Verse', three lectures at the University of Edinburgh (unpublished).
	August	Visit to East Coker.
1939	March	*The Family Reunion.* Lectures on 'The Idea of a Christian Society' delivered at Cambridge.
	October	*Old Possum's Book of Practical Cats.*

7
The design of the drama

... *through* the dramatic action of men into a spiritual action which transcends it.

When we understand necessity ... we are free because we assent.[1]

From 1931 until the outbreak of war in 1939 most of Eliot's writing in verse was directed towards dramatic performance, as his preoccupation with self-perfection expanded into a concern for the perfection of society. The fruition of this development is to be found in the three wartime Quartets; and the main interest of the plays of the 1930s, if it is the poetry one is interested in, is that they enable us to follow the transition from *Ash-Wednesday* to *Four Quartets*. The plays, together with his thinking about the possibilities of poetic drama, can provide an introduction to the new kind of poetry which he wrote during the war.

The action of Eliot's plays arises from no ordinary kind of dramatic conflict, but rather from the contradiction of the sort of experience which is the usual stuff of drama by the religious vision cultivated in his poetry. This is the constant theme of his writings about poetry in the theatre.[2] In the essay on Marston (1934), which is of great interest in relation to *Burnt Norton* as well as *Murder in the Cathedral* and *The Family Reunion*, he wrote:

It is possible that what distinguishes poetic drama from prosaic drama is a kind of doubleness in the action, as if it took place on two planes at once. . . Or the drama has an underpattern, less manifest than the theatrical one.[3]

In his introduction to S. L. Bethell's *Shakespeare & the Popular Dramatic Tradition* (1944) he declared that the contemporary poetic dramatist must create characters

able to perform the same actions, and lead the same lives, as in the real world. But they must somehow disclose (not necessarily be aware of) a deeper reality than that of the plane of most of our conscious living.

The main preoccupation of his lectures on 'The Development of Shakespeare's Verse' (1937) was the way in which the great speeches lift us 'to another plane of reality, or a hidden and mysterious pattern of reality appears as from a palimpsest', so that we 'see *through* the ordinary classified emotions of our active life into a world of emotion and feeling beyond, of which I am not ordinarily aware . . . taking part . . . in no common action, of which I am for the most part quite unaware'. The nature of this mysterious pattern, a perception of which should bring us 'to a condition of serenity, stillness, and reconciliation',[4] is indicated in the Marston essay:

as we familiarize ourselves with the play we perceive a pattern behind the pattern into which the characters deliberately involve themselves; the kind of pattern which we perceive in our own lives only at rare moments of inattention and detachment, drowsing in sunlight. It is the pattern drawn by what the ancient world called Fate; subtilized by Christianity into mazes of delicate theology; and reduced again by the modern world into crudities of psychological or economic necessity.[5]

What one begins to make out in Eliot's idea of poetic drama is something very like 'Our peace in His will'.

It was one thing to say that in the poetry in his own voice and in the forms of prayer of the Catholic Church; but to try to say it in the public theatre was like trying to marry the art of Dante with that of Marie Lloyd. Yet that was more or less what Eliot was after. 'Every poet would like, I fancy, to be able to think he had some direct social utility', he said in 1933, 'a part to play in society as worthy as that of the music-hall comedian.'[6] The worthiness of that role, in the case of Marie Lloyd, was that she not only amused her audience, but succeeded 'in giving expression to the life of that audience, in raising it to a kind of art'.[7] Eliot too wanted to express the consciousness of his audience, of as large an audience as he could command. But I am not sure that he was trying to do quite the same thing as Marie Lloyd. He was rather trying to transform the common consciousness, and to bring his audience to a new and radically different perception of their lives.

He had experimented with this in *Sweeney Agonistes*, the 'fragments of an Aristophanic Melodrama' drafted shortly after the completion of *The Waste Land*, though not staged until 1933 (at Vassar) and 1934 (in London).[8] In that he was seeking to modernise, to make new, a pre-Christian and Primitive ritual drama: one in which the action would evoke certain emotions, and follow out a certain structure of emotion, but without invoking any particular belief or interpretation. When he resumed his experiments with the drama after *Ash-Wednesday* he had come to think that the intellectual interpretation of experience was a necessary stage in the passage from mere experience to the Absolute; and in the plays of the 1930s, as in the Ariel Poems, the apprehension of the meaning

– of the Christian revelation – assumes such importance that all else is subordinated to that end. This is the case not only in the two overtly Christian works, *The Rock* and *Murder in the Cathedral,* but also in *The Family Reunion* which, while it was written for the commercial theatre, may be seen as a Christian version of what he had sketched in *Sweeney Agonistes.*

The two 'Coriolan' poems of 1931 show Eliot working towards his special form of poetic drama. *Triumphal March* was first published as an Ariel Poem, and 'Difficulties of a Statesman' might perfectly well have followed it in that series. Both are concerned, after all, with the revelation of a spiritual vision which exposes the vanity of the accepted order of things; and in carrying that theme into the realm of public affairs they are a natural extension of the series. Eliot's reason for setting them apart from it, and declaring 'Coriolan' unfinished, was that they had been meant to begin 'a sequence in the life of the character who appears in the first part as Young Cyril'.[9] That suggests an impulse towards the drama; and it seems likely that the sequence was left unfinished because the impulse went into the choruses of *The Rock,* which Eliot was commissioned to write in 1933.

The triumphal march is Roman, or in the City of London, or in France after the so-called Great War. The spectators are the usual witnesses of such occasions; and the conquering hero might be, as well as Coriolanus, any general ancient or modern. The world evoked is in the end mainly contemporary. But the glimpsed vision ('O hidden . . .') is altogether remote. More significant than the range of historical times and places – which all merge into each other – is the variety of voices and levels of awareness. A first voice merely registers impressions, like a newsreel; then it generalises them, by simple arithmetic. There is no idea here, let alone an ideal; nor is there any life in the verse. The organisation of mind and feeling is rudimentary. Another voice, presumably observing these observers, ironically reflects: 'The natural wakeful life of our Ego is a perceiving.'

Only when the hero appears is there a clear perception – and it is *his* eyes that are brought into focus –

> There is no interrogation in his eyes
> Or in the hands, quiet over the horse's neck,
> And the eyes watchful, waiting, perceiving, indifferent.

With that line we are no longer looking at but through the hero's eyes; and what is seen then, a purely poetic vision, has the intensity of something absolute. It is apart from the triumphal march, and apart from any particular observer, as it intimates a transcendent order of feeling and being:

O hidden under the dove's wing, hidden in the turtle's breast,
Under the palmtree at noon, under the running water
At the still point of the turning world. O hidden.

That visionary awareness informs the remainder of the poem, but only as an ironical doubling of the merely literal perceiving. 'Temple' and 'sacrifice', and 'Dust/Dust of dust', are seen first with a vacant eye; but then the mind fills in the missing religious associations. The irony becomes explicit and satirical, in a manner that will be carried further in *The Rock*. The world is being mocked for not knowing that its life begins and ends in dust; for its ignorance of the Word (the bell rung at the Communion, and on Easter of all days!); for not comprehending the Light. The irony is left unresolved, even intensified: '*So the soldiers lined the way? THEY LINED THE WAY.*' The emphatic vacuity may make us think of other triumphal progresses, including, just possibly, Christ's entry into Jerusalem and his leaving it to be crucified – and his rising from the tomb which soldiers were guarding.

But even without such specific associations the overall effect is satirical. There is the one moment of intense vision, urgent in rhythm, profoundly evocative in its images. For the rest, the world that is empty of meaning and filled with mere fact and fancy is made to appear simply vacuous. Any possible imaginative response to it is scrupulously excluded, so that there shall be no intensity, no pattern of feeling, and no interesting idea. It is only by the light of a world transcending this that a significant pattern can be made out. The confident opposition of an ideal vision to ordinary perceptions connects this with the fifth poem of *Ash-Wednesday*; and it also exemplifies Eliot's dramatic method. In the plays also the lyrical and the naturalistic elements are separated and opposed, with the one being used to suggest a vision of transcendent reality, and the other to represent the world without vision.

'Difficulties of a Statesman' adopts the viewpoint of 'the eyes watchful, waiting, perceiving, indifferent': now we see things as he sees them. The voice is individual; and in it the satire becomes subordinate to lyricism. The main impression is of a soul suffering in the wilderness of public affairs, and desiring what they deny. The poem has no internal divisions; but the repeated 'What shall I cry?' is an effective punctuation, marking the successive passages of a musical composition. The first three such passages together observe the statesman's sphere of action: the grand, empty, imperial titles; the hypertrophy of bureaudemocracy; the *minutiae* of its *agenda*. This is all presented in its own flat prose, apart from the refrain and the one or two personal interjections. The effect of these latter is to suggest that behind the extreme dryness of statement there might be some private irony. And indeed a reflective mind constrained to submit to these trivia might find amusement in the fact that Cyril, whose name once meant 'Lord', is to be a receiver and transmitter of words, with a bonus at Christmas; and then also in the fact that peace on earth should be a threat to society. At last the wearied mind, as if in a moment of distraction, images what it really thinks of it all: 'And the frogs (O Mantuan) croak in the marshes.' 'O Mantuan' was Sordello's greeting to Virgil in *Purgatorio* VI, and it moved Dante to cry out against the falling away of the Italian city-states from the ideal of the Holy Roman Empire. The reminiscence of that places this suffering statesman with those poets who had known the oppression of the things of Caesar, and who had conceived another Rome founded upon and formed by divine love.

'Fireflies flare against the faint sheet lightning' introduces the other movement of the poem, which is one of inward reflection and feeling. 'Mother mother' states the key term, like a repeated chord; and it initiates a rhythmic pulse which is sustained to the end of the poem. For the stone ancestors and the meaningless formalities it comes with a falling movement, as if wearied out by them. With the remove into vision, and as the images become increasingly immediate, it gathers assurance and attains a moment of serene harmony in the line 'There the cyclamen spreads its wings, there the clematis droops over the lintel'. The vision is now in the present tense, yet it is 'there', not here. When no maternal response comes to support it against the official pieties, the images associated with 'the stillness of noon' give way to those of 'the silent croaking night': a kind of resolution, in this music of images, of the private vision with the public actuality –

> Come with the sweep of the little bat's wing, with the small flare of the
>   firefly or lightning bug,
> 'Rising and falling, crowned with dust', the small creatures,
> The small creatures chirp thinly through the dust, through the night.

This is the light and dust of *Triumphal March* with a different sense and in another pattern: because understood and accepted. It leads to a fully resolved conclusion, exactly reversing the final effect of that first poem. The demand from the *vox populi*, 'RESIGN RESIGN RESIGN', is just what the private vision requires: to be rejected, to be 'a broken Coriolanus', is to be liberated from the empire of the busy, dusty world.

There may be a further meaning in that vain appeal to his mother. The primary allusion to Shakespeare's *Coriolanus* would make her a Volumnia, the Roman matriarch in whom love had congealed into public duty. Then one might think of Virgil's Venus, prototype of the Roman matron, who made her son Aeneas leave Dido in order to found Rome. But there is the difference that she had first brought him to Dido; and if one reads the *Aeneid* as Dante and Eliot did, it was his having loved Dido, and left her, which made him the founder of Rome. Where is Coriolan's love? He has his 'aethereal rumours' in those natural images which have taken on a symbolic value; but he appears to lack the love which drew Dante, and the poet of *Ash-Wednesday*, out of the ruin of the world towards the ideal. That may be his fundamental defect. At least I am prompted to think so by the value given to the awakening of the sexual impulse, with the redirection of it by a loving Mother, in *The Family Reunion*.

The Rock and *Murder in the Cathedral* were both commissioned works, undertaken at a time when Eliot felt he had written himself out as a poet.[10] They are the products of deliberate thought and craftsmanship, and it is no wonder if they lack the inner necessity and fall short of the total integration of his best poetry. What they mainly offer is a clear and full statement of his conscious convictions – his *contemptus mundi* and pattern of perfection – and this can contribute to the understanding of the poetry.

The commission for *The Rock* was to provide the words for a pageant play to be performed in aid of a fund 'to build and endow forty-five new churches, to meet the needs of the rapidly growing suburbs to the north of the Thames'.[11] The scenario called for a series of self-contained scenes in which the building of a church was carried on through various episodes in the history of the Church. These scenes were performed by amateurs, and were mostly in prose. For the Chorus, however, who were trained in choral verse speaking, Eliot was able to write 'a piece of work in verse much longer than any of his previously published poems', and to experiment 'in the attempt to find modern forms of verse suitable for the stage'.[12] His considered judgment was that he had not been very successful: it was his own voice 'addressing – indeed haranguing – an audience, that was most distinctly audible'.[13] Quite properly therefore the choruses – understandably the only part of the work which he thought worth preserving – were included in his *Collected Poems*, where they provide a useful approach to *Four Quartets*.

The argument of the pageant can be summarised as the overcoming of the difficulties of building the Church in the Modern World where it is 'opposed, ignored, or interfered with by the secular tendencies of the present age'.[14] Any and all secular concerns are seen to be against the Church; and the Church to be built is 'the Invisible Church'. ' "Our citizenship is in Heaven"; yes, but that is the model and type for your citizenship upon earth.' Eliot's most powerful poetry is the product of the effort to make such convictions real, inwardly and in the common language. In the choruses of *The Rock*, however, they are not very convincingly realised. The most effective writing is the satire upon the contemporary world, and there is a good deal of that. But the state of the world is not internalised and suffered as his own, as it is in *The Waste Land* and the wartime Quartets; so that 'the world' is not brought into a significant relation with the Word. The affirmations of the Word rather lack substance in consequence, and are left to depend upon dogmatic assertion and the symbolism of Light. The earthly life of the citizen of Heaven, when it is not the life of prayer, is also rather feebly represented:

> Our gaze is submarine, our eyes look upward
> And see the light that fractures through unquiet water.
> We see the light but see not whence it comes.
> O Light Invisible, we glorify Thee!

> In our rhythm of earthly life we tire of light. We are glad when the day
> ends, when the play ends; and ecstasy is too much pain.
> We are children quickly tired: children who are up in the night and fall
> asleep as the rocket is fired . . .

– so the final chorus chants the plangent burden of that lowering and recessive pietism which gets Christianity a bad name. Here Eliot is speaking down to his audience – giving a patronising view of the lives of the devout who are neither poets nor saints – and this means that he is speaking neither for himself nor for them. The writing is therefore fundamentally unreal, both as poetry and as theatre. It makes one more appreciative of the integrity of *Four Quartets*: their truth to the poet's self and to the common experience in the language. And it sharpens the question whether Eliot, being the kind of poet he was, could be a poet in the theatre.

When the evidence of *Murder in the Cathedral* is added to that of *The Rock* the answer appears to be decidedly in the negative. This play was commissioned for the Canterbury Cathedral Festival of June 1935, and was altogether Eliot's own work. He chose to deal with the death of the most outstanding figure in the cathedral's history, the twelfth-century Thomas à Becket, who, having been made Lord Chancellor by Henry II, and then Archbishop of Canterbury, was assassinated by four of the King's men near the high altar a few days after Christmas in 1170. His shrine became a centre of pilgrimage in the succeeding centuries – he is the 'hooly blisful martir' of Chaucer's *Tales*. But Eliot's play is addressed to an audience for whom that is ancient history, and the cathedral an ancient monument. His aim was not just to recall past events, but to show the permanent or universal nature of the conflict between the servants of God and the servants of kings. The play won an immediate success, and has remained one of the most highly regarded and frequently performed of twentieth-century poetic dramas. I have always found it unconvincing in the theatre, and the text only confirms my sense that its 'Christian reality' has much the same validity as 'Soviet reality'.

Eliot summed up the action very neatly: 'A man comes home, foreseeing that he will be killed, and he is killed.'[15] Add that the man is a spiritual as well as a temporal leader, and that his death is explicitly connected with a supreme act of religious sacrifice, and it should give us a profound and universal tragedy. But the theatrical experience is not quite like that, and deliberately not. The ritual action is presented in a form which insistently interprets it; and the interpretation alters the experience. It makes the death not really a death; and it makes the usual feelings of pity and terror merely the infirmities of imperfect understanding. The drama is strictly controlled by the meaning, and the audience must either follow and assent to the meaning, or be left feeling that their response to the death of the hero is being manipulated by the author.

The 'spiritual action' of the play is Becket's martyrdom – his bearing witness to 'the Law of God above the law of man'. This is not at all a dramatic action, since it consists entirely in Becket's apprehending that the 'true martyr is he who has become the instrument of God, who has lost his will in the will of God'. His most telling speeches are metaphysical, and aspire, as one might say, to the poetry of *Burnt Norton*:

> action is suffering
> And suffering is action. Neither does the agent suffer
> Nor the patient act. But both are fixed
> In an eternal action, an eternal patience
> To which all must consent that it may be willed
> And which all must suffer that they may will it,
> That the pattern may subsist, for the pattern is the action
> And the suffering, that the wheel may turn and still
> Be forever still.

The most nearly dramatic expression of that is in the symbolism of the murder: Thomas kneels unmoved, serenely praying, while the four Knights encircle him, their aimed swords setting him at the still centre of their turning wheel.

The main part of the play consists of the interpretation, if it is not the manipulation, of the life of the world in the light of that idea. The Tempters and Knights are declared to be unreal, and are made to seem so. The temptations are put in an antique style, modelled upon the fifteenth-century *Everyman*, and this distances the pleasures of the flesh and the appeal of power, so that they

are indeed the shadows of what Thomas has left behind. Only their own despair
is made actual and given a contemporary voice:

> Man's life is a cheat and a disappointment;
> All things are unreal,
> Unreal or disappointing . . .

The Knights, when they first threaten and then return to kill the Archbishop,
are fixed in a rigid manner of speech and action which makes them the blustering
puppets they are later said to be, unwitting agents of 'the eternal design'. At the
end they are laid aside like puppets:

> Go, weak sad men, lost erring souls, homeless in earth or heaven . . .
> Pacing forever in the hell of make-believe
> Which never is belief: this is your fate on earth
> And we must think no further of you.

That follows their bland self-justification as men of their audience's world and
kind. But the power élite we know, and their propagandists and police, don't
go away when told to. It is the play itself that has left behind what's actual and
probable, for the sake of 'Blessed Thomas', 'the glory of whose new state is
hidden from us'. Even the Knights' appeal to the audience has served this
design. Striking *coup de théâtre* as it is, its effect is to detach us from the murder
itself, and also from the usual issues of guilt and retribution, and to face us
instead with the question: whose side are *you* on? Thus the dramatic crisis is
transformed into a spiritual one.[16]

Becket may be taken to represent 'the order of mind' caught up into 'the
order of charity', and the Tempters and Knights to represent 'the order of
nature'. The Chorus are caught between the two: they belong in the natural
order of things, but sympathy with Becket compels them to suffer and consent
to 'an eternal patience'. Eliot thought of them as 'excited and sometimes hysterical women, reflecting in their *emotion* the *significance* of the action'.[17] So they
express the natural fear at Becket's death:

> God gave us always some reason, some hope; but now a new terror has
>   soiled us, which none can avert, none can avoid, flowing under our
>   feet and over the sky;
> Under doors and down chimneys, flowing in at the ear and the mouth
>   and the eye.
> God is leaving us, God is leaving us, more pang, more pain than
>   birth or death.
>
> Sweet and cloying through the dark air
> Falls the stifling scent of despair;

The forms take shape in the dark air:
Puss-purr of leopard, footfall of padding bear,
Palm-pat of nodding ape, square hyaena waiting
For laughter, laughter, laughter. The Lords of Hell are here.

This hysterical nightmare is a variant of the pathetic fallacy, and might be called the metaphysical fallacy: nature is being made to answer to an idea. The idea, which is stated more or less explicitly in this and other choruses, is the horror and terror of an existence separated from God. The images, if one responds to them directly, express a desperately alienated sense of the natural world; but their real meaning, we are meant to understand, is alienation from God. Moreover, that meaning is what gives rise to the emotion. We have then an idea, which is 'reflected' in emotion, which is expressed as a vision of nature – that is, we have the reversal of the normal procession from direct sensation through feeling to conscious understanding. The emotion may be true to the metaphysical idea, and yet one may feel that it is expressed in a way which is inauthentic as experience. If one does feel that, then one must conclude that the idea is being imposed rather wilfully upon the world we actually know, and that it is not a convincing fit. The final chorus of assent and reconciliation to the will of God – 'We praise Thee, O God, for Thy glory displayed in all the creatures of the earth' – is just the other side of this imposition of an idea upon reality. Acceptable as devotional verse expressing faith and hope, it has not the substance of what Henry James termed 'felt life', in his well-known reflection that there is 'no more nutritive or suggestive truth in this connection than that of the perfect dependence of the "moral" sense of a work of art on the amount of felt life concerned in producing it.'[18] There are two ways in which that can apply. It can underline a deficiency of 'felt life' in the moral sense of the choruses, and of the play as a whole. But it can suggest also that such immediate experience as the play offers – and undoubtedly it does offer much – might lead to a different response and another interpretation. The alienation from nature may remain our primary impression, and we may conclude that the cause of it is the conviction that the metaphysical is the real. This would be to turn the play on its head – unless it is its head that it is standing upon.

The Family Reunion is far and away the most interesting of Eliot's plays, and this has much to do with its being a true development of his poetry. Here one does feel that he has had the experience, and that it is the experience which requires the meaning, not the other way round. This is a play written out of the poet's inspiration and necessities, and it is all the better for that. It was not commissioned, and had to meet no extrinsic requirements apart from the usual conditions of the commercial theatre. First drafted in the summer of 1937, it was produced in March 1939 – the month in which Eliot was delivering the lectures which make up *The Idea of a Christian Society*. The play has proved difficult to bring off in the theatre, but Eliot was right to think it his best 'in the way of poetry'.[19] The most effective medium for it might be radio: it is for the ear, not the eye.

Eliot's account of his intention in *Sweeney Agonistes* applies in a general way to *The Family Reunion*:

> My intention was to have one character whose sensibility and intelligence should be on the plane of the most sensitive and intelligent members of the audience; his speeches should be addressed to them as much as to the other personages in the play – or rather, should be addressed to the latter, who were to be material, literal-minded and visionless, with the consciousness of being overheard by the former. There was to be an understanding between this protagonist and a small number of the audience, while the rest of the audience would share the responses of the other characters in the play.[20]

There is a broader range of characters in the later play, but they do make up a spectrum of the degrees of consciousness. Some exist merely on the plane of appearances, conventionally and more or less ludicrously. One or two have a mild or middling apprehension of another reality. But the only ones who are taken seriously are the three who have entered, or who are entering into, the visionary world through the looking-glass.

The conventions and the stock figures of the theatrical country house drawing-room are used to represent the unreality and banality of a life made up of illusions. To the minor uncles and aunts one could apply Eliot's comment on Marston's minor comic characters: 'there is a kind of significant lifelessness in this shadow-show'.[21] Their formal, 'correct' speech exposes the emptiness of what they have to say; and no chance is missed for putting them down, not even the blank bad pun – 'Excuse me Miss Ivy. There's a trunk call for you.' The nearest approach to consciousness allowed them is Charles' capacity for being surprised by the stuffed bulldog in the Burlington Arcade;[22] or a queasy anxiety expressed in a minor poetry of doom after the style of Kipling and de la Mare and Auden.[23] The childish terrors of these choruses are presumably meant to intimate what they can't face: the void beneath their trivialities. The assumption that many in the audience will be on their level perhaps accounts for the way Agatha sometimes slips into a similar vein of gothique –

> admonitions
> From the world around the corner
> The wind's talk in the dry holly-tree
> The inclination of the moon . . .

Harry, when he is trying to make himself understood by those who cannot understand, speaks of knowing

> The noxious smell untraceable in the drains,
> Inaccessible to the plumbers, that has its hour of the night.

This, he says, is 'trying to give you / Comparisons in a more familiar medium'. And *that* is a way of saying 'You don't see them, you don't – but *I* see them'.

The literal meaning of much that Harry says is strictly for the literal-minded, while his real meaning is beyond any actual formulation. Even his apparently definitive statement at the end of II.ii is only a way of putting it into words:

> Where does one go from a world of insanity?
> Somewhere on the other side of despair,
> To the worship in the desert, the thirst and deprivation,
> A stony sanctuary and a primitive altar,
> The heat of the sun and the icy vigil,
> A care over lives of humble people . . .

Amy thinks he is going to be a missionary, and the uncles and aunts offer practical advice about the climate and the natives. Critics notice the parallel with the life of Charles de Foucauld. But Harry, exasperated at having only his words taken up and his inner meaning missed, declares 'I never said that I was going to be a missionary.' Eliot told Michael Redgrave, who was having understandable difficulties with the part, 'I think he and the chauffeur go off and get jobs in the East End'.[24] What Harry is really saying is all in this line and a half:

> It is love and terror
> Of what waits and wants me, and will not let me fall.

This stands out, after the catalogue of clichés, as a simple and clear statement, enforced by its rhythm, of an inner conviction and a resolved attitude. That is all we need to know, if only we know what he is talking about.

For the more knowing members of the audience there are opportunities for superior amusement. Amy tells Harry, who has been saying that what he needs is purgation, that he will feel better after a bath. One can improve that by thinking of Clytemnestra – is Amy trying to go one better than her prototype, and finish off her Orestes in the same way as her Agamemnon? Then there is the Christian charade of Amy's false expectation: 'Hark, there is someone coming/ Yes, it must be John. [*Enter* HARRY.]' When he is leaving Harry says twice, irrelevantly and therefore portentously, 'Until I come again.' Does that make him the Messiah? He has been at least reborn of Mary, and of Agatha whose name signifies the enabling power of goodness, or the Holy Spirit as one might say. The game becomes silly if it is taken solemnly; yet on a level beyond wit the parallels are seriously meant. These are the jokes, and they keep coming up, of a mind looking down from the heaven of the Christian revelation upon its parodies in the world of appearances. Jokes are not meant to be taken literally, even when their terms are sacred ones. Harry is not Christ – at least no more than he is Orestes – yet the wit does establish a connection.

Harry's comic scene with the policeman gives a dramatic form to the split levels of visionless and visionary awareness. It starts on the merely punning level: whose *birth*day, Harry's or her Ladyship's? Then while the sergeant is stolidly enquiring after his mother's health, Harry refers riskily to his possibly murdered wife. In a way it is an Agatha Christie entertainment. Yet the scene does contrive to work on a double level of feeling and apprehension, and to carry us from the literal to the moral plane. Once we are there the detective interest disappears. Just as in *Murder in the Cathedral* the important matter is not Becket's death, so here the death of the wife is declared merely a matter of appearances –

> What we have written is not a story of detection,
> Of crime and punishment, but of sin and expiation.

That no doubt is to observe 'the capital distinction . . . between representation of human actions which have moral reality and representation of such as have only sentimental reality'.[25] Harry's crime, if he did commit it, is only a symptom of the sin which must be expiated, and which is no mere action but a condition of being – and not of his own being simply, but of his family, of his race. The question of guilt for the murder he might have committed is quite swallowed up in the sense of universal sin.

The spiritual action of the play is worked out through the sequence of Harry's relationships: to Amy, his mother in the flesh; to Mary, whom he could almost love in the flesh; and to Agatha, who proves a spiritual mother and lover. These are the stages in his progression from sin and alienation to reconciliation and expiation. The first is the immediate cause of his predicament; the third releases him from it; and the second enables him to move from the one to the other. What he *does* in the play is simply to reach the decision to leave Wishwood for good. But that involves breaking his mother's will, and renouncing ordinary happiness, in order to follow out his fate.

The relation with his mother is the beginning and the end of the story. Amy is always apart from the family chorus. This is not because she sees what they miss. Indeed she uses her greater intelligence only for a more determined resistance to the dark; and is the more mocked by occult meanings. What distinguishes her is force of character. She is the one person in the play whose existence is not conferred by conventions or by fate. A matriarch with a strong sense of what she wants and a strong will to dominate, she means to make Harry happy as master of Wishwood. But even more important than that, is what she has made of him from his earliest years. She has always imposed her designs upon him, at the expense of his own wishes and feelings. The consequence is that he has never known liberation from himself in love or ecstasy. Even his marriage was only a reaction against what she wanted. It is not only now but always that she has condemned him to her own condition of living without love.

This condition is the family curse, the doom on the house and on Harry and on the world, which he must expiate. It was the condition of his marriage, in which there was no love or ecstasy as there had been none in his parents'; and it is traced back to his having been conceived without love. Ultimately, no doubt, it is Original Sin – all men after Adam being born outside divine love. Yet it is made more specific than that notion usually is with the emphasis falling consistently upon the felt degradation and disease of being out of love.

Harry's liberation from that state begins with his becoming conscious of it. When he enters he is already living on another plane from his mother by virtue of having 'woken to the nightmare':

> The sudden solitude in a crowded desert
> In a thick smoke, many creatures moving
> Without direction, for no direction
> Leads anywhere but round and round in that vapour
> Without purpose, and without principle of conduct
> In flickering intervals of light and darkness . . .

He wakes from 'the partial anaesthesia of suffering without feeling' to accept this alienated vision of human existence as the truth; and that confers the strange freedom which comes from accepting a nightmare as reality – at least it can be faced then.

When he talks with Mary she seems to promise the love and happiness he had missed. She awakens his first feelings of love. Yet he learns at the same moment that there is no going back from the nightmare into ordinary life. Their long lyrical scene is a form of love-duet, musical in the manner of the balcony scene which Eliot especially admired in *Romeo and Juliet*.[26] The two characters are not so much speaking to each other as caught up into a shared consciousness of romantic memories and desires –

HARRY   But do you remember
MARY   The hollow tree in what we called the wilderness
HARRY   Down near the river . . .

That first world was laid waste by a design of Amy's for pleasing the children.
Later, for Harry, all hope was lost:

> The bright colour fades
> Together with the unrecapturable emotion
> The glow upon the world, that never found its object;
> And the eye adjusts itself to a twilight
> Where the dead stone is seen to be batrachian,
> The aphyllous branch ophidian.

But now Mary brings him word of love, as if that childhood Eden could be
regained:

> You bring me news
> Of a door that opens at the end of a corridor,
> Sunlight and singing. . .

At that moment the Eumenides impose their presence, and show themselves
plainly for the first time, 'dissolving all other worlds' so far as he is concerned.
   They thus prevent the *natural* development of the feelings newly awakened
in Harry.[27] This is not meant to imply that the feelings are wrong in themselves;
only that he must move on, into the form of love appropriate to the moral
plane upon which he now exists. To initiate him into this further form of love
is Agatha's role. She is qualified for it by having known the ecstasy of love, and
the necessity for renunciation. More specifically, she has already been a mother
to him in spirit, since her renunciation perhaps saved his unborn life. Now her
strange motherhood is fulfilled in bringing him to birth spiritually. That
requires that the family curse be brought to fruition in him, and that he be
identified with it: 'O my child, my curse,/You shall be fulfilled'. 'It is possible',
she tells him,

> that sin may strain and struggle
> In its dark instinctive birth, to come to consciousness
> And so find expurgation. It is possible
> You are the consciousness of your unhappy family,
> Its bird sent flying through the purgatorial flame.

Being told this makes Harry 'feel happy for a moment, as if I had come home'.
This is his real family reunion: he has found his 'real' mother; and through her
he has discovered what he needs to know of his 'real' father – that is, the way of
His will.

His happiness consists in a development and transformation of his alienated vision in the 'love-duet' he shares with Agatha:

AGATHA   I only looked through the little door
When the sun was shining on the rose-garden:
And heard in the distance tiny voices
And then a black raven flew over.
And then I was only my own feet walking
Away, down a concrete corridor
In a dead air. Only feet walking
And sharp heel scraping. Over and under
Echo and noise of feet.
I was only the feet, and the eye
Seeing the feet: the unwinking eye
Fixing the movement. Over and under.

HARRY   In and out, in an endless drift
Of shrieking forms in a circular desert
Weaving with contagion of putrescent embraces
On dissolving bone. In and out, the movement
Until the chain broke, and I was left
Under the single eye above the desert.

AGATHA   Up and down, through the stone passages
Of an immense and empty hospital
Pervaded by a smell of disinfectant,
Looking straight ahead, passing barred windows.
Up and down. Until the chain breaks.

HARRY   To and fro, dragging my feet
Among inner shadows in the smoky wilderness,
Trying to avoid the clasping branches
And the giant lizard. To and fro.
Until the chain breaks.
The chain breaks,
The wheel stops, and the noise of machinery,
And the desert is cleared, under the judicial sun
Of the final eye, and the awful evacuation
Cleanses.
I was not there, you were not there, only our phantasms
And what did not happen is as true as what did happen
O my dear, and you walked through the little door
And I ran to meet you in the rose-garden.

AGATHA   This is the next moment. This is the beginning.
We do not pass twice through the same door
Or return to the door through which we did not pass.

In these last lines Agatha is no longer speaking 'beyond character', and she makes Harry resume his character also. He realises that in the moment of visionary consciousness he has reached a decision:

> I am still befouled,
> But I know there is only one way out of defilement –
> Which leads in the end to reconciliation.

That means renouncing Wishwood to follow the Furies, now become 'the bright angels', on what Eliot called 'the way of purgation and holiness'.[28]

The play mocks any curiosity about where Harry is going or what he will do because, on the metaphysical plane, he has reached his destination in that moment of illumination. At the same time the play fails to give us the 'spiritual action' in which he has become involved. The final scene merely marks his liberation from Amy's smothering designs by his departure and her death. For the enactment of his new life we have to go on to *Four Quartets,* and more especially to the three later Quartets, since *The Family Reunion* effects the transition from *Burnt Norton* to their more ambitious undertaking.

Because the play does not bring Harry's career to any sort of conclusion we are left to speculate about what Eliot meant. To make out his intention won't make good the deficiency of the play, but it may give us an idea of the design of the wartime Quartets. The primary material of the play has been quite obviously that complex of feelings which we have observed the poet working out from 'La Figlia Che Piange' up to *Ash-Wednesday*; and the mode of organisation is based as ever upon Dante's. What is new is the effort to relate the private experience to a society, and to give it a public value. To be precise, it is the effort to establish a positive relation that is new: in *The Waste Land,* in *Ash-Wednesday* v and *Marina,* there is a relation but it is a negative one. Harry finds that he is not an isolated victim with a merely private problem, but representative of a common experience of disappointment in love or of love-lessness. It is implied then that his following the way of purgation and reconciliation will be the saving of others, that it will be an act of Incarnation valid for the human family.

This development of the vision of the earlier poetry rests upon a striking change in the manner in which love is sublimated. In *Ash-Wednesday* the transition from love of a woman to love of God was effected through an idealisation of the woman, in which her image became identified with that of the 'holy mother'. In *The Family Reunion* Mary, who awakens Harry's natural love, remains quite distinct from Agatha who redirects his love towards God. This changes the process of sublimation from an essentially private and subjective experience, albeit within the impersonal framework of Catholic ritual, into one

179

in which the need for sublimation is understood and assisted by someone who has been through the experience. It is thus made a social rite, in which the individual is joined with another or with others; and in an immediate experience, not the mere formulae of prayers. This distinction between the first beloved and the 'holy mother' corresponds to the distinction Dante is brought to at the summit of Purgatory, between the Beatrice he had seen on earth, and the Beatrice who now instructs him. As the latter she is associated with the Mother of the Word and is the ideal form of 'Holy Mother Church'. Eliot must have intended Agatha to have a similar significance.

These new developments in Eliot's vision indicate a will to expand his love poetry from the essentially personal and lyrical form it had followed up to *Burnt Norton,* towards the scope traditionally associated with the epic. It is the good of a whole society that is becoming his predominant motive, not simply the perfection of his own soul. The ambition, which the play hardly fulfils, is implicit in Eliot's choice of models: the *Oresteia,* the *Aeneid,* the *Divine Comedy,* Shakespeare's *Hamlet* and *Coriolanus,* Racine's *Bérénice.*

The obvious relation with the *Oresteia* is of great importance, but the less obvious relationships may be the more revealing of Eliot's deepest intent. Behind his Christian hero, and superimposed upon Orestes, are Hamlet and Coriolanus who also had socially significant difficulties with their mothers. Hamlet's problem, in Eliot's view, was that his disgust, while apparently occasioned by his mother's behaviour, so exceeded her that he could not understand and objectify it. It remained therefore to poison life and obstruct action; and Shakespeare – whose problem it really was – failed to expand the subject into a tragedy such as that of Coriolanus, 'intelligible, self-complete, in the sunlight'.[29] The success of *Coriolanus,* I deduce, consists in the hero's recognition that in Rome there is no mothering love. With Eliot's 'Coriolan' to point the connection, one can see *The Family Reunion* as his revision of Shakespeare's Roman tragedy; and also as his *Hamlet,* his answer to the Renaissance hero's problem. It renders intelligible, self-complete, in the sunlight, the conviction of what is wrong with the world, together with what is needed to set it right.

Shakespeare's heroes are both representatives of their society: the prince born to set right his disjointed time; the soldier bred to serve the Empire supremely. Hamlet is baffled by evil; Coriolanus is broken by the absence of love, which in Eliot's view is the essence of evil. But his being broken could be the saving of Coriolanus; and possibly it could have been the saving of Rome, if only Rome could have accepted a broken Coriolanus as its true hero. That speculation is suggested by Eliot's account of Virgil's Aeneas, 'a man of destiny'

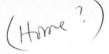

or *fatum,* upon whom depended not only the founding of Rome but 'the future of the Western World'. Eliot regarded him as 'the prototype of the Christian hero': because his heroism is that of 'the original Displaced Person, the fugitive from a ruined city and an obliterated society'; because his submission to the gods, not least when they afflict him, 'is an analogue and foreshadow of Christian humility'; and because, while obeying his fate, he accepts moral responsibility for what has been and must be – as in his 'love affair' with Dido. For Virgil his destiny meant the *imperium romanum.* But 'the Roman Empire was transformed into the Holy Roman Empire', and Virgil's ideal was passed on for 'Christianity to develop and cherish'. In Dante's poem Love is established as 'the principle of order in the human soul, in society and in the universe'. Then there is Racine, the Christian poet best able to emulate Virgil's treatment of Aeneas' fated love.[30] His *Bérénice,* Eliot had said in 1932, 'represents about the summit of civilisation in tragedy; and it is, in a way, a Christian tragedy, with devotion to the State substituted for devotion to divine law.'[31] For Rome's sake Titus must renounce his beloved Bérénice; but it is only when she agrees to renounce him that he is able to do what he must. She bridges the gap between Dido and Eliot's Agatha.

In each one of these cases the ideal Rome is made to depend upon love, but it is only that love which has passed through the looking-glass which gives AMOR : ROMA. And what Love means through the looking-glass is 'sin and expiation'. 'To do away with a sense of sin', Eliot wrote in a letter dated 13 September 1939, 'is to do away with civilisation.'[32] The acknowledgment of sin and the purgation of it are the foundations of his Christian society. Now what characterises his Harry, Lord Monchensey, is precisely that he is possessed by the sense of sin, and that he is saved by the love which makes him see that this is the fate to which he must submit, and which enables him to identify Fate with Love. If I have correctly followed Eliot's thinking, he would have us recognise Harry as the moral protagonist of his society, the founder of its ideal civilisation. He will hardly do as that. But the coming of war in 1939 allowed the poet himself to assume that role. In 'the flame of incandescent terror' he could be the consciousness that it was Love's doing. As his master Dante had made himself successor to Aeneas and pilgrim-founder of a New Rome, he made himself the poet-protagonist upon whom depended the Real City, a metaphysical London 'Bright in dark air'.[33]

8

Dust in sunlight

> Only by the form, the pattern,
> Can words or music reach
> The stillness

Burnt Norton, composed in 1935, is in every sense the central work in Eliot's verse between 1931 and 1939. It grew out of *Murder in the Cathedral*, and it led on to *The Family Reunion*. First published as the conclusion to *Collected Poems 1909–1935*, it seemed the culmination of his 'pure, unapplied poetry', and, to Eliot himself, its end.[1] Only with the war did it prove to have been incomplete, and to require the three further Quartets.

The other poems of the decade, after the 'unfinished' 'Coriolan', are minor, or simply amusements. *Old Possum's Book of Practical Cats*, mostly written in 1934–6, show the poet practising his technique behind the mask of the comic versifier. The eleven minor poems have more to them than that: they reveal in an accessible, even intimate way, something of the author of *Burnt Norton*.

'Five-Finger Exercises', published in the *Criterion* in January 1933, were probably written before Eliot left for America in the autumn of 1932, to lecture at Harvard. There is a mordant wound beneath their wit. The prevalence of animals, and the lightness with which much learning is alluded to, would suggest an unbending towards pleasantry. Yet 'How unpleasant to meet Mr Eliot!' His prim and grim sense of Time and Mortality is the burden of these lines, and they are not disposed to be kind to the animal. The first poem is a relatively straight expression of anguish in unending time, though the tone is rather odd –

> There is no relief but in grief.
> O when will the creaking heart cease?
> When will the broken chair give ease?
> Why will the summer day delay?
> *When* will Time flow away?

The second makes no bones of little dog's mortality, fusing with ruthless rhymes its safe sleep and the endless grave. The third turns kindness to animals upon the kindly: for in our end, trans-substantiated, we shall give 'the feathered mortals' our very flesh to eat. The lines to the delightful Mr Hodgson are deftly barbed by the allusion to Keats' 'Ode on Melancholy': he is so clearly not bursting Joy's grape to taste sovereign Melancholy. Whereas Mr Eliot, self-portrayed in the grimsical manner of Edward Lear, accepts that he is unlovable, having put his animals in their place – notably his 'coat of fur'. How practical, his sense of realities! And what suppressed envy, perhaps, for the cats and dogs so much sooner at the end of their time.

The savagery behind those exercises finds a more direct expression in 'Lines for an Old Man', first published in November 1935. Genesius Jones' associations seem to me helpful: with the serpent, the Fall, and the unregenerate Old Man.[2] That discovers at least natural malice in the allusive imagery; together with a suggestion that instinctive wit should be venomous. If there is no grace, nor is there sentimental kindness in the savage eye. The poem has deeper and wider-spreading associations, in the manner of Mallarmé to whom it was dedicated in a draft.[3] However, Eliot has implied that the meaning in this *symboliste* mode is best left unriddled, since it is not what we think.[4] Part of the meaning, in any case, might be that natural wit does not reach to the order of thought which he cares for.

The three American 'Landscapes' were probably written during Eliot's visit there in 1933; the Welsh and the Scottish probably after his return to England, in 1934 or 1935. Grieving time is dominant, but suffered directly and lyrically, and therefore no occasion for irony. The difference between this set of poems and 'Five-Finger Exercises' surely has much to do with the poet's return, in 'New Hampshire' and 'Cape Ann', to the scenes of his childhood's summers.

The children's voices singing in the apple orchard create an aura of associations about the grief of the grown man. The spring that was is doubled in a present spring, intensifying its appeal, intensifying also the awareness that it is over. Dissonant images are harmonised, not resolved: the sounds chime, but the sense is of contradiction:

> Today grieves, tomorrow grieves,
> Cover me over, light-in-leaves;
> Golden head, black wing,
> Cling, swing,
> Spring, sing,
> Swing up into the apple-tree.

We, with the poet surely, cannot escape the connection of the apple-tree with the Fall. Yet the motif also means much that is positive to him. It occurs in the suppressed 'Ode' of *Ara Vos Prec*; it figures in the coda of *Little Gidding*, an element of 'the end of all our exploring'.

'New Hampshire' and 'Virginia' were printed together in a small pamphlet for distribution by the author, with the title *Words for Music*. They are both almost purely musical, but the second even more than the first. Its images are charged with the intense emotion, as I take it, of the poet's grieving today and tomorrow. The immersion in natural phenomena recalls that passage from *The Education of Henry Adams* which was alluded to in 'Gerontion'. The only relief, if I am correct in thinking the river red with iron ore – though it could be simply red clay – is the finding in it an objective expression of the thought of time that never stays nor passes away. It is not the river of *The Dry Salvages*, and perhaps there is a suppressed wish that it should be. There is no quickness of children's voices here, and not the stillness of an end: only the oppressive drift of the continuous present.

'Usk' and 'Rannoch, by Glencoe' are simpler, perhaps because they are *paysages moralisés* rather than revisited. There is much internal rhyme and assonance, but not that deeper play of sense which characterises the American landscapes. Indeed, the stated preference for 'The hermit's chapel, the pilgrim's prayer' over 'old enchantments', is a reflex as habitual as any ordinary romantic's. There is more pressure of the actual landscape and its historical associations in the other poem, and more intensity of reflection upon it. The rhythm does not gently rock as in 'Usk', but tautly follows out a thought:

> Memory is strong
> Beyond the bone. Pride snapped,
> Shadow of pride is long, in the long pass
> No concurrence of bone.

Though a characteristic response, that is not automatic, but freshly seen.

The moral becomes fully personal in 'Cape Ann'. The known world of natural delight, as it might have been for the boy given the much coveted Chapman's *Handbook of Birds of Eastern North America* on his fourteenth birthday,[5] is recovered and then resigned. That clear dissociation, unblurred by nostalgia, resolves the painful pleasure of 'New Hampshire', and the decaying stillness of 'Virginia'. While the images are very simple, merely an evocation of birds, the verse moves with mature knowledge and feeling. 'O quick quick quick' is a rhythmic motif, which, heard behind the falling rhythm of 'song-sparrow' and the other sparrows, sustains a lifting excitement. When it is echoed in 'Sweet sweet sweet' the immediate sensation has passed into conscious appreciation, a slowed yet unstopping movement, succeeded by deliberate resignation. Then the falling rhythm is absolute:

> resign it
> To its true owner, the tough one, the sea-gull.

That sea-gull will figure among the sea's voices in *The Dry Salvages*. *Palaver* in the last line, 'The palaver is finished', is 'the common word exact without vulgarity': it could be remembered from childhood, but the dictionary records that 'custom applied it to the talking sessions of foreign-tongued natives'. The poet has been in palaver with the natives of a country not his own.

Everywhere in the sequence of 'Landscapes' there is a similarly precise attention to the music of words, an exactitude of image, association and rhythm. By this means feelings are clarified and refined, the old connected with the new, and a calm of mature conviction is attained. Though they are relatively slight sketches, these poems show the poet entering upon the reconstitution of his 'first world' into his final end.

Burnt Norton: the name memorialises a house burnt down, giving a ghostly presence to what has been behind the modern house and garden. Is the garden into which we are led actual, or only dust in sunlight? In retrospect, in *Little Gidding*, we will be told

> Ash on an old man's sleeve
> Is all the ash the burnt roses leave.
> Dust in the air suspended
> Marks the place where a story ended.
> Dust inbreathed was a house . . .

The episode in 'our first world' occurs in an insistent past tense. It is introduced, moreover, as a composition of echoes, in a passage which repeats that word and takes its stressed vowel as keynote:

> Footfalls echo in the memory
> Down the passage which we did not take
> Towards the door we never opened
> Into the rose-garden. My words echo . . .

and so on down to 'follow', which concludes this passage and leads into its development. It will be 'echoed ecstasy', twice removed from us: in the memory only, and of an experience *not* had. It is even, in a way, a fantasy of childhood, this secret garden. Again, the dust is not on the petals of gathered roses, but upon rose-leaves.[6]

For all that the moment is actual and immediate. It becomes present as we are being told that it is past; and it seems to continue in its own present time, the leaves 'containing laughter', when we are compelled to go from it. This *deception* is of a kind to make us scrutinise the word, while recalling how varieties of thrush have figured in earlier visions or hallucinations – the water-dripping song in 'What the Thunder Said', singing down in *Ash-Wednesday* IV, calling through the fog in *Marina*. Here, just as much as in those poems, the illusion has an intensity and immediacy surpassing ordinary reality. Then its passing deceives in the French sense, it disappoints. The dis-illusionment touches the Latin root of the word, a taking away. But the taking away of what is not, reveals what is always real – the permanent and ultimate truth of experience. Thus the *deception* is a very complex moment of truth: a mixing of memory and desire which reaches toward their final resolution.

How strained and disturbed by contradictions the vision is until the cloud resolves it. The imposing presences are invisible, the music is hidden and un-heard; there are roses and vibrant air, but also dead leaves and autumn heat; then the empty alley, and the drained pool. The movement is a balancing of impressions equal and opposite:

> dignified, invisible,
> Moving without pressure, over the dead leaves,
> In the autumn heat, through the vibrant air

There can be no simple flow of feeling in such double vision, where what is most real is not real to sense, and where what is actually seen would contradict it. Nevertheless the fleeting vision does fill the sight and the feeling rides over the caesura at the climax:

> Dry the pool, dry concrete, brown edged,
> And the pool was filled with water out of sunlight,
> And the lotos rose, quietly, quietly,
> The surface glittered out of heart of light,
> And they were behind us, reflected in the pool.

'Dry the pool' gives the rhythmic motif: varied in 'And the pool', turned inside out in 'with water', it re-emerges transformed in 'quietly, quietly', and is fulfilled in 'heart of light'. Then it is worked out to its end in 'and the pool was empty'. This is a movement seeking to grasp and hold what we can almost see, nearly attaining what is ultimately elusive.

Have we seen beyond the seen? 'They were *behind* us, *reflected* in the pool': how can we see that? Are we double, being on this side and yet looking from the further side? Or is it a mysterious effect of sunlight through leaves; the reflection, a reflection of light? This straining uncertainty is of the essence of the experience. The images make us reach into what we have experienced, and so we give substance to the vision. But then the vision alters our sense of what we know, or touches upon imaginings we may ordinarily pay little attention to.

We have been brought to the limit of natural experience, just as far as sense and memory and imagination can reach.

What remains when the moment is over is the immediate sense of loss: the black cloud is real, the pool *is* empty. After such illumination we may feel 'Ridiculous the waste sad time/Stretching before and after'. Yet what release from time has the moment afforded? Only that of being conscious. And if 'To be conscious is not to be in time', still the consciousness has been *of* time. The release is like the catharsis of tragedy: the painful action of desire and memory is resolved in the purging of vain hopes and the acceptance of reality. Yet there is something imperfect, a residue of bitter regret and recrimination, in the close of the garden passage: 'human kind/Cannot bear very much reality'. The mind is not calmed, the passion is not spent.

The last three lines resume the philosophical speculation with which the movement opened, repeating the conclusion that had been reasoned to, and which has now the force of immediate knowledge. That set of propositions could be a form of tribute to F. H. Bradley, in the fusion of passionate feeling with acute intellect, the precision of style, the carrying of empiricism as far as it will go, with the wisdom to know that empiricism is not all.[7] What is the 'one end which is always present'? Is it the Absolute, or annihilation? The sum of experience in the first movement, crystallised in the imagination and analysed by reason, must amount to the latter. That is as far as the natural philosopher can go. Yet Bradley kept his philosophy open to what as a philosopher he could not know, so that his empiricism led on to metaphysics. His Absolute could be unified by an act of faith, when one was able to make it. Later in the Quartets the 'one end' will come to mean God. But it cannot mean that yet.

There is as yet nothing to give that equal and opposite expansion. Certainly there is a feeling for it, but upon no reasonable ground. And revelation is not invoked. This is of the essential character of the poem. It begins in the realm of nature, and for the most part keeps within it. Sense-experience and emotion, imagination and thought, these are carried as far as they can go of themselves, even to a point where they exceed themselves. But the mind does not pass out of nature. And in nature the ultimate reality is death. It may be for this reason that the visionary first movement is imperfectly resolved: its necessary close is not finally satisfying to the poet.

These tensions persist through the lyric which opens the second movement. We may feel drawn to follow this as a simple ascent from the mud towards the stars. As the initial heavy rhythm lightens and quickens, and the images weave a pleasing pattern of associations, it appears that we are placed among the harmonious spheres. Read in this way, the passage could be what the children among the leaves would sing, the children who might have been in an unfallen Eden. But other associations must impose themselves upon our minds which know too much to be so innocent: 'reality' is not so easily transcended. Even as we move in imagination 'above the moving tree/In light upon the figured leaf', we must heed

> upon the sodden floor
> Below, the boarhound and the boar
> Pursue their pattern as before

The resolution, implicit in 'But reconciled among the stars', is not an escape into pure transcendence, but only a perception of the pattern of fate and necessity. Nevertheless, the lyric does indulge the illusion that we may remove ourselves into the realm of pure consciousness; and that even as we perceive the pattern of fate we may be above it.

I suspect that the lyric is Eliot's *hommage et tombeau* for Mallarmé, his modern master in metaphysical poetry; and that, like the tribute to his modern master in philosophy, it is aware of limitation. The vision in the rose garden owes a good deal to Mallarmé; but his method is made to express Eliot's mind, and the art is consecrated not to pure fiction but to 'reality'.[8] One might say that there Eliot was introducing his classical order into modern metaphysical poetry. Here, however, he appears rather to be subdued to Mallarmé's mode and impulse, and to be suggesting the completion which they require only through secondary associations. The allusions to 'M'introduire dans ton histoire' and 'Le Tombeau de Charles Baudelaire' establish the definite link with Mallarmé's metaphysic. But does not 'the sodden floor/Below' recall Dante's looking down upon 'this threshing floor' from the region of the stars?[9] Moreover, each division of the *Divine Comedy* ends with the word *stelle*, the stars, indicating, as the Temple Classics editor put it, 'the constant aspiration of the poem, and of the soul whose journey it depicts, towards the highest things'. But Dante's way to the stars was not by any simple ascent through nature to natural perfection: it was through Hell and Purgatory. Thus even while the lyric follows, and honours, the will for pure transcendence, it bears traces of another ordering of things. Even the 'axle-tree' may include among its many associations, along with the axle-tree of heaven, a funeral cart.[10] 'The trilling wire in the blood' could sing with the fever of *East Coker* IV.

With 'At the still point of the turning world' another voice comes in, unmistakably introducing another metaphysic than Mallarmé's. It might also be completing the philosophy of F. H. Bradley. In his essay on Bradley, Eliot quoted this passage from *The Principles of Logic*:

It may come from a failure in my metaphysics, or from a weakness of the flesh which continues to blind me, but the notion that existence could be the same as understanding strikes as cold and ghost-like as the dreariest materialism. That the glory of this world in the end is appearance leaves the world more glorious, if we feel it is a show of some fuller splendour; but the sensuous curtain is a deception and a cheat, if it hides some colourless movement of atoms, some spectral woof of impalpable abstractions, or unearthly ballet of bloodless categories. Though dragged to such conclusions, we cannot embrace them. Our principles may be true, but they are not reality. They no more *make* that Whole which commands our devotion than some shredded dissection of human tatters *is* that warm and breathing beauty of flesh which our hearts found delightful.

There was an echo from that in 'Whispers of Immortality'; Becket's foiled Tempters find 'man's life . . . a cheat and a disappointment'; Mary will tell Harry, 'Even if, as you say, Wishwood is a cheat,/Your family a delusion – then it's *all* a delusion'. But it is the whole passage which is caught up into and answered by Eliot's 'Neither flesh nor fleshless. . . .'.

The paradoxes, which can be resolved only into a purely metaphysical concept, seek to realise 'that Whole which commands our devotion'. At first they are 'impalpable abstractions'. But then the thinking becomes a commentary upon the experience in the rose-garden, and can be grasped and felt in the light of that experience. The lines from 'The inner freedom' – given as a separate section in the earlier printings, and possibly meant for Becket originally – are the poet's reflection upon his own reality:

> The inner freedom from the practical desire,
> The release from action and suffering, release from the inner
> And the outer compulsion, yet surrounded
> By a grace of sense, a white light still and moving,
> *Erhebung* without motion, concentration
> Without elimination, both a new world
> And the old made explicit, understood
> In the completion of its partial ecstasy,
> The resolution of its partial horror.

If we accept the evidence of poetic experience, this is as empirical an approach to the Absolute as there well could be. It is of course requiring more than reason can apprehend; and the paradoxes do serve elsewhere as analogies for Incarnation. But here we have not the divine but the human aspect of that. Moreover, it is to be observed that the metaphysics is catholic in the broadest sense. It goes back from Bradley to Aristotle, and does not depend upon Christian revelation. We are in the realm of 'hints and guesses'; and although these will be said to mean Incarnation at the end of *The Dry Salvages*, to reach

189

for that *idea* prematurely is to short-circuit the poetry, and to be left with what horrified Eliot as much as Bradley, an 'unearthly ballet of bloodless categories'. The dance at the still point must include all that we have been and might be, earthly flesh with aspiring spirit.

The conclusion, 'Only through time time is conquered', goes beyond Mallarmé and Bradley – and perhaps beyond Eliot's other masters in philosophy[11] – simply by submitting to the realities of life in time. It expresses the desire for transcendence in a form which remains true to experience and to reason, and thus escapes at once the illusoriness of the *symboliste* method, and the limits of philosophy. It recognises – as III will explicate, and *The Family Reunion* also – that the only possible way up is the way down. The whole passage of which this conclusion is the culmination manifests a powerful concurrence of experience, emotion and thought. The style is lucid and rigorously precise; and these prose virtues are raised to a higher power by the versification, which becomes itself a form of syntax, enforcing the stress of sense with the beat of feeling, so that the argument moves with an inner cogency. The conclusion is then the product of a rare integrity of mind: the integration of the whole mind into principle. In the first movement the memory crystallised in vision; here the vision is understood, and the mind is unified on the plane of thought.

The next movement carries meditation towards contemplation, starting from the conclusion just reached. Its *here* is not the intense moment out of time, but only 'the waste sad time'. That is the point of view from which time is accepted and entered into: it is only to be conquered. *Disaffection* is uncompromisingly exact: (1) the absence or alienation of affection; (2) alienation from or discontent with existing authority; (3) physical disorder, or diseased condition (*O.E.D.*). All three senses apply, in various ways, to the place and to the poet. But his dominant intent is to 'cleanse affection from the temporal'. For 'the soul cannot be possessed of the divine union, until it has divested itself of the love of created beings'.[12]

The vision of the world as offering 'neither plenitude nor vacancy' is metaphysical poetry in the common sense. By perceiving likeness in dissimilars it only intensifies the actual: 'Men and bits of paper'. Joyce, in a marvellous epiphany, has the statues in the stonecutter's yard beside the cemetery suggest the shades in the underworld.[13] Here it is the living who are the shades; the London Underground becomes much like the classical underworld; while the hills of the metropolis become a parody of the seven hills of the eternal city, their names a satire. This is a more concentrated treatment of the 'Unreal City' than anything since *The Waste Land*; and it differs from that in being more philosophic. That is, it is not only giving expression to alienated feeling: the alienation is mastered now by a deeper understanding.

'This twittering world' is in every way opposite to the moment in the rose-garden. Its inhabitants have no history or potentiality; they are whirled in an endless passive present, <u>never stilled by consciousness.</u> Yet this is time and place to the poet, inevitable. The partial horror of its unreality can be resolved only by going through it to the end; not by transcendence, but by the negation of the unreal. Here, with a consistency very hard to follow, the end is made present just as it was in the rose-garden, by being conscious, by deliberately seeking to make it now and always. This is to reach towards the Absolute in its negative aspect –

> the aspect of time
> Caught in the form of limitation
> Between un-being and being.

To not be what he is in time is the way towards what he would be out of time. It involves, moreover, not just the annihilation of the world, but of all that he is. The drying out of the world of sense, the evacuation of fancy, the inoperancy of spirit, these mean the end even of the intense and developed consciousness which has been realising itself in the poem.

Plenitude, or vacancy: all or nothing. And if not yet all, then nothingness as the way to the All – that baffling equation of 'the moment of the rose and the moment of the yew-tree'. It is the ascetic imperative, universal, primitive and mystical. It is a matter of personal temperament as much as of any tradition; rather the cause than a consequence of religious practices and beliefs; common to the East and the West, and to ancient and modern times. If it is arrived at by thought and meditation, what is reached would seem to have been the motive behind the thought, and to answer to a need of nature. One may say with Ezra Pound,

> 'But this beats me,
> Beats me, I mean that I do not understand it;
> This love of death that is in them.'[14]

Nevertheless, a perfectly genuine impulse to be liberated from the deceptions of existence must account for Eliot's so willing his world's end.

The lyric which follows completes the meditation, in the poet's equivalent to the mystic's state of contemplation: it is the whole of his consciousness distilled, lucid, perfectly expressed. There are three parts: a closed couplet; a questioning passage; a conclusion. Or statement, response, resolution. Each part has its distinct voice; unless, as in a quartet, the voices are speaking together, but with first one dominant then another.

The couplet reaches back through the 'daylight' lines at the start of III to the passing of the vision in sunlight: it is the heavy, final statement of the end of that reality. 'Buried' is especially weighted and prolonged, taking the extra stress and time of the syllable that has been dropped from the iambic pentameter:

Tíme and the béll/háve   bŭried the dáy

A similar syncopation in the second line double-stresses 'The black cloud'. Now, strangely, these heavy emphases upon the sense are rhythmically dynamic. By the force of their own beat, and by sustaining a cross-rhythm from the reversed feet, they make a formal dance of mortality.

But 'human kind/Cannot bear very much reality.' The passage of questioning might be the response of the natural and nature-loving fancy, seeking consolation in pathetic fallacies. But the sunflower opens to and follows the sun; and when fully ripened it turns earthwards. The clematis is a climber, and its name is not cognate with clemency. An older usage applied it to the periwinkle: 'In early times a garland of this flower was placed on the heads of persons on their way to execution, with which some have connected the Italian name *fiore de morte*, flower of death' (*O.E.D.*). The yew's foliage may suggest immortality; but 'Thy fibres net the dreamless head,/Thy roots are wrapt about the bones'.[15] The questions are thus answered in their own images. The imagination that would 'ascend to summer in the tree', even in this last form of natural hope, is brought down below the earth.

This countering of wishful feeling by a realistic consciousness is very like the double pattern of the 'lost heart' passage in *Ash-Wednesday* VI. But here the hidden sense of the images is unequivocally enforced in the music of the verse. Instead of resting where natural feeling would, upon 'sunflower' and 'clematis', the questioning is carried on to its unwanted answer. The rhythmically matching phrases insist on the falling rhythm, pointing where we are as we question:

Will the súnflòwĕr/túrn tŏ ùs,/will the clémātìs
Stray dówn,/bénd tŏ ùs . . . ?

The wistful 'Will . . .?' is answered in 'Chill', a long note lasting a whole foot or bar; from which we are released only by the rapid sliding beats, with a brief dwelling at the line-end, which gives more weight to the final descent:

Chill
Fingers of yew be curled
Down on us?

The total effect is to resolve the way up of nature – of sense, feeling, imagination – into the way down, and to arrive definitively at its one end.

In spite of that, the conclusion affirms 'the still point of the turning world'. This is to end where the *symboliste* lyric had aspired to arrive. And it is surely a more baffling arrival, by this way of exposing the vanity of natural aspiration, and following out the inevitable descent into the grave. How can that way down lead to this conclusion? Is there not a break here, a discontinuity in the movement? Are we left at the end simply with an abstraction and an act of faith?

It may be that we are. Yet at least they have become part and parcel of the poet's personality,[16] a *Gestalt* structuring perception. In this complex image his whole world is concentrated and organised: it is the essence of what is real to him. 'After the kingfisher's wing' honours the transient beauty which time and the bell bury. Moreover, it is made to escape the hold of 'Cling', and the downward pull of that questioning, precisely by its transience. Then 'still' chimes first with 'Chill', but is altered in 'the still point'. The movement does not rest there however, and 'the turning world' echoes 'curled'. We have been, fleetingly, where the light is still, taken beyond where we are by the assured transition of 'light to light', the confident resting upon 'silent', the definite structure of the sequence

the light is still

At the still point/of the túrning wórld

where the centre is built up to, established, and holds what falls away from it.

Nevertheless, this light at the still point is a reality of a different order from the rest of the lyric: metaphysical, mystical, beyond the order of nature. And it is not continuous with the natural. It concludes the lyric not by following from the statement and question but by imposing upon them an end beyond their reach. The first of the epigraphs[17] from Heraclitus might be applied here. It can be rendered this way: *There is the one centre of all that is, yet men tend to be centred in themselves;* or *though there is the one end of all things, men seek their own ends.* In these terms, the main part of the poem is centred upon the end of nature, the dark chill of the grave. Yet the conclusion asserts the source and end of light, as if it were the centre of the universe. And this is a centre outside the poem, exerting a power of attraction contrary to its gravity.

How can we remove though from the turning world to the still point? In what way can that be a valid conclusion, the end required by the end of nature? The first part of the fifth movement takes up this problem, and its reflections are best understood in the light of the lyric, and as a commentary upon it. The writing, the versification, is pellucid and precise here as much as anywhere in the poem; yet the meaning is veiled. Our first quick impression of what is being said is likely to be false – at least I myself mistook it for a long time. So I go thoughtfully now, one step at a time.

First the main question is put again: how can that which moves only in time conquer time? It is put now in terms of the poem's own words and music; but the earlier discussion must make us see these also as metaphors for the poet's life in time. The form of the poem is the form of his life.

Now time is said to be conquered by silence and stillness – and stillness can mean silence. The silence after speech is like the silence of the kingfisher's wing after it has flashed. This is made to seem desirable, or at least a positive action: words '*reach*/Into the silence'. Yet it must be a negative condition, the absence of discourse and of the light of the Word. But then we were told in *Ash-Wednesday* v that only in perfect silence could the Word be found. Perhaps *the silence* here is simply what it says, nothing mysterious: it is what remains when words have departed.

The *stillness* to be reached 'by the form, the pattern' differs in being not *only* living and not *only* dead. The analogies suggest the mysterious paradoxes of death-in-life and life-in-death. The Chinese jar, like Keats' Grecian Urn, is unliving; and if it appears to move perpetually that is because its form is perfectly finished. Such perfection is not attainable by what lives and must change, as Keats regretfully acknowledged. But Eliot implies a different completion of Keats' thought: it may be attained by ceasing to live and move in time. The lyric, by composing natural life into a formal dance of death, might be aspiring to the condition of the Chinese jar, and as a condition of life as well as art. I take it to be a funeral jar or urn; and I take the lyric to be 'the complete consort dancing together . . . an epitaph'.

This is a stillness beyond that of the held note, which might be that of suspended time, as in 'Chill' or in the timeless moment. It is the co-existence of the passing moment with that ultimate stillness, so that the stillness is lasting, as in 'the time of death is every moment'. This makes the dance of death the perfect form and pattern of living.

To read these analogies less darkly is to be relatively superficial. Their more hopeful intimations lie all the other side of the dark. They do not transcend only living and only dying. All the difference they establish is in making the whole of life conform to death. Liberation from time, as *The Family Reunion* will declare more fully, is through a conscious acceptance of the fate of being mortal.

We have yet to find how the stillness of death may be connected with 'the still point of the turning world'. When the poet attempts to make the connection words strain, crack and break. One cannot say of the violin's note that 'the end precedes the beginning'; nor of the Chinese jar, or the lyric, that 'the end and the beginning were always there/Before the beginning and after the end'. One can feel the strain in the verse, from the attempt to say two quite different things at once. There is a vague sense of analogy, which disintegrates upon inspection. We are left with formulations that will hold only for a being not in time, the metaphysician's and theologian's Alpha and Omega. It may be said that in such a being 'all is always now'. Yet it remains true that 'If all time is eternally present/All time is unredeemable.' And have we not been shown that to redeem time, to attain the Absolute, requires a process of absolution, a purging away, in time and by time, of all that is of time? There is the connection, a negative one.

That is the only form of connection offered in the poem. It is given in the last eight lines of this passage with an appropriate absence of syntactical connection: between the poet's words and 'The Word' is a clean break, as between two planes of meaning and being. Yet a correspondence is implied, between the poet's struggle to make words stay still against the world's usage, and 'The Word in the desert' – a correspondence, in Heraclitus' terms, between the *logoi* of men and the *Logos*. To understand this connection we must remember that the poet would pattern words into stillness, into the silence which *Ash-Wednesday* declared to be the Word. To think forward to *The Family Reunion* is also helpful. One might say that Harry discovers the vanity of the crying shadows, and exorcises them in learning to move in the measure of the funeral dance. 'The disconsolate chimera' could be a creature in his crowded desert: a grotesque union of incompatible natures, a parody of Incarnation because the lower has not been subsumed into the higher nature.

I am not sure that it is altogether orthodox, but certainly the meaning here is consistent with that of all the verse since 1925: that it is only in his death that man can be united with the divine. This is the *human* aspect of Incarnation, the aspect open to poetry. We miss Eliot's meaning if we think only of the divine aspect, which is theology or mysticism. Their ideas are not the same as the poetry, and nor are Eliot's prose statements. 'To the Greek there was something inexplicable in the *logos* so that it was a participation of man in the divine.' 'What poetry should do in the theatre is a kind of humble shadow or analogy of the Incarnation, whereby the human is taken up into the divine.'[18] Those statements do not give us the 'lifetime's death in love', in which 'the darkness shall be the light, and the stillness the dancing'. That is not the perfection of human nature we like to think of, and which ideas of Incarnation usually allow scope for. Eliot's more rigorous sense is that to be taken up into the divine means the end of a man.

It means the end of the poet too. The Mallarmé whose intent was to restore the power of the word[19] – 'to deify the written word' was how Valéry put it – has been a mentor throughout *Burnt Norton*. But now Eliot, seeking the divine

Word which is beyond everything words can express, is moving 'toward a region where that guide can avail us no farther'.[20] As Dante turned from Virgil to theology in the guise of Beatrice, so Eliot now turns for guidance to mystical theology. It appears that the function of this fifth movement has been to realise the use and limits of poetry, and to initiate a process of detachment from it.

The first ten lines of the closing section give brief indications of the realm he is moving into: a note from St John of the Cross, some first principles of theology. The idea is touched upon that the temporal order of existence is, ideally, in process of being drawn up from un-being into the absolute of being. This is not developed, but it gives a context for the coda, which presents the final state of the poet within the realm of poetry:

> Sudden in a shaft of sunlight
> Even while the dust moves
> There rises the hidden laughter
> Of children in the foliage
> Quick now, here, now, always –
> Ridiculous the waste sad time
> Stretching before and after.

It is as if the poet himself were caught between un-being and being; and that painfully unresolved state must remain the condition of poetry, and the condition of his natural life. The shaft of sunlight, catching up earlier images, evokes Plato's shaft of divine light penetrating the material world as its axis.[21] Yet what it reveals is the dance of dust-motes. Though the poet's consciousness may find its image in the shaft of light, he is not pure consciousness, but is made of dust, and must move with it. The echo of the unfallen joy that might have been can only intensify unfulfilled longing. It cannot be 'here, now, always' – not while he is himself, in the flesh, in time. He has far to go before attaining, even in verse, the absolution of complete simplicity. One can see why the hero of *The Family Reunion* is not a poet but an aspirant saint.

One can see, too, why Eliot should have thought that with *Burnt Norton* he had reached the end of his 'pure' poetry, and presented *Collected Poems 1909–1935* as 'the definitive edition' containing 'all Mr Eliot's poetry that he wishes to preserve, with the exception of *Murder in the Cathedral*'.[22]

If he had written no further poems after *Burnt Norton* that work would have stood perfectly well as the completion of his *oeuvre*, and as its masterpiece. In his own view at least, it quite eclipsed *The Waste Land*, that *pièce de résistance* of 'the modern mind'. The fact that both poems have five parts, with the fourth a brief lyric, has led to an assumption that the later was modelled upon the earlier, and that their structures are essentially the same. In fact the resemblance is superficial, and the difference radical. It would be nearer the truth to say that in *Burnt Norton* he realised for the first time a truly unified structure, and one which was the right form for his mind. This is the outstanding achievement of the poem, that it consists of a single complete action, in which the complexities of the poet's experience are progressively resolved into a final disposition of his being.

Near the end of 'The Music of Poetry' (1942) Eliot said, 'I believe that the properties in which music concerns the poet most nearly, are the sense of rhythm and the sense of structure.'[23] Fully to understand what he meant by 'the sense of structure' we should connect that analogy with music with the observation, in his introduction to Valéry's writings on the art of poetry, that 'Music . . . may be conceived as striving towards an unattainable timelessness; and if the other arts may be thought of as yearning for duration, so Music may be thought of as yearning for the stillness of painting or sculpture.'[24] That connects in its turn of course with 'Words move, music moves/Only in time', and so brings us to the source of that stillness –

>   Only by the form, the pattern,
> Can words or music reach
> The stillness

It becomes apparent that his 'sense of structure' has behind it a quite definite order, and that his ambition is to so structure experience in time as to make it conform to the timeless Word.

It must have been because it failed in this respect that Eliot called *The Waste Land*, which Pound had hailed as the longest *poem* in the language, 'structure-less'.[25] In fact that work has a powerful organic structure, of the same kind as *The Ancient Mariner*, and is an impressive demonstration of the self-ordering nature of the imagination which Coleridge celebrated. But a *natural* organisation was just what Eliot did not want in his later work. He was cultivating a metaphysical organisation: one in which nature would be ordered according to a pattern outside and above itself. *The Waste Land* had achieved a unified sensibility; but that process had then to be completed in 'the divine union'.

He can be seen to be working towards that end in the sequences of poems which fall short of being a single whole, *The Hollow Men* and *Ash-Wednesday*.[26] What he needed was a dynamic form to enact the progression from nature through mind to the realm of grace – a single and complete rite for that passage through the looking-glass. I think that when we come to understand *Burnt*

Norton we find that it has this form. Its inner structure is given in the proposition 'the way up is the way down: the way down is the way up'. The second formulation is the mirror-image of the first, and it is arrived at by reversing the natural order in the metaphysical looking-glass. It is the same with the proposition taken from *Burnt Norton* v to give the pattern of *East Coker*: 'In my beginning is my end: in my end is my beginning'. Here the first formulation is true on two levels, one natural, the other metaphysical; but it fully yields the metaphysical sense only when it is reversed by the thinking through of the meaning of *end* until the ultimate beginning is reached.

The first two movements of *Burnt Norton* might be said to work out 'the way up is the way down'; while the other three, answering them in the realm of metaphysical understanding as in a mirror, work out 'the way down is the way up'. The actual symmetry is concealed by the inclusion of the first lyric in II, whereas the answering lyric stands on its own. This may be a deliberate device to throw the weight forward onto the more resolved later movements. But if we allow its due importance to the first lyric we see that it is the centre of the two early movements, as IV is of the other three; and we can see then that these three later movements are like a mirror-image of the first two:

$$
\begin{array}{ccc}
& \text{II.I} & \text{IV} \\
\text{I} & \text{II.2 : III} & \text{V}
\end{array}
$$

The two halves are as it were hinged at the colon, and fold together to give the mirror-image, with v matching I and so on. (If we take account of the fact that, leaving aside the two lyrics, each movement consists of two main sections, then we get the expanded diagram given at the end of this chapter. 'Garlic and sapphires' is marked there as II.1; and II.3 begins at 'The inner freedom' – this was given as a separate section in the early printings. My rough headings – they are of course no more than that – indicate how the five main sections of the second half correspond, in reversed or mirrored order, to those of the first half.) One may wonder, given the likeness of this structure to that of Bartok's Fourth String Quartet (1930), which is sometimes referred to as a Greek ε (or else an AA) quartet form, whether it was a hearing of that work which caused Eliot to reflect that 'It is in the concert room, rather than in the opera house, that the germ of a poem may be quickened.'[27]

Now of course one reads the poem as a continuous progression through its five movements: there is no going backwards in this passage through the looking-glass. Moreover, the progression, once we have resolved the paradoxes of the way up and the way down, can be viewed as a continuous ascent from the realm of the natural towards that of the divine. The poem moves between mere experience at the beginning and the Absolute which would be its end. It moves, that is, in the middle region of mind; and its modes are those of the mind progressing from experience, through thought and meditation, towards prayer and vision.

The co-ordination, or orchestration, of these instrumentalities of the mind must be, surely, what warrants calling the poem a quartet. I don't know whether the analogy with the quartet was already in Eliot's mind when he composed *Burnt Norton*. There is the analogy with sonata forms, and with musical composition in a general way; but he himself warned, in 'The Music of Poetry', against pressing these too far. There is just this one respect in which the term can be applied at all closely: that a quartet is a consort of four instruments or voices. In the case of Eliot's Quartets I would characterise these, tentatively, as the voices of natural experience, of thought which moves into meditation, of meditation which moves into prayer, and of prayer which would culminate in vision.

Clearly, the formal structure of the poem is inseparable from the command of these several voices: it is a quartet form. It is wholly original – at least, I can think of nothing quite like it – and the final product of Eliot's poetic and spiritual development.

The structure of *Burnt Norton*

The way up is the way down : the way down is the way up

IV Nature as the way down: light at the still point

V.1 words in & out of time: the Word in the desert

II.1 Nature patterned as the way up?

III.2 paradoxes of the *via negativa*

V.2 Love in the aspect of time (= coda)

II.2 paradoxes of being in & out of time

III.1 disaffection from the temporal :

I.2 the moment in the rose-garden, in and out of time

II.3 to be conscious, and conquer time

I.1 questions of Time & its end

Part Five

1939–1945

Apocalypse

In that vision Arjuna saw the universe, with its manifold shapes, all embraced in One, its Supreme Lord. . .

    [Arjuna said:] 'Thou seemest to swallow up the worlds, to lap them in flame. Thy glory fills the universe. Thy fierce rays beat down upon it irresistibly. . .'

    Lord Shri Krishna replied: 'I have shown myself to thee as the Destroyer who lays waste the world. . .'
                  (The *Geetā*, ch. XI ('The Cosmic Vision'))

I presumed to fix my look on the eternal light so long that I wearied my sight thereon!
Within its depths I saw ingathered, bound by love in one volume, the scattered leaves of all
    the universe;
substance and accidents and their relations, as though together fused, after such fashion
    that what I tell of is one simple flame.
                  (*Paradiso*, XXXIII)

the only hopeful course for a society which would thrive and continue its creative activity in the arts of civilisation, is to become Christian. That prospect involves, at least, discipline, inconvenience and discomfort: but here as hereafter the alternative to hell is purgatory.
                  (*The Idea of a Christian Society* (1939))

1938

> *March* Germany occupies Austria. *29 September* Munich Agreement – Britain and France cede Czechoslovakian Sudetenland to Germany, thus securing 'peace in our time' (Chamberlain).

1939
January   The last *Criterion*.
March   *The Family Reunion*.
October   *The Idea of a Christian Society*.
December   'Marching Song of the Pollicle Dogs' and 'Billy M'Caw' in *The Queen's Book of the Red Cross*.

> *March* Germany annexes Czech provinces of Bohemia and Moravia. *1 September* Germany invades Poland. *3 September* Britain and France declare war on Germany.

1940
March   *East Coker* (in Easter no. of *New English Weekly*).
May   'Defence of the Islands'.
June   'The Poetry of W. B. Yeats'.

> *April* Germany invades Denmark and Norway; *May* . . . Belgium, Holland, France. *27 May–4 June* Evacuation of B.E.F. and French 1st Army from Dunkirk. *June* Italy enters war. Fall of France. *August* Battle of Britain; *7 September–3 November* London Blitz.

1941
February   *The Dry Salvages*.
December   Edited *A Choice of Kipling's Verse*

> *April* Germany invades Yugoslavia and Greece; *June* . . . Russia. *December* Japan and USA enter war.

1942
February   'The Music of Poetry'.
October   *Little Gidding*.
November   'A Note on War Poetry'.

> *October* 2nd Battle of El Alamein begins defeat of Axis forces in North Africa.

1943
January–February   'Notes Towards the Definition of Culture' – early version of first chapter of the book.
May   *Four Quartets* (1st collected ed.).
July   'To the Indians who Died in Africa'.
November   *Reunion by Destruction* ('Reflections on a scheme for Church Union in South India, addressed to the laity').

> *January–February* Battle of Stalingrad, defeat of German army there; retreat of German forces from Russia. *September* Allied landings in Italy and surrender of Italy.

1944
August   'The Responsibility of the Man of Letters in the Cultural Restoration of Europe'.

> *June* Allied landing in Normandy. *August* Liberation of Paris.

1945
October   'What is a Classic?'

> *May* Germany surrenders. *August* Japan surrenders.

9
Patriot of fire

The designs which haunt my imagination, when I think of what might be done – in this city which Providence has thought fit to visit with fire, and thus prepare for the builder[1]

'The last three of my quartets are primarily patriotic poems.' Although something made Eliot cancel that remark after he had written it in the first draft of 'The Three Voices of Poetry', it comes as near as a single sentence could to providing the key to them. They have a quite different character from all the rest of his poems, including *Burnt Norton*; and their special quality has much to do with their having been written in the war of 1939–45. Eliot recalled that

> *Burnt Norton* might have remained by itself if it hadn't been for the war, because I had become very much absorbed in the problems of writing for the stage and might have gone straight on from *The Family Reunion* to another play. The war destroyed that interest for a time: you remember how the conditions of our lives changed, how much we were thrown in on ourselves in the early days? *East Coker* was the result – and it was only in writing *East Coker* that I began to see the Quartets as a set of four.[2]

What he was thrown in upon was his personal sense of the world crisis. In the final number of the *Criterion*, in January 1939, he had confessed that 'the present state of public affairs . . . has induced in myself a depression of spirits so different from any other experience of fifty years as to be a new emotion'.[3] Then in March he concluded his lectures at Cambridge on *The Idea of a Christian Society* with this statement:

> I believe that there must be many persons who, like myself, were deeply shaken by the events of September 1938, in a way from which one does not recover; persons to whom that month brought a profounder realisation of a general plight. It was not a disturbance of the understanding: the events themselves were not surprising. Nor, as became increasingly evident, was our distress due merely to disagreement with the policy and behaviour of the moment. The feeling which was new and unexpected was a feeling of humiliation, which seemed to demand an act of personal contrition, of humility, repentance and amendment; what had happened was something in which one was deeply implicated and responsible. It was not, I repeat, a criticism of the government, but a doubt of the validity of a civilisation. We could not match conviction with

conviction, we had no ideas with which we could either meet or oppose the ideas opposed to us. Was our society, which had always been so assured of its superiority and rectitude, so confident of its unexamined premisses, assembled round anything more permanent than a congeries of banks, insurance companies and industries, and had it any beliefs more essential than a belief in compound interest and the maintenance of dividends?[4]

A pertinent remark was added when the lectures were published, in a note on 'the attitude of a Christian Society towards Pacificism':

The notion of communal responsibility, of the responsibility of every individual for the sins of the society to which he belongs, is one that needs to be more firmly apprehended; and if I share the guilt of my society in time of 'peace', I do not see how I can absolve myself from it in time of war, by abstaining from the common action.[5]

These statements are important for an understanding of Eliot's patriotism, and of the sense in which his three wartime Quartets are 'patriotic poems'. They go with that sentence from a letter of September 1939 which I quoted earlier, in connection with *The Family Reunion*, 'To do away with a sense of sin is to do away with civilisation.' From his point of view, it is the recognition of sin, ultimately of Original Sin, which should bind men together and be the ground of their common action; and that action should be the expiation of sin, 'an act of personal contrition, of humility, repentance and amendment'. We have to remember that for Eliot 'the one great peril' was, not Hitler, but 'final and complete alienation from God after death'.[6] Atonement with God was what he believed in – a *patria* not of this world.

Patriotism implies a social and political vision; and it is their realisation of such a vision which most of all distinguishes the wartime Quartets from the rest of Eliot's poetry. But his social and political idea, as it appears in his dramatic writings of the 1930s (see chapter 7) and in his philosophy of politics (see appendix c), is not much interested in human fellowship or in human institutions. It would be comfortable to imagine that with the onset of war he at last found himself writing out of a genuinely communal experience and articulating the actual state of the mind of Europe. And after all it was not the case, this time, of a personal breakdown coinciding by accident with the mood of a generation. Yet his 'Note on War Poetry' begins with an emphatic refusal to express the immediate consciousness of the people:

Not the expression of collective emotion
Imperfectly reflected in the daily papers.

The kind of poetry he would affirm instead, in the context of the war, was simply 'private experience at its greatest intensity/Becoming universal'. In that statement only the *intensification* of the private experience mediates between the 'private' and the 'universal'. There is no sense of the value of its being a shared experience, or one suffered in common with other men in other times. If the poet is at one with others, then it is only in the universal. Now 'the universal' can be understood in various ways. It may signify 'the meaning of things', as the sum of experience; or it may signify that which makes all things one, their unifying principle. But for Eliot these two ideas are ultimately one and the same, and meet in the idea of the Logos. I noticed earlier, at the end of chapter 5, that it is precisely the apprehension of its final meaning which so intensifies private experience that it becomes poetry – or, which unifies the mind and brings it towards the condition of the universal or Absolute. Now it is time to emphasise that the 'meaning' is to be understood, after the *Geetā* and Dante, as the divine principle itself; so that 'the universal' is not only the end but also the inspiration of poetry. It is Dante's *amore*, which fuses all that is in one simple flame. This is the active principle equally in Eliot's idea of society and of politics. To grasp his politics we must go back to the Greek root of the word, and recover the sense of that city in which the many are made one – and made one, ideally, by the power of the Logos. Similarly, his idea of society is always the Christian idea of a society made up, not by the fellowship of men with each other, but by their being at one in Christ. It can be truly said that this is a very different conception of society from that which Churchill invoked in his wartime speeches, and that his was the genuinely popular and real one at the time. That qualifies, but it doesn't contradict, the fact that Eliot's Quartets were social and political poems in their own special fashion. The proving comparison is with his previous poems, which remained essentially personal since their effective concern was only with the perfection of the poet's own soul. But the wartime Quartets do effectively realise a concern for a whole society – though it is one existing in 'England and nowhere. Never and always.'

'In my beginning is my end.' This initial proposition in *East Coker* takes its terms from the first and last movements of *Burnt Norton*; yet it marks not a continuation so much as a new state of mind. The intent of the first Quartet was to resolve 'time before and time after' into 'the one end which is always present': that is, to escape or transcend history, by gathering all time to its sum and conclusion 'at the still point of the turning world'. *East Coker* will rather affirm 'the waste sad time/Stretching before and after', having found living *in* time to be not ridiculous but necessary:

> Not the intense moment
> Isolated, with no before and after,
> But a lifetime burning in every moment
> And not the lifetime of one man only . . .

While it is quite consonant with *Burnt Norton*'s invocation of a condition in which 'the end precedes the beginning . . . And all is always now', that is saying something significantly different. Behind the formulations of the earlier poem lies *In the beginning was the Word* . . . ; and it is by a fairly direct appeal to this revelation that its paradoxes are resolved. But in *East Coker* the primary reference of 'beginning' and 'end' is to human life and historical process: the poetry invests them with the experience of time and change before 'intensifying' them towards the theological idea. The poet is now not transcending but entering into history.

Consequently his earlier wish to abstain from movement while the world moves, is altered into 'We must be still and still moving'. The movement is inevitably forward, towards the end of time affirmed in *Little Gidding* v: a redemption from time which is not the cessation but rather the perfection of history. But the way to the end requires a return to the beginning:

> We shall not cease from exploration
> And the end of all our exploring
> Will be to arrive where we started
> And know the place for the first time.

That imperative is in fact the formal principle of the later Quartets: they must progress by returning to origins. The structure of *Burnt Norton* can be represented as 'the way up is the way down : the way down is the way up' – its movement is along the line of 'a shaft of sunlight'. The structure of *East Coker* corresponds to that, only with the difference that its movement is along the line of 'the ground swell, that is and was from the beginning'; so that it should be represented as 'in my beginning is my end : in my end is my beginning', or 'the way forward is the way back : the way back is the way forward'. Whereas *Burnt Norton* was devoted to conceiving 'the one end', the three later Quartets work out the successive stages of the *way* in which it may be attained.

It goes with this that the poetry is not so 'metaphysical' as that of 1925–35: its concern is rather to penetrate than to pass beyond the physical world. The difference can be indicated by observing that the mind of the wartime Quartets is not haunted by what might have been, but is concentrated upon what has been. Instead of the dry pool 'filled with water out of sunlight', it declares

> Ash on an old man's sleeve
> Is all the ash the burnt roses leave

Its method is simply to intensify what has been in order to arrive at what always will be, and its vision is so much the more definite and immediately intelligible in consequence. This is not a new method, this way of conquering history by becoming wholly conscious of it, but a return to that 'historical sense' which was recommended in *The Sacred Wood* and *Homage to John Dryden*, and practised in 'Gerontion' and *The Waste Land*.

Indeed the first paragraph of *East Coker* is so nearly related to 'Gerontion' and to the opening of 'The Fire Sermon' as to appear a conscious resumption of their matter and method. It presents the 'ultimate' facts of life in time, arranged in their inevitable pattern, and shaped towards an undeniable conclusion. The ground of the verse is direct prose statement; but it is a prose formed upon that of the King James Bible and of seventeenth-century preachers; and it achieves a metrical form in the confident emphases of the meaning. By this means the passage creates, over and above its statement of the facts, a traditional consciousness of them – a specific sense of history. This declares itself most obviously in the way each term that is on the side of life is followed by a double insistence upon decay and death. 'Houses rise' is followed by 'and fall, crumble'; 'extended' is followed by 'removed, destroyed'; 'restored' gives place to the rather ambiguous 'an open field, or a factory, or a by-pass'. 'Old stone to new building' may appear to take up the hint of progress, but it is followed by a series of intensifying negations of which the governing term is *earth*, earth which subsumes all else –

> old timber to new fires,
> Old fires to ashes, and ashes to the earth
> Which is already flesh, fur and faeces,
> Bone of man and beast, cornstalk and leaf.

Those lines expand the sense of history from one which ranges back to the time, as it might be, of the original house at Burnt Norton, to that in which human culture is levelled with natural process. The final sentence then assumes the tone and form of the prophetic or universal vision. 'Houses live and die' is the moralised form of 'Houses rise and fall'; and in the development of the theme the emphasis still falls doubly upon its latter term. A line and a half is given to 'a time for building/And a time for living and for generation'; then three lengthened lines declare the aftermath of decay. Now all of this is to read history as a record not of life but of death; and it is not to revive the past in any sense, but only to use it to prove mortality. The beginnings of things, origins both social and personal, are known only as they are now, long dead and gone. So Mary Stuart, whose motto was *en ma fin est ma commencement*, figures in 'the tattered arras'. Eliot's own ancestors are implicit there also, in the allusion to the family motto (used by the Tudor Sir Thomas Elyot) *tace et fac.*

If the repeat of 'In my beginning is my end' were attached to the first paragraph, where it would go perfectly well, it would complete a sonnet upon the Elizabethan model. But that was a form, conventionally, to eternise love. Precisely so: and Eliot's conversion of its structure to serve his own anti-romantic sense of realities will surely have been deliberate, here as in 'The Fire Sermon'. He would refute the sonneteers' assertions that there was an art to preserve human beauty and love from the ravages of time, by proving that it is the nature of all earthly things to change and die. Human beings can live on upon earth beyond their mortal span, not 'in sonnets pretty rooms', he would maintain, but only as dust and ashes.

The actual placing of the repeated statement prevents the closure of the 'sonnet', and very properly: we have not reached conclusion. The ten lines from 'Now the light falls' establish an actual time and place, here and now, shifting out of the continuous present tense of the first paragraph into the simple present. The lane, worn deep before roads were surfaced, is scarcely wide enough for the modern van; the dahlias are a flower introduced since Eliot's ancestors left the village in the seventeenth century; and 'hypnotised' is a relatively recent word for putting the mind to sleep. These slight effects indicate a remoteness, even a severance from the past, and underline the emptiness of the sleepy present day. But there is no especial significance registered in these lines, and it is just that which is their significance. Like the visitor's snapshot they catch only the obvious; while the past he is seeking is become mysterious, and must be patiently attended upon – 'Wait for the early owl.'

The vision 'In that open field . . . On a summer midnight' is one in which ancestral figures are perceived by the historical sense which governed the initial meditation upon ancestral houses. The sentences here are really musical divisions, each one a distinct section in the development of the complete dance. The first combines intimations of folklore and *The Golden Bough* with phrases out of Sir Thomas Elyot's *The Boke Named The Governour*; the second is all from this last; the third resumes the folk ritual, and develops a more immediate sense of the dance, only to end upon the dancers' being long since dead; the fourth sentence then expands the dance of the dead into the dance of nature; and the three short final sentences make a coda, bringing the dance of natural life to its close in 'Dung and death'. It seems to me unmistakable – yet many readers want to have it otherwise – that Eliot's treatment of living and of generation, of both the human and the primordial energies of nature, orders them into a dance of death. A heavy falling measure becomes dominant in the fourth sentence –

Lifting heavy feet in clumsy shoes,
Earth feet, loam feet, lifted in country mirth
Mirth of those long since under earth
Nourishing the corn.

– and this measure persists to its fulfilment in the leaden close –

The time of the coupling of man and woman
And that of beasts. Feet rising and falling.
Eating and drinking. Dung and death.

What is that but a more fully realised vision of 'earth/Which is already flesh, fur and faeces'? It is certainly not *Burnt Norton*'s dance 'at the still point'.

But what of those solemn, celebratory lines from Sir Thomas Elyot? Well, Eliot told John Hayward that 'the public intention is to give an early Tudor setting, the private that the author of The Governour sprang from E. Coker (apparently born in Wilts but his father was the son of Simon E. of E. C.)'.[7] That is worth knowing; but it tells us nothing of what Eliot thought of his ancestor and his book. To find that out we must first look at the book itself, and then consider what Eliot makes of it. *The Governour,* one of the outstanding products of early Tudor Humanism, is a programme for the education of a Christian gentleman and statesman. It recommends dancing as being 'as well a necessary studie as a noble and vertuouse pastyme', and as a mirror of the humane virtues desirable to be cultivated in a Christian society. The chapter from which Eliot quotes explains 'Wherfore in the good ordre of daunsinge a man and a woman daunseth to gether':

It is diligently to be noted that the associatinge of man and woman in daunsing, they both observing one nombre and tyme in their mevynges, was nat begonne without a speciall consideration, as well for the necessarye coniunction of those two persones, as for the intimation of sondry vertues, whiche be by them represented. And for as moche as by the association of a man and a woman in daunsinge may be signified matrimonie, I coulde in declarynge the dignitie and commoditie of that sacrament make intiere volumes, if it were nat so communely knowen to all men . . .

But nowe to my purpose. In every daunse, of a moste auncient custome, there daunseth to gether a man and a woman, holding eche other by the hande or the arme, whiche betokeneth concorde. Nowe it behovethe the daunsers and also the beholders of them to knowe all qualities incident to a man, and also all qualities to a woman lyke wyse appertaynynge.

A man in his naturall perfection is fiers, hardy, stronge in opinion, covaitous of glorie, desirous of knowlege, appetiting by generation to brynge forthe his semblable.

The good nature of a woman is to be milde, timerouse, tractable, benigne, of sure remembrance, and shamfast. . .

Wherfore, whan we beholde a man and a woman daunsinge to gether, let us suppose there to be a concorde of all the saide qualities, beinge ioyned to gether, as I have set them in ordre. . . And in this wise *fiersenesse* ioyned with *mildenesse* maketh *Severitie; Audacitie* with *timerositie* maketh *Magnanimitie;* . . . *desire of knowlege* with *sure remembrance* procureth *Sapience; Shamfastnes* ioyned to *Appetite of generation* maketh *Continence*, which is a meane betwene *Chastitie* and *inordinate luste*. These qualities, in this wise beinge knitte to gether, and signified in the personages of man and woman daunsinge, do expresse or sette out the figure of very nobilitie; whiche in the higher astate it is contained, the more excellent is the vertue in estimation.[8]

Now it must be apparent that Elyot's vision of life is nearly the reverse of Eliot's; and that his phrases have been placed in a context which is jarringly at odds with his Humanism. The difference between their points of view can perhaps be traced back to an earlier chapter in which Elyot glances at an association of dancing with rustic pursuits and country matters. He declares himself to be not of the opinion of those divines who constantly repeat Augustine's saying, 'that better it were to delve or to go to ploughe on the sonday than to daunse'; although he concedes that it might have been well said in idolatrous times, before the pure religion of Christ was everywhere established, when the dancing might have been in honour of such pagan gods as Venus and Bacchus; yet even so, he remarks, Augustine meant no general dispraise of dancing, for 'in his comparison he preferreth nat before daunsing or ioyneth therto any viciouse exercise, but annecteth it with tillynge and diggynge of the erthe, whiche be labours incident to mannes lyvynge, and in them is contained nothynge that is vicious.'[9] There speaks the Humanist. But another mind might have been reminded of Genesis iii, 19 and 23:

In the sweat of thy face shalt thou eat bread, till thou return unto the ground; for out of it wast thou taken: for dust thou art, and unto dust shalt thou return.
Therefore the Lord God sent him forth from the garden of Eden, to till the ground from whence he was taken.

It is in a context very near to this that Eliot places his distinguished ancestor's praise of dancing; and the effect of preserving the antique diction, in the midst of his own 'timeless' statement, is surely to emphasise Elyot's being out of touch with that permanent truth of nature. 'Humanism as a way of life, and in particular as a way of education, is not enough', Eliot said in 1941:

it cannot change the will of those who worship false gods. It is powerless against the drifting desires or torrential passions which turn by turn provide the motive force for the mass of natural men. Humanistic wisdom can provide a helpful, if in the end joyless nourishment for the intelligent educated individual – on another level, there is a comparable wisdom of the countryman rooted in village tradition and the life of the countryside and the procession of the seasons – but it cannot sustain an entire society.[10]

Though its immediate application was to contemporary humanists, that reads like a critique of *The Governour*; and it should correct the illusion that the passage of *East Coker* under consideration affirms a humane vision of life. A final gloss upon the closing lines, from the 1929 essay on Dante, should put the question beyond dispute:

A great deal of sentiment has been spilt . . . upon idealizing the reciprocal feelings of man and woman towards each other . . . : this sentiment ignoring the fact that the love of man and woman . . . is only explained and made reasonable by the higher love, or else is simply the coupling of animals.[11]

Since Elyot, with his sense of the natural nobility of men and women, had nothing to say of this kind of 'higher love', Eliot would be only consistent in regarding his 'association of man and woman in daunsinge' as simply the coupling of beasts.

Some intimation of Eliot's higher love may be discerned in the lines which close the movement. 'Dawn points', by a kind of bilingual pun, suggests both the breaking of day (cf. French *poindre*), and that being a sign. It could be a distant allusion to Arnaut's joyfully seeing before him the day he hopes for, in *Purgatorio* XXVI. In the second sentence there is a clear recollection of the moment when Dante, having left behind the dead air of Hell, turns his steps toward the Mount of Purgatory: 'The dawn was vanquishing the breath of morn which fled before her, so that from afar I recognised the trembling of the sea.'[12] Eliot's version of that anticipates the sea of *The Dry Salvages,* and the view from the promontory on which stands a shrine to the Lady. It is his devotion to her, one may safely suggest, which makes him free from the here and now of the merely living and merely dying, the hell of those alienated from God. But what it means to be thus 'In my beginning' has yet to be realised.

The basically octosyllabic passage which begins the second movement is not so much a lyric as a dramatic chorus. It does not express the poet's own response to the end of the world, but rather a commonplace or conventional response. We should not be put out when he declares it 'not very satisfactory': how could it satisfy the author of *Burnt Norton* IV, failing as it does to perceive the still centre of the whirling world, and falling so far short of the silent Word? The poet's own 'intolerable wrestle/With words and meanings' has another pattern in view than chaos, a pattern at once within and beyond the pattern of nature. But this vision is exclusively natural.

The poetical fashion of the first seven lines is one Eliot has used before: at the start of *The Waste Land*, in certain of the choruses of *Murder in the Cathedral* and *The Family Reunion*, and for the merely natural voice in *Burnt Norton* II and IV. It involves a quasi-identification, if it is not a confusion, of human and natural states, either by a projection of feeling upon natural phenomena, or by a feeling of subjection to them. The trouble with it as a way of putting things is just that it is 'poetical'. We are given no definite fact, and no definite feeling; but simply the vague unease or suppressed panic of a mind caught in a disturbed dream. Is the disorder real? or is it simply a derangement of mind? What we can be sure of is that this vision is very different from that of the first movement. In place of those authoritatively objective perceptions of a final order of human culture and the natural universe, this gives no more than a minor subjective drama, and one which goes no further than the strange sensations of things seeming not as one would expect. The attention has shifted from the facts, and the meaning of the facts, to nervy impressions.

The next ten lines transpose this state of mind into a mode that is specifically of the English Renaissance, which Eliot characterised as 'the period between the decay of scholastic philosophy and the rise of modern science'.[13] The literary models for this mode are in the Tudor translations of Seneca – for example, the choruses which close *Thyestes* IV and *Hercules Oetaeus* III and IV; in some of Marlowe's 'over-reaching' magniloquence; in Donne's *Anatomie of the World*; in the discourses upon cosmic disorder spoken by Titania in *A Midsummer Night's Dream* and Ulysses in *Troilus and Cressida*; and, of course, in Burton's *Anatomy*, and in Milton. In short, the passage becomes a study in the well-worn Renaissance theme, the Decay of Nature. It would appear to be observing the same end of the world as the first movement, only on a grander scale and in a more dramatic fashion. But the critical discrimination to which we are urged – that wrestling with words and meanings which penetrates through the rhetoric to the ethical and moral meaning – discovers a radical difference of attitude. We are faced with the inverse of a paradox: the two things apparently the same are really in contradiction. The end of the world from this Renaissance viewpoint is the opposite of the end of the world in the Christian view. For one thing, the style does not fix the mind on the facts in such a way as to require a personal submission to fate, but rather makes a dramatic spectacle of them, and invites us to adopt 'an *aesthetic* rather than a moral attitude'.[14] We have been here before, with Gerontion, Eliot's first and fullest study of the old man whose wisdom is only 'the knowledge derived from experience'. We may recall also that he considered that attitude to be rooted in a stoicism endemic in periods of 'dissolution and decay', a stoicism which is 'the reverse of Christian humility', and 'the refuge for the individual in an indifferent or hostile world too big for him'.[15] The final lines of the passage carry the allusion to Senecan stoicism into the realm of science or 'the New Philosophy'; and here there is a connection with Eliot's view of the determinism of Hobbes, whom he described as 'one of those extraordinary little upstarts whom the chaotic motions of the Renaissance tossed into an eminence which they hardly deserved and have never lost'. That is to say, he did not allow for man's being able to understand, and then freely assent to necessity:

For a philosopher like Hobbes has already a mixed attitude, partly philosophic and partly scientific; the philosophy being in decay and the science immature. Hobbes's philosophy is not so much a philosophy as it is an adumbration of the universe of material atoms regulated by laws of motion which formed the scientific view of the world from Newton to Einstein. Hence there is quite naturally no place in Hobbes's universe for the human will; what he failed to see is that there was no place in it for consciousness either, or for human beings.[16]

For that last comment to make sense, 'consciousness' and 'human beings' need to be given a quite special meaning, deriving from that moral and theological idea which Eliot is implicitly opposing to the 'scientific' view, as he elsewhere opposes it to the 'aesthetic' attitude.

That view and that attitude are, one gathers from the essays I have been referring to, but two sides of the one state of sensibility, one which arose in the Renaissance and has persisted unabated into the modern world. Its root is the taking a merely natural view of things; or, to put it the other way, its ignoring the Word of God. The consequence is that instead of 'humility', the proper response to the Word, there is submission to mere natural law. This would appear to be what the choric passage as a whole is dramatising, first in a more or less contemporary, and decadent, 'poetical' mode, then in a manner which represents something of its origins in Renaissance 'philosophy'. It is distinctly not the way in which Eliot would choose to put things.[17]

To dismiss it he has recourse, here as in the corresponding section of *Burnt Norton* II, to a style of moral philosophy which might be modelled upon that of Bradley. This second part of the movement, as it meditates upon the knowledge derived from experience, keeps close to the rhythms and diction of current speech; and yet achieves the precision and pointedness of highly intelligent prose as it seeks to penetrate to the value of such knowledge. Then there is what gives it the inner tension and pulse of verse, a passion to reach through accurate knowledge to final wisdom. The passage goes some way towards justifying Eliot's remark, made in 1942, that 'if the work of the last twenty years is worthy of being classified at all, it is as belonging to a period of search for a proper modern colloquial idiom'.[18] But the music of poetry, he observed on the same occasion, while it 'must be a music latent in the common speech of its time', arises at a point of intersection between the present sense and the past history of words. In effect he was restating the argument of 'Tradition and the Individual Talent', in which a main point was that 'the difference between the present and the past is that the conscious present is an awareness of the past in a way and to an extent which the past's awareness of itself cannot show'. Precisely that is likely to be the difference between 'a proper modern colloquial idiom' and 'a worn-out poetical fashion'; that is, the former will be the expression of a timeless or universal point of view.

That this is the case in the main part of this movement is evident from both its overall structure and its style of argument. Although it starts prosaically and with a gesture of dismissal towards poetry, it yet finds its conclusion in two lines of pure poetry. Again, the wrestling with 'words and meanings' proves to be not so much a philosophical investigation of usage and the things words refer to, as a matter of putting a certain construction upon them. The ladder of philosophy is kicked away at the close, as Wittgenstein urged, but it has not actually been climbed; for the action has been no more than a dramatic expression of the poet's own point of view. Thus the question of the value of experience is raised in a form which assumes that the answer is already known; and the deceptions are similarly assumed. Yet to what exactly does 'the autumnal serenity/And the wisdom of age' refer? And who precisely are 'the quiet-voiced elders'? There is no real investigation of the autumnal – such as there is, for example, in Keats' ode. Nor do these phrases really fit anything or anyone so far presented in the poem: Sir Thomas Elyot is hardly to be characterised by them, though Eliot has perhaps done his best to mute him; and the Renaissance poets generically alluded to in the choric lines rather went in for fatalistic magniloquence. What we are being given are not the actual characters of men and things, but simply Eliot's view of them, his sense of their value. That 'the autumnal serenity' is 'only a deliberate hebetude' is not a statement of fact, but merely the assertion of a point of view; and so too is 'The wisdom only a knowledge of dead secrets'.

This point of view is first directly declared in the lines

> For the pattern is new in every moment
> And every moment is a new and shocking
> Valuation of all we have been.

That is to affirm, in the place of 'the knowledge derived from experience' which 'imposes a pattern, and falsifies', just the immediate experience itself; and it is to affirm, moreover, not any value in experience, but just its being a valuation of ourselves. The question of value has been turned, so that man is not now the measure of experience, but is measured in every moment. It would be hard to say of what this immediate experience consists, for *the* pattern is evoked in a sequence of allusions which rather suggest what it is like to experience experience than anything specific. What they amount to is an account of its deceptiveness, ranging from Dante's dark wood of human error, through Brer Rabbit's bramble and Sherlock Holmes' mystery, to 'fancy lights' which could be will-o'-the-wisps or the party decorations in *Le Grand Meaulnes*, and even into the realm of fairy tale. If this is what experience is truly like, in the immediate moment, then its valuation of us must be that so far as we exist in the world of experience our being is unreal and illusory. To be undeceived is to know that all we know is a deception.

The dramatic rhetoric now rises to its climax, in which the dismissal of old men develops a strangely positive irony:

> Do not let me hear
> Of the wisdom of old men, but rather of their folly,
> Their fear of fear and frenzy, their fear of possession,
> Of belonging to another, or to others, or to God.

The folly and the fear are made to point towards what it is clear the poet himself affirms, so that their human failings must be their best wisdom. Moreover, the implicit affirmation is the exact reversal of the natural expectation evoked at the start of the argument. The value looked forward to then was in the possession of what would naturally belong to us – a sense of possession placed in the phrase 'Bequeathing us merely a receipt for deceit'. Now, that value having been changed into a valuation of ourselves, and one that would prove us valueless, there is the further and final turn from seeking to possess to being possessed, and from referring things to ourselves to giving ourselves up to what is other – and ultimately to God. The concluding statement of the argument puts this as if it were an axiom or first principle –

> The only wisdom we can hope to acquire
> Is the wisdom of humility: humility is endless.

So the only acquisition to be realistically hoped for involves dispossession of all that human nature prides itself upon.

The whole passage has been 'criticism from a definite ethical and theological standpoint';[19] and being essentially an assertion of that standpoint, it is most substantive when it presents it most directly. It is not an elucidation of human wisdom to characterise it by deceit, folly and fear: that is evidence rather

215

of the point of view from which it is being judged. As for the evidence of the truth of the wisdom of humility, that is all in the force with which the point of view is maintained, in the wrestling with experience, and in the submission to 'the pattern' and to God. The final proof of it is in the tone of fully resolved assent in the concluding statement of 'The only wisdom'. This is the appropriate form of proof, since its real basis is an act of will, of moral choice: the truth-value is not based upon experience, but is ethical and theological. What the passage has been moving towards, then, by its own imperative logic, is an immediate statement of its basic conviction and assent, and this it achieves in the two lines which close the movement –

The houses are all gone under the sea.

The dancers are all gone under the hill.

That, I take it, is the true, and traditional, music of poetry; in which human history is resolved into a timeless humility. That is to say, it is the order of poetry affirmed by the moral philosopher and the critic within this poem, as well as in his prose writings from 'Tradition and the Individual Talent' up to 'The Music of Poetry'.

It is worth pausing to notice that these first two movements of *East Coker* correspond fairly exactly in structure to those of *Burnt Norton*. Again the first movement presents a natural experience; again the second begins with a way of putting it which is unsatisfactory because incomplete; and again the proper attitude is then defined as a total submission to 'reality'.

The third movement takes up the darkness of those who have lost the light or are blind to it: the dark under the hill; the dark of Milton's blinded Samson; perhaps of Milton himself, as a voice of the new mind formed in the Renaissance; the darkness of mind of old men peering into the darkness or turning their eyes from it; the 'dark in the afternoon' of banal, unilluminated existence; Dante's dark wood, which is the whole way. Just as in *Burnt Norton* III, this darkness is to be so accepted and entered into that it shall become 'internal darkness', which is a 'darkness to purify the soul', being known as 'the darkness of God' – 'So the darkness shall be the light'. The pursuit of the wisdom of humility also follows the way down as the only way up.

Along with this close relation to *Burnt Norton* there is a remarkable difference of tone, amounting to a significant development of sensibility. In the earlier Quartet the attitude to the world seemed that of a man lacerated by a life he could neither accept nor escape, but only negate: 'Not here/Not here the darkness, in this twittering world'. In *East Coker* the actual world of the Underground and the theatre and the hospital is at least allowed to supply analogous forms of darkness and emptiness; with the result that instead of a simple negation of the world of experience, the mind is now carried through its banalities towards 'that which is not world'. Moreover, the poet does not here set himself apart from others in alienated superiority, but includes himself in 'the silent funeral' of existence. The satire in that roll-call of the departing – who are arranged as upon a wheel of fortune – has a certain humour to it, and makes 'a solemn game' of the inevitable, by applying the high-sounding but hollow rhetoric, which Eliot thought Marlowe and Milton especially good at, to hollow worldly pretensions.[20] The attitude to the moments of ecstasy is similarly altered. In *Burnt Norton* it was a matter of all or nothing; but here they are defined in brief, vivid images, and accepted simply as

> echoed ecstasy
> Not lost, but requiring, pointing to the agony
> Of death and birth.

This is indeed to repeat something he has said before – the lines resume the action of *Burnt Norton* – but with the difference, manifest throughout the entire movement, that the attitude which he was then struggling to achieve is now a resolved habit of sensibility, that is, of thought *and* feeling together.

That gives to the movement a calm assurance which is near to stasis: it is not complacent, but nor is it anxious or urgent as the first two movements were, and as *Burnt Norton* was. The mood is that of confident waiting, and not now for the early owl. This mood is broken by the insistence, pedantic or preacherly, upon the idea of the *via negativa*. The violence here must be deliberate, and designed to unsettle any feeling of having already arrived. The passage of doctrine is a paraphrase of chapter 13 of book 1 of John of the Cross's *The Ascent of Mount Carmel*, a treatise upon 'this dark night through which the soul passes in order to attain to the Divine light of the perfect union of the love of God'.[21] This work, and its companion *The Dark Night of the Soul*, have been behind the treatment of the dark throughout the movement, notably in the directives 'I said to my soul be still . . .' But now we are being made to *think* what they mean, and what 'the agony/Of death and birth' means.

Those two prose treatises of John of the Cross are an exposition of his poem *En una noche oscura*, 'wherein the soul sings of the happy chance it had in passing through the dark night of faith, in detachment and purgation of itself, to union with the Beloved'.[22] In his case the song preceded the exposition of the doctrine; but Eliot follows the reverse procedure, which is the one called for in his Clark Lectures, for his fourth movement, the Good Friday lyric, is an attempt to transmute the doctrine by the operation of poetry into immediate feeling. The paradoxes of the dark night are treated in a mode calculated to make them 'a new and shocking/Valuation of all we have been'.

The form of the stanza is adapted from that of John of the Cross's poem, which was an expression of the baroque mode of sensibility characteristic of the Catholic counter-Reformation. Its English exponents included not only Crashaw and Southwell, but Donne in some of his religious verse, and Andrewes in his 'Sermon on the Passion: Good Friday 1604'. But of course it is a mode to be associated with Catholic Europe and not with Protestant England. Now one might think that Eliot's baroque lyric was quite as much a 'study in a worn-out poetical fashion' as 'What is the late November doing'. Yet, in its structure at least, it stands against that unsatisfactory view of the decay of nature, and realises the pattern of humility declared in the intervening parts of the poem. But that it should do this in a mode which has been superseded can be a difficulty even for sympathetic modern readers. To appreciate it, we need to see it as part of the general strategy of the three Quartets, in their effort to re-order 'the mind of Europe', which consists of its historical as well as of its present culture. The mind of *East Coker* is a modern one conscious of its specifically Renaissance origins, of which, on the whole, it has been deeply critical. To revive the poetical mode of the counter-Renaissance, in order to express its own convictions, is to demonstrate their origins in that time; and to essay a contemporary mind founded upon them, which would be the contrary of that which has actually developed out of the Renaissance. It is not just a point of view which is being asserted, but an alternative cultural tradition.

That doesn't mean that Eliot thought the baroque state of sensibility an entirely satisfactory one. In his Clark Lectures he had maintained that the Spanish mystics and the Jesuits, by the very intensity of their efforts to stimulate emotional fervour, had contributed to the cultural disintegration of Europe, and accelerated the transition from the old Europe to the new ('to the Europe, we might say, of 1914'). They had turned religion and theology away from the classic pursuit of metaphysical truth towards psychology; that is, from the apprehension of the universal 'reality' into the analysis of one's own sensations. The consequence – evident to Eliot in Donne, and above all in Crashaw, the typical representative of the religious and devotional mentality of Europe – was 'a separating out of sound, image and thought'; an emphasis upon feeling as against thought; and the presentation of 'a sequence of emotions, or of emotional sensations, rather than a coherent structure of emotions'. And this was a falling away from the definite intellectual structure to be found in Dante. These remarks should lead us to expect that Eliot's intention in taking up the baroque mode was not to celebrate the disorder manifest in its violence and excess, but to correct it. They should alert us, moreover, to the way in which he uses its characteristic wit, not simply to stimulate feeling, but to intensify the apprehension of the metaphysical truth which should have been its object.

The intellectual structure of the lyric is signalled emblematically in the seventeenth-century manner. There are five stanzas of five lines each: five being, as Hopkins conveniently put it, the 'sake/And cipher of suffering Christ'. The first stanza states the theme of a universal sickness that must be its own cure, in immediately human terms (even to having a topical wartime overtone), but with the echo of the biblical 'Physician heal thyself' opening the theological perspective. The second and third stanzas develop the theme through Old Testament and New Testament terms of reference. The fourth brings it home to the personal conclusion. Then that, and the whole, finds its stay in the explicit statement that Christ's dying in the flesh is the saving of our mortal being. In each stanza, and through the lyric as a whole, the wit moves from the striking paradoxes towards the thought which resolves them into simplicity. It moves, that is, away from the baroque fascination with sensational effects and towards wholeness of mind. The rhythm works towards the same end. Each stanza unfolds, through the dynamics of the precisely stressed sense, to reach the thought upon which it may rest; and the succession of stanzas unfolds a progressive structure of thought, driving strongly and confidently to affirm first the necessity and finally the goodness of holy dying. All this is to reunify sound, image and thought; and to do so by using sound and image to make the thought real. There is a telling alteration of John of the Cross's stanza. In *En una noche oscura* it is the second and fifth lines that are longer, and the double contraction and expansion serves a sustained pulsation of emotion. By starting with three taut octosyllabic lines, and then effecting a single powerful expansion through the lengthened fourth into the still longer final line, Eliot makes the feeling reach towards its intellectual conclusion. Each final line, moreover, is controlled by a caesura which at once clarifies the thought, and makes the mind move to its measure. The baroque mode is thus altogether made over from being a predominantly emotional one, into one which is metaphysical in Eliot's special sense.[23]

For all the definiteness of its intellectual structure, the lyric closes upon a statement of unresolved tensions: 'In spite of which we like to think ... Again, in spite of that, we call this Friday good.' Then the first passage of the fifth movement which, just as in *Burnt Norton,* seems to arise out of and have immediate application to the lyric, recognises that this has been just one more raid on the unspoken. It was necessary to attempt to repair the damage done in the Renaissance, so far as that was the beginning of the disintegration of the mind of Europe. Yet while he is implicated in that moment of history, the poet is also 'elsewhere'; and the Good Friday meditation must be taken as just one in the total pattern of timeless moments which constitutes his history of his people. So he moves on from it to the further studies of the timeless moment in the New World of *The Dry Salvages,* and in the 'Now' of *Little Gidding.*

The implicit theme of this fifth movement is the *detachment* which will be more fully developed in the following Quartets, especially in their third and final movements. Now the remarkable thing about this detachment, which may be thought of as the practical side of 'the wisdom of humility', is that Eliot's 'humility' should have a practical side at all. For the acceptance of the ordinary sphere of human action which it involves was just what the poet had been progressively removing himself from in *Ash-Wednesday, Burnt Norton* and *The Family Reunion.* However much he might accept his human fate, there was always that basic contempt for the world which came from setting the Word against all its words and works, and which prevented his taking any real part in it. But now, in the 'So here I am' passage, he presents himself as in the world and of it; and joins his action as a poet – the act of reparation in 'The wounded surgeon', and in the Quartet as a whole – with the activity of Britain at war. The colloquial ease and simplicity are the direct expression of his participation in the war effort. There is none of the strain and difficulty of the corresponding passage of *Burnt Norton,* arising from the impossibility of identifying words and the Word. And there is a very different tone from that of the related lines in Chorus IX of *The Rock:*

> Out of the slimy mud of words, out of the sleet and hail of verbal
>   imprecisions,
> Approximate thoughts and feelings, words that have taken the place
>   of thoughts and feelings,
> There spring the perfect order of speech, and the beauty of incantation.

– that is, as the implicit analogy declares, when it is the Creator who speaks. But the force and the tone of the passage in *East Coker* come from there being no sense of contradiction between the poetry and the war effort. The poet appears to have the same feeling for both, and to be able to view each action in the terms of the other, as if they were really different forms of the same essential struggle.

>   And so each venture
> Is a new beginning, a raid on the inarticulate
> With shabby equipment always deteriorating
> In the general mess of imprecision of feeling,
> Undisciplined squads of emotion. And what there is to conquer
> By strength and submission . . .

The relation there to the current speech and the common action of the early 'phony' phase of the war is very much nearer than in the analogies of III. It is not a case of the known being used to convey the mind towards an unknown which is supposedly more real; but of two things equally real, which the mind must hold together in the one perception. In this way the poet too is taking up his position, along with those noticed in 'Defence of the Islands', and doing his bit to mobilise the nation's resources to save Europe.

That being said, there is something else to be remarked. This familiar use of the common speech depends upon his not declaring just here – what he had been at pains to assert in II – that his idea of what is worth fighting for is an uncommon one. This reserving of his real position, while it enables him to create a sense of community, also makes it a very partial one, and possibly subverts it. For to speak within the limits of a common understanding, but secretly to mean more than will be commonly understood, is to lead others on. A possible justification is given in the argument of chapter II of *The Idea of a Christian Society*, where it is said that while 'a conscious Christian life' is not to be expected of 'the great mass of humanity', 'as their capacity for *thinking* about the objects of faith is small', yet 'their Christianity may be almost wholly realised in behaviour', which 'is as potent to affect belief, as belief to affect behaviour'.[24] Thus to urge detachment upon those who were risking their lives to win the war, in the form of 'For us, there is only the trying. The rest is not our business', was to try to bring those who would not consciously follow 'the wisdom of humility' at least to act as if they did. But this means that the Christian poet's sympathetic participation in the war is strictly delimited: he is joining with his fellows only at the level of behaviour; and only upon condition of being able to place his own interpretation upon their common action. He is all the time conscious of it as 'the one action . . . Which shall fructify in the lives of others'; but this consciousness, the style of the passage implies, is beyond them.

'Home' – which would mean among other things the Home Country, much imperilled in 1940 between Dunkirk and the Battle of Britain – 'is where one starts from.' Other associations overlay that one, so that the personal and private meaning dominates. We are made to think of the poet's own childhood home and the treasured photograph album;[25] and of Andrew Eliot starting out from East Coker for the New World. Then this removal into the private experience becomes a reaching towards the universal –

> Here or there does not matter
> We must be still and still moving
> Into another intensity
> For a further union, a deeper communion

So the poet moves from the temporal ('So here I am') into the timeless, his proper realm, and the basis of his only real community.

The final section of *East Coker* is remarkable for the way in which it gathers up a succession of themes and ideas with an accelerating energy and deepening excitement. It is indeed making a beginning of the end and moving into another intensity. The leading preoccupations of the Quartet are recapitulated, in a manner which recalls their treatment in *Burnt Norton* and marks their further development, and which is at the same time an introduction to the continuing exploration of them in *The Dry Salvages*. In fact, in the final lines we are virtually beyond *East Coker* and entered upon *The Dry Salvages*; so that this is not so much a bridge passage, as a fusion of the coda to the one with the introduction to the next. That is to make of the two Quartets a single, continuous work.

There is a disconcerting flatness about the start of *The Dry Salvages*. Is it a lapse? Or does Eliot know that this is cliché and bathos, and is he doing a straight-faced parody? When the author of *After Strange Gods* begins 'I do not know much about gods' – having just urged us towards 'a further union, a deeper communion' – I think we may take it that he doesn't much want to know about them; nor, for that matter, about the uses of rivers.

At the same time the passage does make a dissociation between the primitive idea of the river as 'a strong brown god', and what is made of it in the march of progress. The leaden periphrases of the record of man's conquest of nature register a progressive alienation from both elemental and human nature: 'Then only a problem confronting the builder of bridges' – 'the dwellers in cities' – 'worshippers of the machine'. The savage's 'strong brown god', though it comes as a rather dull perception, is nevertheless made to stand out against that –

> ever, however, implacable,
> Keeping his seasons and rages, destroyer, reminder
> Of what men choose to forget.

That emphasis is elucidated by some remarks in an introduction to *Huckleberry Finn* which Eliot wrote in 1950:

Mark Twain makes you see the River, as it is and was and always will be . . . As with Conrad, we are continually reminded of the power and terror of Nature, and the isolation and feebleness of Man. Conrad remains always the European observer of the tropics, the white man's eye contemplating the Congo and its black gods. But Mark Twain is a native, and the River God is his God. It is as a native that he accepts the River God, and it is the subjection of Man that gives to Man his dignity. For without some kind of God, Man is not even very interesting.[26]

The river as destroyer (and preserver) becomes explicitly Mark Twain's near the end of the second movement – 'with its cargo of dead negroes, cows and chicken coops'.

In the opening lines it is not so much Twain as Whitman that will be brought to mind: the Whitman who made himself the voice of that America in which the apotheosis of the individual was somehow identified with the conquest of nature by technology. His ambition was, as he put it in *A Backward Glance O'er Travel'd Roads*, with which he closed his last edition of *Leaves of Grass* (1891–2),

to articulate and faithfully express in literary or poetic form, and uncompromisingly, my own physical, emotional, moral, intellectual, and aesthetic Personality, in the midst of, and tallying, the momentous spirit and facts of its immediate days, and of current America – and to exploit that Personality, identified with place and date, in a far more candid and comprehensive sense than any hitherto poem or book.

To Eliot's 'calamitous annunciation' Whitman, with his very different sense of the 'Profession of the calamus',[27] might have retorted in the terms of his Preface to the 1855 edition of *Leaves of Grass*:

Did you suppose there could be only one Supreme? We affirm there can be un-numbered Supremes, and that one does not countervail another any more than one eyesight countervails another . . . and that men can be good or grand only of their consciousness of their supremacy within them. What do you think is the grandeur of storms and dismemberments and the deadliest battles and wrecks and the wildest fury of the elements and the power of the sea and the motion of nature and of the throes of human desires and dignity and hate and love? It is that something in the soul which says, Rage on, Whirl on, I tread master here and everywhere, Master of the spasms of the sky and of the shatter of the sea, Master of nature and passion and death, And of all terror and all pain.

As the self-proclaimed American Bard, Whitman represents pretty well every-thing American and modern from which Eliot is dissociating his own poetry. Yet he meant more than that to him, just as America meant the primitive as well as the modern: 'Beneath all the declamations there is another tone, and behind all the illusions there is another vision. When Whitman speaks of the lilacs or the mocking-bird, his theories and beliefs drop away like a needless pretext.'[28] This is the Whitman of 'When Lilacs last in the Dooryard Bloom'd', an elegy for President Lincoln. A line from that poem, 'With the tolling tolling bells' perpetual clang', is echoed in the sombre and wholly serious later part of the movement; and of course the title itself is alluded to in the closing lines of the first paragraph, which are surely not written in parody.

In fact those lines effect a reconciliation with Whitman and America – a kind of homecoming. They are like four snapshots from the album of memories: intimate, American, dated. They are also, in their being in touch with intimate personal experience and giving it a shape – that of the four seasons of natural life – a return to order after the barbaric yawp. The shape, the pattern, is that of 'the wisdom of humility' stated in its simplest form, at once particular and universal. This is the point at which the inner continuity with the true introduction – 'Home is where one starts from' – is resumed. Musically, it is a matter of finding the home key at last, the right relation of the personal and the primitive, of the natural and the human orders. This vision, and not that other inflated and alienated pride in human achievements, is the America Eliot would explore.

The first ten lines are the kind of study in an unsatisfactory way of putting man's relation to nature, which we would expect to come at the start of the second movement if the structure of the previous Quartets were being followed. Its coming instead as a false start to the Quartet as a whole is a further indication – the first was that its real beginning is in the close of *East Coker* – that *The Dry Salvages* is not simply repeating the now established form. If we keep in mind these hints that there is an 'inner unity which is unique to every poem, against the outer unity which is typical',[29] we will find that the second movement begins, not with an unsatisfactory way of putting it, but with a necessary and accepted patterning of experience, and one which will be not corrected but completed by the fourth movement.

With the shift from the river to the sea the theme announced at the end of *East Coker* is explicitly taken up, to be developed in a continuous progression through to the end of the sestina. The whole of this part of the Quartet is an exercise in calling to mind 'what men choose to forget', in the form of personal, communal and racial memories of the sea. The three sections of the main passage of I enact the rhythm and the sounds of the sea, moving from the seashore, to sailing upon it, to an apprehension of its elemental ground swell; and moving also through the states of mind of the curious child, the sensitive sailor, and the anxious women burdened with the wisdom of experience. The sestina then resumes all such memories in a patterned meditation which, while insisting that the absolute of experience is 'the endless/Journey to no end', yet affirms an end – through the looking-glass, as it were, in a realm of meaning beyond sense.

In the first movement we are caught up in a steadily expanding consciousness of 'reality'. Childish curiosity, which 'searches past and future/And clings to that dimension', is modified by the warning 'It tosses up *our* losses'; and the section closes upon the solemnly drawn out 'And the gear of foreign dead men'. The mind's awed reflex is expressed in a fanciful form: 'The sea has many voices,/Many gods and many voices.' But the two purely musical phrases supervene – rather in the manner of those which closed *East Coker* II – and carry the sense of loss to the heart of personal experience. (Their images connect this awakening of consciousness with those of 'Dans le Restaurant' and *Marina*.) The sea's voices are then heard with an ear sensitive to 'the power and terror of nature', but not yet with full understanding. There may be something of Poe there – from *The Descent into the Maelstrom* – the Poe whom Eliot admired for his emotional sensitivity, and from whom Mallarmé and Valéry learnt something toward their own method of superimposing one reality upon another. But that the sea's many gods are doubled with the voices of dogs, while it directly serves the immediate emotional effect, marks the critical reserve of one who does not know much about them. From 'The distant rote in the granite teeth' – another echo of *Marina* – the mood deepens and develops in the way, according to Eliot, Poe's failed to do.[30] The third section, beginning with a powerful surge in the rhythm at 'And under the oppression of the silent fog', gathers the many voices into the one voice of the tolling bell; with its powerful restless movement as it enters the consciousness of the 'anxious worried women', it connects the elemental rhythm of the ocean with instinctive fear and terror, and the sense of man's helpless subjection to fate.

The sestina continues the treatment of this theme, but in a different mode, and with some significant variations. There is nothing specifically associated with childhood; but the first stanza, which repeats some images from the first section of the preceding account of the sea, has also that striking image of the autumn flowers which is like the mature essence of Eliot's poems of early youth. Even if one takes that stanza as simply an impersonal statement of the theme of the sestina, the answer given to its questioning in the following two stanzas is more individual and personal than anything in the sea-passage of I. In contrast, stanzas four and five express an explicit concern with the life of a community. Here he might be thinking of the fishermen of Gloucester, Mass., about whom he had written in 1928, 'There is no harder life, no more uncertain livelihood, and few more dangerous occupations . . . Gloucester has many widows, and no trip is without anxiety for those at home.'[31] These variations bring us to a rather more immediate experience of the 'sea of life', and a more conscious one, at first on the private level and then on the communal.

The form makes us speak of this as a lyric, though it is not so much the direct expression of feeling, as a meditation upon the feelings just presented. We might just as well call the mode philosophical. But then its thought is of that special, poetic, kind, which is not a thinking about experience but a thinking of it: a thinking in which the intelligence is *realising* what is known. Its function is to complete the experience of the first movement in the understanding of its meaning – to restore it 'in a different form'.

The proper approach to the meaning is through the form. Here, however, there is a small difficulty to be faced. It has become accepted that the form is a variant of the sestina, and I think it profitable to take it as that. One very good reason is that the sestina was the invention of Arnaut Daniel in the *trecento*, as Eliot liked to call the age of Aquinas and Dante; and that its strict discipline is the perfect antithesis of the Whitmanesque free verse sonnet of the opening fourteen lines, and a good example of those Old World traditions which Whitman rejected as 'a denial and insult to democracy'. The difficulty is that Eliot's variation upon the sestina, his repeating the same terminations in the same order in each stanza, happens to correspond with Daniel's usual practice in his *canzoni*; so that he might not have been imitating the sestina at all, but simply following another model. There is just this to support the critical consensus, that Daniel's sestina is the only one of his *canzoni* with a stanza of six lines.

Daniel's one sestina, his 'song of the fingernail and uncle', has six stanzas of six lines each and a coda of three lines. In each stanza the lines end with the same set of six words; but their position alters each time according to a complicated rule. If they are numbered from 1 to 6 in one stanza, then in the next the order will be 6, 1, 5, 2, 4, 3 – *retrogradatio cruciata*. At the end of the series of permutations the word that stood in the first line comes in the last – not counting the coda – so that the poet ends where he began. (Besides this, the terminal words rhyme, in three pairs; and each line of the coda ends with one of these pairs, the two words finally standing next to each other.)

Eliot has departed from this in a number of respects. He has no coda – though his final stanza is something like a coda in the way it gathers up the whole. He uses the same set of terminal sounds only, not words, except for the first and last stanzas, and the recurrence of 'annunciation' in the third. But the major difference is that his terminations are repeated in a fixed sequence, so that there is no progression – and in this lies the most interesting relationship. The only progression beyond the fixed pattern, for Eliot, is by the change of the meaning of the key-word, 'annunciation'; and the effect is to make the end a wholly new beginning.

Daniel's is a poem of sexual desire: Would I were hers in body, not in soul. The rod (*vergua*) is transformed from one he fears into the flowering rod: hence in Paradise will my soul have double joy, if ever a man through fine loving enters there. The coda sends the song to the Desired One. The poem could be regarded as a folly such as Dante had his Arnaut weep for; and Eliot's then would be one in which 'the errors of Arnaut are corrected'[32] – what he should have sung had he come in good time to 'a practical sense of realities'.

Dante also wrote one sestina, 'Al poco giorno ed al gran cerchio d'ombra', closely following Daniel's which he praised in *De Vulgari Eloquentia*. This too is a love poem, but in the spirit of the *Vita Nuova*, affirming an undying and all-quenching love for a Lady dead and in the ground. Here the form enacts the changing seasons of nature only to confirm what cannot be changed: her death and his love. Both Dante and Daniel thus use the form to express, though not at all in the same sense, the constancy of love in a world of change. It would appear that Eliot has used it simply to enforce the constancy of change: to enact the fixed pattern of man's life in nature. Yet if the pattern of fate when rightly understood is a calamitous mode of 'the one Annunciation' – that is, of Love which 'is itself unmoving,/Only the cause and end of movement' – then his sestina too is expressing the constancy of Love in a world of change. He has made it a form for apprehending 'the drawing of this Love and the voice of this Calling'.

If one follows the significance of the sestina in this way, then its end should be 'the sudden illumination' which reveals another pattern in experience than that of the temporal sequence or development, and which stills what is in itself forever unstill. In spite of that, the detail of the pattern remains endless movement: the immediate reality of 'a lifetime's death in love' is the agony of dying. When we enter into the detail we find the poet exercising all the resources of his craft, in imitation if not in emulation of *il miglior fabbro*, in the effort to make the endless movement immediately and totally real. A main effect, everywhere repeated in varying forms, is the doubling of negative impressions – as in 'the soundless wailing', and 'Dropping their petals and remaining motionless' – where the '-less' form takes away the action of loss which yet continues.[33] Again, the lyric is almost wholly composed of words which have a falling measure, upon the pattern of 'soundless', 'motionless', 'emotionless'. As line endings these leave the lines unstopped, the one always lapsing into the next. At the same time the basically four-stress line is drawn out, beyond the eight or ten syllables that would be normal, into eleven or twelve or more. But then this dragging time serves to weight and to ponder over the sense. When we come to that, it is remarkable how plain and firm a statement is being made: there is no failing or falling away in the mind perceiving and meditating upon these things. This is not an anxious, worried mind, but one living and dying without fear and terror, wholly resigned.

The conscious resignation which informs the sestina at every point is what must make the ending right. Without that it would be a mere play upon words, or the imposition of one meaning upon another in the way that Becket's meaning is imposed upon the natural fears and terrors of the women of Canterbury. But the mind in the sestina has been throughout at the point of intersection of the natural experience and the understanding which accepts it as the divine will, in submission to which is our peace. Thus it is not just in the final turn but all the way that the annunciation of death has been pointing to and requiring the Annunciation of Christian birth. However, this reading of the sestina depends on our having followed Eliot's meaning very closely through the later 1920s and the 1930s; and still one may feel that the inner sense all hangs upon the mere addition of a capital letter. One must remember, then, that the lyric does not stand alone: it has its relations with what has gone before; and it will be explicated in the rest of II and in III, and completed in IV.

As in the previous Quartets, the rest of the second movement is given up to thought; but while it grows out of and has direct application to its lyric, as we would now expect, it also rather pointedly resumes the train of thinking of *East Coker* v. When we recall how much that had behind it, we perceive that in fact the thinking in all the more philosophical parts of the work has been continuous and cumulative, and that it has been consistently pursuing the one preoccupation with right knowledge and right action. At this point in *The Dry Salvages* it takes a simpler and more directly practical form, as the thinking comes closer to living. The philosopher criticising knowledge, wanting to *know* what is real, and the poet trying to *see* reality, begin to merge into Eliot's saint, who seeks to be wholly at one with what is. For the saint the stages through which the Quartets move – experience; knowledge, or the critique of experience; wisdom, or the critique of knowledge; vision, or the immediate experience of the 'higher' reality – should culminate in 'right action'. But that, we shall discover, is rather a mode of being than anything we should ordinarily call action.

The argument is not easy to follow; yet it is at bottom starkly simple. The first section (from 'It seems, as one becomes older', down to 'the primitive terror') recapitulates the theory of the two preceding Quartets, and subsumes into it the experience so far encountered in this. If we are to avoid assigning the wrong meaning to 'happiness', we need to bear in mind what has been made of such moments of happiness as 'the laughter in the garden' of *Burnt Norton* I: it has become one item in that brief index of 'hints followed by guesses' which point to 'the agony/Of death and birth'. Here is the place to note, moreover, how 'Pleasure in the wind, the sunlight and the sea' – which shows in many of the earlier poems, and which has behind it, as we can sense, some of Eliot's own most intense sensations of boyhood and youth – has become in *The Dry*

Salvages a totally different experience, being wholly transfigured by the meaning imposed upon it. We have seen the poet working towards this, in the painful emotion surrounding the vivid sea images in *The Waste Land,* the 'confession' of them in *Ash-Wednesday* VI, and the awakening to a new consciousness of them in *Marina.* Yet if the *meaning* of them has been from the beginning 'death by water', that has been most readily, and not altogether satisfactorily, appreciated in the agony of others such as Phlebas and the waiter.[34] In *The Dry Salvages* his own personal feeling of the romantic hope and ecstasy of the sea is at last fully resolved into the meaning, so that it is his own past experience, and not only that of others, which is restored in a different form.

What then takes the place of happiness – which is made to seem so dull after all in the heavy parenthesis – and the place also, in memory, of the original experience, is 'the sudden illumination'. We have seen this in *Burnt Norton,* where the actual experience of the rose-garden is resolved into a consciousness of its ultimate reality. What we have to take in now is that 'the sudden illumination' is the form of experience that is being affirmed: the original experience, and the original happiness, are lost in the ecstatic consciousness of the meaning. Given the nature of that, we may be reminded of Aristotle's observation that we take pleasure in tragedy because in that way of experiencing suffering and death we gather the (universal) meaning of things.

In the second section (from 'Now, we come to discover that the moments of agony') the argument takes a new turn. I don't mean the equating of the moments of agony with the moments of happiness, in that both may be moments of illumination: that, shocking as it may be, follows quite logically, since the meaning to be made out in the happy experience is that it is really the agony. The new development, so far as I can make it out through the parentheses and elisions, is that the moments of agony are being affirmed as an immediate experience of ultimate reality. That is, they differ from what the poet had appeared to be seeking, in that they are not the experience of one drowsing in sunlight and enjoying a sudden illumination of the meaning of things; they are rather moments of primary experience, like the experience before the meaning; only they are a direct experience of the meaning. Consequently 'meaning' as such, which has been mediating between 'experience' and 'experience in a different form', no longer figures here. The 'agony' is all. We may measure the effect of this by thinking again of Aristotle on tragedy, and of the Greek sense of *agony.* The protagonist, as in *Samson Agonistes,* is the hero who acts and suffers – whose action is suffering, as Eliot has Becket put it, and his suffering action. Now the move from affirming 'the sudden illumination' to affirming 'the moments of agony', is a move from the position of the spectator, gathering the meaning, to that of the hero wholly caught up in the action.

'For most of us', however, 'this is the aim/Never here to be realised'; for most of us, there is not the 'lifetime's death in love', but only the moment of illumination, 'The distraction fit, lost in a shaft of sunlight'. The 'agony of others' then assumes its importance, as a timeless moment in which the pattern concealed in our own living is revealed. Thus the relation of 'most of us' to 'the saint' is, after all, that of spectators gathering the meaning to which he bears witness.

The third movement completes the argument by adapting the practical wisdom which the Divine Lord Shri Krishna addressed to the hero of the *Geetā* 'on the field of battle':

> ' "on whatever sphere of being
> The mind of a man may be intent
> At the time of death" – that is the one action
> (And the time of death is every moment)
> Which shall fructify in the lives of others:
> And do not think of the fruit of action.'

One would suppose at first that death is the one action in question. But then that is incorporated into the larger statement: that the one action is that the mind of a man be intent. If we may take it that the sphere of being intended is that of the timeless – which is, after all, what the whole work has been directed towards – then what we are being asked to receive is a reaffirmation of the illuminated state of consciousness, as the state of mind to be cultivated in the immediate experience of being mortal. This adds a new dimension to the agony; or rather, it declares the significant action to be not the suffering of one's fate, not that in itself, but the being in a state of illumination while doing so. This is the antithesis of the old men in *East Coker* II, intent only upon their own sphere of being. It is also a clear stage beyond the darkness and stillness urged upon the soul in *East Coker* III: the *via negativa* has led on to the direct apprehension of the timeless in time.

The argument is carried further yet, by the statement which is Eliot's own extension of the *Geetā*: 'that is the one action . . .Which shall fructify in the lives of others'. Before considering this, however, I would remark the significance of his having had recourse to the *Geetā* at all. It can be taken as an allusion to his reading in the Brahmin scriptures while a graduate student at Harvard; and as a kind of tribute to the Harvard culture of that era, and to the American idealism of which it was a product. One gathers from *After Strange Gods* that Eliot regarded this high-minded interest in the wisdom of the East as a phenomenon of the decay of Protestantism. Nevertheless, he was grateful for having had the opportunity to study the *Geetā*, 'the next greatest philosophical poem to the *Divine Comedy*' within his experience;[35] and one which had, beyond the philosophy and the ideas so different from his own,[36] a wisdom 'the same for all men everywhere'.[37] His use of it in *The Dry Salvages*, characteristically, makes good the suspect modern interest by eliciting this universal wisdom.

The words quoted from it come from chapter VIII, entitled 'The Life Everlasting'; and from that part of it in which Krishna is replying to Arjuna's question: 'and at the time of death how may those who have learned self-control come to the knowledge of Thee?' Eliot has rather abbreviated the reply, possibly because he means to distil just its essential wisdom, and it may help to give it a little more fully:

'Whosoever at the time of death thinks only of Me, and thinking thus leaves the body and goes forth, assuredly he will know Me.
'On whatsoever sphere of being the mind of a man may be intent at the time of death, thither will he go.
'Therefore meditate always on Me, and fight; if thy mind and thy reason be fixed on Me, to Me shalt thou surely come.'[38]

Most of what Eliot's voice descanting has to say, if not directly from the *Geetā*, is at least after its sense and spirit; but his extension of the one action into the lives of others is an exception, and a notable one. It goes quite beyond the exclusive concern for the individual soul shown by Krishna and Arjuna – that the hero alone should be released from the endless cycles of reincarnation into union with the One and All. And it springs of course from Eliot's own sense of communal responsibility, felt intensely at the outbreak of the war and a patent motive in the wartime Quartets. But what is implied by 'the fruit of action' goes very much deeper than would appear – to the very deepest sense of *The Dry Salvages*.

The voice which speaks from ' "Fare forward" ' to ' "this is your real destination" ' is not Krishna's, but one heard 'At nightfall, in the rigging and the aerial'. There is an aural pun to make us think, in the absence of anything more definite, of Ariel, and spirits of the wind and air, who may be angels and messengers of the Lord. In IV the word 'angelus' recalls, from its use in the Catholic devotion, the angel's annunciation to Mary that she would conceive and bring forth the Word of God as the fruit of her womb. An analogy with that is surely implicit in the urging to conceive the supreme sphere of being as the one action which shall fructify in the lives of others. That is to speak, one begins to understand, of Incarnation. The protagonist, hero or saint, dying in communion with Love, brings the Word into being in the world, and so becomes at once like the Mother of God, and an agent of the Holy Spirit. In *The Family Reunion*, Agatha is to Harry both a spiritual mother and a lover who, having conceived the Word in herself, can bring it to fruition in him also. Perhaps Harry's opaque statement of what he is going to do in following the bright angels implies the same action. Within *The Dry Salvages*, the 'anxious worried women' might be receiving, as in an annunciation, the agony of their sons and husbands 'whose bodies/Will suffer the trial and judgment of the sea' – at least their agony is received by the poet in that sense; and he in his turn is both conceiving the action of the Word in the world, and trying to make it fructify in the lives of others.

This allusion to the process of birth – conceiving, bearing and begetting – is fundamental to *The Dry Salvages*, only it has been wholly converted from the natural to a metaphysical sense. What is in question is the regenerative process of the New Life. Now in this there are relationships impossible in nature: 'Figlia del tuo figlio', daughter of thy son; and it is relevant to think of the transitions from a beloved to a divine mother figure in *The Hollow Men*, *Ash-Wednesday* and *The Family Reunion*.[39] These complications arise from the comprehension of Incarnation as meaning the birth of the Word in the world, and not only – as has been hitherto the emphasis in Eliot's work – as meaning the death of the world and the flesh. The simple will to transcend the life of nature involved the negation of it; but this regeneration does it the greater violence, and is the harder to follow. To remove from one sphere of being to another while leaving each essentially unchanged is one thing; but to make *actual* 'the impossible union/Of spheres of existence' is a very different matter. Here words in their ordinary sense must fail. Just as we cannot say 'the end precedes the beginning', we can hardly think of dying as being born, let alone as bringing new life into being in others. Yet 'a lifetime's death in love' means that, means all that it says in its holding in the one phrase 'life' and 'death' and 'love', with their mutual contradictions not cancelling each other but made somehow to fulfil each other: so that life is death, and death in love is life in another sense.

This manner of converting the meaning of things is quite as much in the Christian tradition as, let us say, the denunciation of the world in *Ash-Wednesday* v. Christianity did not simply cast out Venus: it set up the Virgin Mother in her place. Once it was Venus, born of the sea, goddess of love and generation, whose shrine stood on the promontory – as at Terracina in central Italy. In May 1948 the three-day celebration preceding the blessing of the fishing fleet of Gloucester, Mass., opened with the arrival of a wooden statue of Our Lady of

And there shall be signs in the sun, and in the moon, and in the stars; and upon the earth distress of nations, with perplexity. . .
And then shall they see the Son of man coming in a cloud with power and great glory.
(Luke xxi, 25 and 27)

With that somewhere in the air, it is small wonder the verse can proceed so naturally to affirm the apprehension of the saint.

The writing from that modulation through to the end of the movement is musical to a quite extraordinary degree, given that it is a passage of highly concentrated and complex thought. Each sentence has its own distinct meaning and form; yet the whole passage is a seamless statement through which the thinking flows lucidly and powerfully. Reading it, we are compelled to follow the sense by the construction of the verse: the pauses at the line-ends are used for emphasis and impetus –

> The point of intersection of the timeless
> With time

– and by the living movement of the lines which, while equivalent to each other, are constantly varying in their internal stress and pace. The longer line has a basis of five stresses, the shorter of three: if there are fewer than the norm the line slows with the weight, if more it quickens and lightens –

> That it is not heard at all, but you are the music . . .
>
> Here the past and future
> Are conquered, and reconciled

The essence of this art is the mastery of phrasing: the shaping of the sense so that it sounds exactly right. The complement of that is the musical composition of the phrases, so that the whole is organically articulate.

What this art is creating is the poet's wholly distinctive voice and mind – the voice and mind of the Quartets – at its subtlest and strongest so far. We have heard it throughout, of course, but most clearly in those passages of meditation which are here resumed. Yet there has not been before the same degree of completeness and immediacy. A certain assertiveness or strain, as in *Burnt Norton* II and V, could betray a partial realisation; or there could be the sense, as in *East Coker*, that the poet was rather consciously talking to himself or to others. Here the thought is so finally formed that it seems simply to exist 'out there', as much as any lyric vision. It remains thought; but it is surely just as much a crystallisation of the mind, though in the realm of ideas. The mind is absorbed in its thought, and in a state of clarity, wholeness, and immediacy. In the terms of Christian mysticism, this is the state in which the soul, not yet wholly united with its object, is illuminated with the intelligence of it: the state

Good Voyage (Mary, Star of the Sea), which the fishermen had purchased from Lisbon.[40] Eliot had not known of the existence of a statue of the Madonna when he wrote *The Dry Salvages*, though apparently there was one on a church in the town, but had 'thought that there *ought* to be a shrine of the B.V.M. at the harbour mouth of a fishing port'.[41] Eliot's transformation of the associations of the sea is in line with this conversion of Venus. There is its association with the birth of life and of love, and then it is the element into which the residue returns. In Eliot's sestina all this becomes simply an endless dying. But then, when that has been connected with Incarnation, death by water comes to mean again birth and love, only metaphysically.

When we have followed out the argument of II–III in this way, we may find in IV the 'Prayer of the one Annunciation'. It is addressed to 'Figlia del tuo figlio,/Queen of Heaven' as to the first Christian and the model for all others. The phrase from the first line of the final canto of the *Paradiso* is presumably an allusion to all that is said there, in St Bernard's prayer on Dante's behalf, concerning her role in aiding the spirit who would attain the divine vision. It is pertinent to recall also that the prayer is the culmination of Dante's love poetry; and that it is spoken by a Doctor of the Church, as a member of the Church in Heaven. Thus the *dolce stil nuovo* becomes at the last the voice of the communion of saints. In just the same way the voice of the poet, who at the end of *East Coker* I appeared to be alone on the promontory, is now joined in prayer with his fellow Christians, with all who are involved in the one action of Incarnation. The movement has the simple language, direct syntax and deliberate rhythm of a prayer to be said in common (a collect). It is oratory, not as eloquence, but as devotion; and it expresses the feelings, not of an individual, but of a community. The poet's art is subdued to all this; yet it serves to realise the inner form of the prayer. At first we seem to be reading something so close to prose as scarcely to be verse at all. But if we observe the slight pauses at the end of each line, the consequent emphasis upon the terminal words just pulls the apparently formless invocation into a definite shape. We find then that it is formed about ll.9–10 as about a still centre, towards which the first lines reach, and to which the sense of the last returns us.[42]

This is not quite the voice of Dante's communion of the saints in Paradise. It is rather the voice of Eliot's idea of a possible Christian society: 'not a society of saints, but of ordinary men, of men whose Christianity is communal before being individual.'[43] I take it that the prayer is meant to give a Christian form to the natural life of the community represented in the first two movements. And I take that to be an advance, in his view, upon the Christian society of the seventeenth century as represented by the Good Friday lyric; as well as an alternative to modern democracy – the democracy celebrated by Whitman. The prayer bespeaks a community in which a humble submission to fate is distinguished by a serenity arising from the perception of its divine pattern and purpose.

We can now make out more clearly than in *East Coker* v the special sense in which the poet is joining with others in a human society and a common action. That passage left open what was being fought for. In *The Dry Salvages* v it is stated explicitly, dogmatically, that what is in question 'is Incarnation'; and that accounts for the way in which ordinary life and death have been viewed with increasing detachment throughout the Quartet. One measure of this detachment is that the war, actually in progress when the poem was written and published, figures so remotely. One must suppose that 'you whose bodies/Will suffer the trial and judgment of the sea', and the last section of the prayer, include (as 'Defence of the Islands' put it)

> those appointed to the grey
> ships – battleship, merchantman, trawler –
> contributing their share to the ages' pavement
> of British bone on the sea floor

Yet such sailors, like the fishermen, are considered only in their relation to the 'Perpetual angelus'. If not indifferent to the common experience, the poet is certainly preserving his detachment from it; and he is joining with others only so far as their lives conform to the divine order.

We should put with this the fact that in *The Dry Salvages* the natural world has been accepted as expressing the Word. Up to *Burnt Norton* it was the contradiction of the one by the other that was most stressed. *East Coker*, however, perceived the contradiction as a paradox, and resolved it: the darkness of earth, seen as the darkness of God, shall be the light. Thence, in *The Dry Salvages*, 'the dark cold and the empty desolation' is made the direct way to the divine union; so that in the poet's vision, or the saint's, the world now means the Word.

The main part of its fifth movement, stating the metaphysics of Incarnation, comes therefore as the proper conclusion of the double-quartet, *East Coker– The Dry Salvages*. Its function is to establish the *idea* of what the poetry has been exploring and enacting – to supply the doctrine of right action, or orthodoxy. Here the poem shows the dogmatic belief which is from one point of view its ground: the Rock which is the ideal form of 'the ragged rock in the restless waters'. Now it is to be noticed that the poet's struggle with words and meanings is not directly attended to here, as it is at this point in the other

Quartets; instead it is the struggle of the saint to be at one with the Word which is affirmed. But this means that 'Incarnation' is being declared, not as an idea or belief simply, but as a way of life, a mode of existence.[44]

The movement begins with that startling drop from the prayer into a satiric exposure of false witness. 'To communicate with Mars, converse with spirits' is as discordant, following 'the sound of the sea bell's/Perpetual angelus', as was 'I do not know much about gods' after the close of *East Coker*. That was what the poet had to start from in his given world, and here again he is starting from where he is – the world into which the Word is to be received now. The contemporary equivalents of the false prophets, and the teachers and priests who did not know the Messiah when he appeared in the flesh, are a mixture of modern knowledge and ageless superstition. The decadent survivals of primitive religion among the sophisticated and the merely credulous, mingle with the efforts of technology to outdo science-fiction, and of psychoanalysis to explore beyond the limits of conscious experience. This is Eliot's 'modern mind', a mind aware only of the temporal and without 'the historical sense'. Its ways of unravelling the pattern of things are parodied with an appropriately modern sense of style. The mode is not that of the alienated preacher–prophet, crying Woe to these false prophets! or '*Curiosity the finest of the passions*! Vanity of vanities!'[45] It is rather that of the bland satiric turn which the unreflecting victim might take in all seriousness. Yet beneath the straightfaced solemnity there is a disconcerting wit. 'To communicate with Mars' glances at the war and disaster generally, as well as at 'worshippers of the machine'; and conversing with spirits, a back-to-front sort of annunciation, could have unpleasant consequences – as Friar Bacon and Faust discovered. 'To report the behaviour of the sea monster' is a suitably portentous way of noticing the journalists' fun and games at Loch Ness, which are of course a way of choosing to forget reality. The apparently random particulars become unified in the perception that these are all ways of flirting with fate instead of facing it squarely. Beneath the mockery there is the recognition – as with Madame Sosostris – that there is something to them, only it is something which they occlude. The inevitable need be no riddle, and what is ridiculous is to make it one.

The implicit viewpoint from which the satire is directed is that of the Word, and this begins to declare itself at the close of the long first sentence, in the superb modulation from mock-seriousness towards the true intensity of 'But to apprehend . . .'. The change is managed so confidently in the rhythm, and what is said sounds so natural, that one takes in almost unaware what is brought to focus in the Edgware Road. The immensity of it appears only when we catch the echo of Christ's warning of the end of the world:

in which the darkness becomes the light, or in which the meaning is heard so deeply that the soul is the meaning.

The final lines – slowing to make a full close, yet with a strong, even beat that is no dying fall – would have us assent, now that we understand it, to the fate asserted in *East Coker* I:

> We, content at the last
> If our temporal reversion nourish
> (Not too far from the yew tree)
> The life of significant soil.

'Reversion' implies giving back what is left after death to its donor and heir: as in 'dust thou art and unto dust shalt thou return'. But to have it 'nourish ... The life of significant soil' is to attach a value to living and dying in time beyond the mere dust, as in the end of *Burnt Norton,* and beyond the ashes in the earth of *East Coker.* There is now the suggestion of a positive cultural tradition; only it is the tradition of 'old stones that cannot be deciphered', which are part of the 'lifetime burning in every moment' – the tradition affirmed again at the end of *Little Gidding*:

> And any action
> Is a step to the block, to the fire, down the sea's throat
> Or to an illegible stone: and that is where we start.
> We die with the dying:
> See, they depart, and we go with them.
> We are born with the dead:
> See, they return, and bring us with them.
> The moment of the rose and the moment of the yew-tree
> Are of equal duration. A people without history
> Is not redeemed from time, for history is a pattern
> Of timeless moments.

There is Eliot's special view of history, and his idea of a cultural tradition is the same: a Christian culture consists of men united in the one right action of Incarnation. In this action there are but the two perpetual moments, that of the yew-tree with which *East Coker–The Dry Salvages* has been concerned, and that of the rose, introduced in *Burnt Norton* and made one with the yew in *Little Gidding*'s symbolism of fire. Then the temporal is seen as simply the other side – or rather as *this* side – of the timeless. And all this is absolutely the reverse of the democratic vistas opened by Whitman.

Those interconnections point the way into *Little Gidding*; but before entering into it we may well pause to look back over the work of which it is to be the completion. To be clear about what has been achieved is also to form an idea of what yet remains to be done; and we should be in a position now to map out the poem in a way which will project the whole. One dimension of the experience of the final Quartet is how it meets the expectations we bring to it from the preceding ones.

In each Quartet there are images of birds and flowers, and these, through the musical progression of their associations, constitute a pattern of signs. In *Burnt Norton*, the rose and the lotos are 'answered' by the sunflower, clematis and yew; and the thrush by the kingfisher. (There is also 'dust on a bowl of rose-leaves' succeeded by the Chinese jar.) In the later Quartets the bird sequence is a clear paradigm: the early owl – the petrel and the seagull – the dark dove with the flickering tongue. The flowers are more complex, however: the dahlias – the roses and briars of 'frigid purgatorial fires' – the briar rose with the sea salt on it – the transitory blossom of snow, and the white may – the burnt roses – the spectre of a Rose – and the final rose which is fire also, and the full 'answer' to the roses in the garden of *Burnt Norton*. Taking just these signs, even thus abstracted, we can make out an ordered progression through the realm of sense and nature towards a metaphysical vision. At the end of *The Dry Salvages* we can understand what that means; yet it is beyond the orders of experience and philosophy already attained, and to realise that vision fully is going to require a further development, a new order of poetry.

We can guess at its nature from the tendency already observed, for instance, in the topical references to the war. In *East Coker* we were near to the actual war and the Army in training; in *The Dry Salvages* the Navy is nearly merged with all those who are in ships; in *Little Gidding* the Blitz, with allusions to fire-bomb watching and the Air Force, will be inseparably associated with, and subdued to, the operations of the Holy Ghost. Moreover, there will be the shock of learning that the places which also are the world's end were not, in Eliot's mind, the wartime scenes that would have been one's first thought in 1942. According to John Hayward's notes for the French translation, which were compiled with Eliot's help, 'the sea jaws' were associated with Iona (cf. *Murder in the Cathedral*) and with Lindisfarne where St Cuthbert retired to die; 'a dark lake' was Lake Glendalough in Co. Wicklow where St Kevin made a hermitage; 'a desert' was associated with St Anthony of Egypt and other solitaries, and 'a city' was the Padua of the other St Anthony. I suspect that these are likely to remain just Eliot's private associations, but to know of them is to be directed towards the sphere of being upon which his mind was intent.

It is a commonplace that each Quartet has its associated element: earth in *East Coker*, water and fire respectively in the two following. To complete the scheme the element of *Burnt Norton* should be air – and the lyric in *Little Gidding* II does establish that association. But in fact its element, if that is the right word, is light. In the typescript for the printer of *Collected Poems 1909–1935* there were two further very short lines after what is now the final line; the second of these is now illegible, the other was 'Light' – connecting that early Quartet with the two last choruses of *The Rock*. But we should not need that tip to see that air figures only as the vehicle of light, as 'vibrant' or 'faded'; and so to see that the scheme of four elements was conceived only when the three Quartets came to be written. Certainly it is the case that it is only to them that it properly applies. Now the significant thing in this scheme, as in Heraclitus, is the transmutation of the elements, and the moving from one element to another. Earth's bone-fire, stilled, becomes the purgatorial fire; dust and ashes nourish significant soil; water, transmuted, signifies rebirth; the fire, again, becomes tongued, pentecostal, the final element of life and breath and of the multifoliate rose. Thus the scheme gives not a fixed but a dynamic structure, and is the formula for a series of changes which, if rightly followed, resolves all the elements into their quintessence, an ultimate and unchanging whole.

There is a related scheme of correspondences and progressions in the topics of the later Quartets – again *Burnt Norton* does not really belong to it. This can be most conveniently set out in the table below. The correspondences are all progressive; and they plainly indicate, so far as a map can, where the poem is heading.

East Coker	*The Dry Salvages*	*Little Gidding*
The Old World	The New World	The whole History
Old men, forefathers	Mothers	The fruitful dead
The death of earth	Death and Birth by water	The dance in refining fire
Disintegration of the 'mind of Europe'	Re-founding the Christian society	A people redeemed from time in the Communion
Hell: alienation from God	Sanctity: conceiving the Word	Purgatory: right action
The dark night	Illumination of mind	Union with the divine
Absolute paternal care	Annunciation/Incarnation	Pentecostal fire
Christ (the New Man)	The Mother of the Word	The fire is the rose of divine Love

To appreciate the structure as a whole we need to follow the progression both within each Quartet and through their sequence. In each of the three later Quartets – once again *Burnt Norton* remains somewhat apart – the five movements are in effect five steps or stages by which the mind advances towards the absolute which is its goal. These may be roughly labelled: I the world of experience; II the knowledge derived from experience; III the practical sense of history; IV its metaphysics, affirmed in prayer or vision; V the metaphysical, thought out into conscious wisdom. That gives the relatively straightforward structure, founded upon the hierarchy of the instruments or modes of knowledge observed above in *Burnt Norton*. But the structure becomes, not more complicated, but more taxing, when there are three (or four) Quartets composing a single work. For each begins from the level of knowledge and wisdom already attained, and ascends through its own five steps on a higher plane and towards a further level. In the later Quartets these levels may be labelled respectively according to Eliot's three orders of Nature, Mind, and Grace or Charity – which I have shown to be the basis of his mature art. There is the 'lower' experience which breaks down in transitoriness, suffering, death – this is the initial predicament. Then there is the taking thought about it, seeking to penetrate through the natural human understanding to the divine cause which is its 'higher' meaning. Thirdly there is the effort to live according to this meaning and to be at one with the divine. In these terms, *East Coker* proceeds from the merely natural life and understanding into the wisdom of humility; *The Dry Salvages* carries that wisdom on to a positive consciousness of the divine; *Little Gidding,* presumably, will seek to complete the divine union. The difference between one level and another shows not in the outward, 'objective' experience – which remains much the same in kind – but as a development of the understanding, and of the way in which the experience is perceived and accepted. In the light of mere experience, as Eliot would say, the natural world means dung and death; in the light of the wisdom of humility it is a purgatorial fire; and in the full light of Love, in *Little Gidding,* that will become one with the multifoliate rose of Heaven.

The structure I have been making out is hinted at in the coda to *Burnt Norton*, where 'the figure of the ten stairs' is an allusion to John of the Cross's *Dark Night of the Soul,* in which – in chapters 19 and 20 of book II – he explains 'the ten steps of the mystic ladder of Divine love, according to Saint Bernard and Saint Thomas'. The first five are the stages of the Dark Night of Faith, the *via negativa*; the next five are the stages of the illuminative way, by which the soul mounts upward toward the Beatific Vision.

The tenth and last step of this secret ladder of love causes the soul to become wholly assimilated to God, by reason of the clear and immediate vision of God which it then possesses; when, having ascended in this life to the ninth step, it goes forth from the flesh.[46]

Beyond this is a third state, called the unitive way, in which the soul, having left the flesh and the world, is fully and finally oned with God. I do not think that an adequate explication of the Quartets is to be found in John of the Cross; but there is at least a useful analogy between those two sets of five steps which make up 'the figure of the ten stairs', and the two flights of five steps in *East Coker–The Dry Salvages*; and those do lead on to the way of final union.

Another and still more suggestive analogy is to be found in chapter 58 of Julian of Norwich's *Revelations of Divine Love*:

I saw the blessed Trinity working. I saw that there were these three attributes: father-hood, motherhood, and lordship – all in one God...

Our life too is threefold. In the first stage we have our being, in the second our growth, and in the third our perfection. The first is nature, the second mercy, and the third grace. For the first I realized that the great power of the Trinity is our Father, the deep wisdom our Mother, and the great love our Lord... We are God's creation twice: essential being and sensual nature. Our being is that higher part which we have in our Father, God almighty, and the Second Person of the Trinity is Mother of this basic nature, providing the substance in which we are rooted and grounded. But he is our Mother also in mercy, since he has taken our sensual nature upon himself. Thus 'our Mother' describes the different ways in which he works, ways which are separate to us, but held together in him. In our Mother, Christ, we grow and develop; in his mercy he reforms and restores us; through his passion, death, and resurrection he unites us to our being. So does our Mother work in mercy for all his children who respond to him and obey him.

Grace works with mercy too . . . The work is that of the Third Person, the Holy Spirit...

Thus in our Father, God almighty, we have our being. In our merciful Mother we have reformation and renewal, and our separate parts are integrated into perfect man. In yielding to the gracious impulse of the Holy Spirit we are made perfect.[47]

That throws much light, of course, upon the doctrine embodied in *The Dry Salvages*, and it also shows how that doctrine can give rise to the full set of correspondences tabulated above.

Those two connections, with John of the Cross and Julian of Norwich, suffice to demonstrate how essentially and traditionally *Christian* the structure of the Quartets is. To the modern mind it has proved rather elusive; in the Catholic middle ages it would have appeared the obvious and necessary structure for a poem ordered according to the Christian idea. It is the structure of *Piers Plowman*, though there too it has eluded the modern mind, which regards that great work as rambling and formless. And it is unmistakably behind the three divisions of the *Divine Comedy*, where another – and perhaps the most ready – analogy with the Quartets is to be found. Now that connection has the advantage of providing a place for *Burnt Norton*, when we consider the relation of the *Vita Nuova* to the main work: for that first Quartet is also a transmuting of love from its human to its final cause, and so the groundwork for the major argument of Love. For an interesting gloss on the relationship one could draw on Colin Still's account, in his *Shakespeare's Mystery Play*, of the lesser and the greater initiation rites. The lesser is through Mist into the Air of Elysium, or the Earthly Paradise; but the greater initiation is a passage from Elysium, through the experiences of Earth and Water and Fire, to the celestial Paradise.[48] That gives just a glimpse of the more primitive rituals which lie behind the Christian ordering of the universe, and which Eliot was of course fully conscious of. But it was the traditional, which in his view means the timeless, Christian structure which he was enacting in the *Four Quartets*.

It should be clear that the whole work has a fully developed and complex organisation, and that the later Quartets do not simply repeat the structure of *Burnt Norton* three times over. What happens is that the first Quartet is not repeated but expanded and developed into the larger work. *East Coker* does follow it fairly closely – though it begins, not where it has reached to, where the light is, but back in the darkness of the dance of death. The essential likeness is that it proceeds by reversing the natural in the mirror of the divine: 'So the darkness shall be the light'. *The Dry Salvages*, however, does not pass again through that mirror, but goes on from its further side, the natural being now so understood that it can be developed directly towards 'the one Annunciation'. (The cryptic headnote gave the clue: *les trois sauvages* becomes The Dry Salvages, pronounced to rhyme with *assuages*.) *Little Gidding*, we may be sure, will seek to complete the whole. A remark of Eliot's about the *Divine Comedy* is to the point here. 'The *Purgatorio* is the most difficult because it is the transitional canto: the *Inferno* is one thing, comparatively easy; the *Paradiso* is another thing, more difficult as a whole than the *Purgatorio*, because more a whole.'[49] That wholeness is approached in the end of *The Dry Salvages*; and its essential nature was declared in the first draft in two lines which followed 'Are conquered and reconciled' –

> And here is implied Atonement
> And Atonement makes action possible.

The 'right action' which follows from being at one with Christ – that is what we should expect to find in *Little Gidding*.

Little Gidding has its own specific form or 'inner unity'. The two outer movements are its introduction and conclusion; and the three central movements are the successive stages of a single continuous action. The poem starts by passing beyond 'the scheme of generation', with the spirit receiving 'pentecostal fire/In the dark time of the year'. Its central action is a progression from nature's bonfire to the fire of God: 'To be redeemed from fire by fire'. And its end is the ultimate form of 'the tongues of flame'. Its action all takes place, however, at the point of intersection of the timeless with time, and in the moment of 'a lifetime's death in love'.

The title, even more than in the other Quartets, is charged with significance. The place itself, ten miles north-west of Huntingdon, had not the personal associations for Eliot of East Coker and The Dry Salvages, at least so far as I know: I take it to represent a conscious election. John Hayward's notes for the French edition tell us that Eliot visited it on 25 May 1936, and he would have done so for the sake of its history. Nicholas Ferrar, in 1626, established there a small devotional community 'controlled by ideals of Holy Living and Holy Dying'.[50] George Herbert was a particular friend of Ferrar, as Walton records in his *Life*. Crashaw, who died abroad at Loreto in 1649, had been a frequent visitor. Charles I spent a night there after his defeat at Naseby in 1646. With the advent of the Puritan Commonwealth, Cromwell's troops dispersed the community, and the chapel became a ruin. Now it is as Eliot describes it:

> you leave the rough road
> And turn behind the pig-sty to the dull façade
> And the tombstone.

The name, however, preserves something of its timeless meaning. An 'ing' is a fen or water-meadow. 'Gidd' is connected with *guide*; and also with *giddy* meaning to be dazed, out of one's senses, with a root notion of being god-possessed or in a god-spell.

The opening paragraph is an immediate experience of what the name implies. The rest of the movement will present the place and its meaning as it appears to ordinary sense and notion – to what must be put off in order to receive the revelation of the world's end. This is a visionary intimation, as it were in 'The distraction fit, lost in a shaft of sunlight', of divine Love in nature. One of Eliot's best attempts at the kind of metaphysical poetry which 'elevates sense for a moment to regions ordinarily attainable only by abstract thought',[51] it succeeds not by anything mystical but by virtue of what the poetry is and does. The versification, formal and free, based upon but always departing from the pentameter, follows the inner pulse and form of the experience. The first eight lines are fairly sober description, but with the sixth and eighth standing out; then the sentence from ll.9–11 unfolds with a sudden fullness and resonance; the following three short sentences are broken into rather staccato phrases, and then again there is a brilliant lengthened statement, a sinuous unfolding of precise phrases; finally, against the falling rhythm of the close, in counterpoint, the voice rises in longing. The diction deserves special notice. It is a paragraph in which words of very different kinds are made at home with each other. Mostly they are the common words for the common world of nature – 'sodden towards sundown', 'the ice, on pond and ditches' – and these are charged with direct sensation, without any symbolic loading. But then an intensified feeling and a heightened significance, the responses of mind and spirit, are given in uncommon words out of the intellectual and religious heritage. There is the latinate 'sempiternal', in which the 'always' of time is nearly identified with the eternal 'now'. 'Pentecostal', out of the Greek New Testament, encapsulates a history in itself: the transformation of the Jewish Harvest Festival into a Christian occasion 'not in the scheme of generation'. The same history is implied in 'not in time's covenant': for the Old Testament is known also as 'the temporal covenant' of God with men, while the New Testament is the 'eternal covenant'.

Through these effects of rhythm and word the poetry moves in the two distinct spheres of nature and spirit. There is the world of sense, immediately seen; and there is the spirit's response in its own realm of meaning. In their relation lies a third, which is the realm of Eliot's kind of metaphysical poetry. This generates its energy from the co-existence of opposites: 'Midwinter spring', 'sempiternal', 'cold that is the heart's heat', and finally 'the unimaginable/Zero summer'. The passage as a whole, from 'Midwinter spring' to 'Zero summer', is constructed on that principle. Now these co-existing opposites are not like the paradoxes of the *via negativa* ('Our only health is the disease'); and they are very different from the intensifying negatives of the sestina ('the withering of withered flowers'). Their effect is to hold in tension opposing qualities, without resolving or reconciling them, and in such a way that the negative intensifies the positive. Thus the stress falls upon 'spring'; and 'Zero' carries the mind to 'a summer beyond sense'.[52] This is neither negation nor transcendence, but an intensification of what is actual, or an expansion of the actual towards the ideal. 'A glare that is blindness in the early afternoon' is not a mystical 'heart of light', but a quite natural phenomenon; only the spirit's response, receiving it as 'pentecostal fire', carries it on to another plane. Again, the demand for 'the unimaginable/Zero summer' arises inevitably from the precisely characterised 'spring' – how right, above all, 'blanched' is:

> Now the hedgerow
> Is blanched for an hour with transitory blossom
> Of snow, a bloom more sudden
> Than that of summer, neither budding nor fading . . .

244

The complete paragraph enacts what a mind intent upon the timeless sphere of being may see in nature, taking it as the ground upon which sense and spirit intersect.

There is of course a definite set towards what is beyond sense. If the first eight lines are firmly within nature, the next half-dozen are just as firmly out of it; and in the synthesis ('Now the hedgerow') the vision is intent upon what is not in nature. The transition from the one realm to the other is smoothed by the 'And' appearing to be connective, as if 'glow more intense' were another item of the same kind as 'A glare that is blindness'; whereas the 'And' in fact introduces a new development. While the syntax would thus ease the passage through the mirror, we are likely not to follow the poet fully unless we have been inwardly prepared by the preceding Quartets. This vision answers, as the second panel of a diptych to the first, the vision in *Burnt Norton*'s rose-garden; with the difference that it is fully conscious of 'reality'. In the rose-garden the mind was attached still to 'what might have been', and subject to the illusions of unregenerate memory and desire; now it is purged of all such natural feelings, and 'concentrated in purpose'. The poet has arrived at the point where everything means only one thing and is always the same – at an ultimate interpretation of experience.

The statement of this through the rest of the first movement amounts to an epitome of the preceding Quartets. The kinds of sensual experience with which they have been involved, and the usual attempts of the mind to make sense of things, are touched upon only to be summarily dismissed.[53] What remains is simply prayer – 'You are here to kneel/ Where prayer has been valid.' In that one word *valid* is concentrated the essence of *East Coker–The Dry Salvages*, since it contains notions of health and of faring well, and ties them to the idea of being true and right. Prayer, as we have been told, is not just the saying of a prayer: it is the action of receiving and conceiving the divine Word, a 'communication' which is a form of communion. Yet it is not the direct communion with the divine that is affirmed here – there is something of a hiatus where we might expect that, after being warned that prayer is more than it seems. Instead we are told

> And what the dead had no speech for, when living,
> They can tell you, being dead: the communication
> Of the dead is tongued with fire beyond the language of the living.

That is to say, I take it, that the dead are speaking the Word – that their communication is their 'one action', perfected, and fructifying in the lives of others. The implication for the living seems to be that their prayer should consist in receiving this communication, in being in communion with the dead; and that must mean that the life of prayer is Holy Dying. We are being urged then to join the Christian society implied in the prayer of *The Dry Salvages* – a society in which the dying are at one with the dead in the Communion of Saints. It should be observed that the immediate basis for this, in the poetry itself, is not a prayer or a belief, but simply the plain and eloquent statement of the idea – the being able to put it into words, and into current speech.

The lyric which opens the second movement is an ordering of the elements, and of everything in the Quartets belonging to Nature, into a round dance of death. The end, the death of fire, joins with the first word, 'Ash', to close the circle – unless it can break it after the fashion of the sestina. The pattern of changes is a progression which appears to arrive only at its beginning: fire and earth in the first stanza, as ash from the burnt roses and dust; earth and water in the second; water and fire in the third. Implicated in this pattern are the rose garden, the houses of *Burnt Norton* and *East Coker*; the soil and the sea of *East Coker–The Dry Salvages* – to the English rustic scene is added the American Dust Bowl, and *East Coker*'s fields are engulfed in the New England 'death by drowning'; and the first couplet of the third stanza seems to resume the openings of those two Quartets. But then this stanza moves into another dimension with 'The sacrifice that we denied', which might be alluding to the ruin of Little Gidding; or, again, the reference could be to the immediate spectacle of London's bombed churches, the neglect of which had long been a matter of concern to Eliot.[54]

These latter associations complicate the otherwise straightforward pattern of elements. The first stanza might be the experience of death in life, as in *Burnt Norton*. The second is death itself, with its sub-plot of the body, deprived of air and light, corrupting, becoming a grinning skeleton. The third, however, affirms a continuing power, the perpetual triumph of water and fire – they 'succeed', 'deride', 'shall rot'. The verbs move from the present to the future, whereas the governing tenses of the other stanzas were the past and the present. But in the context of 'sacrifice' and 'sanctuary and choir', the natural elements may assume religious overtones, and may just suggest the waters of baptism and purgation, and the fire of purification and the Holy Spirit. In that case the water would be the living not the dead water, and so the answer to the dust and the death of earth; and the final word would not look back to 'Ash', but toward the refining fire and the descent of the dove. This is the wisdom of humility, only it is extended now beyond nature and the personal life into the realm of history and culture – the ruin of the institution of 'the one true Church' in England has been implicitly accepted; and with that is accepted the end of civilisation, if 'the death of water and fire' is taken in the spirit of being 'born again of water and the Holy Ghost'. That this was what Eliot had in mind is made clear by these lines which immediately followed the lyric in an early draft –

Fire without and fire within
Shall purge the unidentified sin.
This is the place where we begin.

The echo of *The Family Reunion*, though it does not make for good verse, does point the meaning. Moreover, the affirmation of fire, in London during the Blitz, recalls the way in which the destruction of London by fire was viewed in *The Rock*: as preparing it for the building of the invisible church of Light.

If there were any doubt of the poet's attitude in 'the death of water and fire', the versification would resolve it. The first stanza has the suggestion of a dance in it, but one in which the feet drag and the tune dies away. There is no dancing in the second stanza, which is regular in its measure like a dead march, and with the heavier beat coming within the line so that there is no sense of a rising progression. In the third stanza, however, the movement becomes taut and energetic; and the lines reach towards their endings where the force is gathered –

Water and fire succeed
The town, the pasture and the weed.

The three final lines modulate from that pattern by the greater weight within the line of 'marred foundations' and 'sanctuary'; and in the different movement of the final line, dwelling upon 'water and fire' instead of upon 'death' as in the previous final lines. All of this enforces a positive progression of feeling, and the positive understanding which breaks the cyclic pattern of nature and makes it the straight way of the Word.

While it gathers up so much of what has gone before, this lyric is also an overture to the three central movements, introducing their themes, implying their development, and requiring the completion of 'The dove descending'. It sums up the end of nature and of human culture 'Now and in England', and it opens towards the other life of the soul atoned with God – as the 'Midwinter spring' passage had done, and as the fourth movement will do. Now the way forward from the one lyric to the other, from the death of the living to a mode of life in death, involves a development of consciousness in which life and death are explored and discovered in their wholeness. The main part of II is concerned with personal existence – a man's relation to himself (hence the 'double'); III is concerned with society – the relation with others; and both these relations are completed in IV, which deals with the relation with God. This final lyric is in every respect the culmination towards which the two preceding movements have been constructed; and we miss their full intent if we try to make sense of them simply on their own.

At the same time the development of the whole has to be traced through the detail of its organisation, and in the way in which we actually experience it as we read. This is something that critical interpretations too often pass over or fail to penetrate to. In particular, in the general praise of Eliot's attempt at 'the nearest equivalent to a canto of the Inferno or the Purgatorio, in style as well as content' that he could achieve,[55] the very significant difficulties that it presents are usually left unremarked; with the result that its real action is rather imperfectly comprehended. To see what is really going on we must attend primarily to the specific qualities of the poetry.

The first thing to be remarked about the 'canto' which is the main part of the second movement, is that the last thirty lines are of a very different quality from the first forty-two, with a difference nearly as great as that between the positive and the negative of a photograph. From 'But as the passage now presents no hindrance' the language is charged with an urgent communication; before that it might be 'last year's language', or the language of the living who have no speech for what the dead can tell.

> In the uncertain hour before the morning
>   Near the ending of interminable night
>   At the recurrent end of the unending
> After the dark dove with the flickering tongue
>   Had passed below the horizon of his homing
>   While the dead leaves still rattled on like tin
> Over the asphalt where no other sound was
>   Between three districts whence the smoke arose
>   I met one walking, loitering and hurried
> As if blown towards me like the metal leaves
>   Before the urban dawn wind unresisting.

Those lines fall upon the ear with a nearly metronomic, mechanical regularity; indeed the fixed metre and the fixed line length are more like the death-mask of blank verse than any live form of it. The one, proving, exception to the steady iambic beat is the fourth line; and what makes that stand out is the enlivening variation of stress, and the natural, musical shaping of each phrase within the line. But such stressing and phrasing, which are the main sources of vitality in English verse, are strangely muted in the rest of this passage and throughout the first forty-two lines. Closer examination discovers that in fact these lines are composed for the most part, not upon the usual basis of stress, but upon the alternation of long and short syllables; and that it is this which evens out and tones down the verse, while still preserving a regular pulsation. Duration is perhaps not a highly developed resource in the music of English, being usually subordinated to accentuation; yet it is not at all foreign to it, and Eliot is not to be accused of trying to write English as if it were Dante's Italian.[56] But what he has done, by subduing stress to quantity, is to lower the life and energy of his language.

The suppression of the natural variations of accent and measure, while it gives an impressively grave, levelled line, prevents the generation of rhythmic energy, so that it is only the syntax which carries the sense on through the prolonged periods. But then of course the syntax itself, with the diction, is left in a rather lowered state. 'The horizon of his homing' seems to be a phrase turned to fit the metre more than for a more precise perception. 'Where no other sound was' hangs loosely between 'the asphalt' and 'three districts'. 'Walking', which is not merely uneconomical but deflationary, seems put in to fill out the line. And is there a specifically 'urban' dawn wind, or is that a procrustean contraction? As to the diction, the levelling out of stress and the fixed line length appear to weaken it towards imprecision, or even plain wordiness. Is there not a smack of Polonius in the first three lines? and is there not rather more art than matter in the later lines following ' "What! are *you* here?" ', and in the prosing about wonder and ease, and thought and theory? The final remark of these forty-two lines, 'For last year's words belong to last year's language/And next year's words await another voice', is, like so much of Eliot's later critical prose, a tired restatement of an insight which had once been an urgent discovery; and it shows the poet dwindled to the man of letters. Then there are some oddly dud words. Dead leaves don't sound like tin: are we meant to think of tinfoil (which is quite different), or is this supposed to be an hallucinatory effect? 'Asphalt', a flat word in a rather empty line, evokes merely the street's surface: is it meant to suggest the asphalt lake where Gomorrah was and the burning marl of Milton's Hell, or are those associations deliberately not brought out? (In the case of the dead leaves, 'tin' effectively prevents our thinking of Shelley's leaves blown in the West Wind 'like stricken ghosts from an enchanter fleeing', and of Dante's souls whirled in the wind of Hell (as in *Inferno* v) – associations in Eliot's mind in 'What Dante Means to Me', so presumably consciously avoided here.) Later there is the patently manufactured 'homely' proverb, 'Last season's fruit is eaten/And the fullfed beast shall kick the empty pail.' I can't believe that anyone would ever actually say that; and if it recalls Dante's earthy metaphors – 'the grass shall be far from the goat's reach. Let the beasts of Fiesole make fodder of themselves'[57] – it is only to be shown up the more as not rooted in common life and the common speech.

The general relation to Dante throughout these forty-odd lines is of the same order as the relation to blank verse and to the language: they neither take over the life that is in his work, nor give new life of their own to the borrowed effects. 'The brown baked features' gets all its force from the context of 'lo cotto aspetto' (*Inferno* xv, 26). 'That pointed scrutiny with which we challenge/ The first met stranger in the waning dusk' is a faint reproduction, lacking the specific reality of 'each looked at us as one looks at another in the evening under a new moon, their eyebrows puckered together as they peered at us as an old tailor does at the eye of his needle' (ibid. 17–21). Many other such echoes can be caught, and always there is more in Dante's lines than in Eliot's.

All this evidence of the poet's failure to make the most of his material points to no ordinary failure: there is something more to Eliot's lines which arrests any simple judgment. The limitations and defects seem to me undeniable. Yet what most readers and critics find, that there is great power and authority in the verse, is not to be denied either. It is an extraordinary kind of inferior writing that can be regarded, as this passage generally is, as a supreme achievement of poetic genius. What we have to reckon with is a mastery which is not infusing new life into the versification and the language; and which shows itself precisely by not doing that – by controlling, repressing, and refusing to enter into the full life of words and of the world. It is a mastery felt as frigidity, as a suppression of feeling, and as a fundamental indifference to experience. It has power, but it is the negatively directed power – which is not the same thing as a negation of energy – of one whose 'life is in the world's decease'. Its poetics of 'detachment' is just the opposite of Coleridge's ideal of the imagination: for here the knower does not find himself in a creative and loving union with the world he knows; but asserts his existence as a soul detached and alienated from an 'unreal' world. This of course was the predicament of Eliot's early personae, and there is a continuity from their states of death-in-life to this culminating *dédoublement*. But then this persona goes on to speak the words of faith and hope in divine Love which Prufrock, Gerontion and Tiresias never thought to speak; and it must be for the sake of those words that the poet refuses his powers to the merely living dimensions of the encounter. That is to say, the first part of the canto is meant not to engage our real interest, but just the reverse. It presents the familiar world of place and time in such a way as to make us feel *dépaysés*, because it would lead us '*through* the dramatic action of men into a spiritual action which transcends it'. Another way of putting it, and the most strictly appropriate, is that the canto begins in the condition of Hell, but proceeds in its latter part to the condition of Purgatory. From the ordinary, unilluminated state of consciousness the poet witholds himself; but into that which is 'tongued with fire' he enters fully.[58]

At the transition from the experience of the living man to that of the dead and the dying the verse begins to come alive –

> But, as the passage now presents no hindrance
>> To the spirit unappeased and peregrine
>> Between two worlds become much like each other

At the end of the first of those lines quantity, instead of being employed to mute stress, is played against it to enforce the sense, and so breaks the dead measure. The line starts with the iambic beat coinciding with the long syllables; but then 'no', which would be scanned as unstressed, is lengthened and dwelt upon because of the relative shortness of the stressed syllables before and after it; and this crossing of a stress-rhythm with a quantitative one enlivens the movement. In the next two lines natural stress and phrasing are allowed their full effect, and the poetic energy can now be felt flowing into the words. 'Peregrine' in particular stands out as the first word in the canto (or at least since its fourth line) to be at all charged with meaning. It suggests first the peregrine falcon – so named, the *O.E.D.* records, by Brunetto Latini in his *Trésor*. It was an apt name for a bird of no fixed habitat, a perpetual migrant, since *peregrinus* had been applied in ancient Rome to visiting aliens. Later it was used of pilgrims seeking there the eternal City of God. Dante has one of his souls in Purgatory remark that an Italian who was a citizen of the true city would be 'peregrine' even in Italy; and elsewhere, in a line which Eliot once applied to himself, he describes someone as 'persona umile e peregrina'.[59] The force of all this makes 'peregrine' an answer to Arnold's sad wandering, in 'Stanzas from the Grande Chartreuse', 'between two worlds, one dead,/The other powerless to be born'. Its energy comes from the action which Arnold could not conceive, seeking the birth in the death, and making the two worlds one.

To do that is the work of the passage disclosing 'the gifts reserved for age'. Having learnt to listen for quantity as well as stress, we find them being used now with constructive mastery, at one point to reinforce, at another to complement each other.

> First the cold friction of expiring sense
>> Without enchantment, offering no promise
>> But bitter tastelessness of shadow fruit
>> As body and soul begin to fall asunder.

In the first of those lines the stressed syllables are also long, and they are further weighted by the departure from the iambic measure, so that all the energy of the line is concentrated in 'cold friction' and 'expiring sense'. In the third line the middle stress (on '-ness') is weak, but it is redistributed as quantity in the drawing out of 'tastelessness'. The sentence closes with a return to the iambic norm as if to the universal form of experience. By such means as these the communication of the dead is animated throughout the remaining lines of the speech.

What Eliot has his dead masters speak here is surely what he would affirm – as his writing does – to be the ultimate of human wisdom. It has been suggested that he must be dissociating himself from this compound double, with a shuddering 'there but for the grace of God go I'. But we have seen that in his work the effect of grace is just to make a man know and accept his mortal fate – 'there *with* the grace of God is where I must fare' is more likely to be his response. And the fact is that if the poet is saved in *Little Gidding*, it is by realising the truth and necessity of this communication of the dead, and by making his mind over to that of his masters who have had the experience and grasped its meaning. Not dissociation, let alone disowning, but at-one-ment is the essential action here. This double is not a Prufrock or Gerontion, not a failed or impotent self; he is the poet's *other* self in the sense that he is what the poet is striving to become wholly conscious of – the timeless mind of Europe. For this is an enactment of the poet's surrender of his own personality to the authority of Tradition.

In the last twenty lines especially we can discern the dead poets, Eliot's chosen ancestors, asserting their immortality. Dante, the supreme master of such communion with the dead, is of course the dominant presence. Then there are echoes of Hamlet's ghostly father; of Milton on Sin and Death; of Swift's epitaph upon himself; of Johnson on the vanity of human wishes; also of Shelley, Tennyson, Arnold; Henry James, of course; and Laforgue and Mallarmé; and lastly – after many others, such as Coleridge, Baudelaire, Bradley and Valéry, who are less distinctly to be made out or merely guessed at – there is Yeats, who emerges (once we have been alerted)[60] as a major presence throughout the entire movement. All these are evoked, however, not in their own genius, but insofar as they contribute to Eliot's wisdom of humility. There is not the least interest in what their works might mean in themselves, or from other points of view; nor is there any sense of Eliot's earlier differences with them. All are merged in the one ultimate and universal mind, that of the conscious dead. Thus Shakespeare, Milton, Mallarmé, Yeats, are 'folded in a single party' with Dante; and their individual apprehensions of life and death are 'completed' by his vision of Arnaut in the refining fire. In the special sense which his context gives to Mallarmé's 'donner un sens plus pur aux mots de la tribu', Eliot has been, as ever, refining others' words into the one Word.

Thus conceived, the Tradition becomes active, 'a *living whole* of all the poetry that has ever been written';[61] and to surrender oneself to it is to pass from merely dying to everlasting life – 'We die with the dying . . . We are born with the dead'. What dies is 'the individual as himself and no more, a mere numbered atom'; what is born is 'the individual in communion with God'.[62] This is what happens within the course of the canto: a transition from the point of view of man alone, apart from God, and so in Hell; to that of 'The souls in purgatory who suffer because they *wish to suffer*, for purgation',[63] and whom the poet enters into communion with in humility and in hope of being united with God. In the last lines he is no longer 'In the uncertain hour', but precisely at the intersection of the timeless moment; which is evoked through the interaction of the associations of Arnaut's prospect from Purgatory, of the connection at the close of the first scene of *Hamlet* of dawn with Christ's birth, and of the blowing of the horn at the world's end (which is every moment).

We may feel that a high price has been paid for all this – that there is so much more to the mind of Europe. Surely *Hamlet* cannot be so simply laid to rest. Neither Milton nor Johnson could really be said to have adhered to Dante's faith; and Valéry consciously did not. Yeats did seek unity of being, but with ı magnanimity not honoured by Eliot – a will to hold in the one vision the work of bringing 'the soul of man to God' and the 'Profane perfection of mankind'.[64] Then there is Dante's exemplary magnanimity, as in the meeting with his old master Brunetto Latini in the canto which Eliot acknowledges as a model in the first part of his own. It was Brunetto who first taught Dante 'how man makes himself eternal'; yet he is damned for having perverted that impulse into a love of earthly fame – he is fixed in the idea that he will live in his *Trésor*, and he thinks of Dante's immortality as earthly. All that Eliot is concerned to communicate in *Little Gidding* is there – the vanity of the world's approval, the true meaning of immortality, and the necessary way to it. But it is presented with a generous recognition of Brunetto in himself, his motives, his achievement, his meaning to Dante; and he is allowed the good he sought, to appear one who wins in the race, even in Hell. The informing quality of the canto is the poet's love for the man his master was: a love fully cognisant of what he has lost in being that; and which is yet quite free of the impulse to convert him into an expression of his own point of view. That is very different from Eliot's treatment of his masters, and especially of Yeats. But the cause of the difference is what we need to appreciate: Eliot is not concerned with the *otherness* of his

253

masters, because he is concerned solely with the process by which the soul is united with God. To prefer Dante's method, to want to know other writers in themselves, is to maintain the healthy interest of the living. But that is the viewpoint which Eliot has been deliberately, and successfully, detaching himself from. The loss that we naturally feel, we are meant to feel – that may be the literary critic's nearest apprehension of his purgatory.

The first section of the third movement is a prosy and somewhat contrived commentary upon what the poetry is about. In part it repeats what has been said before; but now the *via negativa* appears the direct and positive way. Detachment, we are reminded, though the opposite of attachment, is yet like it in being a form of action: it is a willed withdrawal from the objects of affection.[65] That makes it an alternative mode of life, as the 'live' or stinging nettle and the dead-nettle are both flowering plants, and alike in their difference from an unflowering one. (The analogy is itself so detached from the botanical facts that one might well think it referred to a dead stinging nettle – Eliot's interest is only in the pattern of 'metaphysical' associations to be derived from the 'dead' flowering and the 'live' stinging.)[66] Then detachment is declared to be also a form of love, and of an expanded love freed by the exercise of memory from desire – as if *eros* were not a source of energy in love but a constraint upon it. We have been following this process in the immediately preceding canto –

> See, now they vanish,
> The faces and places, with the self which, as it could, loved them,
> To become renewed, transfigured, in another pattern.

There is an instructive gloss in a rough note among the drafts of *East Coker*:

> Alone – the ice cap/separated from/the surfaces of human beings/
> To be reunited in/the Communion

That Communion is being sought now, not only in personal relationships, but in a whole culture. For love in its detached mode takes all History as its 'field of action'.

That phrase, next to 'love of a country', might have referred to the war. However, the second part of the movement – beginning at 'Sin is Behovely', and separated from the rest by a space in the drafts and the early printings – goes back to the seventeenth century for its historical material, and sets that in the perspective of a fourteenth-century mystic. This, presumably, is a properly detached patriotism, using memory, or the historical sense, to expand love of a country into a consciousness of the 'pattern of timeless moments'. The various protagonists of the Civil War 'vanish and return in a different action', as the draft notes put it. In that action it is the defeated who are the true culture-heroes – Charles and Archbishop Laud and Strafford all executed on the scaffold, the Catholic Crashaw who died in exile, and the Puritan Milton who 'died blind and quiet' after the Commonwealth had failed. Their 'symbol perfected in death' means, according to the draft notes, 'the moment of union'; and it means that because they consented to death, and died with their minds intent upon the divine sphere of being. This is to take them as martyrs and witnesses in the only historical event of real interest to Eliot, Incarnation.

In a letter to John Hayward dated 2 September 1942, Eliot said that his purpose in quoting from Julian of Norwich at the beginning and end of this section, and from *The Cloud of Unknowing* in v, was to 'give greater historical depth to the poem by allusions to the other great period' – that is to say, by aligning the seventeenth century with the fourteenth. This would suggest that he was taking the fourteenth century in England as the equivalent of the *trecento* of Dante – as an age of true metaphysical vision and practice. Yet the quotations from Julian of Norwich, although her positive sense of Sin and absolute trust in God are precisely relevant, don't do much more than provide a frame of reference and an emotional groundtone for the seventeenth-century material. Now what gave the later period its great interest for Eliot was this:

The Jacobean–Caroline period has a more civilised grace, and a background of religious belief which casts seriousness and dignity over their lightest lines. It is not insignificant that the monarch who gives his name to the age is dignified with the style of Martyr. On all sides, it was an age of lost causes, and unpopular names, and forsaken beliefs, and impossible loyalties, as Matthew Arnold would have said; the beauty of life and the shadow of martyrdom are the background. . . When I speak of the particular seriousness of the pre-Restoration I am not thinking of one side rather than another: I include Milton, and Bunyan and Baxter as of that age, as men who knew the beauty of life and the possibility of martyrdom and sacrifice for a cause.[67]

That presents, as *Little Gidding* does, an aspect of the seventeenth century which is opposed to that considered in *East Coker*: the side of it which was governed by theology, as against that governed by the new science. As if to declare his own position, Eliot added, in that broadcast talk, 'And I sometimes wonder whether the generation succeeding my own may not be also a generation which has lost faith in lost causes.' I take that to be saying in its gnomic way that a lost cause is truly to be believed in, since to be defeated is to be brought towards the divine union. This corresponds to Julian of Norwich's rejoicing in the humiliating consciousness of sin, because 'through contrition and grace we shall be broken from all that is not our Lord. And then shall our blessed Saviour perfectly heal us, and one us to Him.'[68]

This metaphysical view of history, which is essentially a theological one, was already formulated, though without the explicit theology, in Eliot's thesis on Bradley: 'Ideas of the past are true, not by correspondence with a real past, but by their coherence with each other and ultimately with the present moment.'[69] Fully expanded, that finds the absolute of history in the timeless moment of death in Love. So the seventeenth century, and the fourteenth, and England now, are all one; though what they are in that vision never was. It is, quite frankly, an ideal conception of history.

The aim of the fourth movement is to realise this ideal in the here and now of bombed and burning London, and its lyricism is the direct development of the preceding incantation. That had been as it were the ritual chant of Eliot's Tradition, setting the historical monuments in a new and final order. In the lyric the poet situates himself at the present moment of history, as its consciousness and its protagonist. This is the moment of action – the one right action, which is every moment, and the moment at once of time and of eternity – which the whole work has been affirming and striving towards. The liberating consciousness of 'reality' in *Burnt Norton*, the humble submission to it in *East Coker*, and the conceiving of it as the divine will in *The Dry Salvages*, now culminate in the full experience of the pentecostal/refining fire. What is suffered is understood and assented to all in the one act; and the essential nature of this act is the joining of the human will with the divine, so that the human shall be perfected, i.e. brought to its 'one end'. This is not yet Paradise, of course: it is the human, earthly, experience of that communion of all beings in God which Dante is shown in the final cantos of the *Paradiso*. It is the Beatific Vision in its incarnate form, the Word in the flesh, the act of Love between God and man.

'The dove descending' hardly suggests an ordinary bird at all, so charged is it with poetical and metaphysical associations. It is 'the dark dove with the flickering tongue', at once enemy fighter-bomber and Holy Spirit, bringing the one fire of Incarnation. (It is also *not* 'the lark ascending'.) 'Breaks the air' is similarly charged – partly due to the placing of the main stress of the line upon 'breaks' – as if it meant the destruction of the very element of breath (and of despair). 'Incandescent', echoing and countering 'descending', intensifies the flame to white heat, implying light; but to the earth (*terra*) this means 'terror' – its natural response, associated through the rhyme with 'sin and error', its erring from God. The one hope of redemption from the pyre or bone-fire is to give oneself up to it as to the fire of Love: and this might be termed a rhetorical ultimatum, one in which the choice is determined in the formulation itself. The absence of the element of water may be significant: as implying that we are not now in the realm of the sensuous and passional – the 'daemonic, chthonic/Powers' – but in that of the New Life.

The second stanza enters more immediately into the experience of the fire, and at the same time affirms its meaning in its 'Name'. Julian of Norwich, John of the Cross, and the Christian mystics generally, declare the torments 'woven in the weakness of the changing body' to be the re-creative work of divine Love. It is directly felt, however, as Hercules knew it in the Greek myth reworked by Seneca. 'The intolerable shirt of flame' which he put on unawares was prepared for him by the human passions of love and jealousy; his only way to remove it was to commit himself to the flames of his own funeral pyre – whereupon he was raised to Olympus among the immortals. The lyric does not go that far.

> We only live, only suspire
> Consumed by either fire or fire

is as much as to say that our existence is either hell or purgatory, depending on whether we live according to our own will, or according to 'His will'.

There can be no doubt of Eliot's choice here, nor that he really means it. The movement of the lyric transforms the measure of the round dance of death in II into that of a solemn and serene plain chant. The rhythm arises from the precise formulation of the integrated sensibility; and 'the music' of the poetry is that of 'The complete consort dancing together', celebrating the end of life as the beginning. The poet, responsive only to 'the drawing of this Love and the voice of this Calling', is now 'nel foco che gli affina'.

That makes this the most challenging moment of the poem for the reader. The lyric asks our participation and assent, demands not just elucidation and appreciation but communion in prayer. How we respond is the final and most vital dimension of the experience of the poem, for it is in our response that we discover what it really means to us and where we ourselves stand. The critic's function, in my view, is to elucidate the work so that its readers may know it for what it is, and respond to it truly – that is, with a true as opposed to a false consciousness. Because that must be something each reader discovers and develops in himself, the critic is not in a position to describe or define it. All he can do is help others to form their own response. Just here that means recognising the moment at which *Four Quartets* demands a final response of its readers. Of the implications of its demand I will say something more at the end of the chapter.

The final movement confirms what it would mean to be wholly at one with the poet: it would mean making the end all. The first section here, besides being a direct commentary upon the lyric, as in the corresponding sections of the other Quartets, is a resuming and concluding of the meditation begun in the first movement and continued in the first part of the third. It is thus a recapitulation of the Quartet as a whole at the level of thought. The most striking aspect of the long statement about the poet's *métier* is the sudden pounce at the end, when the Polonius-like theory drops away in the final reality of 'Every poem an epitaph'. That is to make the perfected poem a *symboliste* work, meaning just what is – in the silence after it has been written and read. This goes with the view of History declared in III, which perceives every event as an end. But the silent poem, and the action that is over, having been identified now with the action of the Word, become timeless symbols meaning the true prayer and right action of the soul united with God. And that is what the poet would have 'England' to be now – 'a people . . . redeemed from time' because wholly concentrated in his 'timeless moment', and a community because in communion with God.

The line (taken from *The Cloud of Unknowing*) which stands on its own should be separated from the first section by a double space as in the early printings: for its relation is rather to the *Four Quartets* as a whole than to that section, and it introduces the coda to the entire set. In the coda themes and motifs from all four Quartets are recalled, and resolved into their definitive pattern. This is done very simply and lucidly and lyrically, yet nothing of the total work is forgotten, and through the clear surface may be discerned the depths of its Absolute. To arrive where we started might be, in scholastic terminology, to make our first also our final cause, so that 'all is always now'. But the way to that involves discovering 'the last of earth . . . which was the beginning'; and this, if it suggests Eden, must go further to 'dust thou art, and unto dust shalt thou return'. Yet that co-exists in apparent harmony with the intimations of a happy paradisal state that might have been – the hidden waterfall and the children in the apple tree. These, we have been told however, are not reality but 'echoed ecstasy' and 'hints and guesses'; and they are 'heard, half-heard, in the stillness /Between two waves of the sea', as intimations of an ideal world upon which the mind should be intent even as it suffers death by water.[70] The final sentence repeats the last invocation of *Burnt Norton*, but goes on from the impatience of the neophyte still caught in the temporal, to the patience of the initiate wholly intent upon the eternal. We should know by now all that 'the tongues of fire' mean, and how 'the fire and the rose' may be one. But 'the crowned knot of fire' should give us pause. It is not the mystical 'multifoliate Rose', as I have seen suggested; and it is not a 'crown knot'. It is a knot of fire, and one which is crowned. Elizabeth Drew cites a pertinent sentence from *The Cloud of Unknowing* which speaks of 'the ghostly knot of burning love betwixt thee and thy God';[71] and since we know that this burning Love consumes the man who chooses it, should we not see in the 'knot of fire' the soul itself, burning as do certain souls in Dante's Purgatory, among them Arnaut Daniel. It would be crowned then because he has made perfect his will, as Virgil crowned Dante when he had conducted him to the point 'where art can avail us no farther':[72]

When the stairway was all sped beneath us, and we were upon the topmost step, on me did Virgil fix his eyes,
and said: 'Son, the temporal fire and the eternal, hast thou seen, and art come to a place where I, of myself, discern no further.
Here have I brought thee with wit and with art; now take thy pleasure for guide; forth art thou from the steep ways, forth art from the narrow...
No more expect my word, nor my sign. Free, upright, and whole, is thy will, and 'twere a fault not to act according to its prompting; wherefore I do crown and mitre thee over thyself.[73]

Thus understood, 'the crowned knot of fire' is the state of the individual soul while it is yet itself, a distinct and therefore suffering person, but already in full accord with the divine will – so that the fire it knows and the multifoliate Rose 'are one'. Thus the final word is the properly triumphant conclusion, *one* standing against the complex *all* of the first line of *Burnt Norton*.

Eliot's response to the war, and to the general breakdown of civilisation in which he felt himself implicated, his way of restoring the world to wholeness and peace, was this act of Atonement. For public catastrophe, as it had been for private, his resource was to seek 'Our peace in His will'.

When the four poems, which had appeared separately under their individual titles, were collected as one work, Eliot gave them the name 'Quartets' because, as he wrote to John Hayward,

I should like to indicate that these poems are all in a particular set form which I have elaborated, and the word 'quartet' does seem to me to start people on the right tack for understanding them... It suggests to me the notion of making a poem by weaving in together three or four superficially unrelated themes: the 'poem' being the degree of success in making a new whole out of them.[74]

On the evidence of the work itself, by 'themes' he must have meant what 'all poetry may be said to start from' –

the emotions experienced by human beings in their relations to themselves, to each other, to divine beings, and to the world about them; it is therefore concerned also with thought and action, which emotion brings about, and out of which emotion arises.[75]

That gives a fair indication of the themes of the Quartets. It can be amplified by recalling Eliot's insistence, in his criticism, that his interest in poetry led him on to morals, and to religion, and to politics – and that these could not be kept apart, and that they had to be rightly ordered.[76] That the *poem* should consist in 'making a new whole out of them' recalls his early poetic theory and its debt to Bradley, and is a casual restatement of the poet's lifelong dedication to realising 'the unified totality of his interests'. To use the term 'quartet' as an analogy for this might intimate, given the nature of his 'themes', an aspiration towards the condition in which 'you are the music'.

We have seen in the detail of the Quartets just how much Eliot is seeking to unify. There is the summing up of his own personal experience – though the drafts reveal that this might have been done more fully[77] – and of his life's work in poetry and as a man of letters; there is the gathering of the cultural tradition, in its philosophical, literary and social aspects, into the one present moment; and there is the effort to unite himself with the living and the dead in God. All this is to re-enact the fundamental meaning of *religion*: the binding together of all things, 'To make Cosmos'.[78] That is what the 'poem' is. 'You may call it communion with the Divine, or you may call it a temporary crystal-isation of the mind', Eliot wrote in his essay on Pascal, associating 'artistic and literary composition' with 'religious illumination'.[79] Certainly we may call the final section of *Little Gidding*, taking that part for the whole, a 'temporary crystallisation of the mind'. If we find it to be also 'communion with the Divine', then that would mean that Eliot has succeeded in unifying not merely his own sensibility but that of his culture – that he has created in art the mind of his ideal Christian society.

His language then would be, like Dante's, 'the perfection of a common language':[80] the common speech purified into the communication of fire. The virtue of such eloquence is that it 'can stir the emotions of the intelligent and judicious . . . the emotions which the intelligent and judicious can experience together'.[81] Now such an audience, in the case of *Four Quartets*, would be the Christian Communion in prayer. If we attend to the pronouns which define the consciousness of the Quartets, we can trace the poet's effort to move from a mere individual self, through a range of tentative approaches and withdrawals, into a complete community with his readers. In *Burnt Norton* one is always aware of the poet speaking to others – if it is not just to himself and God: however much he tries to identify the reader with himself, the rather forced 'we' breaks down into 'my words . . . in your mind'. The wartime Quartets for the most part observe the proper distinctions of 'I' and 'you'; with the 'we' reserved for a legitimate generalisation from common experience ('for most of us'), or else for exhortation ('We must be still'). The negative exception is *East Coker* IV, where the 'we' is presumptuous, if not impertinent, because it is not creating a shared emotion but asserting a conception. *Little Gidding* differs positively, and effects a tactful and genuine expansion. In the first movement the subject is open: an implicit 'I' which is near to the impersonal 'one'; then a 'you' which seems to include the poet, as if he were speaking of and to himself as well as for others. In the second movement his 'I' does deliberately dissolve into the other. The 'we' of the three succeeding movements intends a growing in-clusiveness: from the commonplace ('We cannot revive old factions'), to the universal ('We only live, only suspire'); and the final section is governed by a 'we' in which the poet would be speaking in unison with others, and voicing the common consciousness of all who can feel themselves at one in this 'order of words'.

Being united in prayer involves more than a confession of belief, or 'the conscious occupation/Of the praying mind'. The Absolute, Eliot had maintained in his critique of Bradley, remains 'imaginary' so long as it is 'only by an act of faith unified'. It becomes 'real' when the meaning perceived in experience is itself an immediate experience; and it is the function of poetry, in his view, to effect the transmutation of metaphysics into a state of being. 'We are no longer in the same world of discourse' when a metaphysic has been 'transmuted into poetry' – this was how he expressed it in 1952 – and the difference is like that between belief and *behaviour*:

in one aspect our beliefs are those ideas and principles which we maintain consciously throughout our life, and on the other hand, our belief in any particular moment is the *way in which we behave at that moment*. Only, perhaps, in facing and accepting mar-tyrdom, is a man's religious belief completely realised and authenticated.[82]

That is surely no mere analogy for Eliot, who would have poetry too, within its own terms, be a real and authentic witness of the Word. *Little Gidding* in its end comes as near to that as his art could; and so comes nearest to incor-porating his readers into the *action* of Incarnation.

This is to remove poetry from the realm of belief, and from the philosophical problem of the relations of poetry and belief. That is a problem to which Eliot addressed himself on a number of occasions, but always as a philosopher of poetry or as a believer; and his interest in the question arose from his wanting to maintain the necessity of orthodoxy. For the poet the problem does not arise, because in poetry belief is subsumed into behaviour – into the right action of words. The poet is working in the realm of morality, of ethics or conduct; and thence in the realm of practical religion. He confronts his readers not simply with a meaning, such as would challenge their ideas and opinions, but with a mode of being, the challenge of which is existential. The poem makes its meaning really a matter of life and death – 'the choice of pyre or pyre'. To measure its success properly, the reader must ask himself, not whether he agrees with it on the plane of conscious ideas and principles, but whether it brings him to feel what Eliot would have him feel, and to a participation in that one action in which he would unite mankind.

The *poem* offers itself as a religous ritual for the time – as *the* ritual by which a foundering civilisation might be recovered. It does deliberately what *The Waste Land* seemed to do almost unconsciously and accidentally. I concluded that that was a rite to save the poet, himself alone, from the alien world; and that it generates no impulse to renew love or to recover a human city and civilisation. Of the three wartime Quartets one must say that the motive is to save the world also. One great difference is that the poet is not now projecting a private predicament upon the common world in order to be released from it; but is rather taking upon himself the state of the world, in order to identify the common, universal sin, and to bear witness to the way all may be redeemed. This difference proceeds, however, simply from the expansion from the private into the universal of the one motive: the need to make an end of merely living and merely dying, and to find rest in the Absolute.

It is true that this expansion is achieved by making the meaning of the ritual action 'explicit, understood'; and that the conscious apprehension of the meaning is an essential stage in the progression from the mere experience, such as it is in *The Waste Land,* to the intelligible form of 'The Peace which passeth understanding' attained in *Little Gidding*. The *rite de passage* has been attached to an orthodoxy or right teaching, and this not simply as an explanation of it, but as an instrumental part. It is not surprising that readers who don't themselves assent to the Classicist, Royalist and Anglo-Catholic point of view should feel excluded by this, at the points where the doctrine is asserted. Yet, I repeat, the doctrine is not the poetry. Moreover, the poetry enacts the same basic rite as did *The Waste Land,* only it enacts it in a more developed and coherent form.[83] If the earlier poem works, then the wartime Quartets, taken as a poem, ought to work even better. For all that they proceed by taking thought about things, they begin and end in the realm of experience, and bring themselves always to the proof of the immediate experience. They enact a particular way of living the life of the world at a given time and place, 'now and England'; and they affirm and embrace the inevitable facts, just then so insistently present, of human error and mortality. Certainly they do this rather at the expense of everything else that life naturally offers, and with a view to an ideal state of being. But they remain firmly placed in the life and world we all know, and what they would do with that does concern us very nearly. To attempt to order our living into holy dying is truly to challenge us where we live.

The challenge can be stated in the form of a dilemma. There is the one horn for those who find the poem does wholly succeed: do they really enter into its action, as a way of life? That corresponds to the challenge of *The Waste Land* to those who think it the poem of its age. The other horn is for those who think that the rite of *Four Quartets* is not for them: can it really be the case that they maintain another point of view in practice? This is much the harder question, and there are two sides to it. On the one hand there is the fact that what Eliot is expressing has been the main and dominant idea – though by no means the sole idea – of European culture; and that he has realised it in an extraordinarily potent form. I doubt if many of his readers can set against it an alternative ethos so sanctioned by custom, and so definitively formulated. Then there is the fact that his readers must live, whether they like it or not, in a civilisation shaped by the Christian idea – shaped by it still even in its decay. This makes for a certain essential conformity, beneath all differences of belief and ideology, of the poem's action and their way of life. Capitalism and Communism and their variant forms, though apparently alternatives to Christianity, are actually derivatives from it; and remain faithful to its essential character, which is to think that our ideas of things and what we can make of them are more real and valuable than things in themselves; and thence faithful to its prime motive, which is to pursue the ideal at the expense of the actual. The tradition of idealism, the habit of sacrificing personal life and the life of nature for an abstract absolute, is not confined to Christianity: behind the City of God there is the Platonic Republic; and after it there is our own Capital, the ideal absolute of money and power. Our endemic idealism is manifest in the prevailing contempt for the natural world and for the individual; in the abuse of what life can offer, and the consequent dissatisfaction with it; in deep-rooted, and even deliberately fostered, anxiety and fear, which expand into 'distress of nations and perplexity'. These act as powerful pressures, and there are others more direct, to invest our energies in some ideal – whether heaven, or money and power, or simply an idyllic haven. There is so much in our civilisation from which the individual needs to save himself; so much to make him wish to die; and so many ways of death in life – of giving up the life we could live for some deferred return, of sacrificing in order to save, of wasting in order to make more. The traditional Christian habits of feeling and conduct, still strong in the behaviour of the late-Puritan English-speaking world – which has an influence upon much of the rest of the world – make these the normal ways of responding to the social forces which alienate us from ourselves, and from what the Greeks called *Kosmos* and Spinoza *Deus sive Natura*, meaning the actual whole of all that is. That view of life, which is a genuine alternative to the idealist one, is likely to be unfamiliar and even incomprehensible: and in that ignorance there is a measure of our common predicament. We have no real alternative to the way of life enacted in *Four Quartets*. So far as our way of life is governed by the ingrained habits of idealism – and those habits do persist below the superficial hedonism as the 'serious' side of our culture – then we must be susceptible to Eliot's religious rite, and involved despite any conviction that it is alien.

When we come to judge the poem as the ritual for the time that it offers to be, we must take the poem for what it is, and the time as it is: we must set the actual behaviour of the poem with the actual behaviour of its readers. I suggest that there is likely to be at least some degree of essential conformity between the way we live now and the way in which the poem would order life; and to that extent the poem can be said to express, and to give a form to, the sensibility of its age. This conformity of the poem and the prevailing ethos can be indicated summarily through the concept of *alienation*, which touches upon something fundamental in both. Marx's analysis of Capitalist society in terms of alienation is still apt; Eliot, taking a hint from Arnold and making a virtue of that alienation, would have the contemporary alien be a 'spirit unappeased and peregrine', seeking his true home in the ideal. Thus the alienated man of Marx's analysis, and Eliot's spiritual aliens, may be joined in the one action; and in that way the poem may succeed in bringing its society towards 'A condition of complete simplicity'.

Afterwords

'Such are the Laws of thy false Heav'ns; but Laws of Eternity
Are not such; know thou, I come to Self Annihilation.
Such are the Laws of Eternity, that each shall mutually
Annihilate himself for others' good, as I for thee.
Thy purpose & the purpose of thy Priests & of thy Churches
Is to impress on men the fear of death, to teach
Trembling & fear, terror, constriction, abject selfishness.
Mine is to teach Men to despise death & to go on
In fearless majesty annihilating Self, laughing to scorn
Thy Laws & terrors, shaking down thy Synagogues as webs.
I come to discover before Heav'n & Hell the Self righteousness
In all its Hypocritic turpitude, opening to every eye
These wonders of Satan's holiness, shewing to the Earth
The Idol Virtues of the Natural Heart, & Satan's Seat
Explore in all its Selfish Natural Virtue, & put off
In Self annihilation all that is not of God alone,
To put off Self & all I have, ever & ever. Amen.'

(William Blake: Milton ii, 38)

1945–1965

10

The Poet observed

And every moment is a new and shocking
Valuation of all we have been.

With the completion of *Four Quartets* Eliot ceased to be a poet, and became in his art simply a dramatist. His pre-war drama had worked on both levels, the human and the transcendental; but in the three plays produced in the last twenty years of his life the metaphysical poet disappears in the writer of well-made drawing-room comedies. Regrettable as this may be, it was not simply a consequence of failing powers. For one thing, the poet could only have repeated himself, having said all that he had to say in the perfected Quartets. For another, it is just by their not being poetry that the late plays add something to his *oeuvre*. It is not a new vision that they offer, but a progressive revision of that of the poet who would be a saint. *The Cocktail Party* transposes *The Family Reunion* and *Four Quartets* into the audience's own terms, and in doing so significantly alters the emphasis towards the occupations of 'most of us'. In *The Confidential Clerk* the dramatist develops a point of view distinct from that of the poet, and for the first time in Eliot's work the poet is observed in a light other than his own. Then *The Elder Statesman*, which is in certain respects a summing up of the whole of the poet's life-work, brings us at the end to a radical revaluation of it.

This last play gives us something genuinely new and shocking to reckon with. In it the poet, that ideal, elected self, fashioned throughout a lifetime's death in love, who had already turned back to be the dramatist of his world, assumes an ordinary personality and declares himself a human lover like any other. By way of the dedicatory verses with their obvious connection with certain passages in the play, Eliot as good as made a personal appearance on the stage, affirming his need to be loved by a woman and his joy in the liberating experience of sexual love. This was to come back out of the refining fire and through the looking-glass into the secret rose-garden – to go back on the poetry, and to give the last word to the human being whom the poet had all his life been struggling to transform and to transcend. It can't cancel or invalidate the poetry, which remains what it is. But it does establish a new frame of reference, to thus celebrate the union

> Of lovers whose bodies smell of each other
> Who think the same thoughts without need of speech
> And babble the same speech without need of meaning.

That subordination of 'meaning' to the natural communion of lovers affords a new point of view; one which.may detach us finally from the poet's, and enable us to understand the void at the heart of his work – the void which, to borrow Valéry's image, was its source.

THE PLAYWRIGHT'S LATE REVISIONS OF THE POET'S VISION

The happy ending to his life and work must have taken Eliot himself by surprise. But the confining of his drama to the prosaic sphere of human action had been a matter of deliberate effort. Questioned about his intentions in *The Cocktail Party*, he gave the dry understatement: 'I intended to produce characters whose drawing-room behaviour was generally correct.'[1] That was probably the literal truth and not a snub, but it cut deeper than would appear. It needs to be set alongside his altered view of *The Family Reunion*: 'my sympathies now have come to be all with the mother, who seems to me, except perhaps for the chauffeur, the only complete human being in the play; and my hero now strikes me as an insufferable prig.'[2] In 1938 he had regarded Amy as 'merely a person of tremendous personality *on one plane*'; but it was that plane which now interested him most. He was therefore being quite consistent with the theory and practice of his pre-war drama in laying down for himself, when he wanted to represent 'our own sordid, dreary daily world', 'the ascetic rule to avoid poetry which could not stand the test of strict dramatic utility: with such success, indeed, that it is perhaps an open question whether there is any poetry in the play at all.'[3] To adapt his writing to 'the needs of the stage' meant keeping it down to the level of ordinary awareness.

At the same time it does seem perverse to choose to represent ordinary reality according to the artificial conventions of drawing-room comedy. His director and close collaborator, E. Martin Browne, has recorded how studious he was in imitating all its already outworn social and theatrical habits; so much so that Mr Browne felt he had 'placed upon his genius a regrettable limitation', and devoted 'too much of his energy . . . to the correct expression of unimportant social niceties'.[4] This is valuable and just testimony; but I suspect that it misses Eliot's meaning, which would be that it was precisely the vapidity of conventional realism which made it good for his purposes. If it offered only a world of outward appearance and illusion, so too, in his view, did the ordinary world. Its unreality would be the perfect expression of the audience's failure to exist on the moral plane.[5] Moreover, it was the appropriate way to make them aware of that. By giving them just what they expected to find in the theatre he was able, as Pound perceived, 'to make contact with an extant milieu, and an extant state of comprehension'.[6] In a sense they already knew what he had to say to them there, that what they agreed to take as real was mere pretence. To make them fully conscious of this he had only to reveal that this theatrical world was a true expression of their mode of existence.

To bring home the unreality of what we ordinarily call reality— to effect a positive dis-illusionment – had always been an element in Eliot's work, notably in *The Waste Land* and in the satiric treatment of the visionless world in the dramatic writing of the 1930s. But hitherto the aim had always been to dismiss and to transcend it. Now, in the post-war plays, the ordinary human plane, 'unreal' as it is, is accepted as one on which the spiritual action may take place. The development follows on from that of the wartime Quartets, which discovered how consciousness of the 'meaning' could transform the life of the world from a hell into a purgatory. Their dominant concern was the occupation of the saint, whereas the later plays are concerned with more ordinary lives. But the moral is still the same. Whatever one's fate, whether it is to be a martyr or an ordinary person, that is what one must accept in order to be free. 'Resign yourself to be the fool you are', as Sir Henry Harcourt-Reilly advises Edward Chamberlayne, and in that way 'work out your salvation'. That was the odd beginning of the dramatist's finding his peace in human love.

The first thing to be said of *The Cocktail Party* (1949) is that it repeats the essential action of *The Family Reunion*. Celia, a simplified version of Harry, follows out the same 'process by which the human is/Transhumanised . . . on the way of illumination'. By the stages of disillusionment, discovery of solitude, and recognition of sinfulness, she comes to a knowledge of 'the void at the heart of all human relations', and so to the necessity of atonement. She achieves that, we are assured, in accepting her destiny: 'a happy death' in the desert, 'crucified/Very near an ant-hill'. Hers is in every way the strongest part of the play, and it is exactly what we should expect of Eliot. There is one other important respect in which the later play corresponds to the earlier. As Harry was helped on his way by the Eumenides and Agatha, so Celia is directed on hers by the trio of 'Guardians'. Julia and Alex, the intrusive 'kindly ones', save her from error; and Reilly's office, like Agatha's, is to make her understand her fate so that she may assent to it. These three act and advise with the assurance of those who know the law of things – the Logos; and so may be regarded (if we can take them so seriously) as God's messengers and ministers, spreading the conviction of Original Sin and of peace in His will. Thus far the design of the two plays is identical.

But then the Guardians differ from the Eumenides, and even from Agatha, in being thoroughly adjusted to the modern comedy. They are not in the least supernatural, nor are they saints or visionaries. Their air of mystery is as penetrable as that of an average thriller; and Reilly's oracular powers are simply a virtuoso turn for Sir Alec Guinness, and consist of no more than an impressive professional manner combining hints of the shaman, the shriver and the shrink. If they are distinguished from the merely commonplace characters, the Chamberlaynes and Peter Quilpe, then it is by their confident enlightenment or knowingness; and also by their playing the silly social game with the light-headedness of those who don't mind being ridiculous. In a world of fools and saints they belong with the fools, only they would be wise fools. Even the character of Celia, who is to be a saint, is adjusted to the actual world. Eliot surely had in mind the example of Charles de Foucauld, whom he described as 'one Christian witness of our time';[7] and Celia's career is of our time in that the newspapers do occasionally carry such stories. Moreover, Eliot has done all he can to make her experience appear ordinary: the banal affaire; the common-sense way she takes the break-up; the absence of any special vision of 'the boredom, the horror, and the glory'; the distancing of her end, so that it comes as such news generally does into average lives. Altogether, she is changed from a woman of the world into a saint in the most matter of fact way imaginable.

The dramatic effect of Harry's leaving Wishwood to follow the bright angels was to kill Amy and show up the incomprehension of the comic aunts and uncles – that is, it should detach us from the plane of ordinary consciousness. In *Murder in the Cathedral* the effect of the martyr's death, as mediated through the Chorus, was similarly to bring to the common man an apprehension of the ways of God. But the shock of Celia's death in the desert is used for an opposite effect: to confirm the commonplace couple in their mediocrity. 'The dull, the implacable,/The indomitable spirit of mediocrity' is the essential quality of their characters and of their relationship – meaning that they have never been borne out of themselves by the passion of love. Such a marriage without ecstasy was the pollution which made Harry's hell, and from which he had to purge himself. But the Chamberlaynes, once the Guardians have brought them through the breakdown of their illusions and self-deceptions, are simply

reconciled to their condition. It would be hell, as Edward finds and as Reilly
tells Celia, to remain oneself alone 'in the phantasmal world/Of imagination,
shuffling memories and desires'; but honestly to face the fact that one is not
capable of real love, and not really lovable, makes it a purgatory and one way
of salvation. Eliot explained in a letter that when Reilly says these things his
'universe of discourse' is governed by 'two primary propositions: (1) nobody
understands you but God; (2) all real love is ultimately the love of God.'[8] Because she has really loved, Celia is set upon the way of illumination. The
Chamberlaynes' enlightenment is to know that they cannot really love each
other – and that this is why they are bound to each other. Theirs is 'the human
condition' as Reilly describes it:

> tolerant of themselves and others,
> Giving and taking, in the usual actions
> What there is to give and take. They do not repine;
> Are contented with the morning that separates
> And with the evening that brings together
> For casual talk before the fire
> Two people who know they do not understand each other,
> Breeding children whom they do not understand
> And who will never understand them.

'Is that the best life?' Celia asks. 'It is a good life,' Reilly insists; and he adds
later, 'Neither way is better./Both ways are necessary.' That affirmation has to
make all the difference from the putting down of the common man's 'living,
and partly living', in *Murder in the Cathedral*; and from the feeling in *The
Family Reunion* that to be out of love was to be cursed and polluted. The Chamberlaynes are not to be plucked from their burning, but must go on with the
cocktail party as their form – the banal, commonplace form – of the *via negativa*.
Edward understands it thus:

> Oh, it isn't much
> That I understand yet! But Sir Henry has been saying,
> I think, that every moment is a fresh beginning;
> And Julia, that life is only keeping on;
> And somehow, the two ideas seem to fit together.

That is how, being the common fool he is, he grasps the action of *Four Quartets*.

That there should be any degree of reconciliation with 'the human condition'
is a notable advance upon Eliot's pre-war work. But we should not exaggerate
the matter, or take it for something other than it is. When Professor Coghill,
for one, argues that the Chamberlaynes attain the happy fulfilment of natural
human love, he is surely being perverse both in regard to the human and the

natural, and in regard to the play itself, which does not claim after all that theirs is a life of love.[9] It rather shows that the essential point about them is that it is their fate not to know what real love is. Furthermore, there is nothing in the play as a whole to suggest that Eliot had altered his view of what human life and love offered just in themselves. For example, some remarks in his Clark Lectures, in a passage discussing Donne's 'The Ecstasy,' would provide an apt commentary:

the conception of the ecstasy of union between two souls is not only philosophically crude but emotionally limiting. The expression of love as contemplation of the beloved object is not only more aristotelian, it is also more platonic, for it is the contemplation of absolute beauty and goodness partially revealed through a limited though delightful human object. . . Donne, the modern man, is imprisoned in the embrace of his own feelings. There is little suggestion of adoration, of worship. And an attitude like that of Donne leads naturally to one of two things: to the Tennysonian happy marriage – not very different from Donne's own – which is one sort of bankruptcy; or to the collapse of the hero of Huysmans' *En Route: Mon dieu, que c'est donc bête.*

Celia is saved by just such a collapse; and the Chamberlaynes are saved by the bankruptcy of their Tennysonian happy marriage. That they are saved by it makes a difference between the play and the tenor of the lectures; but that is all the difference. 'The best of a bad job is all any of us make of it', says Reilly, 'Except of course, the saints' – which leaves most of us stuck with a life that is not any the less a bad job for being made the best of. The change that has taken place in Eliot's work is simply this: that from fear and terror of the ordinary human lot, he has come to accept it as inescapable, and therefore as necessary for ordinary mortals. This is the very reverse of an escape from or transcendence of mediocrity. It is a coming to terms with it, by comprehending it within the pattern of fate. 'The waste sad time' becomes in the simplest way 'ridiculous', to be laughed at; and the importunate negative is discovered to be the absurd side of Providence.

This should make the play a comedy in a deeper sense than is intended by the term 'drawing-room comedy'. Yet what sort of comedy is it? Celia's death, from the Christian viewpoint, is certainly a sort of happy ending. Possibly, still from that point of view, the fate of the nun who escaped but 'Will never be fit for normal life again' should evoke 'a tremor of joy'. But this is the comic sense of the saint. The comic sense which would reconcile us to the human condition differs from it as it has a different object. Its basis appears to be the conviction that in this world we are all of us fools, and that the wisest are those who laugh at themselves for being 'only human'. To them is granted the assurance that in the end 'all shall be well, and all manner of thing shall be well', and this makes them glad to be ridiculous. But this means that, ultimately, both fool and saint are seen in one and the same Christian vision. A natural association of ideas might lead one to speak of this comedy as introducing a new humanity into Eliot's work; but to look at it from a humane point of view is to discover its limits. Erasmus' *Praise of Folly* would be a useful guide to the play's discriminations of the different kinds of fool there may be in the world; and at the same time, fully understood and taken with his Dialogues and other writings, it gives a measure of how far short the play falls of a complete Humanism. Erasmus, without being any the less Christian, was genuinely in touch with the Greek sense of man – which Eliot repudiated even while drawing upon Greek sources for his plays. He was, moreover, a genuine precursor of the Shakespearian comic vision, in which Puck's 'Lord, what fools these mortals be!' is only one note in the gamut, and one fully resolved in the final harmony of nature, when 'all the story of the night . . . grows to something of great constancy'. The truly humane sense of comedy does not leave out of its sense of life all that makes for life, for its power and substance and intensity. In its light, the human wisdom of *The Cocktail Party* is only that of the void heart, conscious only of failure and defeat and alienation; a wisdom valid for lightening the burden of *Angst* by giving it a meaning and a purpose; but hardly one which ministers to the sane and joyful fulfilment of mankind in its own nature. From the point of view of a comedy which celebrates the possibilities of our world, the Guardians look like a bunch of creeps, dangerous because they think they know all, and because their cure is to confirm the disease. The spreading of their 'enlightenment' to the Chamberlaynes, and from them to Peter Quilpe – and from the play to its audience – calls for Blake's penetrating critique, in *Songs of Innocence and of Experience*, of the passing on of the oppressive evangel of sin and sorrow like death itself from generation to generation. Even from a point of view near to Eliot's own the humanity of the play must appear very restricted: Dante's *Divine Comedy* does not make fools of us.

The Confidential Clerk (1953), though it is generally regarded as the lesser play on account of having even less 'poetry' in it, is both more of a comedy, and a more humane one. This is because it doesn't merely reconcile the mediocre to their lot; but does this on the basis of their having something worthwhile to be reconciled to – a positive human potential which the play works to release and fulfil. Moreover, from that there follows a surprising further reconciliation within the deep and tangled complex of emotions which had dominated Eliot's poetry up to *The Family Reunion*, and which had seemed to be finally, if rather violently, resolved there. Most surprising of all, there is a distinct suggestion, which becomes a fairly definite conviction by the end, that his typical hero is not being taken so seriously as hitherto, and that he is being exposed in a not wholly flattering light.

The most obvious advance upon *The Cocktail Party* is that here Eliot committed himself, for the first time, to making a play that would work in purely worldly terms. Certainly the worldliness is kept on a tight rein, by the artifice of the plot, which owes even more to Plautus and to Oscar Wilde than to its declared 'point of departure',[10] the *Ion* of Euripides; and also by the seeding in of images, puns and allegorical hints to intimate the existence of another world. Nevertheless, it was a great leap for Eliot to do without a saint and martyr. The several characters who are in search of themselves and of their children or parents, have all to find their real identities and relationships in the actual world. Along with this, Eliot brought down his divine agents to the level of the everyday, making the one a tightly rolled confidential clerk, devoted to his duties and his suburban garden; and the other a prim widow in a flowery hat and drab coat who minds other people's children. Eggerson's part is simply to bring to light the facts that must be faced; and Mrs Guzzard's is simply to spell out the facts and their consequences. He is a comic sort of Apollo or his priest, and she is a sort of Fate or Sybil. They have affinities with the Guardians too, and with the Eumenides; and they act as god-father and god-mother to the hero. But all that is merely 'in the air'; and what directly characterises them, first and last, is their ordinariness, and their possessing no special wisdom or mystery. If they represent the Christian way of life, the one in its positive and the other in its negative phase, they do it in the forms of normal worldly behaviour.

The action of fate as they unravel it appears relatively simple, its complications only those of a romantic tale designed to bring us through confusions to the truth which makes a happy ending. Sir Claude Mulhammer thinks Colby Simpkins is his son; Lady Elizabeth, his wife, persuades herself that he must be *her* long-lost son; in fact he belongs to neither of them. Their real children are, respectively, Lucasta Angel – whom Sir Claude would like to be rid of, and of whom Lady Elizabeth does not approve – and B. Kaghan, whom she doesn't approve of either. When Lucasta and B. decide to marry, Lady Elizabeth has to accept them both together; while Sir Claude fears that he is losing Lucasta just when he has found that she is all the children he has. Colby was Mrs Guzzard's son; but she had given him up to Sir Claude so that he might have a better start in life, and she does not mean to reclaim him now. Instead she sets him free to follow his wanting to be an organist in spite of knowing he will not be first-rate, by telling him that his real father was an undistinguished musician.

Thus far we appear to be in the realm of *The Cocktail Party*'s ordinary good life. Colby is happily resigned to being the mediocre musician he is; and the rest of the household are composed into a contented family group, tolerant of themselves and of each other, and reconciled to 'the human condition' in just the way Reilly prescribed.

It makes an immense difference, however, that instead of this condition being reserved for the loveless, all the characters are moved by love in one way or another, while the facts they must adjust to are the real substance of their loves. Sir Claude and Lady Elizabeth in losing their illusory children discover their true ones; and they also discover each other. Lucasta finds the kind of love she needs with B. Kaghan – one which has the security of being without illusions. Eggerson, in looking after Colby, seems to find again his own son who was 'lost in action'. (Colby and Mrs Guzzard also follow the leading of their loves – but that is another story, to be returned to in a moment.) The larger group of characters are composed in the finale into a family tableau, united in the spirit – if not quite in the same tone – of this speech which was drafted for Monica in *The Elder Statesman*:

> any words are silly between people like ourselves
> Who've no vocabulary for love – but is there one
> For love within a family? That love is most in silence,
> For it's the love on which all else depends, the love
> That stands between us and destruction, love that's lived in
> But not looked at, love within the light of which
> All else is seen, the love within which
> All other human love finds speech. . .[11]

That quality of love is not explicitly stated in *The Confidential Clerk*, but it is both the end towards which it progresses, and the ground of its action. This of course is a striking development in Eliot's work, that instead of unfamiliar Love being all, there should be a positive valuation of love as men and women commonly know it in their human relationships.

Colby and Mrs Guzzard are got off stage before the final tableau, and they don't belong in the family group. They rather enact 'the pattern' of the earlier works; but with a difference that arises in part from the way in which they do it, and in part from the way in which the pattern is woven into the 'ground' of the family relationships. As in *The Family Reunion*, the son's life is made to depend upon his mother's love, but Colby is given no cause to kill Mrs Guzzard. The analogies with Orestes and Oedipus, and with Hamlet and Coriolanus, simply don't apply. Thinking back to the earlier play in 1951, Eliot reflected, 'we are left in a divided frame of mind, not knowing whether to consider the play the tragedy of the mother or the salvation of the son.'[12] In *The Confidential*

Clerk, written about that time, the two things are reconciled. This is done by allowing the mother to be to the son both an Amy and an Agatha, so that her tragedy is his salvation. As his natural mother she showed her love in sacrificing her own claims for the sake of his worldly prospects; when she renounces that hope and reveals the truth of his origins, she brings him to birth in his spiritual existence. So the son seeking his soul's fulfilment, and the mother who wants him to do well, are reunited in a common action. This amounts to a reconciliation of the two realms of flesh and spirit, such as seemed inconceivable in *The Family Reunion*. But there is still the persistent suggestion of a division between the natural and the spiritual, and of the natural life being set right only by an action on a 'higher' plane. Mrs Guzzard, at least, is required to follow the negative way, in consciously sacrificing her own will to her son's destiny.

Colby's destiny is to follow his love of music, and there is something supernatural about this too, although it is brought down to earth. It seems that in order to be sure about it he needs to know who was his real father, and here the connection with the *Ion* becomes illuminating.[13] Young Ion's problem is that he doesn't know whether he is of divine or human origin, and he can find no answer in the evidence offered by both gods and men. But that drives him back upon his own nature, and there he finds his answer: he must follow what Arnold would call his best self. His divine father, Apollo, having absconded, the divine inspiration is to be sought within the human spirit itself. In his own fashion, by having Colby become an organist, though an indifferent one, Eliot also rediscovers the divine principle within the human.

The play makes much of the passion for music, and for art in general – we need to remember that Apollo was the god of music and the arts. Colby's music, and Sir Claude's love of ceramics, enable them to pass from the unreal into the real: the form, the pattern, transports into the realm of immediate experience which is 'life itself'. More than that, the creative impulse is understood as an impulse towards the absolute – that is, towards the unification of all one's being into a single intense and perfect whole. The terms used recall *Burnt Norton*'s analogy between the shaping power of human art which is inspired by love, and divine Love which shapes all things. But in this case it is the likeness which is brought out, not the disparity: what is affirmed is simply the creative principle within human nature. Moreover, the quest for integrity no longer requires the annihilation 'of all that's made'. 'Life itself' does not lie through a metaphysical looking-glass, but is realised within the mirror of a natural love raised to the power of art. This means that the aspiration towards the condition of music should not be at odds with the human condition – as it had been in all of Eliot's work since 'Portrait of a Lady' and 'Prufrock'. Colby is clearly right to want his music to be not merely ideal and shut off from his ordinary existence, as Sir Claude's collection of china has been.[14] Even the world of finance and material power could be 'life itself', as it was for the latter's father, if only one had the right passion for it and could make an art of it. Eggerson in his humble way does that, making a single world of his garden and his confidential duties. So we gather that the one thing necessary is to practise the divine art of making oneself whole, the essential inspiration of which is love.

Now we come to the heart of Colby's problem. He loves his music, which Lucasta calls his secret garden; but being alone there makes even it unreal, as well as everything else. 'If I were religious,' he tells her,

> God would walk in my garden
> And that would make the world outside it real
> And acceptable, I think.

When he says that he is beginning to hope that Lucasta might walk there with him. But just as they are finding that they could love each other, the natural development of their feelings is prevented – exactly as in *The Family Reunion*, though by nothing so sensational as the Eumenides – by the discovery of the 'fact' that they are brother and sister. The shock serves to make them sublimate their love for each other, even after the supposed fact is disproved; and Colby is confirmed in his solitude. His impulse to love another person thus follows the pattern adhered to from 'La Figlia Che Piange' right up to *The Cocktail Party* – though with the modifications that he does not have to suffer a terrible disillusionment and conviction of sin, that his separation from Lucasta is not violent and absolute, and that his being impelled towards the divine union is merely hinted at.

This leaves him rather undeveloped in the end, and rather exposed to criticism. The design of the earlier drama and of *Four Quartets*, which I have been tracing out here in a distinctly humanised and more comic form, would lead us to expect that he has been detached from the human object of his love, and born again in the calling of his real father, in order that he might conceive the Word. But we don't see him in that ideal relation: we see him in his human relations, and in a context where human relationships have been given an unprecedentedly positive value. In this perspective it becomes possible to reflect that if his real self can walk only with God, the reason might be that his natural development has been arrested. The quest for integrity of self, which involves separating himself from unreal or falsifying relations, is undeniably a virtue; but it becomes vicious if it leads to being self-enclosed and incapable of entering into real relationships with other persons. Eliot accurately described Colby as having 'a certain deliberate ambivalence: egotist and ascetic';[15] and while we may choose to regard him as a potential saint, we are shown him as actually something of an egotist. That must make us a bit dubious about his budding sanctity.

The doubt is enforced by the way the play is shaped towards the final family group, from which Colby stands aside; and even more by the treatment of Lucasta, the *jeune fille* as Eliot would once have called her. She is the first of his characters to be a truly *other* person, and not a projection of his hero or of his own feelings and preconceptions about others. (Mary in *The Family Reunion* perhaps comes nearest to her; but even she, though not required to be a Beatrice, exists only within Harry's subjective drama.) Lucasta is the product of sympathetic observation and understanding, and becomes a thoroughly real woman trying to be true to herself in a world that seems to consist mainly of artifice and false relations – Eliot's 'Roaring Girl', as one might say.[16] Now such a recognition of another person could be the first step towards, as it is the necessary basis for, a true union of a man and a woman. Lucasta's feeling for Colby is primarily in her recognition of what he is in himself; and her relationship with Kaghan is founded upon their mutual recognition of each other. But Colby doesn't seem capable of that. He is really rather afraid of Lucasta; is willing to meet her only upon his own terms – in his own private garden; and is so bound up in himself that he has no real sense of her as a person at all. Looked at in this light, his love appears to be in the immature, narcissistic stage – one of the stages of adolescence. And his sublimation of it would be a way of keeping his ego intact from a woman who was too grown-up for him.

None of this invalidates his quest for integrity, but it does question the form it seems likely to take. So far as he has the character of the metaphysical poet who would be a saint, he is a portrait of that poet as a young man. A first principle in reading Eliot is: the poet is not to be identified with his personae. Now we discover that the dramatist is not to be identified with the poet, but has become the detached critic observing him. He has not disowned the poet, nor the occupation of the saint; but his interest in human characters and human relationships has developed into a new point of view, and so arrived at a new understanding of the impulse towards the ideal. Instead of making that impulse the measure of all else, he has shown it in a way which allows it to be measured by other possibilities. One consequence is that the self-perfecting alien ceases to be the unquestioned hero of the drama, but is seen to be making the best of a bad job after his own fashion. Another is that human beings are found to have rather more to offer than the poet had been willing to credit.

The interest of *The Elder Statesman* (1958) is all in its relation to its author: to the poet he had been, and the man he now showed himself to be. Eliot's remark that its model was Sophocles' *Oedipus at Colonus*[17] recalls what he had said in 1938 about *The Family Reunion*: 'Harry's career needs to be completed by an *Orestes* or an *Oedipus at Colonus*.' That was because Harry had not fully understood what the Furies were telling him, that 'the only way out is the way of purgation and holiness'.[18] The poet had followed that way to its end in the Quartets. But when Eliot came to write his *Oedipus at Colonus*, for performance in his seventieth year, he rather abruptly took another way out. His view of life had of course undergone a significant alteration since 1938. But a revolutionary change seems to have followed upon his falling in love with and marrying his secretary, Valerie Fletcher, at the stage when he was writing and she was typing Acts I and II. The dedication draws attention to the reflection of that event within the play, where the discovery of love does appear to supervene upon an action quite differently conceived. It was to have shown the process of Lord Claverton's purgation and finding the way to die in peace. The celebration of the love which unites his daughter and her fiancé is superimposed on that, and in rather an awkward fashion, since their love for each other is somehow made to fulfil his need to be loved for himself. The awkwardness prompts us to see through the dramatic illusion to the private reality, where there were not two relationships but only one; and where the need which had been turned towards purgation and self-transcendence, was answered by an unhoped for love, and satisfied in a relationship not allowed for in the initial conception. For the play itself this is quite shattering – I don't see how it can be pieced together into a convincing whole. But it becomes all the more eloquent on that account as a human document, and one which suggests a shocking revaluation of Eliot's life-work.

The play remains concerned with the Elder Statesman's purgation except at its beginning and its end.[19] Lord Claverton is an ambitious, successful and honoured public man. Retired because of bad health, he finds himself for the first time since he was plain Dick Ferry with a blank engagement book, 'contemplating nothingness' and terrified of solitude. The self he had been in public life is a thing of the past, yet it is all that he is in the eyes of others: where is his real, his authentic self? For the first two Acts it seems that he must rediscover that through coming to terms with the ghosts of his youth who return to haunt him.

The first of these was a friend whom he helped go to the bad, but who has since changed his name and made good in a Central American republic where corruption is a respectable way of life. This Federico Gomez is clearly Lord

Claverton's double; most of all in having so thoroughly changed his identity as to lose himself and become cut off from others. He hopes to be restored to reality by having his old friend accept both the man he used to be and the one he has become – that is, the hollow man he knows himself to be. When Claverton refuses to admit the likeness, Gomez tries to bring it home by recalling the occasion when Dick Ferry ran over a body on the road and didn't stop: thus reviving the shameful, sordid memory of a moment of truth when he had thought only of saving himself. As in *Little Gidding*, his double is offering 'the rending pain of re-enactment/ Of all that you have done, and been'. By refusing to meet him on their common ground of humiliating egotism and error, he must be confirming his own imprisonment in unreality. For he needs exactly what he is denying Gomez: to be recognised as the small soul he really is, and to be loved as that.

His second visitant cuts nearer to the heart. If Mrs Carghill is a woman with a past, then, in the same sense of the phrase, she is his past. But he had thought to buy her off and bury the affair; whereas she makes no secret of having been Maisie Montjoy the musical comedy star, and of his having been her first lover. She has to remind him:

> There were the three of us – Effie, Maudie and me.
> That day we spent on the river – I've never forgotten it –
> The turning point of all my life! . . .
> I said 'there's a man I could follow round the world!'
> But Effie it was – you know, Effie was very shrewd –
> Effie it was said 'you'd be throwing yourself away.
> Mark my words' Effie said, 'if you choose to follow *that* man
> He'd give you the slip: he's not to be trusted.
> That man is hollow'. That's what she said.
> Or did she say 'yellow'? I'm not quite sure.
> You do remember now, don't you, Richard?

He is prepared to remember only 'a brief infatuation' and 'a lucky escape'. But for her their relationship, though brief, was intense and remains a permanent reality:

> It's frightening to think that we're still together
> And more frightening to think that we may *always* be together.
> There's a phrase I seem to remember reading somewhere:
> *Where their fires are not quenched.*

Mrs Carghill is a very near relation to the women of *The Waste Land*; and Claverton seems to have belonged with the loitering heirs of City directors. He has not let 'The awful daring of a moment's surrender' bring him into existence as a moral being; and still, in refusing to acknowledge any relation with her, he is preferring to keep up appearances. Yet Mrs Carghill touches more deeply than Gomez his terror of being irredeemably unreal because hollow at heart – incapable of loving another, and justly unloved. This, his most deeply repressed anxiety, is his worst shame and original sin. That means, according to the example of *The Hollow Men* and the later poems, that it is what he needs to confess and accept as his purgatorial fire. What he is refusing in rejecting Mrs Carghill's ambiguous·advances could be his salvation.

Because he will not acknowledge them, these two ghosts can only turn the key upon his imprisonment within an unreal public image – they prove ineffectual Eumenides. A third encounter, with his son Michael – a second self – exposes his present cowardice and hypocrisy. Michael is not impressed by his father's public image, and feels falsified by the expectation that he should live up to it. He wants to be himself and make his own way; which seems to mean taking after Gomez. Shocked and disappointed, Lord Claverton accuses him of being 'a fugitive from reality', of trying to hide from his past failures. What he will not admit is what he most needs to admit – it is the only way to remove the barrier between them – that he has himself been doing the same all his life; and that what really shocks him is Michael's frankly confessing to being no better than he ought to be – like the true son of his shameful, secret self. For the third time he refuses to come clean, and rejects the opportunity to set right his relations with himself and with others.

Nevertheless, at the end of that second Act, he does begin to acknowledge his hypocrisy, in admitting to his daughter Monica that he is himself a·coward trying to escape himself and his past, and that he should set himself to be schooled by his humiliations. He must have been moved to this by her declaration, following his scene with Michael, that there must be 'love within a family', and that she would give her life for him. It is a short speech – simply the gist of the draft version from which I quoted in connection with *The Confidential Clerk* – but it is the crucial moment for Claverton and for the play. Up to this point the governing 'reality' has been that there is no love and no truth in his relations with himself and with others. By the established pattern of Eliot's work, the way out of his hell of loneliness and shame should be through suffering it in full consciousness. But everything is altered by the sudden discovery that he is loved after all; and the most profound change is that this enables him to get scot free of his unreal and shameful selves, and to enter directly into 'the illumination/Of knowing what love is'.

The first thing love means to Claverton is confession – showing one's real self to another person, and being really known by that person. But then his confession proves to be essentially a mode of communion, or an approach to communion, in which all sense of self is lost. His shames and failures come to seem unimportant; and what gives release from them is simply the being able to confess to the one person who loves him. Moreover, the meaning of the confession is that he loves that person:

> If a man has one person, just one in his life,
> To whom he is willing to confess everything . . .
> Then he loves that person, and his love will save him.

The manner in which it saves Claverton has little to do with the confession of sins, or with the liberation from humiliation by humiliation called for in the early notes and drafts.[20] While he sees himself 'emerging/From my spectral existence into something like reality', he dismisses Gomez and Mrs Carghill as 'not real' –

> They are merely ghosts:
> Spectres from my past. They've always been with me
> Though it was not till lately that I found the living persons
> Whose ghosts tormented me, to be only human beings,
> Malicious, petty. . .

That, one might have thought, is to strip them of their moral reality, and to conceal the fact that they are his Furies. He goes on in that fashion, admitting only that he nourished faults and weaknesses the friend of his youth had been born with; and as for the woman who 'had a peculiar physical attraction/Which no other woman has had', and whose first lover he was,

> Maisie loved me, with whatever capacity
> For loving she had – self-centred and foolish –
> But we should respect love always when we meet it;
> Even when it's vain and selfish, we must not abuse it.
> That is where I failed. And the memory frets me.

What a paltry phrase, and what a patronising 'confession'! He is really setting himself in judgment upon the others whom he fears and wants to be rid of, while taking as little as possible upon himself. In regard to himself, he is mainly appealing for Monica's 'protective affection' – asking for her love to save him from himself and from his past. Her response answers precisely to his need. Aided by her fiancé, Charles, a rising politician, she shows loving devotion towards him, and drives off the 'intruders' with legal menace and chilling snobbery. So far as they are concerned the confession is in effect an exorcism. For the rest it is a confession of love: of his need for love, and the difference it makes to be loved.

The most striking measure of the difference is that in his end he becomes the first of Eliot's personae and protagonists to find his peace in human love, and not by the way of purgation and holiness. It is revealing to observe the stages by which he brought the play to this conclusion. At first the love theme was quite undeveloped, though the daughter's 'protective affection' was already important in a synopsis written while he was working on Act II. Then the play was to end in this way:

ELD ST. begins to unburden his heart to DAUGHTER. She is happy to find him so changed, and instead of contemning him, as he expects, she exhibits a new protective affection. He is still further affected by her response. He feels the end approaching. . . But he feels released – wants to take a walk. Goes out. Dies offstage. Thunderclap?[21]

The thunderclap could suggest a connection with 'What the Thunder Said'; but the nearer connection was likely to have been with Oedipus' death in the grove of the Eumenides at Colonus, when 'the earth groaned with thunder from the god below'. In a later outline of Act III, drafted after Eliot's marriage, the thunder is replaced by: (1) the voices of his Furies in the dusk taunting him; and (2), after he has answered them, and collapsed, by the daughter and fiancé in a 'Love duet finale'.[22] Then this last became the end on its own; and that meant the complete elimination of the original conception of the play as a ritual of purgation and union with the divine. Claverton's Furies are not transformed into Kindly Ones, but are discarded as merely his alter ego, his old flame and his black sheep, as if they were to be associated rather with Sophocles' Creon and Polyneices. He joins himself instead with his truly loving daughter and his new son – which is rather as if Oedipus were not to pass into the other world, but were to enter into a marriage of Antigone and Theseus. The manner in which he enters into this human communion is perhaps slightly veiled; yet an acquaintance with Eliot's habit of using personae and doubles should make it transparent. The 'daughter', by a reversal of the mode of sublimation practised in *Marina* and *Ash-Wednesday*, becomes his beloved; and the man she loves is himself, his 'real self' brought into being at last in love.

POSTLUDE

I

In the 'Love duet finale' of *The Elder Statesman* – as also in the discovery of love in its first scene[23] – Eliot was making a transparent confession of his own personal happiness. The characters of Claverton, Monica and Charles all dissolve into Eliot himself, and the words they speak are 'private words addressed to [his wife] in public'. In these passages, as in the 'Dedication', the writing breaks the decorum of impersonal art, and becomes awkwardly intimate:

CHARLES   Oh my dear,
        I love you to the limits of speech, and beyond.
        It's strange that words are so inadequate.
        Yet, like the asthmatic struggling for breath,
        So the lover must struggle for words.
MONICA   I've loved you from the beginning of the world.

The mawkish sincerity of the writing enforces the declaration that it was Eliot himself, the man who suffered among other things from emphysema, who had been 'brushed by the wing of happiness'.

That was 'In spite of everything, in defiance of reason' – and in complete contradiction of his life's work. The basic premise and inspiration of that had been the conviction that the 'barriers between one human being and another' were indestructible; that there was an 'awful separation between potential passion and any actualisation possible in life'; that 'the void . . . in the middle of all human happiness and all human relations' could be filled by only one thing – Atonement with Christ. The final Act of *The Elder Statesman* breaks that pattern, and affirms the contrary. It finds a new life in the human union, the being at one with each other of a man and a woman in love, 'conscious of a new person/Who is you and me together'. In this love is found the peace of a complete communion here and now:

        Age and decrepitude can have no terrors for me,
        Loss and vicissitude cannot appal me,
        Not even death can dismay or amaze me
        Fixed in the certainty of love unchanging.
                                        I feel utterly secure
        In you; I am a part of you.

'The divine union' is simply not in question here, one way or the other. That underlines the wonderful fact that Eliot should end his career as an artist by asserting as actual what his writing over fifty years had maintained to be impossible in life.

So the positive purpose broke at last from the seemingly negative life-work –

                        And what you thought you came for
        Is only a shell, a husk of meaning
        From which the purpose breaks only when it is fulfilled
        If at all. Either you had no purpose
        Or the purpose is beyond the end you figured
        And is altered in fulfilment.

Its end proved to be the immediate experience of love – which had to be, if it were to be had at all in life, actual human love – and the recovery of the ecstasy lost or sacrificed because not believed in, which had been the beginning. The need for self-transcendence in love can now be seen to have been the deepest and most consistent motive in all his work. When it seemed unattainable, frustration and failure grew and were deliberately cultivated into 'the death motive': *Angst*, alienation and the sense of sin; then suffering and death embraced as the way of purgation into the realm – mystical, transcendental, ideal – of perfect Love. Yet all this pursuit of the Absolute through negations is exposed, by the actual experience of love, as necessary only because he was out of love, and only for so long as he remained in that state. When he found himself in love, he found the fullness and harmony of being for which he longed – and his poetry could be seen for what it is, a supreme expression of the negative phase of desire. He might have said with Aquinas, though with a rather different application, 'It seems to me but straw.' What he did say, by his wife's account, was that 'he felt he had paid too high a price to be a poet'.[24]

2

Some other reconsiderations would have been in order. He might have said, what he never did say publicly at least:

that his poetry was true and valid for one experience of life, and for that experience only;

that he had found in the end that another experience was possible;

that this was not the news to the human race that it was to him.

His discovering that it was possible to be whole in the love of another person should have been the occasion for an acknowledgment that there was a wisdom deriving from such love, which he had done his utmost to put down in the name of 'the wisdom of humility'; and that there was a poetry, a making of a life in love, which neither meant death – nor was meaningless babble. It was the moment too for a contrite nod to those authors, especially the friends and contemporaries and near elders, whom he had denounced – correcting those he might well have been corrected by – for honouring the powers of nature and of human nature.

'What does Mr Pound believe?' he had asked, having just confessed, 'I am seldom interested in what he is saying'. He simply didn't want to know about the *religio*, the making Cosmos in the *Cantos*, or about achieving the possible *paradiso terrestre*. Pound told him: 'Given the material means I would replace the statue of Venus on the cliffs of Terracina' – meaning that he would recover, as in Canto XXXIX, the *natural* vision of the Lady 'whose shrine stands on the promontory'. 'I believe', he added, 'that a light from Eleusis persisted throughout the middle ages and set beauty in the song of Provence and Italy.' To Eliot's way of thinking this was heresy. It was the idea of Original Sin which gave the middle ages their significance for him; and *amore* meant a heaven in the light from which a natural life was hell, or at best purgatory.[25]

All his modern heretics he condemned on such grounds. Yeats would have had more than 'lust and rage' to spur him into song in his old age, had he but subdued and disciplined them by religion, and so brought himself to sing like Arnaut in the purgatorial flame.[26]

Lawrence, being 'an ignorant man in the sense that he was unaware of how much he did not know', drew 'the wrong conclusions from the insights which came to him from below consciousness'. He had not been taught that a life lived in conformity with nature involved seeing the world not only 'with the eyes of a Mexican Indian', but 'as the Christian Fathers saw it' – that is, as Eliot saw it in *East Coker* and *The Dry Salvages*. So long as 'his early belief in Life [failed to pass over], as a really serious belief in Life must, into a belief in Death', then 'the man's vision was spiritual, but spiritually sick' – an instrument of 'the daemonic powers'.[27]

Eliot found the same sickness in Hardy, and worse, an 'intrusion of the diabolic': in *Oedipus Rex*, *Heart of Darkness* and *Turn of the Screw* 'we are in a world of Good and Evil – in *Barbara of the House of Grebe* we are introduced into a world of pure Evil'. That story (in *A Group of Noble Dames*) is a study in the sort of perversion which fascinated the author of *Sweeney Agonistes* and some of the fragments among the drafts of *The Waste Land*; but it failed to satisfy him, one must suppose, because Hardy doesn't suggest that any good can come of such horrors – his morals had ceased to be 'a matter of tradition and orthodoxy'.[28]

That judgment is passed again on George Eliot's dreary, provincial, puritanical rationalism – the adjectives are Eliot's. A comparison of *Felix Holt* with *The Family Reunion* might elucidate his meaning. The two works have such similarities that it seems possible that Eliot was reshaping George Eliot's material according to his own very different moral sense. Esther's soul is born in the moment she renounces the Transome estate, which is her Wishwood; but hers is a very different spiritual birth from Harry's. It is only the giving up of a self-seeking false consciousness, and the attaining of a more enlightened and true selfhood – a self of the sort Arnold would have approved. There is no provision of 'bright angels'; and the love which waits and wants her, and does not let her fall, is the love of Felix Holt. The moral failure in *Middlemarch* would have been the letting Dorothea off the hook of her fate by having Casaubon so conveniently die. Eliot, one can guess, would have preferred the spectacle of her purgation to George Eliot's attempt to imagine the adjustment of her aspirations to the actual world.[29]

Eliot's criticism in these instances is hardly 'the common pursuit of true judgment'. He gives at best a very partial account of others' works and visions; and the only thing that is made fully clear is his own point of view. This is true of his criticism as a whole, which has three main components. (1) Deep interest in writers who were good for expressing 'the horror, the horror', the death motive of a world without God – for example, the Senecan element in Elizabethan and Jacobean drama. (2) Homage to writers who added to that sort of dis-illusionment with life a vision of how it might be made to serve as a way towards beatitude. Here Dante is the great master, then Racine, Baudelaire and the later James; also writers, ranging from Mallarmé to Kipling and de la Mare, who gave 'Free passage to phantoms of the mind', or carried the mind beyond the frontiers of ordinary experience. (3) Denunciation of the heresy of those who did not conform to his 'practical sense of realities' – some examples of this have just been noticed. Its function is to close a defensive ring around Eliot's own vision of the world. But his needing to do that is a symptom of neurosis: for it is a neurotic vision, one arising from some disorder or disease of the personality – or of his culture – which has this compulsion to impose itself upon all the world, and to require of everyone and everything else that they confirm its particular order. In his attacks upon those who affirmed what life in love could offer Eliot was demanding – in a manner searchingly diagnosed by Blake (another whose education he found defective) – that because he was alienated, all must be; and that all minds should be possessed by fear and terror – for only in fear could he see any hope.

Eliot did frankly declare throughout his career, and in his 1961 critique of the critic he had been, that his criticism went with his poetry as the expression in another mode of the one sensibility and point of view – he had always, as Leavis has put it, 'his axe to grind'.[30] One can accept that. But then one would expect all the more that when his point of view had undergone so great a change as we have seen in *The Elder Statesman* he would have revised some of his earlier judgments. Instead he appeared still content in 1961 to let them stand. A little of Pound's magnanimity would have been more welcome:

> Many errors,
>   a little rightness,
> to excuse his hell
>   and my paradiso.

To admit that others had been right about the positive experience of love could only have expanded and given authority to his own.

The author of *The Elder Statesman* would have done well, for example, to set himself to school with George Eliot's profoundly wise – wise in its knowledge of the human spirit – study of the banker Bulstrode, with its culmination in the breaking down of his public image and ego, his confession to his wife, and her compassionate love. Again, appreciation of some of the things Lawrence did know could have saved the exchanges of love from being so shallow and stilted.

In Hardy, specifically in *Tess of the D'Urbevilles*, he might have found a liberating diagnosis of the neurosis behind his life's work. Hardy is finely aware of the natural forces at play in Tess and Angel Clare; and he observes how they are thwarted by the pressures of social and religious false consciousness, especially as these operate upon the temperaments of Alec D'Urbeville and Angel Clare. Those two might represent the twin aspects of Eliot's own temperament, the sensual and the ascetic.[31] Hardy's view is that both these are against nature; that they are twin products of an after-Christian society, alienated from the natural world and from the deep sources of humanity; and that they contribute equally to the destruction of 'a pure woman' – one who is whole and true in her own nature. That Tess is finally driven to murder Alec and pay the penalty exacted by society and religion is not, for Hardy, an entry into the real world of Good and Evil, but the ghastly triumph over nature of a very sick mentality. What would have seemed right, had it been possible, would have been the natural fulfilment of their love promised in the moment when Tess's beauty, to Angel, was 'like an annunciation from the sky' – but there's the symptom of what prevents it! – and there was 'the gravitation of the two into one... which changed the pivot of the universe for their two natures'.[32] Eliot, at the end of *The Elder Statesman*, just reaches to a moment of that sort, but with none of Hardy's grasp of the natural universe and human traditions. That means that his late affirmation of human love fails to honour the powers which Hardy shows to be of its essence, and essential to its fulfilment. It also means that he failed to reach an adequate understanding of how and why his life-work had gone against nature and against human love.

3

The neurosis of which Eliot's work is the expression must have been first of all a personal one. But if it were merely that it would be of no great interest.

What makes his neurosis significant is that it is one endemic in our culture, and so common that it can be regarded as a perfectly normal state of mind. It is probably this more than anything else that gives him his common ground with his readers. Moreover it is what makes him a classic, a true type of the mind of Europe: for it is not simply a modern phenomenon, but one deep-rooted in our history, and perpetuated and sanctioned by our traditions. To comprehend it fully we must trace it back beyond the Christian era, at least as far as the profound transformation of primitive Greek religion within the Athenian civilisation.[33]

Our knowledge of Eliot's private history is uncertain, the available facts being few, thin and fragmentary, and leaving us too much to our own interpretations and speculations. However, it is possible to piece together a bare outline, and to arrive at a notion of its basic structure. It is clear at least that he was a deeply sensitive and intelligent child, and closely bound to a mother whose powerful influence promoted a precocious mental and moral development. It is fairly clear also that in adolescence his awakening to sexual love was complicated by her influence and that precociousness. Through the poems of 1905–12, with the aid of the very scanty biographical data, there can be made out the disillusionment of the idealist, preceding and preventing experience, rationalising anxiety and reinforcing inhibition, and making 'sublimation' the only way of love that felt right. When he did commit himself in marriage, his mother (and father) refused their sanction, and the marriage turned into nightmare. If we may read through the poetry to the personal life which remains in darkness, we may deduce that he felt he had fallen into hell, and that only the way of purgation and holiness could cleanse him of the pollution of frustrated love. That involved the transference of love from a human to an ideal object; and to one which is not only an idealisation of the imperfect beloved, but which is ultimately the ideal Mother. This is the process which the poet entered upon in *The Waste Land*, worked out through *The Hollow Men* and *Ash-Wednesday* to its most explicit and expanded form in *The Family Reunion*, and re-enacted in *Four Quartets* as *the* ritual of a Christian culture.

When we notice how the relationship with the mother is always the dominant one – with a mother who becomes both the object of desire and the Divine Mother; and how the usual relationship with a woman is always the deeply wrong form of love; and then how the father-figures are disposed of . . . – then we must be struck by the resemblance to the Oedipus Complex, Freud's key to 'the understanding of human history and the evolution of religion and morality'. Eliot was thoroughly acquainted with Freud's work;[34] but he adapted its diagnosis of civilisation to his own purposes, and drew his own conclusions from it. He did follow Freud's fundamental perception that sexual energy, when prevented in its instinctive action, becomes a dynamic factor in human culture: that is, the neurosis, with its symptoms of guilt and anxiety, is a source of morality, art and religion. Eliot might have been echoing that when he wrote, 'To do away with a sense of sin is to do away with civilisation.' But it was his own bent – though one confirmed by Christianity – which made him take the description as prescriptive, and seek the cure for the neurosis in converting human energies wholly towards the ideal and the Absolute.

In Freud's version of the Oedipus Complex, the son's natural desire for the Mother's love is frustrated by the presence of the forbidding Father: thence the drama of the Ego, a conflict between the powerful impulse of the Id and the authority of the Superego. One way of resolving that conflict – the way we tend to think 'modern' though it is perennial – is to liberate the sexual energies from the repressive morality. Eliot's way is by sublimation, which he liked to think of as traditional and classical, though it is practised as much as ever – only now perhaps with a vision rather materialistic than beatific in view. In Eliot's form of sublimation, the conflict is resolved by the apotheosis of the Mother: as the Divine Mother she not only subsumes the beloved ('Blessed sister, holy mother'), but she also assumes the authority of the Father through being identified with the Logos. This is to reinterpret the Oedipus Complex in the light of a mystical Christianity such as Julian of Norwich's: 'In our Mother, Christ, we grow and develop; in his mercy he reforms and restores us; through his passion, death and resurrection he unites us to our being.'[35] To be thus absolute for the ideal which prevents us everywhere is, within Eliot's work, the salvation of the neurotic. But from the outside that appears to be rather the imperative of the neurosis itself, driving towards its most extreme form.

It is not easy to attain a detached view of the neurosis which is like a dominant gene in our culture. It is a matter, as I observed at the end of the previous chapter, of the alienation of man from that to which he properly, of his nature, belongs – his being cut off from the vital universe, from others, from much in himself. The symptoms, if they are not also the causes, are: the exaltation of mind over matter, reason over nature; then the exploitation of the world in a rather narrowly conceived human interest; then the anxiety and sense of sin consequent upon going against nature, and upon being impoverished and baffled in one's relationships and in oneself. Consequent upon *that* there is likely to be a desperate feeling that there must be a redeeming purpose behind it all, and a raising of the question of personal immortality. There we come back to the fixation in Eliot's work upon the Mother–Redeemer; and I am prompted to suggest that at the root of all is an immature state of personality, one that has remained essentially recessive, self-regarding and self-saving. But for understanding the neurosis which Eliot in his poetry took as a way of life we need to get at a distance from ourselves; and for this we can hardly do better than go to some of the Greek plays which he used as points of departure for his own. These afford us a view of man getting above himself and so falling into error, from within a culture still possessed by a vision of Kosmos – of one life in all things, and all things bound together in the one life.

Euripides' Alcestis saves the life of her husband by taking his death upon herself; and is then herself recovered from death by Heracles. She is of the type of Persephone, whose yearly descent into the earth and vernal return sustains, according to the rites of Eleusis, the life of man and of the entire universe of nature. She re-enacts the rite in which the living and the dead, and the realms of Apollo and Thanatos, sunlit world and dark earth, are bound together in the one process by the one power – the chthonic and solar energy. Admetus, her husband, type of rational, civilised, self-preserving Man, proudly above nature, fails to perceive any of this, even when his own continued existence has been shown to depend on it. He is a rather absurd figure in consequence; and the effect of the comedy is to liberate the mind of the audience from its civilised notions into a deeper comprehension of the nature of things. That the play is made to work in this way must mean of course that its audience was civilised, and needed to be checked, however lightly, in its tendency to become alienated from the sources of life.

Eliot's *Cocktail Party*, having departed from the *Alcestis*, might be said to attain the terminus of that tendency. It enacts no rite of life, nor does it honour the powers which 'make Cosmos'. Instead Alcestis–Persephone is split into Lavinia, the society hostess and fit partner for her Admetus-like husband; and Celia, the heavenly one, who becomes a bride of Christ. Dionysiac Heracles, agent of the solar force bringing living things forth from the earth, is made over into One-Eyed Reilly and his assistant Guardians. The rite which they celebrate is one of merely personal salvation, and a saving of the soul from nature: a confirming and perfecting of alienation, which is just the reverse of Euripides' reuniting man with the powers of his nature.

In Eliot's rehandling of the Oedipus myth there is a similar conversion of a rite of ultimate reconciliation with the daemonic, chthonic powers into one of

Atonement with Christ. This myth, as given in Sophocles' two plays, is possibly the next most important model for his work after Dante – the connection goes far beyond that of *The Elder Statesman* with *Oedipus at Colonus*. It is the major model for *The Family Reunion*, though this is disguised by its being crossed there with the *Oresteia*, and with *Hamlet*. It provides a groundplan for *The Waste Land*, though here it is even more overlaid: there is the 'murdered' father, the sinful marriage, the cursed city; to whom but Oedipus should Tiresias tell what he sees? with whom else, in the context of that allusion, must the poet–protagonist be identifying himself, as he assumes the burden of the waste land, wanders in exile and finds his Colonus? But Eliot no more read Sophocles 'straight' than he read him in Freud's way. In effect, and quite possibly in fact, he read him through Seneca, who had changed the primitive terror – i.e. awe at earth's powers – into mere horrors; and these horrors – Sweeney's, Tiresias's, the Sybil's, Kurtz's – he made into a horror of life itself. He also superimposed upon the myth the Grail Romance, which he probably knew best in Malory. 'The incest of Arthur is the foundation of the plot of the whole book', he once wrote, and went on to approve its 'profound, tribal, Sophoclean morality' – 'Certain acts were sins, and had deadly consequences, and those consequences must follow whether the acts were committed in ignorance or not. They demanded purgation.'[36] In 'What the Thunder Said' the form of purgation leads to the empty chapel of those who seek the vision of the Grail, and the thunder finds out their unworthiness: it is far from Sophocles' Colonus. By such over-readings Eliot assimilated Sophocles' vision to his own view that the state of nature was a state of Original Sin, and that the use of Mind was to save the soul by directing it towards the ideal Love.

In Sophocles, on the contrary, sin is the consequence of Mind acting in ignorance of the nature of things, and so against nature; and Love flows when the mind is at one with Nature. Oedipus is a man characterised by clear reason and the will to act morally; and who is fated to commit, just by following his reason and will, the very crimes he would avoid. He kills the King, unaware that he is his father, because he blocks his way – the way which leads, as it happens, to his marrying the Queen his mother. He comes to that by quelling the terrible Sphinx with the answer 'Man', a feat which seems to justify man's pride in reason as setting him over primitive nature; but the hubris of that appears in his incest, and in his bringing upon Thebes a plague far worse than the Sphinx. His answer was after all only a half-answer, and missed the full meaning of the riddle – 'what is it that in the morning goes upon four legs, at noon upon two, and upon three in the evening?' – that man's life is a process in and of nature. Then it is brought home to him that he has all blindly violated the fundamental bonds of natural society. Not only has he reverted to the savage custom, long suppressed in civilised societies, whereby the new man of power must kill the old one and marry the reigning queen; but it is his own father that he has killed – the worst of sins in patriarchal Athens – and his own mother that he has married, breaking the deepest of human taboos. His self-blinding is like the putting out of the light of pure reason, so that he may learn the ways of the 'dark' powers to which he has been blind. It is with these that he makes his peace in the grove of the Eumenides at Colonus. Kerényi suggests that he should be understood to behold Persephone, as in the crowning vision of the Mystery at Eleusis.[37] In his end he is gathered lucidly and gladly into the generative process of life itself.

'This primitive morality was refined by Christianity', in Eliot's view,[38] and in his own art; but the Sophoclean vision affords a profound criticism of that refinement. What Eliot would perfect, the setting of mind against nature, he shows to be the very source of human error and tragedy. What Eliot rejects, in fear and horror until he can convert them into 'hounds of heaven', he shows to be truly the *kindly* ones: that is, of nature, and therefore loving.

Yet Eliot's refined velleities may be not altogether remote from those current in late fifth-century Athens. They have something in common at least with those of Aeschylus' *Oresteia*, which was written half a century before *Oedipus at Colonus*, and which represents and glorifies the Athenian institution of the rule of reason. In Eliot's mind the stories of Oedipus and Orestes – and of Hamlet too – seem to have been composed into one. But the myths are not fully congruent; and in the versions of Aeschylus and Sophocles they lead to quite opposite conclusions. In the *Oresteia* the will to subdue nature to civilising reason is made to prevail, and the primitive powers are allowed a place in the state only when they have been tamed to serve its purposes.

The first part of the trilogy, a supreme instance of 'the historical sense', gathers up into a single irresistible fate the history of the House of Atreus and of the Trojan War as seen from Argos, and brings it to a moment of truth in the murder of Agamemnon. But then the aftermath is no final catharsis, but a resumption of the old bloody and unnatural tale – Orestes kills Clytemnestra, the Furies demand his death. All of this, it is made clear, is the work of the violent, irrational, uncontrollable powers of the sea and earth and passionate blood – Eliot's 'daemonic, chthonic powers'. In the final play of the trilogy, exactly in his manner, revulsion from 'the immense panorama of futility and anarchy' is made to reinforce the felt need for a law and order answering to human reason above mere natural necessity. The issue is not worked out in actual experience, but is brought to trial before the supreme court of Athens. Apollo argues that there was no blood-guilt in Orestes' killing his mother, since the father is the true parent of the child and there is no blood-tie with the mother. Athene, born from the head of Zeus, is the proof of that. She supports 'the father's claim and male supremacy in all things',[39] and her casting vote carries the verdict against the Furies and the natural order of things. The Furies threaten to lay waste the land with plagues and sterile blight; but are soon soothed and coaxed with promises of honours and offices into accepting the honorific role of Eumenides, and taking a place in the great symbolic procession of the Panathenaic Festival.

This fulfilment of the wish for order lacks all substance. The pastoral idyll of the Eumenides breathing blessings in wind and sunlight throughout the land is too simple to stand up against the earlier anti-pastoral of the storm destroying the Greek fleet on its way home from Troy; or against Clytemnestra's identification of herself, as she exults in the rain of Agamemnon's blood, with the sown earth exulting in the bright showers of spring. She is of course primitive and savage to excess; but the Athenian exaltation of man's mind and reason is excessive too – as Sophocles observed. The trilogy is really deeply divided between the familiar extremes: sweetness and light on the one side, on the other an anarchy of the dark powers; ironic Blake's satanic energy against heavenly reason; Christian Eliot's original sin against the divine union. Aeschylus seems to bring us, as Eliot would, to an ideal order. Yet that appears to involve institutionalising the neurosis, and making it – as in *Four Quartets* – the basis of civilisation.

4

Applied to *Hamlet*, our universal mirror which looks backward and forward and seems always to show the beholder his own image, the ancient diagnosis illuminates the modern form of the neurosis.

The Athenian dramatists, with their awareness of the rites of Eleusis, prompt us to see Hamlet as a man fatally proud of his human nature, and fatally alienated from Nature. He has his Renaissance conceit of what it is to be Man; and behind that is the Christian conceit of Everyman, representative of the supreme importance of man in himself, for whom Hell and Heaven contend on the stage of the fallen world.[40] To Hamlet's immensely heightened self-awareness the drama is all in his own mind, and is the drama of the mind itself – the mind which makes its universe a theatre:

indeed, it goes so heavily with my disposition that this goodly frame, the earth, seems to me a sterile promontory; this most excellent canopy, the air, look you, this brave o'erhanging firmament, this majestical roof fretted with golden fire, – why it appears no other thing to me than a foul and pestilent congregation of vapours. What a piece of work is man! how noble in reason! how infinite in faculty! in form and moving how express and admirable! in action how like an angel! in apprehension how like a god! the beauty of the world! the paragon of animals! And yet, to me, what is this quintessence of dust?

In the dizzying play of wit in the first sentence – a vision of the universe, and the actual theatre with its stage, hangings, painted roof and breathing audience, dissolving the one into the other – which is the reality? or does it all become merely what Hamlet's thinking makes it? As for man in himself, summoned forth out of the foul and pestilent congregation of vapours to stand against this backdrop of the world, he can seem all things and the sum of all – and then mere dust. Hamlet's *Angst* is just the other side of his idealism: his world appears rotten because he is only looking on at life with the eyes of an intensely refined egotism.[41] The fathering powers of earth have become in him – after the moral refinement of Christianity, and the return to Seneca – his ghostly father, imperative for justice, but expressing a very confused and baffling sense of the ultimate sources of life. The full measure of his loss, and ours, is given in Ophelia's madness and death: through the evocations of ancient rituals in her snatches of old songs and the elegiac account of her drowning. She was the Rose of May, the May Queen, and should have been bride to 'Th'expectancy and rose of the fair state'; but is blighted with Hamlet's 'blown youth/Blasted with ecstasy'. Instead of a midsummer marriage bringing the natural process of life to its human fulfilment, there is the blood sacrifice of her father; and she herself is given over to that ritual of death, with the whole latter part of the play. The order of life, which her idiom is always seeking to recover, and which is traced out in the structure of the first scene of the play only to be left unfulfilled by the play as a whole – the order of life has been violated by Hamlet's idealism. That proves to be the death motive, Eliot's importunate negative, about its dirty work.

Hamlet failed to satisfy Eliot, so far as I can make out, only because it lacked the intellectual completion which would have carried Hamlet on to his beatitude. Like the Hyacinth Girl who is associated with her – and whose very name, like an antonym of Rose of May, recalls Hyacinthus whom Apollo loved and killed – Ophelia, being saved from madness by drowning, should have been metamorphosed into 'the third who walks always beside you', the figure of perfect Love in the desert, 'I do not know whether a man or a woman'.

Modern readers in general are unlikely to follow Eliot there. The usual responses involve a greater or less degree of self-identification with Hamlet:

an agreement that the play is *his* tragedy; and a failure to see (what Hardy would not have missed) that really the tragic victim is Ophelia, and that she is sacrificed to Hamlet's 'sovereign reason'.

5

Man just as a mind and will, immature in that he has not realised himself as a
    mode of life, a part in the whole process,
    seeks self-fulfilment and self-transcendence through his 'sovereign reason'
    and his strength of will,
    – whence Idealism (dreams of the apotheosis of the Ego), and its twin –
    Materialism (dominations of the Other).

Idealism and Materialism alike express the alienation of men from the one
    life within us and within all things;
    both, by repressing exploiting and perverting the energies of man and nature,
    turn life against the living.

Man's existence as just a mind and will seeking his own absolute is contrary
    to nature, and contrary to his own nature –
    his thought annihilates and his touch kills.

Eliot is expert in this state of existence:
    he is its consummate poet, having brought it to a fully conscious realisation;
    and its prophet, bearing witness to how it may be perfected.

Idealism takes many forms: the Platonic, the Christian; even the City when speculating in values which have no substantial existence is idealist; International Capital in its mysterious working is very like Providence and Fate; and our leading thinkers – economists, nuclear physicists, Parisian critics – are all engaged in the realms of the Ideal. But the form most immediately relevant to Eliot and to Art is that of the *Symbolistes*.

Mallarmé dreamed of transmuting everything in words into a book that would *be* the world. Valéry reckoned what it cost to practise that alchemy of Mind: the fatal divorce from Nature which left the man a shade in a void – dissolved in his own thinking. Eliot once praised Valéry's 'poetic statement of a definite and unique state of the soul dispossessed', meaning dispossessed of God; though one might have thought, with Valéry himself, that it was Nature he had lost. Eliot's conscious contribution to the *symboliste* movement – in whose writings he had so steeped himself that they seem to echo with reminders of his – was to reconnect it with its origins in classical and orthodox idealism. 'Valéry was not Pascal', he wrote, having set himself to be both of them at once: to be god-possessed through the praxis of Atonement with the Word.

He could commit himself to the Zero and renounce the passing summer of sense, not as if he were giving himself up to mere thought, and not only in speculation. *He really meant it*, as few idealists do – meant it enough to make it his way of life. He refined his language until it made living mean only separation from God; and he ordered his sensibility so that it became absolute for death, as the form in which the living might know and be at one with God. This required him to realise what the ideal meant in his actual existence: not instant bliss and the beatific vision on earth – precisely not that; but angst and suffering and death. His making his ideal real in this way, and telling the whole truth about life in the ideal, gives his work a substance, seriousness and dignity, and a permanent value, beyond that of most other idealists.

Eliot – to adapt to himself what he said of Dante's Brunetto – is excellent in idealism: so admirable a poet, and so perverse.[42]

Materialism, in the loose sense in which one may speak of this as a materialistic age, is not the opposite of Idealism, but rather the practical (as against the contemplative) mode of self-seeking. It is quite commonly an attempt to make the world serve or conform to an ideal. The Crusades and the Inquisition, and the conquests of empires such as the Spanish or the contemporary American hegemony, these have been the material consequences of ideals. Kurtz is a universal type. There are ideals behind *laissez-faire* Capitalism, behind the Communist State, behind Fascist Republics. Behind Pure Technology lies Pure Science. The perception of something as material to man is the other side of a perception of man as outside and above nature.

To master nature by the exercise of will and intelligence, to make it serve our needs and dreams, isn't that what it is to be human? Is it not godlike to use the energy of the nucleus, to make of the ocean a generator, to synthesise sunlight? Has not every man the right to his personal paradise, as good or better than the next man's? And don't I deserve to be loved all for myself?

But the actual experience of the attempts to make these ideals materialise is a desolating discovery of the hollowness, and corruption and pettiness and misery, of man in himself alone. Our mastery of nature makes a waste land of it, and neurotics of ourselves.

In general – but in the particular lie blessed exceptions – the way of life in the civilisation to which most readers of this book will belong is one of sacrifice.

Not quite – not directly – blood sacrifice, but still the sacrifice of life to an ideal that is always promising to materialise; and which does materialise in a far from ideal actuality.

Because he was a master of the actual experience of the ideal, Eliot's poetry can speak for and to this civilisation. His poetry articulates the woe that is in the marriage of alienated neurotic egos; the atrophy and perversions of spirit in the crowd that flows over London Bridge; the pitifulness of its recreations, and the depressed resignation of humble people who expect nothing; the waste of living and partly living, of loving and partly loving; the sense of life turning to dust and ashes in the mouth; the anxiety, and fear, and sick loathing; the conscious impotence of rage at human folly, and the consequent self-contempt; and the death-wish. He had a certain real knowledge of the world –

> the strained time-ridden faces
> Distracted from distraction by distraction
> Filled with fancies and empty of meaning
> Tumid apathy with no concentration
> Men and bits of paper, whirled by the cold wind
> That blows before and after time,
> Wind in and out of unwholesome lungs
> Time before and time after.
> Eructation of unhealthy souls
> Into the faded air, the torpid
> Driven on the wind that sweeps the gloomy hills of London...

The essential experience of Eliot's poetry is the essential experience of an actual state of civilisation, but in an extraordinarily refined and intelligent form. The interpretation he put upon it, and the cure he recommended, may seem out of touch with the common way of thinking. Yet by thus connecting the current form of the drive for the absolute and ideal with its relatively recent origins, and with a traditional form, he has rendered it the more intelligible. He is a true voice of our Western world.

Appendices

Appendix A

About the text of the poems

Since Eliot was himself a member of the firm which published his poetry in
England, from *Poems 1909–1925*, one might reasonably expect that the Faber
text would be authoritatively established, and correctly printed. Up to now that
expectation has been disappointed. There is evidence to suggest that Eliot did
attempt to establish 'the definitive edition' of his poetry up to *Burnt Norton* in
Collected Poems 1909–1935,[1] and then of the whole of his poetry in *Collected
Poems 1909–1962*. These are the most nearly authoritative editions that we
have. Yet confidence in them is shaken by some obvious errors and some
dubious readings; by the rather random and half-hearted fashion in which
earlier errors have been corrected and persistent sources of error removed; and
by the fact that besides the emendations and revisions which are probably
Eliot's own latter thoughts, there are certain other changes which he called for
but which have never been made. Thus even the best text, that of *Collected
Poems 1909–1962*, remains in need of a certain amount of correction, and is
somewhat open to question – or even, in a few places, to serious doubt. There
have been two further English editions since Eliot's death. The *Complete Poems
and Plays*, first published in 1969, is a convenient, indeed a necessary collection,
which I should expect to be bought, used and valued by the common reader
as well as the student. All the more to be deplored therefore are its many careless
misprints; and it is these alone which have to be noted here, since its text is not
otherwise significant, being simply a reprint of the then current editions of the
poems and the plays. A new edition of *Collected Poems 1909–1962* was
published in 1974, replacing that of 1963. Though reset, this exactly copies its
predecessor page for page, only fitting the thirty-two lines per page into the
space formerly given to thirty-one – a saving effected wherever possible by
reducing the spacing between paragraphs. There are a few bad misprints. It is
of textual significance, however, because there has been some editing of the
text of *Collected Poems 1909–1962*, in a few instances happily, but otherwise
uncertainly and unsatisfactorily. It is really a step away from the much needed
definitive text; and it opens a discouraging prospect, since the publishers seem
always to prefer, when preparing a new edition, simply to copy their latest,

without taking the trouble to compare it with the earlier and now more authoritative ones.

The purpose of this note is to remark the main sources of error in the texts of Eliot's poems; to note the alterations in the various editions of the *Collected Poems* which can reasonably be accepted as Eliot's deliberate revisions; and to list the *corrigenda* for *1909–1935*, *1909–1962*, *Complete Poems and Plays*, and *1909–62* (1974). For *Four Quartets* note has been taken also of the first separate edition of each Quartet, of the English first collected edition of 1944, and of the new edition first printed in the Faber Paperback series in 1959 (eighth impression 1974). For the other poems the texts in the various *Collected Poems* have been compared with their printings in separate editions (*The Waste Land*, the Ariel Poems and *Ash-Wednesday*), in the early collections (*Prufrock and Other Observations*, *Poems* [1920], and *Poems 1909–1925*), and in periodicals; mention has been made of these, however, only where they throw light on doubtful readings in the four principal collections. I have excluded from consideration *Sweeney Agonistes* and the choruses from *The Rock*.

Eliot's collections of poems from *1909–25* have been published in the United States by Harcourt Brace and these American editions have their own publishing history and textual tradition, one influenced by the Faber editions and yet with a measure of independence. I take note here only of the two collections in print in 1993: *The Complete Poems & Plays 1909–1950* (1952), and *Collected Poems 1909–1962* (1963) – both have been frequently reprinted. *1909–50* of course does not contain 'The Cultivation of Christmas Trees' (1954) or the 'occasional verses' first collected in *1909–62*; but it does include Old Possum's *Practical Cats*. It neither gives Eliot's late emendations nor suffers from the misprints and errors found in the later English editions. It does have misprints and errors requiring to be corrected, some inherited and a very few of its own. Among its welcome advantages are a handsome format with a wider page so that there are relatively few turned lines, and an effective system for marking off verse paragraphs. *1909–62* (US) differs from the English edition only in its typesetting and pagination, and in having fewer misprints and errors. It incorporates very nearly all the late emendations. It also copies *1909–62*'s misprints in l.40 of 'Gerontion' and l.26 of 'Whispers of Immortality'. But it does not follow that edition into error in half a dozen other places. It reproduces five misprints and spacing errors common to most editions. Otherwise its setting of the text is exemplary. The more to be regretted therefore is its abandoning both the handsome format and the systematic indenting of verse paragraphs of *1909–50*.

A brief account of the publishing history of *The Waste Land*, although it is rather the extreme than the typical case, will illustrate how a text can lose authority, and how difficult it can be to recover exactly what the author himself intended.[3] The poem was published in 1922, in the *Criterion* in October, in the *Dial* in November, and as a separate volume (in which the notes first appeared) by Boni and Liveright of New York in December. Each of these three texts has its peculiarities, and it is not clear that one is more authoritative than another. All three could well derive from the one final draft; but Eliot evidently allowed himself to introduce slight alterations into each copy as he typed it, without ensuring that the others were changed accordingly. The earliest of these copies must have been the one sent about 19 July to John Quinn for Boni and Liveright.[4] The next would be the one given to the publisher of the *Dial* in August.[5] The latest was the one for his own *Criterion*. This ought then to be the best text; but in fact while some of its new readings are improvements, others are merely maverick afterthoughts which remind one that Eliot was still under great mental and emotional strain.[6] In any case, the Boni and Liveright edition was preferred as the copy-text for the English separate volume edition hand-printed by Leonard and Virginia Woolf at their Hogarth Press in 1923. A very few of the *Criterion* revisions were incorporated, but most were forgotten; and a few new revisions were made. These were forgotten in their turn, along with those which had appeared in the two periodicals, in *Poems 1909–1925*, which exactly reproduced the text of the Boni and Liveright edition, except only that it omitted a comma at the end of l.153, inserted two commas instead of spaces in l.308, and changed 'aetherial' in l.415 to 'aethereal'. The subsequent collected editions followed *1909–25*, but with each in turn introducing its own slight alterations and corrections. Thus the earliest of the several texts of 1922–3 became established as the base text; and the changes made in the two latest of those texts, which were the ones Eliot himself saw through the press, were simply forgotten. There were further complications in the later history of the text. In a proof copy of *Collected Poems 1909–1935* now in the Hayward Collection at King's College, Cambridge, there are a number of corrections and revisions to *The Waste Land* in Eliot's own hand, with every appearance of their having been intended as directions to the printer. They were not printed, however. Yet there can be no doubt that Eliot meant them: should they not be incorporated now? Again, what should be done about the new line which Eliot inserted after l.137 in 1960, when he was making a holograph copy for sale on behalf of the London Library? Though it was in the draft it has never been included in any of the printed versions: did Eliot mean it to be restored, or was he simply giving that copy a unique value? Perhaps the answer here has to be in the fact that he did not restore it in the 1961 limited edition printed for Faber by Giovanni Mardersteig on the hand-press of the Officina Bodoni, since this, Eliot told Daniel H. Woodward in June 1963, might be taken to be 'the standard text'.[7] Yet again, in spite of that, the text of *Collected Poems 1909–1962* published in September 1963 is not completely in accord with the Mardersteig edition, although it does follow it fairly closely. One change not followed is the perhaps unnecessary and there-fore merely pedantic correction of the line from Verlaine by the insertion of the comma after 'Et'. But another, the removal of the stop at the end of l.272, does make a difference to the music of the passage. The same might be said of the line from Verlaine. In both cases one has to ask, did Eliot mean that to be the 'standard' reading, or did he not? Thus we are left in the end with an author's final text that fails to be quite final, just as the base text fails to be a true *editio princeps*. What is to be done? My *corrigenda* show what I think can reasonably be achieved; but I suspect that there will never be complete agreement about some of the finer points.

For all that a bit of negative capability is, in the end, necessary, there is still good reason for demanding as correct a text as may be possible, if only so that one can forget about the letter and attend to the life of the poetry – that life which is *in* the letter. The 'letter', in the case of Eliot's poems, can be literally that: 'the Hyacinth garden' is not 'the hyacinth garden'; 'and still she cried' is not 'and still she cries'; 'arras', in *East Coker* l.13, lacks the archaic quality of 'aresse' which Eliot had wanted to use. However, most of the details which remain to be settled are matters of punctuation and spacing. 'I only hope the printers are not allowed to bitch the punctuation and spacing', Eliot wrote to John Quinn when sending him the copy of *The Waste Land* for Boni and Liveright, 'as that is very important for the sense.'[8] The 'sense' in question of course is the poetic sense, not just the prose meaning. In general the punctuation in Eliot's poetry has to be taken more as a musical than as a syntactical pointing. He told Quinn,

I see reason in your objection to my punctuation; but I hold that the line itself punc-tuates, and the addition of a comma, in many places, seems to me to over-emphasize the arrest. That is because I always pause at the end of a line in reading verse, while perhaps you do not.[9]

It must have been for the sake of the music, in this case to mark the arrests more definitely, that he authorised three changes in the punctuation of 'Gerontion' – changes which are still, however, requiring to be made. But did he intend the full stop after 'Horn', near the close of that poem, which appeared in *Collected Poems 1909–1962*? A number of problematic readings of that sort are remarked in the *corrigenda*.

The problem which needs the most careful attention is that of the spacing between the paragraphs of the verse, and in some cases between the lines or half-lines. I suspect that the significance of the spacing is not always appreciated: i.e. that it is a way of marking the music. The problem arises from there being no established convention for marking a new paragraph in verse. The first line can of course be indented, as in prose; but generally a space is left instead, and this serves perfectly well for regular stanzas and verse forms. Unfortunately spacing alone has proved inadequate for Eliot's unpredictable verse forms. When a space falls at the foot of a page there is often no way of knowing whether one is intended or not. The space that was intended may be lost in the next edition; or one that was not may appear. Both consequences of marking off the verse paragraphs only by spacing are found in the successive editions up to and including *Collected Poems 1909–1935*. In *Collected Poems 1909–1962* some indenting was introduced, but so inconsistently that instead of clearing things up it created a new source of uncertainty. In the poems preceding *The Waste Land* only 'Prufrock' and 'Portrait of a Lady' were indented, and in 'Prufrock' the last three paragraphs were overlooked. Indenting was introduced into *The Waste Land*, but the second and third paragraphs of part III were overlooked. The Ariel Poems of 1927–30 were indented, but *The Hollow Men* and *Ash-Wednesday* were not, and nor was the minor and unfinished verse. In *Four Quartets* the inconsistency is such that any idea of a convention seems to have been abandoned. It has to be recognised that awkwardnesses and inelegancies can arise from indenting the first line of each verse paragraph, and each line that stands on its own. Yet some clear convention is absolutely necessary, for Eliot's poems at least, and none better seems to offer itself. The model edition in this respect is the American *Complete Poems & Plays 1909–1950* which introduced 'an attractive new format of indentation' and carried it through consistently. Its system was *not* followed in the setting of the American edition of *Collected Poems 1909–1962*. Indenting is not, of course, a substitute for spacing: the great need for it is precisely in order to preserve the spacing which marks a main pause or arrest. Two special forms of the problem come up in *Four Quartets*. In a few places different degrees of space are called for, as in *Little Gidding* V where there should be a triple space before the line which stands on its own, and a double space following it. Then there are the broken lines, which in some cases occur within the paragraph, as in *Burnt Norton* I; and in others coincide with a paragraph break, as in *East Coker* III ('You say I am repeating'). But there are still others where the variations from one edition to another leave uncertain whether the broken line marks a division within a continuous passage, or a division between one passage and the next. These distinctions should be perceptible. If the passage is continuous, the second half-line should be dropped to the line below with no extra spacing and without being moved either to right or left; if it begins a new passage or paragraph it should be dropped the appropriate extra space and moved as many ems to the right as for indenting. Comparison of the several texts of *Four Quartets* shows that an editor needs to be especially clear-minded and vigilant about this.

SOME LATE EMENDATIONS, PROBABLY AUTHORIAL

'Prufrock': *1909–62* reads 'To roll it towards some overwhelming question', where earlier editions had 'toward'.

'Preludes': *1909–62* first separated final line of I; and restored the break after l.5 in II (lost through falling at the foot of the page in *1909–25*).

'Rhapsody on a Windy Night': l.7, *1909–62* 'precisions.' – 'precisions,' in earlier editions.

'The "Boston Evening Transcript"': *1909–62* 'La Rochefoucauld' – previously 'Rochefoucauld'.

'Mr Apollinax': *1909–62* corrected the misplacing of l.13 in *1909–35* (which first divided the poem); and in l.19 changed ' "unbalanced," ' to ' "unbalanced." '.

'Gerontion': *1909–62* in l.8 gives 'Jew' – previously 'jew' – and in 6th from last line 'Horn.' – previously 'Horn,'.

'Burbank with a Baedeker: Bleistein with a Cigar': *1909–62* gives 'Jew' in l.23 – previously 'jew'.

'A Cooking Egg': l.3, *1909–62* '*Views of Oxford Colleges*' – previously '*Views of the Oxford Colleges*'.

'Journey of the Magi': *1909–62* alters previous 'vegetation;' to 'vegetation,' at l.22, and previous 'sky,' to 'sky.' at l.24.

'Cape Ann' and 'Lines for an Old Man': *1909–62* (following *1909–50*) gives a full line break before the final line of both poems. But *1909–62* (US) does not!

Burnt Norton: 1.51, *1909–35* & 1941 separate edition 'And reconciles', emended to 'Appeasing' in *4Q*.; space after l.69 deleted in *4Q* and following English editions but not in US editions; ll.161–75 indented 1941, *4Q*. and later impressions of *1909–35* – but not *1909–62*.

The Dry Salvages: l.19, 'hermit crab' emended after 1944 to 'horseshoe crab'; l.160, 1st edition 'should fructify' emended in *4Q*. to 'shall fructify'; l.177 1st edition 'suo figlio' emended in *4Q*. to 'tuo figlio'.

CORRIGENDA

N.B. Wherever possible only the correct reading is given; the edition(s) in square brackets are those in which there is an error requiring to be corrected. In doubtful cases the various readings are given. A few of these notes are not, strictly speaking, *corrigenda*, but rather questions or suggestions.

'Prufrock': l.24, *1909–35* et seq. have no comma after 'street' [*1909–50*]; l.49, *1909–25* has final colon, *1909–35* et seq. have dash – *1909–50* has both in error? 10th from last line, read 'Do I dare to eat' [*1909–62* (1974)].

'Portrait of a Lady': II, first paragraph ends with l.15 [*1909–62* et seq.]; II.8, read 'and has no remorse' [*C.P.P.*, *1909–62*(1974)]; II.33, read 'I remark' [*C.P.P.*]; III, 'And I must borrow . . . in a tobacco trance –' is a separate paragraph [*1909–35*].

'Preludes': III.8, 'shutters' in *1909–35*, *1909–50*, *1909–62*, *C.P.P.*, but *1909–62* (1974) gives 'shutters,' (as in *1909–25*).

'Rhapsody on a Windy Night': should not the second paragraph run from 'Half-past one' down to 'ready to snap', in line with the other distinct sections each of which is introduced by telling the time? The break within the second section appears to derive from *1909–25*, the turn of the page coming just there. l.17, read 'toward you' [*C.P.P.*]; l.24 read 'things;' [*1909–50*]; l.39, read 'quay.' [*C.P.P.*].

'The "Boston Evening Transcript"': title should read thus [*1909–35*, *1909–62*, *C.P.P.*].

'Gerontion': epigraph, Shakespeare's text reads '...an after-dinners sleep/Dreamimg on both' [all editions]; l.40, read 'or if still believed' [*1909–62*, *1909–62* (US)]. Eliot gave his authority to these three emendations which have yet to be made:[10] l.1, delete final comma; l.35, read 'And issues;'; l.37 read 'distracted,'. *1909–50* gives a space before l.26 ('By Hakagawa') as in *1909–25* – in *1909–35* et seq. this falls at the turn of the page; but it and *1909–62* (US) are probably wrong in setting as a separate line 'Vacant shuttles' which in all English edns. is part of the previous line (l.29).

'Dans le Restaurant': 20/21 no break after 'vautour!' [1909–50].

'Whispers of Immortality': 1.26, read 'arboreal' [*1909–62, 1909–62* (US), *C.P.P.*].

'Mr Eliot's Sunday Morning Service': 1.12, 'browned' in editions before *1909–62* (1974), which gives 'browned.' – in error? 1.20, all editions give 'pence.', thus breaking the syntax – delete the stop? 6 lines from end read 'pistillate' [*1909–50*].

'Sweeney Among the Nightingales': 3rd from last line, *1909–62* et seq. omit the comma given in previous editions – should it not be restored?

The Waste Land:

13, read 'archduke's' [all editions except *1909–50*] – TSE called for the deletion of the hyphen in the set of proofs for *1909–35* now in the Hayward Collection.

35–7, *1909–35* (following earlier editions) gives 'hyacinths . . . hyacinth girl . . . Hyacinth garden'; in *1909–62* the capital disappeared from this last; *1909–62* (1974) follows, but gives the first as 'Hyacinths' – in error, surely. Was *1909–62*, 'hyacinth garden', an Eliot emendation?

102, read 'And still she cries' [all editions] – the reading in the Hogarth edition (1923), called for by TSE in the set of proofs for *1909–35*.

111–38, a much confused passage in which whatever conventions are adopted for marking paragraphs and direct speech need to be applied consistently: ll.112–14 should not be inset [*1909–62*(1974)], l.113 should not be indented [all editions]; l.123, *1909–62*(1974) should read, by its convention, 'Nothing?"'; l.131, delete quotation-mark at end of line [*1909–35, 1909–50, 1909–62, 1909–62* (US) *C.P.P.*].

122, read 'Why do you never speak?' [*1909–35, 1909–50, 1909–62, 1909–62* (US) *C.P.P.*].

130/1, early printings give a space here – in Boni and Liveright it fell at the turn of the page, and so disappeared in *1909–25*.

137/8, should one insert the line 'The ivory men make company between us' as Eliot did in the holograph copy he made in 1960?

153, read 'said,' [all editions].

162, read 'are' [*1909–50*].

180, Mardersteig gives 'directors –' – but this is a case where the pointing is primarily musical, and where the syntax will be clear if the pauses are correct: 'directors;' is probably the more exact musically.

186/7, space [omitted in *1909–35* and *1909–50*]; *1909–62* et seq. fail to mark new paragraph, as also at l.203.

202, Mardersteig gives Verlaine's line according to his text (as against the poet's ear): 'Et, o ces voix d'enfants chantant dans la coupole.'

307

214/5, *1909–62* introduces extra spacing – *1909–62* (1974) fails to follow.

255, read 'smoothes' [*1909–62* (1974).

259, read 'O City, City' [all editions] – called for by TSE in the set of proofs for *1909–35*, and found in the *Criterion* and Hogarth printings.

263, read 'fishmen' [*1909–62* (1974) – corrected in later impressions].

272, Mardersteig gives 'spar' – all other editions 'spar.'.

275, why not 'Greenwich Reach' [all editions]?

278/9, delete space – as called for by TSE in proofs for *1909–35*, and as in early printings up to *1909–25* (*Criterion* excepted).

307–11, since they are not part of the Thames-daughters' song (266–306) these lines should not be inset with it, but aligned with l.265.

340, read 'can neither stand' [*C.P.P.*].

376/7, space [*1909–35*].

423–33, set as one block in all editions from *1909–25*, but the division of the lines in the typescript drafts and the early printings deserves consideration: the 'London Bridge' line stands on its own, and the final line also stands apart (with its three words widely spaced – as still in US editions).

The Hollow Men: IV.9, read 'Gathered' [*1909–62*].

Ash-Wednesday: Should not the first edition dedication 'To My Wife' be restored? III, there should be a space before the final line [*1909–62* et seq.]; V.8, read 'Against the Word' [*1909–35*]; VI.24/5, space – *C.P.P.*'s error derives from the falling of the space at the foot of the page in *1909–35* et seq.

A Song for Simeon: l.3, read 'has made stand' [*C.P.P.*, *1909–62*(1974)].

Marina: the spacing between paragraphs is inadequate in *1909–62*(1974).

Triumphal March: ll.13–23, type should not be leaded [*1909–50*, *C.P.P.*, *1909–62* (1974)].

'Difficulties of a Statesman': l.24, read 'dice on the marches' [*1909–35*]; l.39, read 'lintel' [*1909–62* (1974)].

'Eyes that last I saw in tears': l.6, read 'affliction [*1909–62* (1974)].

Four Quartets

Burnt Norton: I consists of one paragraph, in which the two broken lines should be set according to the principle defined above – as they are in *1909–35*, first separate edition (1941) and *4Q*. [*1909–62* and *1909–62*(1974) have drifted away from the simple clear setting called for here].

2, read 'future,' [*1909–62* (1974)].

64, read 'fixity,' [*1909–35*, 1941 separate edition].

IV consists of one paragraph [Faber Paperback edition].

East Coker: 23, is this a broken line (as in Faber Paperback), or does 'In that open field' begin a new paragraph (as in *1909–62* et seq.)? In first edition and *4Q.* the break fell at the foot of the page and there is no indication of the extra space; however the second half-line is set off to the right. *1909–50* agrees with Faber Paperback.

24, read 'summer' [*1909–50*].

31, read 'commodious' [Faber Paperback].

103, read 'men of letters,'[*1909–62* et seq.].

105, read 'chairmen' [*C.P.P.*, *1909–62*].

128/9, space (before 'Whisper of running streams') – as in *New English Weekly* and *Partisan Review* first printings. The break coincides with the turn of the page in most subsequent editions, which fail to indicate the new paragraph; in Faber Paperback and *C.P.P.* it quite disappears.

129, 'lightning.' in all editions from *4Q.*; but *New English Weekly* and first separate edition read 'lightning,' – an alternative to be reckoned with.

133/4, insert line break between lines [*1909–50*].

203, read 'Here or there does not matter' [*4Q.*, *1909–50*, *1909–62*, *1909–62* (US), *C.P.P.*].

The Dry Salvages: 7, read 'implacable,' [*1909–62* (1974)].

28, read 'heard:' [*1909–50*].

46, read 'the ground swell' [*1909–62* (1974)].

84/5, there should be a double space after the lyric, according to Gardner, *Composition of Four Quartets* (1978), p.133.

106–7, read 'Having hoped ... not in question' [*C.P.P.*].

216, read 'union' [*1909–50*].

Little Gidding: 10, read 'dumb' [*C.P.P.*].

39, in first edition this is a broken line, not a paragraph break as in *4Q.* et seq. – the earlier is perhaps the more exact setting?

95, should be indented; 96, should not be indented; 141, should not be indented [*C.P.P.*].

112, read 'My thought' [*1909–62* et seq.] – or is 'thoughts' Eliot's deliberate emendation?

160, read 'Begins as attachment' [*1909–62*(1974)].

165/6, space (before 'Sin is Behovely') [*4Q* and following English editions].

214, read 'is often' [*C.P.P.*].

224, read 'an end' [*C.P.P.*].

237/8, triple space required [*1909–50*, *C.P.P.*, *1909–62* (1974)].

Appendix B

The drafts of 'The Waste Land'[1]

Valerie Eliot's facsimile edition of the drafts makes a real contribution to the understanding of the poem's evolution and inner process; and it enables us to give a meaning to Eliot's saying that he wrote *The Waste Land* simply to relieve his own feelings. Yet it leaves us guessing still about some of the basic matters of fact. What is the precise chronology of the various materials which Eliot presented to John Quinn in 1922 as 'the MSS of the Waste Land'? The arrangement in the edition corresponds as closely as possible to the finished version, with the extra pieces following in no particular order. But this has the effect of concealing the stages of the poem's evolution. Moreover, the clues by which we might recover them have been effaced in the process of photographic reproduction. The originals appear to have been enlarged or reduced, and intensified or lightened, in order to achieve a nearly uniform size of page and degree of inking; and the editorial description of them doesn't give all the necessary detail. For accurate scholarship of course there can be no substitute for the originals; and criticism based upon facsimiles should in any case be cautious. But we need not be left quite so much in the dark. Then there is the problem of the exact form in which Eliot placed the materials before Pound in Paris in December 1921. Some things included here were surely not in that version; and others that were in it are probably missing. We know that at least three and probably more lyrics which were finally excluded, and which there-fore are placed here outside the poem proper, were in fact interspersed within it at that stage – but it seems that we cannot tell where. This not knowing clearly and fully what Eliot conceived his poem to be at the moment before Pound got to work on it means that we are ignorant about one of its most interesting phases. It matters less, but it is still a loss, that the end of part III as it was shown to Pound appears to be missing. Nor do we have the final, nineteen-page version, which Eliot sent Pound in January 1922.[2] For a complete record, account must be taken also of the three known typescripts made after that version and before publication.[3] In short, the edition supplies rather less than the whole story of the making of *The Waste Land*.

My own tentative reordering of the drafts would put first the miscellaneous

330

pieces which we can be fairly certain were not part of the draft Pound saw in Paris. Three at least of these can be dated as of 1914 or earlier: (1) 'After the turning of the inspired days'; (2) 'I am the Resurrection and the Life' – a brief collocation of the New Testament and the *Bhagavad-Gita*; (3) 'So through the evening, through the violet air'. These were written in the same hand on the same sort of paper; the first and third are thematically related; and they anticipate a considerable section of 'What the Thunder Said'. That was the part that gave Eliot the greatest difficulty, and which he was unable to compose until late 1921. Yet these pieces were certainly written years before; and they could well have been the additions to 'Prufrock', drafted about 1912, which Conrad Aiken persuaded Eliot to suppress.[4] Certainly the image of drowning at the end of the third of them connects 'Prufrock' and 'Death by Water'. But what this earliest layer of thematic material mainly shows is that *The Waste Land* was conceived in embryo nearly a decade before it was successfully delivered by Pound.

Next in order must be (4) 'The Death of St Narcissus', written no later than August 1915, and possibly considerably earlier. Some of this went into ll.25–9 of the finished poem; but it has also a close connection with the last part, for which those lines prepare. With this I would associate the lyric 'Exequy', which was included in the 1921 version (and referred to by Pound in his letter as 'the sovegna'). In her notes Valerie Eliot quotes from a letter of Eliot's from Marburg dated July 1914, in which he shows a curiosity about 'pudibund', a word used in the draft. Then there is 'The Death of the Duchess', which can't be certainly dated, but which is likely to have been written in London, and so in 1915 or 1916. Pound's annotations on these leaves must have been made before they were drawn on for part II – the 'My nerves are bad tonight' scene is first and fully sketched here – but there is no way of telling how long before. He observed 'cadence reproduction from Pru[frock] or Por[trait]', and the relationship is a real one. Here is the same need to escape from a situation in which love seems to confer only a more anguished awareness that 'It is impossible to say just what I mean!' In 'So through the evening, through the violet air' that is expressed as a quest for 'The one essential word that frees/The inspiration that delivers and expresses'. Now in 'The Death of the Duchess' there is the terror of being alone with another person and finding nothing to say. But there is a significant new development, in the attempt to dramatise the predicament: with the assistance of Webster, a relevant objective situation is found for the otherwise merely subjective and self-consuming hysteria. This introduces a tone hardly heard before in Eliot's verse: sympathy, feeling for another. Here it is perhaps hardly more than the pathos generated by the quotations from Webster. But that marks an expansion both of material and of response which was to make all the difference between the self-enclosed monologues of the earlier poetry, and the breakthrough to an impersonal lyricism in *The Waste Land*. The fact that the 'bad nerves' passage is genuinely dramatic means a first step towards that sympathy with others which is the basis of coming to terms with oneself.

It would seem that Eliot started serious work on the poem in 1920, when he had 'Gerontion' and the poems in quatrains off his hands. His New Year's resolution for that year, he told his mother, was 'to write a long poem I have had on my mind for a long time'. Probably he already had a good deal of material in rough drafts and disconnected fragments. But he had still to discover how to make a *poem* of them – something that perhaps was not to be altogether clear to him until he had done it, and Pound had shown him what he had done. As late as January 1922 he seems to have been regarding it as a collection or sequence of poems, which could stand the excision of 'Death by Water', the adding on of the miscellaneous lyrics at the end, and the printing of 'Gerontion' as a prelude. He might have had in mind as a model Tennyson's *Maud,* or the *Satyricon* of Petronius. However the case is not so simple as those first impressions would suggest. Something of the essential structure of the poem is already apparent in 'He do the Police in different voices', i.e. the nearly finished drafts of parts I and II, which are so typed and pinned together as to appear the first stage to have been more or less satisfactorily completed. There are the centres of intense personal experience which are the source and heart of the entire work – the dramatic lyrics of the hyacinth garden and the enclosed room; there are the phantasmagoric visions of the Unreal City, *symboliste* (or Expressionist) projections of the personal drama; and there is the application of the historical sense to discover its relevant past and so arrive at the universal form. In the successfully completed poem this process culminates in a return to the personal predicament with an intensified, because more conscious, apprehension of it; and its resolution is a direct, lyrical and objective expression of the poet's state. But 'He do the Police in different voices' seems to be moving away from that, towards 'objective correlatives' which are neither direct expressions of the emotion nor elucidations of it, but more nearly an escape from it. The roistering night out in Boston, which was the start of the poem at this stage, and the pub monologue at the end of part II, while they assume the mode of realism, are in fact a kind of illicit generalising from the poet's own feelings. The disorder and futility which they observe is not necessarily 'out there' in contemporary life, but is the reality of his own inner world.[5] (There is a telling note by Pound against the four lines beginning the 'My nerves are bad tonight' section – alongside which Vivien Eliot had pencilled her 'WONDERFUL':

photography? he queried – *there* was the reality Eliot had to express, in his own life, not in the lives of others.) Eliot cancelled the Boston episode, without any prompting from Pound so far as one can tell, but it is not clear why. That the writing was thin and factitious would have been reason enough; but did he perceive that such satire was a false solution to his problem? The pub monologue, which is preserved, though a *tour de force* in its way, is just as much an evasion of the personal predicament. He may have seen it as the objective correlative of his emotion; but it is not the direct, lyrical expression in which the emotion could find its own true form, 'intelligible, self-complete, in the sun-light'. 'He do the Police in different voices' looks like an attempt to practise the theory put forward in the Hamlet essay of 1919. But the evidence of the drafts as a whole goes with that of the finished poem to show that what Eliot needed for the satisfactory expression of his baffling emotion was not some pseudo-objective 'equivalent', but simply to find his own true voice of personal feeling. Yet that was no simple matter for him, because his way to it had to be through the conscious understanding of his state. It is that need which explains his cultivating an objectivity which was not the right objectification of his emotion.

Part III, on which Eliot seems to have been still at work when he showed it to Pound in December 1921, was hopelessly given over to the kind of satire which indulged the poet's sickness of soul without doing anything to observe and cure it in himself. There was no centre of intense personal experience here; instead there was the idea of correlating contemporary decadence with the myth of a decay of English sensibility since the seventeenth century. But no idea could save the bad writing and bad feeling from Pound's justly savage attack. Out went the seventy lines of couplets, a brutal and trifling sketch of the character of women from the Restoration to emancipation, sadly wanting in the substance and force of the corresponding passage which opened part II. Out went the prophet–preacher's apostrophe to London, which fully merited Pound's rude word. The typist passage was salvaged by skilful surgery which cut through the eighteenth-century quatrains to remove its grosser crudities. Thus 'The Fire Sermon' was reduced from a draft of about 200 lines to the 75 lines which Pound could accept as *echt*. The inferior quality of the rest was symptomatic of insincerity, or of the diseased condition of the poet's own sensibility: his genuinely creative powers were either disengaged or impotent.

I would guess that when Eliot went to the Lausanne clinic towards the end of November 1921 he had with him the typescript drafts of parts I–III, and that he wrote out there the fair copy of part IV containing the shipwreck and drowning episode and the 'Dirge'. (These latter are on the same graph-ruled paper as was used for the first draft of part v.) Pound found 'Dirge' doubly doubtful, and with good reason: there is no healthy motive to be discerned in 'Full fathom five your Bleistein lies'. The shipwreck narrative was not bad in the same way, its trouble being rather that it was devoid of any particularly significant feelings. On straightforwardly technical grounds the translator of *The Seafarer* and author of Cantos I and II saw that it wouldn't do, line after line, until only 'Phlebas the Phoenician' survived – the lyrical formulation. That, we know, had been written in its French version by 1916; and it is probable that the narrative also had been written some time before. What he had still to write when he had his breakdown was part v, the conclusion which had haunted him from the first stirrings of the thematic material, and which he had been finding himself ever more desperately unable to get onto paper. Early in that winter he told Conrad Aiken 'that although every evening he went home to his flat hoping that he could start writing again, and with every confidence that the material was *there* and waiting, night after night the hope proved illusory'.[6] From Margate, where he had gone to begin his rest cure, he wrote on 6 November: 'I am satisfied, since being here, that my "nerves" are a very mild affair, due not to overwork but to an aboulie and emotional derangement which has been a lifelong affliction.'[7] At last at Lausanne the piece of writing 'meditated apparently without progress for months or years' suddenly took shape and word: 'What the Thunder Said' was produced very rapidly and in a form requiring only the slightest revision.[8] By an extraordinary coincidence Rilke, in the same winter and less than a hundred miles away, was to complete the *Duino Elegies* and write the *Sonnets to Orpheus* in a similar (though more sustained) burst of creativity after his ten years of patient effort.

So far as one can tell from the facsimile Eliot appears to have written the first sixty-four lines (down to 'exhausted wells') without a break and with scarcely a hesitation or afterthought. Then there are three lines which threaten to repeat the preceding effects and which were struck out. When he resumed he wrote out the next forty lines (from 'In this decayed hole' down to 'set my lands in order'), again without a break, though with not quite the same degree of sureness. At the end of this passage there is a significant hesitation over a line which would have linked the *Damyata* section not only to the hyacinth girl but to the Thames-daughter on Margate sands, and which would have sounded again the note of personal loss and guilt: 'I left without you/Clasping empty hands I sit upon the shore'. He took the short way out of the difficulty by simply suppressing that note, which is really the introduction to *The Hollow Men* and *Ash-Wednesday*. But for the moment at least he was relieved of his burden, as one can see in the firmness with which he set down 'Shantih shantih shantih'.

Pound passed the manuscript at first sight: 'OK from here on I think'; and on the typescript fair copy he made only half a dozen minor suggestions.

Eliot regarded part v as 'not only the best part, but the only part that justifies the whole'. Moreover, in his view there were 'about 30 *good* lines in *The Waste Land*' – i.e. 'the water-dripping song' (ll.331–58) – 'the rest is ephemeral'. That song is undoubtedly the vital new element in the poem, and its true conclusion. The difference it makes when compared with the earliest drafts (1, 3, and 4 in my numbering above) is partly that what was there inarticulate and confused is now clearly and fully voiced; but more that the poet is now at one with his experience and in himself. Even the images of terror and nightmare carried over from the early drafts find a new rhythm, which counters their disturbing effect with calming detachment – compare 'A woman drew her long black hair out tight' in the two versions. The proper development from this was not the Laforguian 'infant hydrocephalous', roughly corresponding to 'one withered by some mental blight' in (3), and rightly cancelled. It was rather the acceptant serenity of

> In this decayed hole among the mountains
> In the faint moonlight, the grass is singing
> Over the tumbled graves . . .

The newly achieved integrity informs the responses to the thunder, where instead of the guilt and terror of the earlier parts of the poem, or the denunciation of the vanity of the world, there is honest self-recognition. This brings a relief which is not the escape the poet appeared to be seeking in the earlier stages of the poem, but the correlative of being able at last to integrate into the psyche the painful experience which had been alienating him from himself and from life. With the water-dripping song he had found what he most deeply needed to say: what his life really meant to him and how he must live it. Such saying, to paraphrase Rilke, is a mode of being – the lyric is knowledge become power.

There is further evidence of recovered powers in the revision of part III after Pound's attack upon it in Paris. To replace the couplets Eliot drafted on the verso of that sheet the dozen lines of the new opening. Genuinely a fusing of the present with a relevant past, these observe the litter of the nymphs' lives, not now in alienated disgust, but sympathetically and with elegiac intensity. Then to complete part III with an appropriate music he added the song of the three Thames-daughters. There are difficulties here which, for want of information, may be insoluble. It is not clear just when the song was written. Presumably, since it was shown to Pound in pencil draft, it was either not drafted or not considered for III when the typescript version of that was prepared. The reference to Margate makes it reasonable to suppose it was written later than Eliot's stay there in October 1921. (There is a like reference to Lac Léman in the new opening lines.) The probability is that it was composed in Paris or upon his return to London. In the second place, one would like to know what it replaced – what was the now missing conclusion to the typescript version? Having to guess, and with only the materials in the facsimile to go on, I find 'Song for the Opherion' the most likely – the one Pound referred to as 'sweats with tears' when he advised Eliot not to work it into the nerves monologue but to let it wait. (Revised, it became 'The wind sprang up at four o'clock'.) The song which took its place – assuming that that was to have been the conclusion – does show a certain affinity; but it has also the essential difference, that instead of being in the voice of the self-concerned observer, Ferdinand–Tiresias as it were, it allows the women to speak honestly and movingly in their own voices. In the draft one can see its lyricism, at once objective and compassionate, being refined out of Eliot's first relatively gross perceptions with help from Dante and to the standards set by Pound. It becomes the most eloquent passage in the whole poem; and its sympathetic realisation of others' fates is the concomitant of the self-realisation and integration achieved in part V. The transformation of 'The Fire Sermon', early in January 1922, from an attack by a sick seer upon a world of the living dead, into an inwardly felt expression of the desolate aftermath of merely sensual passion, is really the final stage in the poem's evolution. The new and more just perception of the external world could only follow upon the proper ordering of the poet's self.

I can see why Eliot could tell Aiken in November 1922 that *The Waste Land* was already a thing of the past so far as he was concerned, and why he should think most of it ephemeral. When he had at last tapped that deep source of self, in which the being is integrated and regenerated in song, the rest of the work would appear merely symptomatic of the diseased states he had passed through, or at best as evidence of the struggle for the living words. Having composed the truly integral songs, he had found the mode of the 'dream song' proper to his next phase of development. To have continued writing in the voice of Tiresias would have been a denial of the vital achievement of the poem.

Eliot's persisting in trying to find a place for the miscellaneous lyrics, which Pound clearly saw would not go with the rest, may have sprung from his conviction that that was the mode that mattered. Valerie Eliot's notes confirm that the three particularly mentioned in Pound's letter of January 1922 were 'Exequy', 'Dirge', and 'Song for the Opherion'. Another, 'Elegy', is among the drafts and might also have been intended for insertion. I have suggested that 'Dirge' seems likely to have gone into 'Death by Water'; and that the 'Song' could have come at the end of 'The Fire Sermon'. Pound's comment on 'Exequy', that some lines are 'Laforgue not XVIII', might indicate that it was meant to go between the couplets and the quatrains. It could have been inserted between pages 2 and 3 of the draft typescript, after 'Et o ces voix d'enfants', since Pound renumbered pages 3ff. as if to accommodate an extra sheet there. It might then have been seen to have links with Parsifal; and to associate Arnaut's words with the crying of swallows and nightingales in the manner of the fragments at the end of part v. However, the plain fact is that none of these lyrics would really do. That leads to the less simple consideration of why, though in the lyrical mode, they were unsatisfactory. Beyond the practical difficulties of placing them and reconciling different styles, the basic reason is that they are not truly in the voice of impersonal lyricism. 'Dirge', as I have said, goes with the negations of the disintegrated mind. So too do the other pieces. Though they are charged with the guilt and terror of failed love which Eliot was struggling to express, their forms are at once too personal and too literary – the inadequate objectification and the undigested verse rhythms go together. As the elision in the *Damyata* lines indicated, at its most intimately personal level his experience had still to find its full expression. These rightly discarded lyrics remain as tokens of the urgent motives which had been as yet only partially worked out.

It was Pound, according to Eliot, who turned *The Waste Land* 'from a jumble of good and bad passages into a poem'.[9] But he did that simply by bringing to the drafts the critical faculties which Eliot could not command while he was immersed in the struggle to express himself. He added nothing – less than Wordsworth to *The Ancient Mariner* or Johnson to *The Deserted Village* – and suggested few variants. His main work was to discriminate between what was *echt* and the factitious or otherwise bad writing. His test of the genuine was directly technical: a weak word or rhythm, a facile or false effect, was evidence of insincerity or of inadequately realised feeling. Applying this test he discovered the poem within the drafts. There is nothing to suggest that he tried to understand the poem, in the sense of seeking an interpretation or explanation of its meaning. Eliot, on the contrary, would seem to have been wanting to preserve the invalid parts just because he did have conscious ideas of what he was after. Pound's contribution was to elicit what he had actually achieved – the poem in itself. Perhaps the only way that could be done was by attending wholly to the direct evidence of poetic quality. When one reads the drafts through his annotations the nearly unerring sureness of his judgment is exemplary. Faced with this quite original work in a still unfinished state, he picked out at once the weak parts – the relapses into mechanical pentameter, or into a too easy or too eccentric usage. To watch him going through the shipwreck passage is an education in his own verse principles; his work on parts II and III is a demonstration of practical criticism at its best.

The major lesson is in the correspondence of Pound's critical method to Eliot's creative process. If the poem now runs (as Pound thought it did) without a break from 'April' to 'Shantih', that is because its complex of feelings has been progressively ordered and integrated. But its sources are deeper than any conscious account of them, so that the adequate expression must be finally a lyrical one. The end of the process is not understanding in the common sense, but rather to find for what is unintelligible a form which will have the clarity of immediate experience. Pound's criticism treats the poetry not as something to be explained but as immediate experience. Its axiom is that 'technical' rightness will be the enactment or creation of right feeling and perception – that the perfect song is a well-ordered mind. The function of criticism then is simply to approve the genuine, and to clear away what would obstruct the expression and the experience of it.

Appendix C

The Christian philosopher and politics between the wars

> I am no traitor, no enemy of the state . . .
> The law of God is above the law of man,
> The Kingdom of God above the kingdom of man.
> (Thomas in *Murder in the Cathedral*)[1]

T. S. Eliot was not a political philosopher, and he had no political philosophy as such: he was a philosopher who took a certain interest in politics. Much confusion and misunderstanding has been generated by those interested in his politics who have failed to observe the distinction. What it means is that his thinking about politics is not simply dependent upon its object, and is not defined by its object – what is ordinarily called the subject-matter. Rather it is the expression of the point of view from which he examines the object; and his point of view is dependent upon and only defined by theology and revelation.[2] He is, strictly speaking, a metaphysician, one who in observing politics is always trying to see through the actuality to the ideal. Consequently, if we really want to understand his remarks about politics – as distinct from engaging in political polemic, the purpose of which is rather more practical – we will need to penetrate beyond their relations to actual events and to rival political ideas, and to elicit their governing point of view, their metaphysic. The purpose of this note is simply to direct attention towards the philosophy of Eliot's politics.

One finds it already manifest in April 1926, in a note on Mussolini in his *Criterion* 'Commentary', which was sub-headed 'The Future of the Roman Empire'. The Fascist regime had come to power in Italy with the march on Rome in October 1922; but, as G. M. Gathorne-Hardy wrote in his *Short History of International Affairs 1920–1939*, 'The movement was generally regarded as of mainly domestic importance, and in spite of the intermittent truculence of Mussolini's utterances and actions, faith was put in the remark which he only tardily repudiated in 1930, that Fascism was not a commodity for export.'[3] Eliot's way of putting the case was characteristic:

The point upon which we ought to insist is this, that the Roman Empire does concern us, but that whatever use may be made of that idea in Italian politics as an incentive to Italian action is a local matter which does not concern – in either way – those persons who are interested primarily in European ideas. The old Roman Empire is an European idea; the new Roman Empire is an Italian idea, and the two must be kept distinct. . . The general idea is found in the continuity of the impulse of Rome to the present day. It suggests Authority and Tradition, certainly, but Authority and Tradition (especially the latter) do not necessarily suggest Signor Mussolini. It is an idea which comprehends Hooker and Laud as much as (or to some of us more than) it implies St Ignatius or Cardinal Newman. It is in fact the European idea – the idea of a common culture of western Europe.[4]

This was to set aside the actual Rome, and indeed the historical Roman Empire as well; and to invoke in their stead the ideal Rome of Virgil and Dante – an empire founded not upon Caesar, but upon divine Love. That is the idea of a Christian society, one that is essentially a church and only contingently a state, which underlies all Eliot's thinking about politics.

In his *Criterion* Commentaries he declared his approach quite explicitly, first as that of a philosopher simply, but later as that of a Christian philosopher. He wrote in June 1928,

In the theory of politics, in the largest sense, *The Criterion* is interested, so far as politics can be dissociated from party politics, from the passions or fantasies of the moment, and from problems of local and temporary importance. Which party is in power at home, or what squabble may be taking place in the Balkans, is of no interest, nor is jockeying for position in treaties and peace-pacts. But the general relations of civilized countries among each other should be examined; and the philosophies expressed or implicit in various tendencies, such as communism or fascism, are worthy of dispassionate examination.[5]

Thus, in the issue for December of that year, he reviewed five books about Fascism as one 'interested in political ideas, but not in politics'. Of the actual practice of Fascism in Italy he had very little to say: it might, or it might not, prove feasible as a working programme for that country. But for democracy elsewhere, he suggested, the only new thing it appeared to offer was 'excitement and military salutes', and a 'comfortable feeling that we shall be benevolently ordered about'. He questioned whether it might not be, like Communism, something of 'a substitute for religion, and therefore a muddle'; and whether, moreover, it could be compatible with Catholicism, given 'that the Catholic conception of the State was ultimately theocratic'. Christian order and authority, he went on to imply, were not at all the same as those of any mere state; and the impulse towards them might be just the reverse of the impulse towards the totalitarian state:

Order and authority are good: I believe in them as wholeheartedly as I think one should believe in any single idea; and much of the demand for them in our time has been soundly based. But behind the increasing popular demand for these things, the parroting of the words, I seem to detect a certain spiritual anaemia, a tendency to collapse, the recurring human desire to escape the burden of life and thought.

It was the failure of democracy which he thought explained the fascination of Fascism, or at least the prevalent disillusionment with democracy, and from that he dissociated himself:

it is manifest that any disparagement of 'democracy' is nowadays well received by nearly every class of men, and any alternative to 'democracy' is watched with great interest. This is one point on which intellectuals and populace, reactionaries and communists, the million-press and the revolutionary sheet, are more and more inclined to agree; and the danger is that when everyone agrees, we shall all get something that is worse than what we have already. I cannot share enthusiastically in this vigorous repudiation of 'democracy'. . . The modern question as popularly put is: 'democracy is dead; what is to replace it?' whereas it should be: 'the frame of democracy has been destroyed: how can we, out of the materials at hand, build a new structure in which democracy can live?'

He concluded that the answer was not to be found in the practice of either Fascism or Communism: 'I cannot believe that enthusiasm for Russian or Italian "revolution" has any intellectual value here.'[6] In the next issue he deplored the tendency, which he detected in Shaw, Wells and Wyndham Lewis, to incline towards 'some kind of fascism', 'some kind of autocracy'. 'We must prepare', he urged, 'a state of mind towards something other than the facile alternative [to failed democracy] of communist or fascist dictatorship.'[7] They would not do because 'the Russian and the Italian seem to me mechanical rather than spiritual communities'.[8]

The spiritual community which he invoked as the right alternative to the dictatorships, and to the decadent democracies, was an ideal royalism in which the idea of kingship is derived from the idea of the ultimate kingship of Christ. This was not quite the royalism of Charles Maurras, to whose writings he acknowledged a real debt; for Maurras was a free-thinker, a heretic, and 'made no pretence of Christian belief'.[9] The difference is like that between the royalism of Hobbes, and that of John Bramhall, Bishop of Derry under Charles I and Primate of Ireland under Charles II:

Superficially their theories of the kingship bear some resemblance to each other. Both men were violently hostile to democracy in any form or degree. Both men believed that the monarch should have absolute power. Bramhall affirmed the divine right of kings: Hobbes rejected this noble faith, and asserted in effect the divine right of power, however come by. But Bramhall's view is not so absurdly romantic, or Hobbes's so soundly reasonable, as might seem. To Bramhall the king himself was a kind of symbol, and his assertion of divine right was a way of laying upon the king a double responsibility. It meant that the king had not merely a civil but a religious obligation toward his people. And the kingship of Bramhall is less absolute than the kingship of Hobbes. For Hobbes the Church was merely a department of the State, to be run exactly as the king thought best.[10]

That 'religious obligation', with all that it implies, marks the fundamental difference between Eliot's idea of a king and every modern dictator. The same distinction makes it impossible for his royalist to be the follower of any merely political dictator:

what is to be the attitude of a royalist towards any system under which absolute submission to the will of a Leader is made an article of faith or a qualification for office? Surely the royalist can admit only one higher authority than the Throne, which is the Church.[11]

In short, Eliot's being 'royalist in politics' is inseparable from, and consequent upon, his being 'anglo-catholic in religion'. 'We feel convinced', he told the Anglo-Catholic Summer School of Sociology at Oxford in 1933,

that our spiritual faith should give us some guidance in temporal matters; that if it does not, the fault is our own; that morality rests upon religious sanction, and that the social organization of the world rests upon moral sanction; that we can only judge of temporal values in the light of eternal values. We are committed to what in the eyes of the world must be a desperate belief, that a Christian world-order, *the* Christian world-order, is ultimately the only one which, from any point of view, will work.[12]

It should be clear to any mind not closed by ignorance or prejudice that Eliot was not 'fascist' in any meaningful sense of the term. But nor was he really democratic. Democracy might be the best system for the temporal realm in which he found himself; but his first and ultimate allegiance was to the realm of the eternal and the ideal. He was an absolutist, with the absolutism of the Christian faith, and his conception of the State was 'ultimately theocratic'. That is what makes his political position so difficult to understand, as it made it difficult to maintain in practice. There is the strain, apparent in the previous quotation, between the apparently open and various 'any point of view' of the temporal realm, and the unarguable absolute implicit in 'ultimately'. The sentence makes sense only if 'any point of view' is subordinated to the ultimate; that is, if all points of view which are possible are reduced to the one viewpoint of man's final end. But that would mean viewing temporal affairs as if from eternity, *sub specie aeternitatis*. Precisely that is Eliot's intention, as it is the intention of his poetry. His was not, it was quite deliberately not, a worldly or a humane way of looking at things.

When authors were asked to take sides on the Spanish Civil War, by replying to the question: 'Are you for, or against, the legal Government and the People of Republican Spain? Are you for, or against, Franco and Fascism?', Eliot answered

While I am naturally sympathetic, [meaning, presumably, that he shared the sympathies of the left-wing questioners for 'the People of Republican Spain'] I still feel convinced that it is best that at least a few men of letters should remain isolated, and take no part in these collective activities.[13]

In a 'Commentary' concerned with the Spanish Civil War and dated 'November 1936', he had already declared his determination to maintain, among conflicting policies, each tending to an extreme, a central position based upon eternal values. Yet, he conceded, 'that balance of mind which a few highly civilized individuals, such as Arjuna, the hero of the *Bhagavad Gita*, can maintain in action, is difficult for most of us even as observers'.[14]

What it came down to in effect, was a defence of detachment against all committed 'sides'. When he defended Jacques Maritain in October 1938 against an attack by one of Franco's ministers, the quality he approved in him was 'the just impartiality of a Christian philosopher'; a quality not manifest, he added, among 'the irresponsible anti-fascists', 'the heirs of liberalism, who find an emotional outlet in denouncing the iniquity of something called "fascism" ', and who by doing so 'distract attention from the true evils in their own society'.[15] That was rather a shotgun blast, directed against a scattering of targets; but its stand is upon the principle that while the pure intellectual analysis of the philosopher may terminate in emotional conviction, emotional conviction should not interfere with his analysis.[16] What this could mean showed most frigidly in his reproof to the University of Oxford, in 1937, for refusing to participate in the bicentenary celebrations of the University of Goettingen in protest against its dismissal of Jewish academics. 'It seems hardly credible', he wrote, 'that the motives of the authorities of Oxford University in deciding not to send representatives to the celebration could have been to express disapproval of the German Government.'[17] His point would seem to have been – it is not easily made out in the exceptionally tortuous prose – that while it might be permissible for individuals to express their disapproval, it was not right for a public institution to do so. Now this has been represented as evidence of Nazi, or at least vaguely fascist sympathies; but that misses the point. What it reveals is an extreme concentration upon an *idea* of public institutions, to the exclusion of the political and the human actuality. Eliot was not approving the Nazis; he was simply not thinking about them, nor yet of their victims – or, to be exact, he was maintaining that it was not for the authorities of Oxford University to allow their feelings about the dismissal of Jewish academics to affect their official relations with the German university in question.[18] I am not at all sure that the Foreign Office would have disagreed with him, then or now. To the objection that it is inhuman to be so detached, Eliot might well have answered that as a philosopher it was not one's business to be human; but that, on the contrary, it was to examine human affairs justly in the light of eternal values. 'Not that it is possible, or even right, for any individual to regard such matters from the point of view of pure intelligence alone; but it is well that we should all regard them from that point of view now and then.'[19] But 'now and then', in his own work, was virtually always.

That he felt the isolation of his position is apparent in the hint of a personal apologia in his defence of Wyndham Lewis in 1937.

As for Mr Lewis's politics, I see no reason to suppose that he is any more of a 'fascist' or 'nazi' than I am. People are annoyed by finding that you are not on their side; and if you are not, they prefer you to surrender yourself to the other; if you can see the merits, as well as the faults, of parties to which you do not belong, that is still worse. Anyone who is not enthusiastic about the fruits of liberalism must be unpopular with the anglo-saxon majority. So far as I can see, Mr Lewis is defending the detached observer. The detached observer, by the way, is likely to be anything but a dispassionate observer; he probably suffers more acutely than the various apostles of immediate action. The detached observers are in theory the philosophers, the scientists, the artists, and the Christians.[20]

And there is no observer so detached, one may conclude, as he who is all at once Christian, artist and philosopher. In 1960 the apologia was more bitter and more barbed. 'The less respectable' – among the intellectuals to whom Lewis is a stumbling-block – 'vociferate the cry of "fascist!" – a term falsely applied to Lewis, but flung by the *massenmensch* at some who, like Lewis, choose to walk alone.'[21] I take that to be the retort of the Coriolanus who is the obverse of the would-be Arjuna. It has its truth, not only as to the facts of the case, but in the tone. The tone is one in which isolation, so deep as to be alienation, is the correlative of an inward sense of superiority. The cause is his electing to be the citizen of no earthly city: to be a voluntary alien in human society, and to be at home only in the City of God.[22]

That made his criticism of *all* existing political systems essentially negative. In April 1924 he remarked upon 'that meanness of spirit, that egotism of motive, that incapacity for surrender or allegiance to something outside of oneself, which is a frequent symptom of the soul of man under democracy.'[23] Later, in the 1930s, it appeared that from the point of view of the Christian observer there was little to choose between democracy and the dictatorships: 'The fundamental objection to fascist doctrine, the one which we conceal from ourselves because it might condemn ourselves as well, is that it is pagan.'[24]

Instead of merely condemning Fascism and Communism, therefore, we might do well to consider that we also live in a mass-civilization following many wrong ambitions and wrong desires, and that if our society renounces completely its obedience to God, it will become no better, and possibly worse, than some of those which are popularly execrated.[25]

. For the expression of the positive idea which lies behind these observations we must go beyond *The Idea of a Christian Society* – though that is the fullest and best approach to it afforded by the prose writings – to 'Coriolan', *The Rock*, *Murder in the Cathedral* and *Four Quartets*. For example, there is this statement by the Chorus at the end of part I of *The Rock*:

> There is no help in parties, none in interests,
> There is no help in those whose souls are choked and swaddled
> In the old winding sheets of place and power
> Or the new winding sheets of mass-made thought.
> O world! forget your glories and your quarrels,
> Forget your groups and your misplaced ambitions,
> We speak to you as individual men;
> As individuals alone with GOD.
> Alone with GOD, you first learn brotherhood with men.[26]

But that is not a political idea, so much as a removal from the realm of politics to that of theology.

Eliot confessed as much in his 'Last Words' in the final number of the *Criterion*:

I have felt obscurely during the last eight years or so . . . the grave dangers to this country which might result from the lack of any vital political philosophy, either explicit or implicit. . . For myself, a right political philosophy came more and more to imply a right theology – and right economics to depend upon right ethics.[27]

I am not sure, however, that he developed from his theology anything that could properly be called a political philosophy; and I rather think that his criticism of politics is the negative side of his theology, just as his treatment of the world in his poetry expressed 'the necessary and negative aspect of the impulse toward the pursuit of beauty'. Yet there was a positive and practical expression of it, which might be thought of as a kind of individual politics, in his conduct as a man of letters and as poet in the war against Nazi Germany and its allies. He wrote in September 1939, in a letter to the *New English Weekly*:

Our position at this moment is, I am sure, the right one. But if we are to maintain it, we must make a further effort toward rectitude and intelligence. We cannot effectively denounce the enemy without understanding him; we cannot understand him unless we understand ourselves, and our own weaknesses and sins. . .

If we limit our thinking to opposition to Germany, we shall get no further than 1918. In order to get beyond that point, we must venture on constructive thinking which may be as critical of ourselves as it will be of Germany.[28]

That is what he did, for his own part in the war, in his three wartime Quartets. These, properly understood, are the work in which he was really politically committed; and they remain – though of course they are more than this – his true political testament.

Appendix D

The secret history of 'Four Quartets'[1]

The drafts of *The Waste Land* directed attention upon a crisis of personality. They exposed the diseased state of sensibility which Eliot had to express, and they made it clear that the essential action of the poem was the process by which the sensibility gradually made itself whole. Its predicament was that of being conscious, and only conscious, of ' "the horror, the horror" ' of life; and its cure was to become wholly possessed by the horrors. The personality of the poet, in that poem, needed to realise itself through the intensification of suffering and death. *Four Quartets* appears to re-enact the same process, and most of all in the second and fourth movements of *Little Gidding*. Yet the drafts of the Quartets, and especially the drafts of those two movements, show the process being re-enacted not out of urgent personal necessity, but from the head and as the working out of an idea. They reveal, moreover, that Eliot tried to give *Little Gidding* a grounding in private experience, and failed. This raises the question, which Henry James put so well, of how far the mastering moral sense is substantiated by felt life. The truth of *The Waste Land* is primary: whatever its larger cultural and human significance, it is rooted in and empowered by immediate experience and psychic energies. Is it the case that, in the end, the truth of *Four Quartets* is rather of the secondary sort: the product of thought more than experience; and a matter of congruence with a governing idea, and internal self-consistency? Furthermore, does Eliot's failure to realise his idea of life in immediately personal terms suggest that, however much it may be a traditional and dominant idea of our culture, it may be not wholly true to life, and not wholly true even for himself?

Helen Gardner's book is an edition of all the known drafts, with a very substantial introduction and commentary in which Eliot's correspondence about the poem is made full use of. The various readings of the drafts are presented in an analytic apparatus, in the manner of the Oxford English Texts. This is a necessary economy in dealing with a succession of drafts – a dozen or more in the case of *Little Gidding* – but it does make it difficult to recover any one state of a Quartet or of a sustained passage. However, for the passages that underwent a lot of revision the several versions are usually given in full in the commentary which runs along with the text; and the first version of *Little Gidding*, which differs very significantly from the final one, is printed in full as an appendix. There are no facsimiles, and this is most unfortunate in the case of the holograph notes and drafts, for three reasons: these are the primary documents; the reduction of them to type has all the inevitable inadequacy of translation or paraphrase; and the transcription of them is not always accurate – there are perhaps a dozen misreadings (or misprints). The editing of the typescripts appears to be faultless. There are only two other editorial lapses. In the critical apparatus and in the commentary for *Burnt Norton* there is some confusion and inaccuracy over the alteration of the fifth line of part II. This must be due to using a reprint of *Collected Poems 1909–1935*, and assuming that it had not been altered from the first edition; but in fact the text was silently altered after 1944 to agree with that of *Four Quartets*.[2] Then there is no mention of the two cancelled lines at the end of the typescript of *Burnt Norton* – one is the single word 'Light', and the other a word now indecipherable. These are very minor flaws in a major contribution to scholarship.

Not much is known about the composition of *Burnt Norton*. Only the final typescript, sent to the printer of *Collected Poems 1909–1935* in which it first appeared, has been preserved; and this of course reveals just the last-minute corrections and refinements. Beyond that all there is to go on is some information about the personal occasion of the poem, and its well-attested relationship to *Murder in the Cathedral*.

The occasion, as T. S. Matthews first reported and Helen Gardner now amply confirms, was Eliot's visit to the rose-garden of Burnt Norton, in the autumn of 1934, with Emily Hale who had been a close friend since his Harvard days. Rather too much has been made of this, given that the exact nature of their relationship is a well-preserved secret, and given that Emily Hale is really not present at all in *Burnt Norton*. At the most she could only be the person addressed in the first movement; but the pronouns 'you' and 'we' can't be restricted in that way, being in effect addressed to the reader, to any and every reader, and being at the same time a kind of communing in which individual personalities are forgotten. There is a cognate scene in *The Family Reunion* in which Harry and Agatha similarly lose themselves, and discover 'reality', in their moment of vision and communion. The moment in the rose-garden of *Burnt Norton* is so much more than the record of a romantic visit with an old flame, as are Virgil's and Dante's and Hardy's encounters with theirs. It is an extraordinarily complex experience, in which the whole mind is engaged – memory, imagination, knowledge, and immediate sensory experience; and what we are given is no single or simple event, but the crystallisation of that whole in vision. The ostensible occasion may well have precipitated this, but it is also quite consumed in it.

The crystallisation of the poet's mind, which is the main episode in the first movement, is first introduced and then concluded by lines taken over from *Murder in the Cathedral*. Eliot used to say that the poem began with bits that had to be cut out of the play, and Helen Gardner has tracked down the bit, originally written for the Second Priest to speak after Thomas's speech at the close of the Second Temptation, which became the opening fourteen lines. Then there are several obvious common passages, notably 'human kind/Cannot bear very much reality', at the end of I, and the philosophical part of II. These are all in the metaphysical mode used in the play to interpret human experience according to the 'eternal design' of God; and they are being put to the same use in the poem. Here we have as good a clue as we are likely to find to the method of composition which is the basis of Eliot's quartet form. The vision of life arrived at in I by what we would ordinarily call the poetic imagination, is subjected in II to philosophical – or, more precisely, metaphysical – investigation. One may gather from Eliot's unpublished Clark Lectures of 1926 that he thought the proper basis for metaphysical poetry was given in Richard of St Victor's account of the stages of religious contemplation: natural imagination being put aside by cogitation, and that succeeded by meditation, the ideal culmination of which was contemplative vision. In those terms, the third movement of the poem is the stage of meditation, in which the mind is fixed upon the reality discovered by the intelligence, and the affections willed into accord with it; and the lyrical fourth movement is the attempt to *see* the world as it has been understood to be. In the fifth movement 'the complete consort' resumes the work of the preceding movements, and concludes it in an intuition of human existence in the light of eternity – a radical re-vision of the moment in the rose-garden. The process of the poem has been a progression by distinct stages from a natural sense of human existence to a metaphysical one; and of course this transformation of vision implies the transformation of the poet's mode of being.

There is the answer to the great unsolved problem of the Quartets: in what sense are they 'quartets'? It is because they use these four instruments of the mind, imagination, reason, meditation (which involves the will and affections), and contemplation (in which the seer is at one with what he perceives). Their formal structure corresponds to the traditional order of these mental functions. This is something that the drafts don't reveal in any obvious way – like the finished poems they simply practise what Eliot thought the proper method of metaphysical poetry. But the drafts do show that he knew with complete certainty what kind of writing was called for at each stage of the three later

Quartets. They show, that is, that with *Burnt Norton* he had arrived at a perfectly clear and definitive form for his mind in poetry.

While the three wartime Quartets use the same instruments as *Burnt Norton*, and correspond to it in method and form, they differ from it in that the experience they start from is not so much the poet's own as the common or universal experience. It should be remembered that *Burnt Norton* was published as the concluding poem of Eliot's *Collected Poems 1909–1935*, and that that collection was not expanded to include the later Quartets until 1963. For nearly twenty years his poems were published in the two distinct groupings, with *Burnt Norton* closing the one and opening the next.[3] The distinction thus marked was between the poems in which he had been working out his own salvation in poetry, and those in which he was trying to work out the salvation of others and of his society. His commitment to this latter task had led him to turn from writing poems to writing for the theatre, as the more promising medium for working upon the mind of the age. The war suspended his play writing, while making him feel that his society needed to be recalled more urgently than ever 'to values beyond those of politics and power struggles'. It was in this spirit that he wrote the three later Quartets. He referred to them once as 'patriotic poems'; and they were his particular contribution, as a poet, to the war effort. This sets them quite apart from *Burnt Norton*, and the distinction needs to be stressed because it has been generally overlooked.

A further distinction will emerge between the first two of the wartime Quartets, which are a firmly linked pair and in effect one continuous work, and *Little Gidding* which, in the drafts at least, can be seen aspiring to be a personal as well as a patriotic poem. For that reason I will consider *East Coker* and *The Dry Salvages* before tackling the really interesting case of *Little Gidding*. In those first two it is pre-eminently the complex and confused apprehensions of experience formed by others that he is bringing into his own ideal order. He does of course place himself in a personal relation to them, through his descent from the Elyots of East Coker, and his having grown up beside the Mississippi and on the Massachusetts coast. But the emphasis is upon the common experience of life in the Old World and the New; while his own vividly personal memories are presented briefly and in symbol. His own intense moments can be presented in that way because their meaning has been understood: 'Whisper of running streams, and winter lightning . . . requiring, pointing to the agony/Of death and birth'; and again, towards the close of *The Dry Salvages*, 'These are only hints and guesses . . . The hint half guessed, the gift half understood, is Incarnation.' That understanding governs the treatment of human experience in general, from the living and dying of generations now in the earth of East Coker and elsewhere, through that of those who have to do with the sea and all that it is made to stand for, up to that of those engaged in the war 'Now and in England'.

Apart from a few manuscript jottings, only the typescript drafts of *East Coker* and *The Dry Salvages* have been preserved, and in these both poems appear in a relatively finished state. For the most part the revising is a matter of polishing and perfecting, and there is no evidence of false starts or uncertain gropings. The unusual rapidity of the composition leaves no room to suppose that the missing manuscript drafts would contradict the impression that Eliot knew exactly what he had to do, and did it in a thoroughly systematic and orderly fashion. Some time in February 1940 John Hayward noted that Eliot had 'drafted the first two out of five sections' of 'a new poem in succession to "Burnt Norton" '. *East Coker* was finished within that month, and was published in the *New English Weekly* on 21 March. The first Hayward knew of *The Dry Salvages* was when he received the first draft on 1 January 1941, and by the 29th Eliot had corrected the proofs for its publication in the *New English Weekly*.

The only really revealing revisions are those in which Eliot can be seen struggling to get beyond some first formulations so bare and explicit as to be statements of a preconception or a prejudice. In *The Waste Land* drafts much of what had to be cut out or refined was the crude expression of bad feeling; in the case of these two Quartets what most needed to be cut, or else substantiated, was crude thought. Some simple examples of these first thoughts: 'Before the *patient* ice-cap reigns' (my italics); 'the efflorescence of the April suburbs', which became 'the rank ailanthus of the April dooryard'; 'And through the fog the pretemporal ground swell'; and as an instance of the abstract becoming didactic,

> We content and should be
> If the temporal aspect of the soul
> Nourish (not too far from the yew-tree)
> The life of significant soil.

A fuller example of how Eliot worked is afforded at the close of *East Coker*. For this there is a manuscript jotting: 'Alone – the ice cap/Separated from the surfaces of human beings/To be reunited in the Communion'. (For 'in' Helen Gardner gives 'and'). The entire closing paragraph can be seen to be an expansion of that idea, or a set of variations upon it. The first ten lines are little altered from the first draft to the final text, but the rest required more than one attempt. The first typescript followed 'The evening with the photograph album' with this:

> Here or there does not matter. We must be still
> And be still moving. The mind must venture

Where it has not been, be separated
For a further union, a deeper communion,
Aranyaka, the forest or the sea
The empty cold with the desolation
The wave cry, the wind cry
With the understanding and the consolation
Of the petrel and the porpoise. In my end is my beginning.

Eliot then crossed that through and typed this in its place:

Love is itself unmoving
But love is most nearly itself
When now and now cease to matter.
Here or there does not matter.
We must be still and still moving
Into another intensity
For a further union, a deeper communion,
Through the empty cold with the desolation,
The wave cry, the wind cry, the vast waters
Of the petrel and the porpoise.

'In my end is my beginning' was added in pencil; and, also in pencil, the third last line was altered to read 'Through the dark cold and the empty desolation', and 'Old men ought to be explorers' was added for insertion after the third line. The final text was arrived at by cancelling the first line, which had been taken over from the end of *Burnt Norton*, perhaps as a cue; and correcting the third line to read 'here and now'. What the process of revision amounts to here is essentially an effort to make the thought real to sense, or to express the meaning in the terms of experience.

In the case of *Little Gidding* the complete series of drafts has been preserved, from the first rough note to the final proof, except for the manuscript draft of I. Helen Gardner's reconstruction of the notepad used for drafting both *The Dry Salvages* and *Little Gidding* shows that he proceeded directly from the one to the other; and that for the latter as for the former he first jotted down brief notes outlining the Quartet as a whole, and then drafted the successive movements each in its turn, sometimes starting from a prose draft and sometimes achieving at once a more or less rough but still impressively formed verse. A first complete version was sent to Hayward on 7 July 1941 – less than six months after the completion of *The Dry Salvages*. But this time, instead of moving swiftly through a final revision to publication, Eliot first expressed grave doubts about it, then set the poem aside for a full year; and finally, in July, August and September 1942, he radically altered the parts where he had felt the poem broke down. In a letter to Hayward on 14 July 1941 he wrote:

My suspicions about the poem are partly due to the fact that as it is written to complete a series, and not solely for itself, it may be too much from the head and may show signs of flagging ... The question is not so much whether it is as good as the others (I am pretty sure it is not) but whether it is good enough to keep company with them to complete the shape. If the problem is more than one of improving details, it will have to go into storage for some time to come.

On 5 August he wrote:

The defect of the whole poem, I feel, is the lack of some acute personal reminiscence (never to be explicated, of course, but to give power from well below the surface) and I can *perhaps* supply this in Part II.

Earlier in the same letter he had written, 'this part needs some sharpening of personal poignancy: a line or two might do it.' He then went on to answer Hayward's asking why the meeting with the ghost was 'in the autumn weather' (a detail later dropped):

'Autumn weather' only because it *was* autumn weather – it is supposed to be an *early* air raid – and to throw back to Figlia che piange ... but with less point than the children in the appletree meaning to tie up New Hampshire and Burnt Norton ...

Given such intentions, one might well wonder if the 'autumn weather' was meant to throw back also to 'the autumn heat' of *Burnt Norton*.

What all this points to is a strong preoccupation, such as is not to be discerned in the two preceding Quartets, with his personal and even private experience. And it is to be noted that it was the failure to achieve a satisfactory expression of this preoccupation that was the cause of the poem's breaking down in 1941.

This was the preliminary note for *Little Gidding*:

Winter scene. May.
Lyric. air earth water end – & daemonic fire. The Inferno.

They vanish, the individuals, and our feeling for them sinks into the flame which refines. They emerge in another pattern & recreated & redeemed, reconciled, having their meaning together not apart, in a unison which is of beams from the central fire. And the others with them contemporaneous.

Invocation to the Holy Spirit.

(For 'unison' Helen Gardner gives 'union'.)

The note for the first movement at this stage suggests only its main theme; and it does this in a way that could well be recalling the passage in the first temptation in *Murder in the Cathedral* which clearly lies behind the fully worked out 'midwinter spring' opening:

THOMAS You talk of seasons that are past. I remember
        Not worth forgetting:

TEMPTER   And of the new season.
               Spring has come in winter. Snow in the branches
               Shall float as sweet as blossom. Ice along the ditches
               Mirror the sunlight. Love in the orchard
               Send the sap shooting . . .
THOMAS   The impossible is still temptation.
               The impossible, the undesirable,
               Voices under sleep, waking a dead world,
               So that the mind may not be whole in the present.

There were echoes there, probably deliberate allusions, from 'New Hampshire' and 'Marina' and the suppressed 'Ode' of 1918; and Eliot had wanted to bring these in again later in the first movement. In the section dealing with 'May' and its 'voluptuary sweetness', his early version had the line 'In the may time, the play time of the wakened senses'. This was altogether in the style of *Murder in the Cathedral*; and when Hayward objected to the 'jingle' Eliot said that he had 'wanted the Children hint again'. Another telling hint in the early version threw back to 'What the Thunder Said' and *The Hollow Men*: 'The words of the living are wind in dry grass,/The communion of the dead is flame on the wind'. It is no surprise to learn that Eliot's private associations for those 'other places/ Which are also the world's end' – 'the sea jaws,/Or over a dark lake, in a desert or a city' – had nothing to do with the war: he was thinking of sainted hermits and the desert fathers, the models for his juvenile 'Saint Narcissus' and for Celia in *The Cocktail Party*. This theme of passion and its purgation is of course woven in with the other themes of *Little Gidding*, with the socio-political (the perpetual present moment of England's history), and with the religious (the descent of the Holy Spirit in pentecostal fire). But what the drafts up to the version of July 1941 show is that it was of far greater importance in the early conception than one would have guessed from the final version.

The theme of sensual life and love was at first the predominant, and virtually the exclusive concern of the second movement. The lyric of the four elements, compounded of allusions to *Burnt Norton* and the other Quartets, was to insist simply and unequivocally upon their end; and the fire was to be only 'daemonic', the fire of nature which, in Eliot's view, is the fire of hell if it is not accepted as purgatorial. There was a statement of this alternative, as a coda to the lyric, in one early draft: 'Fire without and fire within/Shall purge the unidentified sin./ This is the place where we begin.' That would have brought to mind what Harry learns from Agatha in *The Family Reunion*. It was cut before the version of July 1941, perhaps because it was another jingle, perhaps also because at that stage the second movement was to go no further than the natural wisdom of experience, while the progression from 'The Inferno' to 'the flame which refines' was to be effected in III. The Dantescan 'canto' was to lead up to the communication of the dead master, and this was to have been a confessional examination of the poet's past life under the guise of the *dédoublement* of personality:

'Remember rather the essential moments
    That were the times of birth and death and change
    The agony and the solitary vigil
Remember also fear, loathing and hate,
    The wild strawberries eaten in the garden,
    The walls of Poitiers and the Anjou wine,
The fresh new season's rope, the smell of varnish
    On the clean oar, the drying of the sails,
    Such things as seem of least and most importance.
So, as you circumscribe this dreary round,
    Shall your life pass from you, with all you hated
    And all you loved, the future and the past.
United to another past, another future,
    (After many seas and after many lands)
    The dead and the unborn, who shall be nearer
Than the voices and the faces that were most near.
    This is the final gift of earth accorded –
    One soil, one past, one future, in one place.
Nor shall the eternal thereby be remoter
    But nearer: seek or seek not, it is here,
    Now, the last love on earth. The rest is grace.'

In the first manuscript draft the third line of this speech read, 'The dark night in the solitary bedroom'. One would have thought that had just the 'acute personal reminiscence' and 'sharpening of personal poignancy' which Eliot thought the poem needed more of. Perhaps it was too open to the kind of explication he wanted to avoid, in that it might direct attention upon his private experience and away from his meaning. Would it suggest a dark night of the soul? The revised line, 'The agony and the solitary vigil', errs on the other side, forcefully expressing the general idea but no specific experience. The passage as a whole suffers from an excess of the general idea, and a lack of specifying experience – of experience felt in such a way as to require these ideas. The facts of the poet's life are really quite sufficiently indicated, but they remain the bare facts, lacking the essential feeling, and lacking therefore the power to move the mind towards another life.

Waking alone
At the hour when we are
Trembling with tenderness
Lips that would kiss
Form prayers to broken stone.

There was the agony of love in an intense and urgent form – what the dead master, and double, was merely prosing about at this stage in the composition of *Little Gidding*. His communication was not 'flame on the wind'.

A manuscript note for III recapitulates the idea set down for this movement in the outline for the whole Quartet – the same idea as that in the rough note for *East Coker* V ('Separated from the surfaces of human beings/To be reunited in the Communion') – and implicitly connects it with the 'Remember rather the essential moments' speech: 'The use of memory   to   detach oneself from one's own past – they vanish & return in a different action   a new relationship. If it is here, & now, why regret it?' (Helen Gardner gives 'then' for '& now'.) The first manuscript draft was already near to the final version, except for one significant emphasis –

> This is the use of memory,
> In liberation, not less of love but extension
> Of love in the death of desire

The movement, in that draft and still in the 7 July version, went on to seek this 'extension of love' in 'The life only death transmits', and affirmed 'the motive/ Which the moment of death brings to life'. It ended with this variation upon a Christian prayer:

> Soul of Christ, sanctify them,
> Body of Christ, let their bodies be good earth,
> Water from the side of Christ wash them,
> Fire from the heart of Christ, incinerate them.

The first and third of those lines are near to the prayer, but the other two are really all Eliot's own. The conclusion of the prayer was doubtless in his mind –

> In the hour of my death call me,
> And bid me come to Thee,
> That with Thy Saints I may praise Thee.
> For ever and ever. Amen.

That may be connected with the line from *The Cloud of Unknowing* inserted in the final movement in 1942, 'With the drawing of this Love and the Voice of this Calling'.

The idea that love must look to death for its fulfilment was expressed in the earliest draft of IV rather more starkly than in the final version:

> The dove descending breaks the air
> With breath of crepitative fire
> Of which the tongues declare
> The culmination of desire,
> Expectancy, hope, doubt, despair.

> Beneath those never resting feet
> All aspirations end and meet.

The last four lines imply the nexus of romantic memories which the first two movements attempted to deal with, and they reach back to one of the unpublished poems found among the drafts of *The Waste Land*. 'Elegy', in which the shade of 'the injured bride' becomes a fury, expands its nightmare into this:

> God, in a rolling ball of fire
> Pursues by day my errant feet.
> His flames of anger and desire
> Approach me with consuming heat.

The second stanza in the earliest draft of *Little Gidding*'s lyric also seems to reach back to that earlier phase of Eliot's work. It was to conclude the several variations in the poem upon the conceit of the four elements by evoking the water of baptism, the brand of those touched by the Holy Spirit, and 'The gambler between death and birth/Whose climax is a pinch of earth'. The persona was first called 'The miserable athanatos', which could be an allusion to the predicament of the Sibyl of Cumae, deathless in life; next it was 'The votaries of Thanatos', meaning those dedicated to death; the third and uncancelled form of the line was 'The votary of Soledos', which – if one accepts Helen Gardner's convincing suggestion that Eliot ('who did not know Spanish') meant 'Soledad', the Spanish for 'solitude' – is a link at once with John of the Cross and with the hermits and desert sages Eliot had in mind in the first movement. Altogether, this first draft of the lyric can be seen to be working out 'the culmination of desire' as meaning death. But then in the draft of July 1941 that key line became 'The one restorative from error'; and the echoes of personal passion were removed. The second stanza was replaced by two new stanzas of forced conceits based upon accountancy – 'The deficit that is complete,/Or cancelled by the Paraclete', and so forth. Eliot knew it had gone wrong. He told Hayward, 'It may be that the attempt to give a XVII flavour is a mistake (having previously done it successfully)'; and he cancelled the more conceited of the two stanzas in August 1941. But it seems obvious from the drafts at that stage that he had lost touch with the motive and inspiration of the poem, and instead of working out his deep personal feelings had gone off into some contrived moralising.

The poem seemed to have broken down and disintegrated at that point. Yet Eliot was able to go on, in mid-1941, to write the final movement in a form very near to its final state. Moreover, this last part was the true conclusion to the Quartet as he had intended it to be. Its first section resumed the socio-historical theme; and the second, bringing together motifs of passionate personal experience from the whole set of Quartets, achieved the fusion of private experience and religious meaning which had been Eliot's ambition in *Little Gidding*. He had brought the poem successfully to its conclusion, but he had failed at two of the stages in his approach to the communion of the fire and the rose. In the second and fourth movements he had approached the meaning, but had not recovered the experience in thought or in vision.

In his 'rescension' of the poem in the summer of 1942 Eliot made two unsuccessful attempts at what the dead master had to say, and then at the third had him speak of 'the gifts reserved for age'. In place of 'the essential moments' of his own life, he was drawing now upon his thinking about Yeats in his 1940 memorial lecture. The first attempt had the ghost change form and feature to become 'the spirit unappeased and peregrine', and to characterise himself as having 'spent my life in that unending fight/To give a people speech'. Then, after a brief confession of error – 'As who, in imperfection, can avoid . . .?' – he was to conclude:

> 'Those who knew purgatory here shall know
> Purgation hereafter: so shall you learn also,
> In the embraces of that fiery wind
> Where you must learn to swim & better nature.'

One remarkable thing about this draft version is that the effort to make a personal confession has been totally displaced by a socio-political confession from a distinctly *other* poet. But equally remarkable is the fact that when this other addresses himself to Eliot's case it is in images which recall, not Dante's political figures, but his lovers – Francesca and Paolo in *Inferno* v ('Caught in the coils of that strong fiery wind' was an alternative form of the penultimate line), and Arnaut Daniel plunging back into the refining flame. The recurrence of these images, which had of course haunted Eliot all his life, show him trying to preserve at least a hint of the kind of purgatory he had meant to write.

The second attempt cut back the socio-political statement more or less to what it is in the final text ('But as the passage now presents . . . and foresight'). Then Eliot drafted a variation upon Yeats' 'The Spur', which he had cited in his 1940 lecture 'as a personal confession . . . of a man who was essentially the same as most other men', except for his 'greater clarity, honesty and vigour' –

> You think it horrible that lust and rage
> Should dance attendance upon my old age;
> They were not such a plague when I was young:
> What else have I to spur me into song?

'To what honest man, old enough, can these sentiments be entirely alien?' Eliot had asked in 1940, 'They can be subdued and disciplined by religion, but who can say that they are dead?' Then he added, 'The tragedy of Yeats' epigram is all in the last line.' His variation upon it was an attempt to bring it into accord with his own orthodox morality (viewing it much as Thomas viewed his First Temptation in *Murder in the Cathedral*):

> You shall know old rooted sin puts forth again
> Even in exhausted soil, after many seasons,
> When the starved unflowering growth shows still more foul
> Without luxuriance . . .

This particular attempt to subdue and discipline 'his personal animal feelings' went no further than the first rough manuscript draft. But it found effective expression in the form of a disclosure of 'the gifts reserved for age'. In this conclusion to the movement, as it stands in the final version, one can detect traces of the previous attempts. First there is the traditional spiritual discipline of viewing life under the aspect of death – generating a morality from mortality. Then there is the echo of 'Remember rather the essential moments' in 'the rending pain of re-enactment/Of all that you have done, and been'. That, with its echo of Francesca's 'There is no greater pain than to recall a happy time in wretchedness', shows what the first version had failed to achieve: the memories there, because they had no life in them, could not hurt enough to make a hell or purgatory. But then what we are given in the final version is simply a powerful statement of the idea: Eliot has triumphed over the earlier failure by intensifying the thought and letting go the experience. What substantiates the idea and gives it such force is not 'acute personal reminiscence', but the sense of a tradition of moralists weighting the formulation. Finally, at the close of the speech, there is the correction and saving of Yeats through the implicit identification of his images of the dance of the soul in the refining fire with Dante's Arnaut – a dying into the artifice of eternity in Eliot's sense, and not his own.

Eliot worked over the second section of the third movement in 1942, but the consequence was only to make the expression of the thought less assertive and more incantatory, and to add the quotation from Julian of Norwich to introduce it and to serve at the end in place of his variation upon the 'Anima Christi'. He seems to have revised the final movement next, since Hayward had received the revised versions of that and of the first three movements by 27 August, but first saw the revised form of the lyric in the 'Second Complete Draft 2 Sep. 1942'. That suggests that Eliot left the lyric to last. In the 1942 working drafts there is no sign of the two over-conceited stanzas; and the first draft for the new second stanza appears to take its cue from the second movement, connecting its opening lines with its (revised) conclusion:

Who heaped the brittle roseleaves? Love.
Love put the match; and blew the coals.
Who fed the fire? Love,
To torture and to temper souls
In that consumption from above
    Where all delights & torments cease
    The will is purified to peace.

'Endless consumption, which is love', presumably a variant of the third from last line, provides a further gloss upon the conceit. This draft recovers the notion from the earliest of the drafts that the 'culmination of desire' is the purgatorial fire. Then Eliot hit upon the allusion which perfectly combined this idea of love with the close of II, and which crystallised the whole complex of his feelings about love –

The intolerable shirt of flame
Which human power cannot remove.
We only live, only suspire
Consumed by either fire or fire.

With that said the difficulties of the composition were at last overcome. A 'Final Recension' is dated 19 September 1942; the proof for the *New English Weekly* was corrected by 28 September, and *Little Gidding* appeared there on 15 October.

The record of the composition of *Four Quartets* reveals that there were three distinct stages in the growth of the work. *Burnt Norton*, conceived and written as a self-complete entity, was a setting in order of the poet's own passional experience. *East Coker* and *The Dry Salvages* appear to have been conceived and written as a pair of Quartets setting in order the natural history of his culture. They are intimately bound together and could stand as complete in themselves: the coda to *The Dry Salvages* is the full conclusion to the themes they have been working out, and there is nothing in them that obviously requires the further development of *Little Gidding*. What did require that further development was the disparity between *Burnt Norton* and *East Coker–The Dry Salvages*, and Eliot's seeing the possibility of integrating his personal quest for order with his attempt to set his society in order. This called for a personal witness to the working out of God's will in the world: a confession, and interpretation, and envisioning of his own experience in such a way as to implicate and to illuminate the English experience of life. *Little Gidding* was to 'complete the shape' by making a new whole out of the distinct achievements of *Burnt Norton* and of *East Coker–The Dry Salvages*. The dark secret of this history is that Eliot was unable to make that personal confession, and had recourse instead to an impersonal tradition to enforce his conception.

I don't think that this made *Little Gidding* imperfect, or marred *Four Quartets* as a whole. On the contrary, it was probably the right way to complete what Eliot really had to say. That was the conviction that the final and absolute truth about life is death, and that only in death is to be found the satisfaction of human desires. This of course is not a truth of experience, but a metaphysical idea. And what the buried failure shows up is that the idea is not true to the whole experience of life and love. Because the end is only the end, and not the being alive and in love, to view life and love only in the aspects of disenchantment and death is to falsify the experience, and to lie against life. Was something in Eliot resisting that lie when he tried to present his own life – as he had presented the life of the folk of East Coker and of the Massachusetts coast – as meaning only death? An answer may be given in the fact that when, fifteen years later, he found himself loved and in love, he did manage to make his confession at last, in *The Elder Statesman*. And what he confessed there, beyond the oppressive consciousness of failure in love, was not the aspiration of the saint committed to 'death in love', but the basic human need to be sustained by love in life. His intellectual discipline had not purged that; but in *Little Gidding* it did effectively repress it.

Appendix E

Artful Voices: Eliot's Dramatic Verse[1]

It is not for me, but for the neurologists, to discover...why and how feeling and rhythm are related. The tendency, at any rate, of prose drama is to emphasise the ephemeral and superficial; if we want to get at the permanent and universal we tend to express ourselves in verse.[2]

We distinguish on sound technical grounds between prose and verse. But the non-technical distinction between prose and poetry is more difficult to sustain, and may be fundamentally unsound, because the difference, in a healthy state of mind and language, is a matter of degree and not of kind. However, if one does make that distinction, then of course it follows that poetry can be written in either verse or prose, and so too can prose; or, to put it another way, it follows that verse can be a medium for both prose and poetry. We naturally think of verse as getting more out of words than prose, as heightening or intensifying the prosaic into the poetic. But verse may also be used to keep language down to a prosaic level by flattening out or repressing possible meanings and intensities.

Eliot was one who did distinguish between prose and poetry, that is, as he saw it, between the prose of ordinary consciousness and the poetry of metaphysical thought and vision. He therefore made his verse at once a medium for the better realisation of both, and an instrument for discriminating between them. This makes his verse 'dramatic' in a double sense, for not only does it find appropriate voices for the matter of fact and the metaphysical, but it also acts out their fated relations.

At a basic level, drama is a matter of actors in action – or, as we usually think of it, of characters in action. Verse, as it can specify and differentiate states of mind and feeling, can create distinct characters very effectively. A specific verse style is a voice, and hence, potentially, an actor. And the interaction of a set of verse-voices, if only we are sensitive to them, can constitute a dramatic action. So verse, through its variety of modes and styles, can be a theatre in itself. In 'Portrait of a Lady', 'Prufrock', 'Gerontion' and *The Waste Land*, the versification is such a theatre.

For example, Prufrock's drama, a crisis of identity occurring in his effort and failure to transcend his all too actual world, is acted out in the shifts and

342

progressions of the versification. He begins in a form of verse that is open to and charged with apprehensions; but he drops, after the neutralising couplet ('In the room the women come and go...'), into a form which subdues those apprehensions to a predictable, and soothing, development and closure. This foreshadows the main action: the tautening of the verse into nervy stanzas as he wonders if he dare disturb his universe; and the drop, after his failure to say what he felt and meant, into the anti-climactic stanzas in which his anguish is muted by his antagonist's refrain ('That is not what I meant'). His end is a collapse into pastiche blank verse and the elegiac rhythms of decadent romanticism: having failed to live out his capacity for apprehending the tedium and terror of his existence, he has lapsed, wittingly, into cliché.

In his earlier poems Eliot was already using verse with what he called, in a *Criterion* 'Commentary' in July 1932, a 'dramatic intent': 'The greatest deficiency in most of the contemporary verse which comes to my eye is the lack of any dramatic intent, which might help to correct its imperfectly conceived philosophies and its imperfectly objectified emotions.' So the use of verse is to objectify emotions or responses to experience, in order that they may be observed, seen for what they are and diagnosed; and in order that a philosophy based upon imperfectly apprehended experience might thereby be corrected.

In *The Waste Land* the verse creates many voices, many characters. However, the essential action of the poem is the resolving of all the voices into one voice, and that one increasingly impersonal, 'beyond character'. It might be called the true voice of Eros in Angst, of desire that will not be satisfied. It is heard at the centre of each of the first two parts (the hyacinth garden, 'My nerves are bad tonight'); then opening and closing 'The Fire Sermon' (11.173-84, 292ff.); and through much of 'What the Thunder Said'. The verse in which this voice is realised is at once closer to plain speaking than any other in the poem – more immediately in touch with and possessed by experience – and more lyrical than any other:

> 'On Margate Sands.
> I can connect
> Nothing with nothing.
> The broken fingernails of dirty hands.
> My people humble people who expect
> Nothing.'

And again: '. . . The sea was calm, your heart would have responded/Gaily, when invited...' As this voice becomes the dominant one, the others are placed by it as relatively unreal, as symptoms of the predicament, but not effective expressions of what it feels like and means to be in it. They belong on the whole to literature – we have 'known them all already, known them all' – and what they are saying, with all their trailing allusions, is simply that life is death. But the voice of Eros in Angst is saying, with its immediacy and intensity, what Prufrock could not manage, that to suffer that state, really to suffer it, is life.

The creation in verse of a natural voice for what he had to say was the basis of Eliot's *stil novo,* the new form and style of *The Hollow Men,* the 'Ariel' poems and *Ash-Wednesday.* Yet in these poems it ceases to be a dramatic voice, and becomes rather a lyrical one; and it is superseded, moreover, by the mode which Eliot aptly called 'dream song', in which the substance of experience is dissolved into phantasmagoric symbols. The natural voice of passion is heard in section III of *The Hollow Men* ('Waking alone/At the hour when we are/Trembling with tenderness'), in *Ash-Wednesday:* VI ('And the lost heart stiffens...'), and again in the 'love-duets' in *The Family Reunion;* but it is always placed as the merely natural voice that must be subdued to the further revelations of symbols and beliefs – of symbols explicated by beliefs, and beliefs made real in symbols.

'A verse play', Eliot wrote in 1944, in his introduction to S. L. Bethell's *Shakespeare & the Popular Dramatic Tradition,* 'is not a play done into verse, but a different kind of play: in a way more realistic than "naturalistic drama", because, instead of clothing nature in poetry, it should remove the surface of things, expose the underneath, or the inside, of the natural surface appearance.' That is a formula for such dualistic verse as this, from 'Triumphal March':

> What a time that took. Will it be he now? No,
> Those are the golf club Captains, these the Scouts,
> And now the *société gymnastique de Poissy*
> And now come the Mayor and the Liverymen. Look
> There he is now, look:
> There is no interrogation in his eyes
> Or in the hands, quiet over the horse's neck,
> And the eyes watchful, waiting, perceiving, indifferent.
> O hidden under the dove's wing, hidden in the turtle's breast,
> Under the palmtree at noon, under the running water
> At the still point of the turning world. O hidden.

This is a fair sample of Eliot's dramatic verse and method in the 30s. The simple opposition of 'poetic' images to 'prosaic' facts is enforced by breaking up the continuous prose sense into rhythmically isolated phrases, and making each phrase a bored cadence; and then giving the 'broken images' in a coher-ent, rising rhythm, which first establishes a musical pattern of feeling, and then attaches it to the metaphysical idea. This may not be what is normally meant by drama, but it is of the essence of Eliot's theatre.

In writing for the theatre Eliot was always very conscious of the need to avoid the least echo of Shakespearean blank verse, and to establish communi-cations with the living language. Yet a striking feature of his experimental and apprentice drama is the deliberate avoidance of the natural speaking voice, or the reserving of it for his metaphysical vision. *Sweeney Agonistes* was a successful experiment, insofar as it showed how low-life material could be objectified by regularising its idiom into a sort of automatic ragtime. But it also discovered that verse alone could not make that idiom yield the vision indicated by the epigraphs from Aeschylus and St John of the Cross. In the choruses for *The Rock,* and in *Murder in the Cathedral,* the versification is quite as artificial – it really needs the trained verse-speakers it was written for – but it is in the service of an explicitly Christian idea of things. It is strictly rhetorical, more and less subtly enforcing a preconceived morality, and hardly at all responsive to any immediate experience. But it is of great interest for its technical virtuosity, for the range of styles deployed, and for the subtle adjust-ments of the verse to express and to discriminate among a variety of attitudes and philosophies. At the same time the basic technique is very simple, as in the doubling of a falling stress ('Living and partly living'), or in the opposing of a doubled rising stress to it ('In the vacant places/We will build with new bricks'). The general effect is to estrange the audience from their ordinary world, and to give the authority of ordinary speech to the confessions of dis-enchantment ('Man's life is a cheat and a disappointment'), and to Thomas' philosophic statements ('It is out of time that my decision is taken/If you call that decision/To which my whole being gives entire consent'). But what would the Women of Canterbury have to say if they were allowed their proper Kentish speech?

The Family Reunion (1939) was Eliot's first play for more or less normal speaking voices, and it required a considerable development of verse tech-nique. Speaking about this in *Poetry and Drama* (1951), he said

my first concern was...to find a rhythm close to contemporary speech, in which the stresses could be made to come wherever we should naturally put them, in uttering the particular phrase on the particular occasion. What I worked out is substantially what I have continued to employ: a line of varying length and varying number of syllables, with a caesura and three stresses. The caesura and the stresses may come at different places, almost anywhere in the line; the stresses may be close together or well separated by light syllables; the only rule being there must be one stress on one side of the caesura and two on the other. [3]

A 'rule' allowing so much freedom is no more than a minimal requirement; and in fact it serves less as a rule than as a basis from which to depart, (as the iambic pentameter is the basis from which the verse departs in Eliot's earlier poems). In the plays from *The Family Reunion* on there is great variation in the verse line: in the number of stresses; in their weights, whether light or heavy; and in their pattern, whether regular or informal. This variety is the major resource of his theatre. But of course the uses to which he puts it are what really count, and in this connection the really interesting remark is the one about placing the stresses 'wherever we should naturally put them'. What is 'natural' in a given case will depend upon the nature of the thing said, on the nature of the speaker, and also on the nature of the dramatist.

So an artificial 'Society' way of speaking is natural for the shallow aunts and uncles in The Family Reunion:

> *Well*, as for *me*,
> I would *never* go south, no, *definitely never*,
> Even *could* I do it as *well* as *Amy*:
> *England's* bad *enough*, I would never go *south*,
> *Simply* to *see* the *vulgarest* people

The degree of stress, and even the exact placing of a stress, is of course not precisely fixed in such verse, and one can only mark the words where a stress would be likely to fall. But the trick of this habit of speech is to accentuate the qualifying/intensifying words rather than verbs and substantives. Eliot catches this very well, and uses it to expose the vanity of those who are merely the creatures of their habits. In Amy's speech, because she is conscious of the vanity of things, the verse alters from the self-assertive accentuation into a stressing of sense:

> You *none* of you *understand* how *old* you are
> And *death* will come to you as a *mild surprise*,
> A momentary *shudder* in a *vacant room*.
> Only *Agatha* seems to discover some *meaning* in *death*
> Which *I* cannot *find*.

Those two passages show how differently Eliot's rule can be applied – in the one to stress the sense, and in the other to stress the lack of it. The verse given to Agatha and Harry shows how the rule can be departed from. Agatha commands a more formally weighted line, of which the basis is four stresses.

Harry's normal line is also a four-stress one, but his speech fluctuates a great
deal in intensity, and there is always liable to be an extra stress or two:

> *You* do not *know*
> The *noxious smell untraceable* in the *drains,*
> *Inacessible* to the *plumbers,* that has its *hour* of the *night*; you do not *know*
> The *unspoken voice* of *sorrow* in the *ancient bedroom*

In Harry's 'love-duet' scenes, first with Mary, later with Agatha, the verse is
as much a musical composition as that of *Four Quartets,* and consists, like the
Quartets, of variations upon a basic four-stress line:

> I *only looked* through the *little door*
> When the *sun* was *shining* on the *rose-garden*:
> And *heard* in the *distance tiny voices*
> And *then* a *black raven flew over.*

These passages of 'pure poetry', in which the speakers are rapt beyond their
ordinary characters, are effective – although I think they would be most convincing when spoken by disembodied, radio voices. But the passages to be
spoken by various characters in chorus seem to me unsuccessful, and for the
same reason that the Eumenides are unsuccessful: they are merely rhetorical
devices, not voices arising naturally from the given world.

Of the versification in the three postwar plays the main thing to be noticed
is that each play has its own distinctive and specific style. One cannot generalise about them. *The Cocktail Party* is in a developed form of the verse created for Amy and the aunts in *The Family Reunion,* but in this case there is no
departing from it into impersonal poetry. The verse modulates between intensely superficial Society party talk, and such serious conversation and
thought as the members of that same society can command when they are
being cultured. The range is from

> You've missed the point *completely,* Julia:
> There *were* no tigers. *That* was the point.

through Celia's

> You see, I think I really had a vision of something
> Though I don't know what it is. I don't want to forget it.
> I want to live with it. I could do without everything,
> Put up with anything, if I might cherish it.

to Julia's

> Oh yes, she will go far. And we know where she is going.
> But what do we know of the terrors of the journey?
> You and I don't know the process by which the human is
> Transhumanised: what do we know
> Of the kind of suffering they must undergo
> On the way to illumination?

There are moments when the language is less abstract – generally when the 'commonplace' human condition is in question – but that is characteristic of the most serious and intense parts of the play. Consequently there is scarcely any question of the verse working for 'poetic' effects. All that is required of it is that, as in the philosophical passages of the Quartets, it should clarify the thought and impress it upon the thinking mind.

A note on the dust-jacket of *The Confidential Clerk*, probably written by Eliot himself, said that it is 'in the same kind of verse as *The Cocktail Party*'. But in fact it is even nearer to conversational prose. There is so minimal a sense of verse-pattern, or of stresses counting in any way, that the verse is really no more than a marking of breathing and phrasing. I should have thought that this was verse drama on a quite new principle – one in which the verse was no longer the medium and theatre of the action, but was so effaced as to leave only the trace of its formal patterns. The reason for this is that the play is a romance comedy committed to making the most of the human condition. In Eliot's book the exclusion of metaphysics requires a prosaic verse.

Having gone about as far as he could from formal verse, Eliot seems to have set himself in *The Elder Statesman* to put his sort of contemporary speech as nearly as possible into blank verse. Its basis is a fairly regular four-stress line, equivalent to the normal dramatic 'pentameter'; and the effect is to formalise and to give a traditional weight to the contemporary 'correct' speech. An appropriate strategy for his *Oedipus at Colonus*.

Notes

Abbreviations

A.S.G.	*After Strange Gods* (1934)
C.C.	*To Criticize the Critic* (1965)
C.P.	*Collected Poems 1909–1962* (1963)
C.P.P.	*Complete Poems and Plays* (1969)
Hayward Collection	The T. S. Eliot Collection bequeathed to King's College, Cambridge, by John Davy Hayward
P.P.	*On Poetry and Poets* (1957)
P.R. interview	'The Art of Poetry I: T. S. Eliot', *Paris Review* no. 21 (Spring–Summer 1959), pp. 47–70.
S.E.	*Selected Essays* (3rd English ed., 1951)
S.W.	*The Sacred Wood* (2nd ed., 1928)
U.P.U.C.	*The Use of Poetry and the Use of Criticism* (1933)
W.L. Drafts	*'The Waste Land': a facsimile and transcript of the original drafts including the annotations of Ezra Pound*, ed. Valerie Eliot (1971)

For all bibliographical information about Eliot's published writings see Donald Gallup, *T. S. Eliot: a bibliography* (2nd ed., 1969).

In these notes the place of publication is London unless otherwise specified.

Notes

Introduction

1 'A Brief Introduction to the Method of Paul Valéry', *Le Serpent par Paul Valéry*, with a translation into English by Mark Wardle (1924), pp. 12, 14.
2 'Shakespeare and the Stoicism of Seneca' (1927), *S.E.* p. 137.
3 'Tradition and the Individual Talent', *S.E.* p. 18. The notorious phrase comes between two others which significantly qualify it, and make the emphasis fall upon the word *more*: 'The mind of the poet . . . may partly or exclusively operate upon the experience of the man himself; but, the more perfect the artist, the more completely separate in him will be the man who suffers and the mind which creates; the more perfectly will the mind digest and transmute the passions which are its material.'
4 'A Brief Introduction . . .' (see n.1 above).
5 *Measure for Measure* III.i, 118–22.
6 'Religion and Literature' (1935), *S.E.* p. 388.
7 'The Perfect Critic', *S.W.* p. 11.
8 'Studies in Contemporary Criticism', *Egoist* V.9 (October 1918), p. 113.
9 See, for example, 'The Serious Artist', *Literary Essays of Ezra Pound*, ed. T. S. Eliot (1954), pp. 41–57. See also F. R. Leavis, 'Eliot's "axe to grind" and the nature of great criticism', *English Literature in Our Time and the University* (1969), pp. 83–108.
10 *U.P.U.C.* p. 154.
11 'Mr Chesterton (and Stevenson)', *Nation & Athenaeum* XLII.3 (31 December 1927), p. 516.

1 The growth of the poet's mind

1 'Wordsworth and Coleridge', *U.P.U.C.* p. 79.
2 *P.P.* p. 209.
3 *Literary Essays of Ezra Pound* (1954), p. 391.
4 'The Influence of Landscape upon the Poet', *Daedalus, Journal of the American Academy of Arts and Sciences* LXXXIX.2 (Spring 1960), p. 422.
5 'The Unfading Genius of Rudyard Kipling', reprinted from *The Kipling Journal* XXVI, no. 129 (March 1959), in *Kipling and the Critics* ed. Elliot L. Gilbert (1966), p. 120.
6 *C.C.* p. 44.
7 *P.P.* p. 124.
8 Reproduced from the manuscript now in the Hayward Collection in *T. S. Eliot: a symposium* ed. Tambimuttu and Richard March (1948), between pp. 116 and 117.
9 As a safeguard against simplification at this point the reader might consider the distance between the poet and his small soul in *Animula*.
10 *U.P.U.C.* p. 78.
11 *On Poetry: an address* (Concord Academy, Massachusetts, 1947), p. 14. Cf. *U.P.U.C.* pp. 32–6, 'On the development of taste in poetry'.

12 Recorded in Valerie Eliot's 'Note' to *Poems Written in Early Youth* (1967). See also *P.R. interview*, p. 49.

13 *P.P.* p. 193. The verses were 'A Fable for Feasters'. *Beppo* looks a likelier model.

14 From a Prize Day Address at the Methodist Girls School at Penzance, 'sometime in the '30s', the typescript of which is in the Hayward Collection.

15 'The Unfading Genius of Rudyard Kipling', *Kipling and the Critics*, p. 119 (see n.5 above).

16 'Goethe as the Sage' (1955), *P.P.* p. 208.

17 'The Education of Taste', *Athenaeum* no. 4652 (27 June 1919), p. 521.

18 *P.P.* p. 208. See also 'The Perfect Critic' in *S.W.*

19 It may have been for this reason that Eliot doubted whether literature should, or could, be taught – cf. *S.E.* p. 512, and *U.P.U.C.* pp. 35–6.

20 *Egoist* IV.11 (December 1917), p. 167. Cf. *U.P.U.C.* pp. 78–9 and 148.

21 Quoted in 'The Eliot Family and St. Louis', an appendix to 'American Literature and the American Language' when published in June 1953 as *Washington University Studies* new series, *Language and Literature*, no. 23, pp. 28–9.

22 Ibid. p. 28, quoted from TSE's Preface to Edgar A. Mowrer, *This American World* (1928).

23 *P.R. interview*, p. 70.

24 'The Influence of Landscape upon the Poet', *Daedalus* (Spring 1960), pp. 421–2.

25 'Yeats' (1940), *P.P.* p. 252.

26 Introduction to *Selected Poems of Ezra Pound* (1928, 1948), p. 8.

27 'To Criticize the Critic', *C.C.* p. 18.

28 Ibid. p. 22.

29 'Reflections on Contemporary Poetry', *Egoist* VI.3 (July 1919), p. 39. See also *C.C.* p. 126.

30 'What Dante Means to Me' (1950), *C.C.* pp. 126–7. Elsewhere, TSE mentioned James Thomson's *City of Dreadful Night* and John Davidson's 'Thirty Bob a Week' as two poems which influenced him deeply in his formative years between 16 and 20, and helped him with the 'good many dingy images [he had] to reveal' (Preface to *John Davidson: A Selection of his Poems*, ed. Maurice Lindsay (1961)).

31 Quoted from *La France Libre* VIII.44 (15 June 1944), p. 94, by E. J. H. Greene, *T. S. Eliot et la France* (Paris, 1951), p. 10.

32 *P.R. interview*, p. 56.

33 'American Literature', *Athenaeum* no. 4643 (25 April 1919), p. 237. My speculation is prompted by TSE's prose contributions to the *Harvard Advocate* in May 1909, and by some remarks in later essays.

34 'Henry James: The Hawthorne Aspect' (1918), reprinted in *The Shock of Recognition* ed. Edmund Wilson (New York, 1955), p. 865.

35 'A Commentary', *Criterion* XIII.52 (April 1934), pp. 451–2. The friend was Jean Verdenal, to whom TSE dedicated *Prufrock and Other Observations* and *Poems* (1920).

36 In the Hayward Collection.

37 *C.C.* pp. 20–1.

38 'A Commentary', *Criterion* III.9 (October 1924), pp. 1–2. In 1916 TSE remarked that the labour of the Ph.D. thesis 'is fatal to the development of intellectual powers. It crushes originality, it kills style' (*New Statesman* VII.173 (29 July 1916), p. 404).

38a *Letters of T. S. Eliot* I, 1898–1922, ed. Valerie Eliot (1988), p.139.

39 *On Poetry*, p. 7 (see n.11 above).

40 *New English Weekly* XXXIV.14 (13 January 1949), p. 164.

41 *On Poetry*, p. 7.

42 'The Aims of Education' (1950), *C.C.* p. 101.

43 Ibid. p. 83.

44 'Our Inaccessible Heritage' (letter), *Athenaeum* no. 4669 (24 October 1919), p. 1076.

45 Extracts from letters included in Valerie Eliot's introduction to *W. L. Drafts*.

46 *P.R. interview*, p. 65.

47 'The Value and Use of Cathedrals in England Today' (1951), an address printed in *Friends of Chichester Cathedral Annual Report 1950–51*. I quote from the typescript in the Hayward Collection.

48 *The Bookseller* no. 2450 (6 December 1952) pp. 1568–70.

49 In *Revelation*, ed. John Baillie and Hugh Martin (1937), p. 30.

50 *On Poetry*, pp. 8–11 (see n.11 above). 'Nothing but a brilliant future behind me' – TSE in a letter to Bonamy Dobrée, in July 1934, quoted in Bonamy Dobrée, 'T. S. Eliot: a personal reminiscence', *Sewanee Review* LXXIV.1 (January–March 1966), p. 99.

51 Cf. T. S. Eliot, 'Introduction: 1928' to *Selected Poems of Ezra Pound* (1948), p. 16.

52 *P.R. interview*, p. 56.

53 'T. S. Eliot talks about Himself . . .', an interview with John Lehmann, *New York Times Book Review* (29 November 1953), reprinted in *T. S. Eliot: Four Quartets, A Casebook*, ed. Bernard Bergonzi (1969), p. [23].

54 Cf. T. S. Eliot, 'Introduction: 1928' to *Selected Poems of Ezra Pound* (1948) p. 16.

55 *U.P.U.C.* p. 144. Cf. *S.E.* p. 405.

56 Ibid. p. 155.

57 'Shakespeare and the Stoicism of Seneca' (1927), *S.E.* p. 137.

58 *U.P.U.C.* p. 69.

59 *S.E.* p. 275.

60 'Beyle and Balzac', *Athenaeum* no. 4648 (30 May 1919), p. 393. (Evelyn Underhill: the editor, translator and scholar of medieval Christian mystics.)

61 Quoted in John D. Margolis, *T. S. Eliot's Intellectual Development* (Chicago, 1972), p. 142.

62 In a review of Murry's *Son of Woman*, *Criterion* X.41 (July 1931), p. 771. Cf. TSE's remark in *Revelation*, pp. 1–2 (see n.49 above): 'I take for granted that Christian revelation is the only full revelation; and that the fullness . . . resides in the essential fact of the Incarnation'. I am also drawing upon remarks in *Criterion* V.2 (May 1927) p. 256, and *A Sermon* (1948); a quotation from a 1933 address in Kristian Smidt, *Poetry and Belief in the Work of T. S. Eliot* (1949), p. 243; and a letter of 1930 from which extracts are given on p. 233 of Nevill Coghill's edition of *The Family Reunion* (1969).

63 'Religion without Humanism', *Humanism and America*, ed. Norman Foerster (New York, 1930), p. 110.

64 From the typescript in the Hayward Collection of a speech delivered 15 November 1951 at the Bibliothèque Nationale, at the opening of an exhibition ('Le Livre Anglais').

65 'The Unfading Genius of Rudyard Kipling', *Kipling and the Critics*, p. 123 (see n.5 above). The poem is 'The Appeal'.

66 'For T.S.E.', *Sewanee Review* LXXIV.1 (January–March 1966), p. 109.

2 *Prufrock observed*

1 'Imperfect Critics', *S.W.* p. 31.
2 *S.W.* p. 152.
3 Herbert Howarth, *Notes on some Figures behind T. S. Eliot* (1965), p. 102.
4 The edition Eliot bought in 1909 would have been *Oeuvres Complètes*, ed. Camille Mauclair (3 vols., Paris, 1901–3). The most accessible recent editions are *Poésies Complètes*, ed. Pascal Pia (Livre de Poche, Paris, 1970), and *Moralités Légendaires* (Mercure de France, Paris, 1964).
5 In his notebook now in the Berg Collection of the New York Public Library, 'Conversation Galante' and 'Humouresque' are both dated November 1909. For this and other information about the notebook I am indebted to Donald Gallup's 'The "Lost" Manuscripts of T. S. Eliot', *Times Literary Supplement* (7 November 1968), pp. 1238–40.
6 Cf. TSE's letter to Pound dated 2 February [1915], in *Ezra Pound: Perspectives*, ed. Noel Stock (Chicago, 1965), p. 110, in which he says he has had a Christmas card from the lady – 'It seemed like old times.'
7 'Henry James: In Memory', reprinted from *Little Review* (August 1918) in *The Shock of Recognition*, ed. Edmund Wilson (New York, 1955), p. 856.
8 'Browning', in *Essays from 'The Guardian'* (1901), pp. 44–5.
9 *Literary Essays of Ezra Pound*, ed. T. S. Eliot (1954), pp. 419–20.
10 *Autobiography* (New York, 1956), p. 594 – *The Middle Years*, part VI.
11 Preface to Charles-Louis Philippe, *Bubu of Montparnasse* trans. Laurence Vail (Paris, 1932), pp. x-xi. Eliot had read the novel in Paris in 1910, when to him '*Bubu* stood for Paris as some of Dickens' novels stand for London.'
12 'Henry James: In Memory', pp. 856–7 (see n.7 above). For related remarks on Blake's 'naked vision' see *S.W.* pp. 151–5.
13 'The Genteel Tradition in American Philosophy' (1911), reprinted in *Selected Critical Writings of George Santayana*, ed. Norman Henfrey (1968), vol. II, p. 96. Cf. Arnold's 'On the Modern Element in Literature'. Eliot's affinities with Santayana, who was one of his teachers at Harvard in 1909 and 1910, seem to be very close, and to be much more significant than Herbert Howarth's account suggests; at the very least, Eliot's work is given an illuminating background in Santayana's 'The Poetry of Barbarism' (1900), 'Platonic Love in some Italian Poets' (1896) and *Three Philosophical Poets* (1910), 'The Genteel Tradition in American Philosophy' (1911), 'The Philosophy of M. Henri Bergson' (1913).
14 See part II, v.i.
15 'The Poetry of Barbarism', *Selected Critical Writings* vol. I, p. 113.
16 'The Perfect Critic', *S.W.* p. 11.
17 *Syllabus of a Course of Six Lectures on Modern French Literature* (1916) – reproduced at the end of this chapter.
18 Henri Bergson, *Mélanges* (Paris, 1972), pp. 845ff. A report of the lectures on Personality is given on pp. 847–75.
19 'Lettre d'Angleterre', *Nouvelle Revue Française* XXI.122 (1 November 1923), p.620, and see Piers Gray, *T. S. Eliot's Intellectual Development 1909–1922* (Sussex, 1982), p.2.
20 Quoted in F. O. Mattheissen, *The Achievement of T. S. Eliot* (3rd ed., New York, 1958), p. 183.

21 'Sa troublante promesse d'immortalité (". . . même la mort . . .") ne participe-t-elle d'aucune méthode de séduction?' ('Lettre d'Angleterre', p. 623 – see n.19 above). Santayana concluded his critique of Bergson, in *Winds of Doctrine* (1913), with a powerful attack on his 'voluptuous whiffs of immortality'.

22 *A Sermon preached in Magdalene College Chapel* (Cambridge, 1948), p. 5.

23 Eliot gave the date as 'Paris 1910' in his annotation of John Hayward's copy of *Poems 1909–25*, but this seems improbably early.

24 Gallup, 'The "Lost" Manuscripts of T. S. Eliot', p. 1240 (see n.5 above).

25 *Matter and Memory*, authorised translation by Nancy Margaret Paul and W. Scott Palmer (1911), pp. 322–4. Cf. *Oeuvres* (2nd ed., Paris, 1963), pp. 371–2.

26 *An Introduction to Metaphysics*, authorised translation by T. E. Hulme (1913), pp. 78–9. Cf. *Oeuvres*, p. 1432.

27 *Creative Evolution*, authorised translation by Arthur Mitchell (1911), taken from the Modern Library reprint (New York, 1944), pp. 291–2. Cf. *Oeuvres*, pp. 721–2. For 'elle se ranime' this translation gives 'glimmers': I have altered this to 'lights up'.

28 'Baudelaire' (1930), *S.E.* p. 427.

29 *C.C.* p. 126.

30 *S.E.* p. 426.

31 *Essay on Rime* (New York, 1945), p. 17. Shapiro attaches the remark to *The Waste Land*, but would perhaps not dispute my application of it to 'Prufrock' also. He remarks in the same place: 'The clean/Conversational voice of the American/Once and for all outlawed the late-Victorian/Lilt.'

32 *Literary Essays of Ezra Pound*, p. 3. In the draft of a lecture on 'The Last 25 Years of English Poetry' which Eliot was to have given for the British Council in Italy in 1939, he wrote: 'The English verse line is better conceived on the analogy of a musical phrase, composed of bars of equal value though not of an equal number of notes.'

33 *Moralités Légendaires* (1964), p. 136. ('O world of the quite content, you enjoy the beatitude of blindness and silence, while we are in agonies for the supra-terrestrial. Why are not the antennae of our senses closed in by the Blind, the Opaque, the Mute, why will they reach out for what is beyond us? Why do we not have this trick of growing a shell in our own little corner, there to sleep off this state of being dead drunk on our little ME?')

34 There is a specific connection with *Maud*, which, as it happens, Tennyson thought of as his *Hamlet*, as 'Prufrock' might be Eliot's.

35 See *S.E.* p. 275.

36 In the notebook drafts ll.1–69 have as (cancelled) epigraph the final two lines of *Purgatorio* XXVI – Arnaut's 'Sovegna vos'. A further point of interest is that the drafts of what became ll.70–4 ('Shall I say, I have gone at dusk') were titled 'Prufrock's Pervigilium'. For TSE's placing of Laforgue in relation to Dante, in 1926, see p. 128 below.

37 'A Prediction in Regard to Three English Authors . . .', *Vanity Fair* XXI.6 (February 1924), p. 29.

38 'It was Pound who took pains, Eliot recalled 40 years later, over the arrangement of *Prufrock and Other Observations*' (Hugh Kenner, *The Pound Era* (1972), p. 355).

3 *Gerontion, and the historical sense*

1 In a letter to Pound, printed in *Letters of Ezra Pound*, ed. D. D. Paige (1951), p. 236.
2 'The Method of Mr Pound', *Athenaeum* no. 4669 (24 October 1919), p. 1065.
3 *Letters of Ezra Pound*, p. 235. In his *A Lume Spento* (1908) Pound gave the title 'Fistulae' to a group of lyrics, the last of which has the line '[man's] soul is a hole full of God'.
4 *P.R. interview*, p. 56.
5 Ibid. p. 55, and Preface to his selection of Edwin Muir's poems (1965), p. 10.
6 Quoted from a letter of Pound's to H. B. Parkes in Donald Gallup, *T. S. Eliot & Ezra Pound* (New Haven, 1970), p. 11. Cf. Pound in *Pavannes & Divagations* (1960), p. 161: 'I took Parson Elyot to see the Prima Ballerina and it evoked "Grushkin" '.
7 'Marivaux', *Art and Letters* II.2 (Spring 1919), p. 81.
8 The neat formulation is Northrop Frye's, in his *T. S. Eliot* (1963), p. 14. Meredith's poem mentioned in the next sentence is 'Lucifer in Starlight'.
9 'Do you know T. S. Eliot's little poem about me called "Mr Appolinax"?' – Bertrand Russell, in a letter sold at Sotheby's 17 December 1974 (from the Sale Catalogue, p. 77).
10 The title is from Corbière's 'Épitaphe'.
11 The prose sense is something like this: Woe unto the woeful Thames which flows by the *Spectator*. The conservative editor of the *Spectator* plagues the breeze. The reactionary shareholders of the conservative *Spectator* lope along arm-in-arm, taking a turn or two. In a drain a little girl in rags, snub-nosed, stares at the editor of the conservative *Spectator* and is dying of love. (Corbière refers to death as La Camarde, the snub-nosed or noseless.)
12 'Try to put into a sequence of simple quatrains the continuous syntactic variety of Gautier or Blake' (TSE (as 'Apteryx'), 'Professional or . . .', *Egoist* V.4 (April 1918), p. 61).
13 *The Letters of Henry Adams*, ed. W. C. Ford (Boston, 1930–8), vol. II, pp. 110–11.
14 Cf. 'The Function of Criticism' (1923), *S.E.* pp. 32–3. Donald Davie has some pertinent reflections in his contribution to *Eliot in Perspective*, ed. Graham Martin (1970), pp. 74–81.
15 *S.W.* p. 43, and *C.C.* p. 122.
16 From B. C. Southam, *A Student's Guide to the Selected Poems of T. S. Eliot* (1968), p. 62.
17 'Where the souls of the devout/Burn invisible and dim' combines allusions to Henry Vaughan's 'The Night', Browning's 'The Statue and the Bust', and John iii.
18 I am grateful to Brigadier Peter Young, editor of Purnell's *History of the First World War*, for supporting my supposition.
19 Letter to *The Sunday Times* (6 April 1958), p. 4.
20 *The Art of the Novel*, Critical Prefaces by Henry James, with an introduction by R. P. Blackmur (New York, 1934), p. 222.
21 See Canto IX, and *Hugh Selwyn Mauberley* IV. Pound's 'Malatesta' Cantos were first published in the *Criterion* in 1923, and might well not have been drafted in 1919. I am pointing to a likeness, not suggesting a source.
22 *The Education of Henry Adams* (Boston, 1918), p. 268.
23 *S.E.* p. 163.
24 *S.E.* pp. 130–1.
25 'Baudelaire' (1930), *S.E.* p. 423. While there is an interesting comparison to be made

with Newman's *Dream of Gerontius* (in which the decayed body of the dying man is called 'the mansion of the soul'), the connection with Henry James' tale *The Beast in the Jungle* is of greater interest still.

26 'London Letter', *Dial* LXXI.4 (October 1921), p. 455.

27 'Introduction', *S.W.* pp. xv-xvi.

28 'A Sceptical Patrician', *Athenaeum* no. 4647 (23 May 1919), p. 362 – a review of *The Education of Henry Adams*.

29 'Shakespeare and the Stoicism of Seneca' (1927), *S.E.* p. 137.

30 The original title was 'Experience and the Objects of Knowledge in the Philosophy of F. H. Bradley'. The new title was given when the thesis was published in 1964 – my page references in the text are to this edition. The book consists of the thesis, from which the conclusion has been lost, and two articles published in *The Monist* in 1916. Since the appended articles appear to be a version of the lost conclusion I treat them as one work with the thesis.

31 'The Perfect Critic', *S.W.* p. 15.

32 'Hamlet and His Problems', *S.W.* p. 102.

33 'Preface to the 1928 edition', *S.W.* p. viii.

34 *A.S.G.* pp. 28, 26.

35 *S.E.* p. 273.

36 *U.P.U.C.* p. 69.

4 *Tiresias transformed*

1 'Dante' (1920), *S.W.* pp. 168–9.

2 'Cyril Tourneur' (1930), *S.E.* p. 190.

3 *S.E.* p. 137.

4 A 'real German', from Lithuania, in Munich, would be a stateless person. Lithuania had been for a long period before 1917 subject to Russia; the German claim to it began and ended with the brief occupation of 1917. 'Arch-duke' was an Austro-Hungarian title; the murder of the last, at Sarajevo in 1914, was made an excuse for the war.

5 *P.P.* p. 110.

6 In an essay written at Harvard c.1913–14 on 'Is a science of religion possible? – the problem of interpretation' (now in the Hayward Collection).

7 For Eliot, as for Dostoyevsky in *Crime and Punishment*, which Eliot had read in a French translation, the interesting question about a murder was not who did it, but that the murderer has done something eternal – see further p. 117.

8 Cited in *W. L. Drafts*, p. 125.

9 The striking image is of course from Baudelaire. Eliot quoted it in a Commentary in *Criterion* III.10 (January 1925), p. 163.

10 'It is terrible to be alone with another person' is a line in 'The Death of the Duchess' (*W. L. Drafts*, p. 104), an early draft towards 'A Game of Chess'. The drafts, and a late typescript of 1922, said explicitly after l.124 'I remember/The hyacinth garden'. The present note keyed to l.126 – presumably an error for l.125 – still connects this couple with those lovers.

11 Cf. 'The Metaphysical Poets' (1921), *S.E.* p. 288.

12 Cf. 'Hamlet and His Problems', *S.W.* pp. 100–1. In the *Egoist* of 2 November 1914 – and reprinted in *Catholic Anthology*, though without its commentary – was a scenario by John Rodker entitled *FEAR*. He presented it as a specimen of how to evoke primitive emotions at the level of 'race-memories', and to effect the liberation of whole complexes of buried feelings. In it Pierrot and Columbine play chess in silence. Steps sound in the house, then at the door. But there is nothing there. It happens again. And again. Each time Pierrot wearily resumes the game. Then Columbine breaks down. They rush from the room, pursue the steps, which seem then to pursue them. . .

13 This places the pub monologue with the many passages in the drafts which reveal Eliot's own alienated states in untransmuted forms. However its 'unreality' does not prevent it from being of considerable interest technically and otherwise. One may note, for instance, the anticipations of *Sweeney Agonistes*; a relation emphasised in Eliot's recorded reading by the suggestion of ragtime rhythms.

14 Tiresias, in Tennyson's poem, was struck blind because he saw Pallas Athene bathing naked – an analogue to Actaeon's fate in Ovid. The version of 'Song for the Opherion' in *W. L. Drafts*, p. 98 – later 'The wind sprang up at four o'clock' – alludes to this.

15 *S.E.* p. 297.

16 *S.E.* p. 274.

17 Swinburne's Tiresias says 'I am a soul outside of death and birth.'

18 *Dante* (1929), *S.E.* p. 252.

19 The Fire Sermon is given nearly complete as a kind of preface to William Empson's *Collected Poems* (1955). Vachel Lindsay gave this short version among his 'Poems to be chanted' in *Poetry* iv.4 (July 1914), p. 129:

> Buddha thus addressed his disciples: – 'Everything, o mendicants, is burning . . . With what fire is it burning? I declare unto you it is burning with the fire of passion, with the fire of anger, with the fire of ignorance. It is burning with the anxieties of birth, decay and death, grief, lamentation, suffering and despair. . . A disciple . . . becoming weary of all that . . . divests himself of passion. By absence of passion . . . he is made free.'

20 *Dante* (1929), *S.E.* p. 256.

21 Donald Gallup reports an eight-line poem 'The Little Passion from "An Agony in the Garret" ' in the notebook, probably written in 1915 – 'The "Lost" Manuscripts of T. S. Eliot', *Times Literary Supplement* (7 November 1968), p. 1240. The allusion could be to Dürer's *Little Passion*.

22 The allusions in this paragraph are to: 'Swinburne', *S.E.* pp. 324, 327; 'Massinger', *S.E.* p. 211; 'The Metaphysical Poets', *S.E.* pp. 286–7.

23 *Egoist* iv.7 (August 1917), p. 103.

24 The connection with Conrad's novel was noticed by Leonard Unger, *T. S. Eliot: moments and patterns* (Minneapolis, 1966), pp. 148–51. See also Jane Harrison, 'The Rite of the "Thunders" ' in ch.iii of *Themis* (1911), on the association of thunder with the voice of the God and with purification in initiation and fertility rites. (TSE mentioned this work in his essay written at Harvard *c.* 1913, 'Is a science of religion possible?'.)

25 The phrase is from a review by Eliot quoted on p. 11 above.

26 Cf. Eliot's remarks on Blake's freedom from conventionality: *S.W.* pp. 151–5.

27 Cf. Iona and Peter Opie, *Oxford Dictionary of Nursery Rhymes* (1973), pp. 270–6.

28 In some early printings l.426 (London Bridge) is set in isolation; one printing also

gives a space after l.429 (Le Prince d'Aquitaine), which would set off ll.427–9 as a unit within the coda.

29 Ezra Pound's rendering, *Spirit of Romance* (1952 ed.), pp. 18–21.

30 *Oxford Companion to English Literature*, under 'Upanishad'.

31 *P.P.* p. 98.

32 *P.P.* p. 87.

33 See *S.E.* pp. 334–8.

34 *U.P.U.C.* pp. 106, 103.

35 *U.P.U.C.* p. 69.

36 'Thoughts after Lambeth' (1931), *S.E.* p. 368.

37 'In Memoriam' (1936), *S.E.* p. 334. The advertisement for *Poems 1909–1925* on the dust-jacket of *Ash-Wednesday* gave this quotation from a review by I. A. Richards: 'Some readers find in his poetry not only a clearer, fuller realization of their plight, the plight of a whole generation, than they find elsewhere, but also through the very energies set free in that realization a return of the saving passion.'

38 *U.P.U.C.* pp. 118–19.

39 Cf. 'The Death of Saint Narcissus', *Poems Written in Early Youth*, and *W. L. Drafts*, pp. 90–7.

5 *The poet saved from himself*

1 *W. L. Drafts*, p. xxv.

2 Ibid. pp. 100–1.

3 *U.P.U.C.* pp. 144–5. Cf. *S.E.* p. 405, and Valerie Eliot's introduction and notes to *W. L. Drafts* where the connection of these passages with the writing of 'What the Thunder Said' is confirmed.

4 *W. L. Drafts*, pp. 78–9. Eliot cancelled in the manuscript the last two half-lines.

5 Ibid. pp. 116–17. My text follows Eliot's revisions.

6 'Eeldrop and Appleplex: i', *Little Review* IV.1 (May 1917). p. 9.

7 'Fragment of an Agon', *C.P.P.* pp. 124–5. Although first published in the *Criterion* in 1926–7, *Sweeney Agonistes* was drafted not later than April 1923 – see Donald Gallup, *T. S. Eliot & Ezra Pound* (New Haven, 1970), p. 28. The draft synopsis in the Hayward Collection reveals a close relation with the thematic preoccupations of the 'dream songs' and the other poems up to *Marina*, as well as with *The Family Reunion*. One cancelled title was 'PEREIRA/or/THE MARRIAGE OF LIFE AND DEATH/ A Dream'. Sweeney was to 'do in' Mrs Porter, who was then to stage a resurrection.

8 *S.E.* p. 137.

9 See *The Letters of Ezra Pound*, ed. D. D. Paige (1951), pp. 236–7.

10 *W. L. Drafts*, pp. 98–9. A revised version was published as 'Song to the Opherian' in April 1921. Valerie Eliot helpfully notes that while there is no word 'opherion' nor 'opherian', an 'orpherion' (Orpheus + Arion) is described in *Grove's Musical Dictionary* as 'the poor man's lute'. This is mentioned as an alternative to the lute in a number of Elizabethan song books (Campion's, Dowland's, and others).

11 Eliot wrote of that experience as if it had been his own also – see *S.E.* p. 273. His interest in Joyce's story *The Dead* is also revealing – see *A.S.G.* pp. 37–8.

12 Cf. Eliot's remarks on Baudelaire and the imperfect sublimation of passion, *S.E.* pp. 429–30.

13 'A Note on Richard Crashaw', *For Lancelot Andrewes: essays on style and order* (1928), p. 125 (p. 98 in 1970 reset ed.): 'just as Crashaw is deficient in humanity . . . so we feel at times that his passion for heavenly objects is imperfect because it is partly a substitute for human passion. It is not impure, but it is incomplete.'

14 'Note sur Mallarmé et Poe', *Nouvelle Revue Française* XIV.158 (November 1926), p. 525.

15 *S.E.* p. 275.

16 Cf. *S.E.* p. 277. Eliot's interest in the 'phantasmagoric' – in Dante and Baudelaire, and see the related 'phantasmal' in *W. L. Drafts*, pp. 42–3 – is elucidated by Aristotle's *De Anima* III.iii, 427b27–429a9 and III.vii, 431b1–431b9, where the term is used for the mind's projection of an image of something feared or desired or willed: the hermit-thrush singing in the pine trees in *The Waste Land*'s water-dripping song would be an example, and much of *Marina* also. (For this gloss upon Eliot's term I am indebted to Ian Bell – see his 'The Phantasmagoria of Hugh Selwyn Mauberley', *Paideuma* V.3 (Winter 1976), pp. 361–85.)

17 'Baudelaire' (1930), *S.E.* pp. 424–5.

18 'Baudelaire in Our Time' (1927), *For Lancelot Andrewes*, p. 90 (p. 71 in 1970 ed.).

19 *C.C.* p. 127.

20 *S.E.* p. 416.

21 Lancelot Andrewes, in his sermon for 5 November 1616 on 'The Gunpowder Treason', spoke of the abortive plot, whence came for those saved a new birth of prayer and praise to God. See *Ninety-six Sermons* (Oxford, 1841: Library of Anglo-Catholic Theology), vol. IV, pp. 341–60.

22 In a note on the typescript draft now in the University of Texas, and again in a letter to the *Times Literary Supplement* in 1935, Eliot said the title alluded to Kipling's poem 'The Broken Men', and also to William Morris' prose tale *The Hollow Land*. There may be a further allusion to the conspirators in Shakespeare's *Julius Caesar*, where the phrase 'hollow men' occurs (IV.ii, 22).

23 The most useful work is the unpublished Clark Lectures of 1926, 'On the Metaphysical Poetry of the Seventeenth Century'. Also of special interest are: 'Shakespeare and the Stoicism of Seneca' (1927), *Dante* (1929), and 'The *Pensées* of Pascal' (1931); 'Dante' (1920), 'A Brief Introduction to the Method of Paul Valéry' (1924), 'Note sur Mallarmé et Poe' (1926), 'Leçon de Valéry' (1946), and 'Introduction' to Paul Valéry, *The Art of Poetry* (New York, 1958).

24 'Donne in Our Time', *A Garland for John Donne*, ed. Theodore Spencer (Cambridge, Mass., 1931), pp. 8–9. The idea is repeated from the Clark Lectures. The other quotations in this paragraph are from the typescript of those lectures in the Hayward Collection. I am deeply indebted to Mrs Valerie Eliot for permission to paraphrase and to quote from this unpublished work. My next paragraph is mostly drawn from it.

25 'che a considerar fu più che viro' (*Paradiso* X, 132).

26 The passage is from book 1, chapter 3, of the *Benjamin Major*, but both that work and the *Benjamin Minor* expound these ideas. A convenient selection in English translation is Richard of St Victor, *Selected Writings on Contemplation*, trans. Clare Kirschberger (1957).

27 Jacques Maritain, 'Poetry and Religion', *Criterion* V.2 (May 1927), p. 225. The trans-

lation is credited to F. S. Flint, but Donald Gallup states that it was Eliot's (*T. S. Eliot: a bibliography* (2nd ed. 1969), under item C203a).

28 Quoted by F. O. Mattheissen, *The Achievement of T. S. Eliot* (3rd ed., New York, 1958), p. 90.

29 'Leçon de Valéry', *The Listener* XXXVII.939 (9 January 1947), p. 72.

30 'A Brief Introduction to the Method of Paul Valéry', *Le Serpent par Paul Valéry*, with a translation into English by Mark Wardle (1924), p. 13.

31 'Leçon de Valéry' (see n.29 above).

32 'Introduction' to Paul Valéry, *The Art of Poetry* (New York, 1958), p. xxiii.

33 Richard of St Victor, *Benjamin Minor* ch. 86, in *Selected Writings* p. 126 (see n.26 above).

34 Cf. 'A Brief Introduction', and 'Leçon de Valéry' (see nn. 30 and 29 above).

6 Love through the looking-glass

1 *Dante*, in *S.E.* p. 276.

2 The Ariel Poems were a series of single poems by various poets, published in pamphlet by Faber & Gwyer and then Faber & Faber. About half a dozen were published each year from 1927 until the mid-1930s. The title no doubt had a special significance for Eliot – cf. Shakespeare's Ariel, and Laforgue's – and so was used in his *Collected Poems* as the generic title for his own contributions to the series.

3 *U.P.U.C.* p. 148.

4 The passages are given in part in *S.E.* pp. 259–61.

5 In Eliot's own collection of photographs as preserved in the Hayward Collection there is a faded poor snapshot of a Christmas tree.

6 Ezra Pound's text and translation of the Cavalcanti *ballata* are in *The Translations of Ezra Pound* (1953), pp. 120–3. His notes on Cavalcanti there and in his *Literary Essays* present a point of view from which Eliot may have been reacting. It is an illuminating exercise to try to hold together in the mind *Ash-Wednesday* and 'Donna mi pregha' as rendered by Pound in Canto XXXVI: all three poets being concerned, though with different ends in view, with the power of love to refine vision. For Dante's references to Cavalcanti see the *Vita Nuova* sect. iii, *Inferno* x and *Purgatorio* XI. For Eliot's parallel though elliptical remarks see *S.E.* pp. 275–6. The Lancelot Andrewes sermon is given in his *Sermons*, selected and edited by G. M. Story (Oxford, 1967), pp. 119–42.

7 XI, 14.

8 *S.E.* p. 262.

9 *S.E.* p. 343. On Dante's debt to Aquinas see 'Shakespeare and the Stoicism of Seneca', *S.E.* pp. 135–6.

10 Cf. *S.E.* pp. 26–9. In this essay, 'The Function of Criticism', Eliot begins to separate Orthodoxy from Tradition; in *A.S.G.* the former becomes explicitly the corrective of the latter.

11 Cf. *S.E.* pp. 261–8. These pages with the section on the *Vita Nuova*, are the best guide to the relation of *Ash-Wednesday* to Dante.

12 *S.E.* p. 262.

13 *S.E.* p. 274.

14 *S.E.* p. 273.

15 Taken from the facsimile on p. 20 of the Catalogue for the Exhibition of T. S. Eliot's Books and Manuscripts held at the University of Texas in June 1961. These two lines follow 'not as lost' – i.e. as ll.16–17.

16 *Essay on Rime* (New York, 1945), p. 17.

17 'For the boy whose childhood has been empty of beauty, the boy who has never learned the *detached* curiosity for beauty, . . . the sexual instinct when it is aroused may mean the only possible escape from a prosaic world' (TSE *International Journal of Ethics* XXVII.1 (October 1916), p. 127).

18 There may be a buried connection between the hyacinth garden and 'blue of larkspur': the blue larkspur is the Greek hyacinth, which has markings on the base of its petals interpreted as AI, meaning 'woe' or 'alas' (Robert Graves, *The Greek Myths* (Harmondsworth, 1957), vol. II, pp. 324–5). For the colour symbolism see also John of the Cross, *Dark Night of the Soul* II, xxi.

19 'Swinburne as Poet' (1920), *S.E.* p. 326.

20 *S.E.* p. 137.

21 There may be a hint of explanation in the remark that when Baudelaire wrote 'Mon enfant, ma soeur' in 'L'Invitation au Voyage', 'The word *soeur* here is not, in my opinion, chosen merely because it rhymes with *douceur*; it is a moment in that sublimation of passion toward which Baudelaire was always striving' (*For Lancelot Andrewes: essays on style and order* (1928), pp. 94–5 (pp. 74–5 in 1970 reset ed.)).

22 *S.E.* pp. 427–30.

23 'Thoughts After Lambeth' (1931), *S.E.* p. 387.

24 Cf. *S.E.* p. 137.

25 *S. Swithun's Prayer Book* (38th impression, n.d.), p. 26. Eliot's penultimate line is from the 'Anima Christi' on p. 53. I have the impression that Eliot used this Prayer Book from a remark somewhere in his published writings which I have been unable to track down again. (I am indebted to Mr Robin Grove both for the suggestion to consult this book, and for a copy of it.)

26 From the letter quoted on pp. 11–12 above.

27 It requires little ingenuity to identify the animal emblems with Anger, Envy, Ambition, Pride, Sloth, Greed and Lust. *The Book of Common Prayer* gives among the rites and ceremonies of the Church 'A Commination or denouncing of God's anger and judgment against Sinners'. I owe to Professor Bernard Harris the connection of these lines with a charm in Carmichael's *Carmina Gadelica*, a collection of Highland folk poetry from which, Eliot said, he had 'got a good deal of stimulation' ('Ezra Pound', reprinted from *Poetry* LXVIII (September 1946) in *Ezra Pound: a collection of critical essays*, ed. Walter Sutton (Englewood Cliffs, N.J., 1963), p. 22).

28 Shakespeare's *Pericles* v.i, 80–236.

29 See *The Family Reunion* I.ii, 238–90 and II.ii, 183–223 (in *C.P.P.* pp. 309–311, 334–7).

30 See E. Martin Browne, *The Making of T. S. Eliot's Plays* (Cambridge, 1969), p. 98. In the typescript in the Hayward Collection which I have followed here, 'a word' is not cancelled; and in the second line 'under sleep, in the deep, in the abyss of light' has been added in Eliot's hand, with 'under sleep' then struck through.

31 *Murder in the Cathedral* I, 319–22.

32 The source of this paragraph is 'Baudelaire', *S.E.* pp. 419–30.

33 In a postscript to his letter presenting the draft of *Marina* to the Bodleian Library, Oxford, Eliot wrote: 'I intend a criss-cross between Pericles finding alive, and Hercules finding dead – the two extremes of the recognition scene – but I thought that if I labelled the quotation it might lead readers astray rather than direct them. It is only an accident that I know Seneca better than I know Euripides.'

34 'Baudelaire', *S.E.* p. 427.

35 *Paradiso* XXVII, 82–6.

36 Seneca, *His Tenne Tragedies*, ed. Thomas Newton, with an introduction by T. S. Eliot (The Tudor Translations second series, 1927), vol. II, p. 255. The line quoted earlier in this paragraph, 'What heavenly harmony' etc., will be found on p. 241; and the analogue to Dante's Arnaut on p. 250.

7 *The design of the drama*

1 *S.W.* p. 11. The first epigraph is from the unpublished lectures, 'The Development of Shakespeare's Verse', given at Edinburgh University in 1937. The sentence begins: 'The personages in *Cymbeline*, *The Winters Tale*, *The Tempest* and *Pericles* are the work of a writer who has finally seen . . .'

2 A select list of Eliot's writings on poetic drama would include half a dozen of the essays in *S.W.*, all of them included in *S.E.* except 'The Possibility of a Poetic Drama'; the essays in sects. II and III of *S.E.*, with 'Marie Lloyd' and 'Wilkie Collins and Dickens'; a note, 'The Romantic Englishman, the Comic Spirit and the Function of Criticism', in *The Tyro* no. 1 (1921); 'Dramatis Personae', *Criterion* 1.3 (1923), pp. 303–6; the introduction to his mother's verse drama *Savonarola* (1926); the introduction to G. Wilson Knight, *The Wheel of Fire* (1930); *U.P.U.C.* pp. 152–4; 'Audiences, Producers, Plays, Poets', *New Verse* no. 18 (1935), pp. 3–4; 'The Need for Poetic Drama', *The Listener* XVI.411 (25 November 1936), pp. 994–5; the unpublished lectures, 'The Development of Shakespeare's Verse' (1937); the introduction to S. L. Bethell, *Shakespeare & the Popular Dramatic Tradition* (1944); *Poetry and Drama* (1951). In 1959 Eliot said: 'I am no longer very much interested in my own theories about poetic drama, especially those put forward before 1934. I have thought less about theories since I have given more time to writing for the theatre' (*P.R. interview*, p. 62).

3 *S.E.* p. 229.

4 *P.P.* p. 87.

5 *S.E.* p. 232.

6 *U.P.U.C.* p. 154.

7 *S.E.* p. 457.

8 E. Martin Browne, *The Making of T. S. Eliot's Plays* (Cambridge, 1969), pp. x, 38, has some notes on the first production by The Group Theatre in 1934. For the Vassar production see Hallie Flanagan, *Dynamo* (New York, 1943), pp. 82–4. Mr Browne's invaluable companion is referred to hereafter as 'Browne'.

9 From Eliot's commentary when reading from his poems on NBC radio, printed in *University of Chicago Round Table* no. 659 (12 November 1950).

10 Cf. *P.P.* p. 91.

11 Browne, p. 3.

12 From the note on the dust-jacket of *The Rock* (1934) – it may well have been written by Eliot himself.

13 *P.P.* p. 91.

14 From 'The Story of the Pageant', signed by TSE and Martin Browne, in the Programme for the production at the Sadlers Wells Theatre, May–June 1934, p. 7.

15 *P.P.* p. 80.

16 Eliot told George Hoellering, who made the film of *Murder in the Cathedral*, that his main reason for writing the play was in the Knights' self-justification and challenge to the audience, and he asked for that to be spoken straight at the cinema audience – see George Hoellering, 'Filming *Murder in the Cathedral*' in *T. S. Eliot: a symposium for his 70th birthday*, ed. Neville Braybrooke (1958), pp. 83–4. The filmscript puts the question directly: 'Then ask yourselves, who is more representative of the thing you are: the man you call a martyr, or the men you call his murderers?' (*The Film of Murder in the Cathedral* (1952), p. 117).

17 *P.P.* p. 81 – italics added.

18 Preface to *The Portrait of a Lady* in *The Art of the Novel: critical prefaces* (New York, 1934), p. 45.

19 *P.R. interview*, p. 60.

20 *U.P.U.C.* p. 153. There are some further pertinent remarks in the lectures on 'The Development of Shakespeare's Verse':

> It is permissible and right to speak primarily to a small audience, if that audience has its organic place in society, if that audience is really representative of the most highly developed intelligence and sensibility of the people – but not an audience which has become completely cut off from the rest of society. A great writer may appeal only to a small audience, but if so, it must be an audience which has a functional importance in the whole society.

However, 'It was the work of Shakespeare, more than any other writer, to appeal to every audience, and so to keep them cohering: to overcome the separation between the courtly group of Senecans, and the crowd at the fair.'

21 *S.E.* p. 225.

22 Eliot thought that this 'just saves Charles' – letter to E. Martin Browne, quoted in Browne, p. 108. This letter, previously published in F. O. Mattheissen, *The Achievement of T. S. Eliot* (2nd ed., New York, 1947), is a very revealing statement of Eliot's point of view.

23 See the choruses which close i.i, ii.i and ii.iii.

24 Richard Findlater, *Michael Redgrave, Actor* (1956), pp. 49, 50 – as quoted in Browne p. 136.

25 *S.E.* p. 180.

26 *P.P.* pp. 87–8.

27 Eliot's letter to Browne (see n.22 above) is very interesting on this.

28 Browne, p. 107.

29 This and the previous sentence are of course a paraphrase from TSE's 'Hamlet' – see *S.E.* pp. 143ff.

30 This paragraph has been paraphrasing 'Virgil and the Christian World', *P.P.* pp. 127–31.

31 *U.P.U.C.* pp. 41–2.

32 Quoted in Nevill Coghill's Introduction to his edition of *The Family Reunion* (1969), p. 44.
33 From the Builders' Song in *The Rock*.

8 *Dust in sunlight*

1 See ch. 1, n.53 above.
2 Genesius Jones, *Approach to the Purpose* (1964), pp. 228–9.
3 From F. O. Mattheissen, *The Achievement of T. S. Eliot* (3rd ed., New York, 1958), p. 192.
4 *P.P.* p. 30.
5 From Eliot's note in his copy.
6 Two associations: 'Rose leaves, when the rose is dead,/Are heaped for the beloved's bed' (Shelley, 'Music, when soft voices die'); 'and the china bowls full of dead rose leaves dried with bay salt. All has long since vanished and become a memory, faded, but still fragrant to myself' (Samuel Butler, *The Way of All Flesh*, ch. 1).
7 Cf. 'Francis Herbert Bradley' (1927), in *S.E.*, for this sentence and for the paragraph.
8 See in particular the conclusion to Mallarmé's 'Crise de vers' (in *Variations sur un sujet*).
9 *Paradiso* XXII, 124–54; XXVII, 82–6.
10 See Herrick's 'Men mind no state in sicknesse'.
11 'Enchainment', in the French sense, would bring Bergson to mind; '*Erhebung*' suggests Eliot's reading in German philosophers.
12 Epigraph to *Sweeney Agonistes*, from John of the Cross.
13 *Ulysses* (1937), p. 92.
14 Canto XXIX. Eliot is present in the episode and may have occasioned the remark.
15 Tennyson, *In Memoriam* II.
16 'Ordinary writers of verse either deal in imagination or in "ideas"; they escape from the one to the other, but neither one nor the other nor both together is truth in the sense of poetic truth. Only old ideas "part and parcel of the personality" are of use to the poet' (TSE, *Egoist* IV.6 (July 1917), p. 90).
17 Eliot's first thought and his last was to attach these epigraphs to *Burnt Norton*, not to *Four Quartets* as a whole.
18 'To the Greek . . .' from 'Second Thoughts about Humanism' (1929), *S.E.*, p. 485n.; 'What poetry should do . . .' from 'The Aims of Poetic Drama', *Adam* XVII.200 (November 1949), p. 12.
19 Cf. 'Note sur Mallarmé et Poe', *Nouvelle Revue Française* XIV.158 (November 1926), p. 525.
20 *P.P.* p. 87.
21 *The Republic* X.616–17.
22 Faber & Faber 'Christmas Books' Catalogue, 1936; dust-jacket of *Collected Poems 1909–1935* as first issued.
23 *P.P.* p. 38.
24 'Introduction' to Paul Valéry, *The Art of Poetry* (New York, 1958), p. xiv.
25 In *P.R. interview* p. 54. See also 'From Poe to Valéry', *C.C.* pp. 34–5.

26 *Ash-Wednesday* was a 'sequence of six poems' according to its dust-jacket. The printer of *Collected Poems 1909–1935* was directed *not* to begin each part of *Burnt Norton* on a new page.
27 *P.P.* p. 38.

9 *Patriot of fire*

1 *The Rock*, p. 82 – the speaker is Wren.
2 'T. S. Eliot Talks about Himself . . .', an interview with John Lehmann, *New York Times Book Review* (29 November 1953), reprinted in *T. S. Eliot: Four Quartets, A Casebook*, ed. Bernard Bergonzi (1969), p. [23].
3 'Last Words', *Criterion* XVIII.71 (January 1939), p. 274.
4 *The Idea of a Christian Society* (1939), pp. 63–4.
5 Ibid. pp. 73–4.
6 Ibid. 'Appendix', p. 96.
7 Letter in Hayward Collection.
8 *The Boke Named The Governour* [1531], book I, ch. xxi; ed. H. H. S. Croft (1883), vol. I, pp. 233–8.
9 Ibid. book I, ch. xix; p. 209.
10 'The Christian Conception of Education', in *Malvern, 1941: the life of the Church and the order of society, being the Proceedings of the Archbishop of York's Conference* (1941), p. 207. See also 'Rudyard Kipling' (1941), *P. P.* pp. 247–50.
11 *S.E.* p. 274.
12 *Purgatorio* I, 115–17.
13 'John Bramhall' (1927), *S.E.* p. 355.
14 'Shakespeare and the Stoicism of Seneca' (1927), *S.E.* pp. 130–1.
15 *S.E.* pp. 131–2.
16 *S.E.* pp. 355–6.
17 There is a fascinating, and rather complicated, relation between this passage of *East Coker* and I. A. Richards' *Science and Poetry* (1926) – a bare hint of it is given in the essay on Bramhall (see *S.E.* pp. 356–7). Richards had noticed a tendency in English poetry, especially in that preceding *The Waste Land*, to confuse human sentiment and natural fact. A certain piquancy is added by his having also praised Eliot's 'complete severance between his poetry and *all* beliefs' – a statement which Eliot found 'incomprehensible' (*S.E.* p. 269).
18 *P.P.* p. 38.
19 'Religion and Literature' (1935), *S.E.* p. 388.
20 See 'Milton' (1936), *P.P.* p. 144. Re TSE's 'vacant interstellar spaces' see ibid. p. 141: 'Here *interlunar* is certainly a stroke of genius, but is merely combined with "vacant" and "cave", rather than giving and receiving life from them.' Eliot was perhaps superimposing upon Milton's image Pascal's 'Le silence éternel de ces espaces infinis m'effraie'.
21 'Prologue', *The Complete Works of St John of the Cross*, trans. and ed. E. Allison Peers (rev. ed., 1953), vol. I, p. 11. John of the Cross (1542–91) was declared 'Doctor of the Church Universal' in Rome in 1926.
22 Ibid. p. 10.

23 In 1926, in his Clark Lectures, 'On the Metaphysical Poetry of the Seventeenth Century' Eliot placed John of the Cross with the *romantic* mystics; but in a 1952 lecture he associated him with Dante, and said: 'the emotion is so directly the consequence of the idea that the personality of the author is somehow annihilated: in experiencing his poems we seem to be in direct relation with what he saw, without any mediation through the personality of the author himself'. 'Scylla and Charybdis', *Agenda* 23, 1–2 (1985), p. 15, originally published in French as delivered in *Annales du Centre Universitaire Méditerranéen*, Nice, V (1951/2), pp. 71–82.

24 *The Idea of a Christian Society*, pp. 28–30. The habit of speaking in a deliberately restricted sense has to be watched for in much of Eliot's writing about the relations between contemporary society and the Christian idea; it can clear away some of its opacity and apparent confusion to recognise that what is put forward as a reflection upon society is really the expression of his religious idea.

25 Now in the Hayward Collection.

26 Introduction to Samuel L. Clemens (Mark Twain), *The Adventures of Huckleberry Finn* (The Cresset Press, 1950), pp. xiv–xv. Another paragraph is of great interest:

> It is Huck who gives the book style. The River gives the book its form. But for the River, the book might be only a sequence of adventures with a happy ending. A river, a very big and powerful river, is the only natural force that can wholly determine the course of human peregrination . . . the river with its strong swift current is the dictator to the raft or to the steamboat. It is a treacherous and capricious dictator. At one season, it may move sluggishly in a channel so narrow that, encountering it for the first time at that point, one can hardly believe that it has travelled already for hundreds of miles, and has yet many hundreds of miles to go; at another season, it may obliterate the low Illinois shore to a horizon of water, while in its bed it runs with a speed such that no man or beast can survive in it. At such times, it carries down human bodies, cattle and houses. At least twice, at St Louis, the western and the eastern shores have been separated by the fall of bridges, until the designer of the great Eads Bridge devised a structure which could resist the floods. . . The river is never wholly chartable; it changes its pace, it shifts its channel, unaccountably; it may suddenly efface a sandbar, and throw up another bar where before was navigable water. (pp. xii–xiii; see also *C.C.* p. 54).

27 The phrase, in TSE's 1918 'Ode [on Independence Day]', *Ara Vos Prec*, may have some reference to the 'Calamus' section of *Leaves of Grass*.

28 'Whitman and Tennyson', *Nation & Athenaeum* XL.11 (18 December 1926), p. 426. Besides the obvious allusion, Whitman's 'Out of the Cradle Endlessly Rocking' is behind *The Dry Salvages* I–II; his 'Passage to India' could be behind III.

29 *P.P.* p. 37.

30 See 'From Poe to Valéry', *C.C. Rote*: the sound of surf breaking (USA).

31 Publishers' Preface to James B. Connolly, *Fishermen of the Banks* (1928), p. viii.

32 *S.W.* p. 167.

33 I find groundless the objections of Donald Davie (and others) to 'emotionless', 'devotionless', 'oceanless', 'erosionless' – especially given his admiration for Hardy, who could go even further, as with 'existlessness' in 'The Voice'. Eliot's are not false coinages, since the language allows one to take away pretty well anything one has just thought of by means of this formation: 'thoughtless', 'loveless', 'waterless', 'painless', 'endless'.

34 New England sailors also figured in the draft of 'Death by Water': that was an unsuccessful attempt to write an equivalent to Dante's Ulysses canto, something successfully achieved in *The Dry Salvages* I–II.

35 *S.E.* p. 258.

36 *George Herbert* (1962), p. 24.

37 'Goethe as the Sage' (1955), *P.P.* p. 226. In his 'Preface' to *Thoughts for Meditation*, selected by N. Gangulee (1951), Eliot said that he attached 'a special value to an anthology which places side by side passages from Christian, Jewish, Moslem, Hindu and Buddhist scriptures and devotional writings':

> They are intended for everyone who is curious about those emotions, and states of soul, which are to be found, so to speak, only beyond the limit of the visible spectrum of human feeling, and which can be experienced only in moments of illumination, or by the development of another organ of perception than that of everyday vision.

'It is salutary', he added, 'to learn how frequently contemplatives of religions and civilizations remote from each other are saying the same thing' – but, 'what they say can only reveal its meaning to the reader who has his own religion of doctrine and dogma in which he believes' (pp. 11–14).

38 *The Geetā*, trans. Shri Purohit Swāmi (new ed., 1942), p. 51. This version, published by Faber & Faber, first appeared in 1935.

39 Cf. Julian of Norwich, *Revelations of Divine Love*, chs 58–60 – quoted from on p. 241 below.

40 From a cutting in the Hayward Collection, from an unidentified newspaper dated 28 May [1948].

41 From TSE's typescript note, signed and dated '14.8.47', attached to a postcard which Charles Olson had sent to Ezra Pound with the comment: 'Here is my Lady that Possum stole.' 'Mr Olson', Eliot recorded, 'is in error. I have never returned to Cape Ann or to Gloucester Mass. since 1915.'

42 'There may be Ministers of the Gospel who do not realize that the music of the phrase, of the paragraph, of the period is an essential constituent of good English prose, and who fail to understand that the life of a reading of Gospel and Epistle in the liturgy is in this music of the spoken word' (TSE, *Sunday Telegraph* no. 98 (16 December 1962), p. 7, as reprinted in *The New English Bible Reviewed*, ed. Dennis Nineham (1965), p. 101). It is interesting to compare Eliot's prayer with the 'Litany for those at Sea' in *Hymns Ancient and Modern* (no. 624).

43 *The Idea of a Christian Society*, p. 59.

44 'What poetry proves about any philosophy is merely its possibility for being lived . . . For poetry . . . is not the assertion that something is true, but the making that truth more fully real to us; it is the creation of a sensuous embodiment. It is the making the Word Flesh . . .' (TSE, 'Poetry and Propaganda', reprinted from *The Bookman* LXX (February 1930), pp. 595–602, in *Literary Opinion in America*, ed. Morton Dauwen Zabel (New York, 3rd ed., 1962), vol. I, p. 106).

45 TSE (mocking a remark in Gerald Heard's *Science in the Making*), in his contribution to *Revelation*, ed. John Baillie and Hugh Martin (1937), p. 7.

46 *The Complete Works of St John of the Cross*, vol. I, p. 441 (see n.21 above).

47 Julian of Norwich, *Revelations of Divine Love*, trans. Clifton Wolters (Harmondsworth, 1966), pp. 165–6. (I have corrected Wolters' 'he has united' to 'he unites').

48 See the chapter 'The Meaning of Initiation' in *Shakespeare's Mystery Play: a study of 'The Tempest'* (1921).

49 *S.E.* p. 264.

50 Charles Smyth, reviewing *The Ferrar Papers* (ed. B. Blackstone), *Criterion* XVIII.71 (January 1939), p. 369.

51 From TSE's unpublished Clark Lectures of 1926 'On the Metaphysical Poetry of the Seventeenth Century'.

52 This phrase is from the version published in *New English Weekly*, where it was part of a line preceding 'Zero summer'.

53 The first draft was more explicit: 'And the speech of the living is wind in dry grass/And the living have no communication with each other'; instead of the second line a later draft has 'The communion of the dead is flame on the wind'.

54 The drafts show that Eliot had the dead in mind as well. Before finding the word 'sacrifice' he wrote 'Water and fire shall rot/The skeletons that we forgot', and, in another version, 'Water and fire deride/The skeletons that we denied.'

55 'What Dante Means to Me', *C.C.* p. 128.

56 Though TSE's 'canto' may give an impression of the supposed smoothness of Italian, Dante's versification is not so utterly regular in its metric. See *Literary Essays of Ezra Pound*, ed. T. S. Eliot (1954), pp. 169–70.

57 *Inferno* XV, 72–3.

58 In a letter to John Hayward, dated 27 August 1942, TSE wrote that he wanted the effect of the 'canto' as a whole to be 'Purgatorial'.

59 *Purgatorio* XIII, 94–6; *Paradiso* VI, 127–42. TSE applied to himself the phrase from the latter passage in his speech accepting an honorary degree at Aix-en-Provence in December 1947 – typescript in Hayward Collection.

60 I am indebted to Professor Kristian Smidt for the information that Eliot told him in a letter in 1961 that 'he was thinking primarily of William Yeats' when he referred to 'a familiar compound ghost'. In the drafts the identification was virtually explicit, and Eliot was afraid, as he told John Hayward, that readers would identify his 'visionary figure' with Yeats, when he did not mean anything so precise as that. See Kristian Smidt, 'T. S. Eliot and W. B. Yeats', *The Importance of Recognition: six chapters on T. S. Eliot* (Tromsø, 1973); Helen Gardner, *The Composition of 'Four Quartets'* (1978), pp. 64–9 and 171–96; also my Appendix D.

61 *S.E.* p. 17 (italics added).

62 'Francis Herbert Bradley' (1927), *S.E.* p. 453.

63 *Dante* (1929), *S.E.* p. 256.

64 'Under Ben Bulben'.

65 Cf. *The Geetā*, p. 25 (see n.38 above).

66 'You know as well as I do', Eliot wrote to Hayward in his letter of 27 August 1942, 'that the dead nettle is the family of flowering plant of which the White Archangel is one of the commonest and closely resembles the stinging nettle and is found in its company. If I wrote "the live nettle and the dead" it would tend to suggest a dead stinging nettle instead of a quite different plant, so I don't see that anything can be done about that.' TSE had similar difficulties with 'hermit crab' – which had to be changed to 'horseshoe crab' – and 'waning dusk', as he revealed in 'Scylla and Charybdis'. It seems to me that in all three cases the difficulty arose from his being intent, not upon the things in them-

selves, but upon the 'metaphysical' associations: not upon the crab but the 'hermit' – which wouldn't do because the hermit-crab has no shell of its own, and so leaves no hint 'of earlier and other creation'; and not upon the direct perception of dawn, but upon the sensations of a mind attuned to the dark night.

67 'The Minor Metaphysicals: from Cowley to Dryden', *The Listener* III.66 (16 April 1930), p. 641. In an earlier talk in the same series TSE had said: 'In its religious sensibility the seventeenth century seems to me the third most interesting period in the history of Christianity; the others being the early period which saw the development of dogma in the Greek and Latin churches, and the thirteenth' ('Thinking in Verse: a survey of early seventeenth-century poetry', *The Listener* III.61 (12 March 1930), p. 442).

68 *Revelations of Divine Love, Recorded by Julian, Anchoress at Norwich*, a version . . . by Grace Warrack (1901), p. 190. The quotations in *Little Gidding* are from the thirteenth revelation (ch. 27): 'Synne is behovabil, but al shal be wel & al shal be wel & al manner of thyng shal be wele' (Warrack, p. 56, n.1); and the fourteenth (ch. 41): ' "I am Ground of thy beseeching: first it is my will that thou have it; and after, I make thee to will it" ' (ibid. p. 84). In the final chapter the Lord repeats ' "I am the Ground of thy beseeching" '; then he answers Julian's desire to learn his meaning – ' "Love was His meaning. Who shewed it thee? Love. What shewed He thee? Love. Wherefore shewed it He? For Love" ' (ibid. p. 202).

69 *Knowledge and Experience* (1964), p. 54.

70 A remark in TSE's letter to Hayward dated 7 September 1942 shows that he intended the echo of a speech of Harry's in *The Family Reunion* (I.ii, 239–46): but the images have been somewhat transvalued.

71 Elizabeth Drew, *T. S. Eliot: the design of his poetry* (New York, 1949), p. 199.

72 *P.P.* p. 87.

73 *Purgatorio* XXVII, 124–42.

74 Letter dated 3 September 1942.

75 *C.C.* p. 38.

76 Cf. 'Preface to 1928 Edition', *S.W.* p. x, and 'Preface' to *For Lancelot Andrewes* (1928).

77 In the first draft version of *Little Gidding* II (that of July 1941) the main action of the 'canto' was to have been a discharging of the burden of remembered personal experience. See my 'The Secret History of *Four Quartets*', *Cambridge Quarterly* VIII. ii (1978), pp. 164–79 – reprinted here as Appendix D.

78 Ezra Pound, Canto CXVI. Pound's sense of Cosmos is, of course, very different from Eliot's, as it seeks to recover the original Greek idea and *praxis*.

79 *S.E.* p. 405.

80 *S.E.* p. 252.

81 *P.P.* p. 188.

82 'Scylla and Charybdis' – from the typescript in the Hayward Collection.

83 The parallel is not altogether exact, but one can see a correspondence between *East Coker*, and 'Gerontion' and the first two parts of *The Waste Land*; between *The Dry Salvages* and the next two parts – especially when one thinks of the full draft version of 'Death by Water'; and then between *Little Gidding* and 'What the Thunder Said'.

10 *The Poet observed*

1 'Comments on ... *The Cocktail Party* ...', *World Review*, new series no. 9 (November 1949), p. 21.
2 *Poetry and Drama* (1951), *P.P.* p. 84.
3 Ibid. p. 85 – the preceding quoted phrase is from p. 82.
4 E. Martin Browne, *The Making of T. S. Eliot's Plays* (Cambridge, 1969), (hereafter Browne), pp. 342–3.
5 Cf. 'Marie Lloyd', *S.E.* p. 458.
6 'The Art of Poetry v: Ezra Pound', *Paris Review* no. 28 (Summer–Fall 1962), p. 37.
7 'Towards a Christian Britain', *The Listener* xxv.639 (10 April 1941), pp. 524–5. In this broadcast talk TSE describes de Foucauld as a man born to wealth and social position who abandoned a life of pleasure and dissipation, first to travel in unexplored French Morocco and Algeria, then having found a vocation for the religious life, to be a missionary in a solitary African outpost. 'His aim was not primarily to convert by teaching, but to *live* the Christian life, alone among the natives ... Almost by an accident, he was killed at his prayers in 1916 by a marauding band.' TSE concluded:
> This is not, as the world judges, a life of striking success. Yet ... I think that it is through such men as Foucauld that the reborn Christian consciousness comes; and I think that from the point of view which we should take, there is no higher glory of a Christian consciousness than that which was here brought into being by a death in the desert.
8 'Some Comments on the Play, taken from the author's private correspondence', *T. S. Eliot's 'The Cocktail Party'*, ed. Nevill Coghill (1974), p. 192.
9 Nevill Coghill, 'An Essay on the Structure and Meaning of the Play', pp. 237–9 (see n. above).
10 *P.R. interview*, p. 61.
11 From the revised first draft as given in Browne, p. 325.
12 *P.P.* p. 84.
13 I am indebted to Philip Vellacott's translation of *Ion*, and to his introduction, in Euripides, *The Bacchae and other plays* (Harmondsworth, 1954).
14 In the Hayward Collection there is a sheet of typescript notes correcting errors in an *Evening Standard* review of *Poetry and Drama*, in which TSE recorded that his own father 'did not want to be a minister (his father would have been highly pleased, I am sure). He wanted to be a painter. He was not the owner of a brickworks. He was Pres. and Chairman of the Hydraulic-Press Brick Co. Inc. which owned brickworks in various parts of the USA.'
15 In discussion with E. Martin Browne – see Browne, p. 286. Cf. Lucasta to Colby in Act III (*C.P.P.* p. 502).
16 See 'Thomas Middleton', *S.E.* pp. 161–70.
17 *P.R. interview*, p. 61.
18 Browne, p. 107.
19 My summary account is based on TSE's synopses as given in Browne, as well as on the printed text.
20 See Browne, pp. 333–5.

21 Browne, p. 310. (I have corrected his 'condemning' to the typescript's 'contemning'.)

22 Browne, p. 329.

23 Browne, pp. 316–17, states that this scene was written after TSE's marriage.

24 Valerie Eliot, in an interview with Timothy Wilson, *Observer* (20 February 1972), p. 21.

25 For TSE's views see: 'Isolated Superiority', *Dial* LXXXIV.1 (January 1928), pp. 4–7; *A.S.G.* pp. 41–3; *Dante* (1929). For Pound's see: 'Credo', *Selected Prose*, ed. William Cookson (1973), p. 53; *Literary Essays of Ezra Pound* (1954), p. 85; *Guide to Kulchur* (new ed., 1952), pp. 294, 299–301.

26 'Yeats', *P.P.* pp. 257–8; *Little Gidding* II.

27 I have synthesised TSE's view of Lawrence from: *A.S.G.* pp. 35–7, 58–61; *The Idea of a Christian Society*, p. 62; 'Foreword' to Father William Tiverton, *D. H. Lawrence and Human Existence* (1951), pp. vii–viii. (The connection between *Burnt Norton* I and the critique in *A.S.G.* of Lawrence's story 'The Shadow in the Rose Garden' is of great interest.)

28 *A.S.G.* pp. 54–8.

29 TSE's view of George Eliot is drawn from: *S.W.* pp. xiii, 43; *A.S.G.* p. 54; *Revelation* ed. John Baillie and Hugh Martin (1937), pp. 4–5; *A Sermon preached in Magdalene College Chapel* (Cambridge, 1948), p. 5.

30 E.g. 'I am aware that prejudice makes me underrate certain authors: I see them rather as public enemies than as subjects for criticism; and I dare say that a different prejudice makes me uncritically favourable to others' (Introduction to Marianne Moore, *Selected Poems* (1935), p. 6). Of 'the artist–aesthetician' in general he wrote, in his Preface to Leone Vivante's *English Poetry . . .* (1950): 'If he himself practises some art, he will be strongly moved to direct other artists to practise, and the public to applaud, those styles that he thinks right for his own time and the immediate future' (p. viii).

31 See letter to P. E. More quoted pp. 11–12 above.

32 *Tess of the D'Urbevilles*, ch. XXIV.

33 The pioneering and still indispensable account is Jane Ellen Harrison's *Prolegomena to the Study of Greek Religion* (Cambridge, 1903, 1908), and *Themis: a study of the social origins of Greek religion* (Cambridge, 1912, 1927).

34 TSE considered Freud's work complementary to that of Frazer in throwing light upon the complexities of the human soul – see 'Lettre d'Angleterre', *Nouvelle Revue Française* XXI.122 (1 November 1923), pp. 622–3 – though his references to it were rare and oblique. His essay on Hamlet (1919), in its latter half which is the original part, is a critical development of Freud's observations in *The Interpretation of Dreams* (1900). That book, together with *Totem and Taboo* (1913) – especially the part dealing with Oedipus and Shakespeare – must surely have contributed to *The Waste Land* at least as much as *The Golden Bough*.

35 Julian of Norwich, *Revelations of Divine Love*, trans. Clifton Wolters (Harmondsworth, 1966), p. 166.

36 'Le Morte Darthur', *Spectator* CLII.5513 (23 February 1934), p. 278. Malory was a 'favourite author' (*A.S.G.* p. 27n.).

37 C. Kerényi, *Eleusis: archetypal image of mother and daughter*, trans. Ralph Mannheim (1967), pp. 84–5, 88. Another, and extraordinarily illuminating interpretation of the Oedipus plays, is to be seen in Pasolini's film.

38 In review of *Le Morte Darthur* (see n.36 above).

39 Aeschylus, *The Oresteian Trilogy*, trans. Philip Vellacott (Harmondsworth, 1956), p. 172.

40 Carlyle, in *Past and Present*, book II, ch. xv, contrasted Abbot Samson's 'practical–devotional' Catholicism of the twelfth century with 'the *Isms* current in these poor days', such as 'Methodism with its eye forever turned on its own navel; asking itself with torturing anxiety of Hope and Fear, "Am I right? am I wrong? Shall I be saved? shall I not be damned?" – what is this, at bottom, but a new phasis of *Egoism*, stretched out into the Infinite; not always the heavenlier for its infinitude!' Cf. Pound's 'I offer for Mr Eliot's reflection the thesis that our time has overshadowed the mysteries by an overemphasis on the individual . . . Eleusis did not distort truth by exaggerating the individual, neither could it have violated the individual spirit' (*Guide to Kulchur* (1952), p. 299).

41 See D. H. Lawrence's discussion of *Hamlet* in 'The Theatre', *Twilight in Italy* – profoundly suggestive; and yet persistently dualistic.

42 *S.W.* p. 166.

Appendix A: About the text of the poems

1 The dust-jacket stated: 'This volume contains all Mr Eliot's poetry that he wishes to preserve, with the exception of *Murder in the Cathedral*.' The Faber & Faber 'Christmas Books' Catalogue, 1936, described it as 'the definitive edition, including *Burnt Norton*'.

2 It is disappointing to find in 1993 that Faber have still not corrected the many faults in *1909–62* (1974), apart from the single instance of 'fishmen' (*W. L.*, 263), even though there have been frequent reprintings. A start was made upon the study of the English text by Robert L. Beare, 'Notes on the Text of T. S. Eliot: variants from Russell Square', *Studies in Bibliography* IX (1957), pp. 21–49.

3 For a fuller account see Daniel H. Woodward, 'Notes on the Publishing History and Text of *The Waste Land*', *Papers of the Bibliographical Society of America* LVIII (July/September 1964), pp. 252–69; (hereafter Woodward, *Casebook*, since my references are to the reprint in *T. S. Eliot: 'The Waste Land', a Casebook*, ed. C. B. Cox and Arnold P. Hinchliffe (1968), pp. 71–90). This needs to be supplemented, and in a few details corrected, by Valerie Eliot's Introduction to *W. L. Drafts*.

4 See *W. L. Drafts*, p. xxiii. (N.B. The text printed with the drafts as that of the Boni and Liveright first edition has been silently 'corrected' in half a dozen places, and fails to observe the correct spacing in half a dozen more. It falls somewhere between the text it purports to be, and the most recent Faber text.)

5 See *W. L. Drafts*, p. xxiv, and Woodward, *Casebook*, p. 75. My dating 'in August' is not certain; but it is supported by the fact that the *Dial* text is slightly further removed from the drafts than that of Boni and Liveright.

6 E.g. the change from Lower to Upper Thames Street at l.260 – the latter is on the wrong side of London Bridge from Billingsgate Fish Market.

7 Woodward, *Casebook*, p. 81.

8 *W. L. Drafts*, p. xxiii.

9 From a letter dated 9 May 1921 quoted in Woodward, *Casebook*, p. 81.

10 See William Marshall, 'The Text of T. S. Eliot's "Gerontion" ', *Studies in Bibliography* IV (1951–2), pp. 213–17.

Appendix B: The drafts of 'The Waste Land'

1 This is a revised version of my review of '*The Waste Land': a facsimile and transcript of the original drafts including the annotations of Ezra Pound,* ed. Valerie Eliot (1971), which appeared as 'Broken Images/Voices Singing' in *Cambridge Quarterly* VI.1 (1972), pp. 45–58.

2 For their correspondence see *The Letters of Ezra Pound,* ed. D. D. Paige, under December 1921 and January 1922 and *The Letters of T. S. Eliot* I: 1898–1922, ed. Valerie Eliot (1988), pp. 497–507. (N.B. Pound's dating of the first of his letters concerning *The Waste Land,* '24 Saturnus, An I', should be read as equivalent to 24 January 1922. An agreement between Pound and Liveright was dated '4 Jan. a.d. 1922' and alternately '4 Saturnus An I' – see Charles Norman, *Ezra Pound* (New York, 1960), p. 253. In March 1922 Pound wrote to H. L. Mencken: 'The Christian Era ended at midnight on Oct. 29–30 of last year. You are now in the year 1 p.s.U.' – meaning *post scriptum Ulysses,* Joyce having finished writing that work on 29 October 1921, by happy chance the day before Pound's own birthday.)

3 One typescript is in the Hayward Collection; another is in the Houghton Library at Harvard; a third is among the *Dial* papers in Yale's Beinecke Library.
communication to Daniel H. Woodward, see Woodward, *Casebook,* p. 75).

4 In a letter in the *Times Literary Supplement* no. 3045 (8 July 1960), p. 433, Eliot wrote: '*Prufrock* was written ... over a period of time in 1910–11, that is to say all that survives in the printed version. I did, I think, in 1912, make some additions to the poem and I am grateful to Mr Aiken for having perceived at once that the additions were of inferior quality. The suppressed parts, however, have not disappeared from view like the script of *The Waste Land;* I am pretty sure that I destroyed them at the time, and I have enough recollection of the suppressed verses to remain grateful to Mr Aiken for advising me to suppress them.' I persist in my harmless speculation in spite of Eliot's being 'pretty sure' he had destroyed the additions. It may be to the point that as published in 1915 'Prufrock' ended with a line of dots, as if another section were to follow.

5 I take this to be the esoteric sense of Eliot's remark that Joyce's 'mythical method' was 'simply a way of controlling, of ordering, of giving a shape and a significance to the immense panorama of futility and anarchy which is contemporary history' – see last paragraph of '*Ulysses,* Order, and Myth' (1923), reprinted in *Selected Prose of T. S. Eliot,* ed. Frank Kermode (1975), pp. 177–8.

6 Conrad Aiken, Prefatory Note to 'An Anatomy of Melancholy', as reprinted in *Sewanee Review* LXXIV.1 (January–March 1966), p. 189.

7 See 'Introduction', *W. L. Drafts,* p. xxii.

8 See 'Editorial Notes', *W. L. Drafts,* p. 129.

9 'On a Recent Piece of Criticism', *Purpose* X.2 (April/June 1938), pp. 92–3.

Appendix C: The Christian philosopher and politics between the wars

1 These lines appear only in the Acting Edition of *Murder in the Cathedral* (Canterbury, 1935), p. 27. The speech from which they are cut is on p. 63 of the first Faber edition, and p. 269 of *C.P.P.*

2 See 'Introduction by T. S. Eliot' to Josef Pieper's *Leisure the Basis of Culture* (1952), pp. 11–17.

3 (4th ed., 1950), p. 152.

4 *Criterion* IV.2 (April 1926), p. 222.

5 *Criterion* VII.4 (June 1928), p. 3.

6 'The Literature of Fascism', *Criterion* VIII.31 (December 1928), pp. 280–90.

7 'Commentary', *Criterion* VIII.32 (April 1929), pp. 378–80.

8 'Commentary', *Criterion* XI.45 (July 1932), p. 681. As regards the British Fascism of Oswald Mosley: in *Criterion* VII.3 (March 1928), pp. 196–7, Eliot dismissed its programme as 'a sentimental Anglo-fascism' from which he wished England to be preserved; in X.40 (April 1931), p. 483, he objected to Mosley himself for his lack of 'profound moral convictions'. In a letter headed 'The Blackshirts' in *The Church Times* (2 February 1934), p. 116, he raised the question 'whether the Christian and Catholic idea and the Fascist idea are, in themselves, compatible', by inviting 'every Catholic who inclines to sympathize with Fascist politics' to meditate upon these propositions extracted from Mussolini's *The Political and Social Doctrine of Fascism*: (1) 'War alone brings up to its highest tension all human energy, and puts the stamp of nobility upon the people who have the courage to meet it.' (2) 'Absolute monarchy has been, and can never return, any more than blind acceptance of ecclesiastical authority.' (3) 'Fascism conceives of the State as an absolute.' To anyone acquainted with his writings, Eliot's opposition to these principles should be self-evident: they appear to have been selected as the exact contrary of what he would maintain.

9 *The Christian News-Letter* no. 44 (28 August 1940), p. [2]. For Eliot's various remarks on Maurras see also: *Athenaeum* no. 4657 (1 August 1919), p. 680; *Times Literary Supplement* (28 October 1920), p. 703; 'The *Action Française*, M. Maurras and Mr Ward', *Criterion* VII.3 (March 1928), pp. 195–203; 'The Literature of Fascism', *Criterion* VIII.31 (December 1928), especially pp. 288–90; *S.E.* pp. 480, 499; dedication to *Dante* (1929); *Aspects de la France et du Monde* II.8 (Paris, 25 April 1948), p. 6; *Time and Tide* XXXIV.3 (17 January 1953), p. 82; *C.C.* pp. 17, 142–3.

10 'John Bramhall' (1927), first collected in *For Lancelot Andrewes;* quotation from *S.E.* p. 360.

11 See *Criterion* XIII.53 (July 1934), pp. 628–30.

12 'Catholicism and International Order', *Essays Ancient and Modern* (1936), pp. 113–14. Cf. *The Idea of a Christian Society* (1939), p. 63:

> To the quick and simple organisation of society for ends which, being only material and worldly, must be as ephemeral as worldly success, there is only one alternative. As political philosophy derives its sanction from ethics, and ethics from the truth of religion, it is only by returning to the eternal source of truth that we can hope for any social organisation which will not, to its ultimate destruction, ignore some essential aspect of reality. The term 'democracy', as I have said again and again, does not contain enough positive content to stand alone against the forces that you dislike – it can easily be transformed by them. If you will not have God (and He is a jealous God) you should pay your respects to Hitler or Stalin.

13 Reprinted from *Authors Take Sides* (1937) in *And I Remember Spain*, ed. Murray A. Sperber (1974), pp. 203, 206.

14 *Criterion* XVI.63 (January 1937), p. 290.

15 *Criterion* XVIII.70 (October 1938), pp. 58–9.

16 In his definition of his critical attitude in *Criterion* VII.4 (June 1928), p. 3, Eliot remarked: 'In religious controversies, again, *The Criterion* can take no side. It can only examine the ideas involved, and their implications, their consequences and their relations to the general problems of civilization; but at the point where intellectual analysis stops, and emotional conviction begins, our commission ends.'

17 *Criterion* XVI.65 (July 1937), pp. 669–70. For a reply by Herbert Read see XVII.66 (October 1937), pp. 123–4.

18 Eliot's alleged anti-semitism was set in its proper perspective by George Orwell, in a letter dated 29 October 1948:

> It is nonsense ... about Eliot being anti-semitic. Of course you can find what would now be called anti-semitic remarks in his early work, but who didn't say such things at that time? One has to draw a distinction between what was said before and after 1934. Of course all these nationalistic prejudices are ridiculous, but disliking Jews isn't intrinsically worse than disliking Negroes or Americans or any other block of people. In the early '20s Eliot's anti-semitic remarks were about on a par with the automatic sneer one casts at Anglo-Indian colonels in boarding houses. On the other hand if they had been written after the persecutions began they would have meant something quite different. (*Collected Essays, Journalism and Letters of George Orwell*, ed. Sonia Orwell and Ian Angus (1968), vol. IV, p. 450).

The remarks in his early work amount only to the allusions in 'Gerontion' ('And the jew' – later editions read 'Jew' – 'squats on the window sill, the owner'); 'Burbank with a Baedeker: Bleistein with a Cigar', in which the latter is identified as 'Chicago Semite Viennese', and mention of the Rialto is followed by 'The rats are underneath the piles./ The jew is underneath the lot' – later editions again give the capital letter; and to these we can now add 'Dirge' in *W. L. Drafts*. These betray a rather more virulent form than Orwell's letter might suggest of the anti-semitism endemic in Christian–Capitalist Europe, but his main point holds. It might be added that the stupidity of this kind of prejudice is that it perceives a whole race as one type of person, when that type in fact exists in all races, and when all types are to be found in that race.

The first two of those poems were published by 1920; the third was never published by Eliot. There is just one other remark which can legitimately be construed as anti-semitic, and its date is right on Orwell's dividing line. In the course of the first of his lectures given at the University of Virginia in spring 1933, and published in February 1934 as *After Strange Gods*, Eliot said:

> You are hardly likely to develop tradition except where the bulk of the population is relatively so well off where it is that it has no incentive or pressure to move about. The population should be homogeneous; where two or more cultures exist in the same place they are likely either to be fiercely self-conscious or both to become adulterate. What is still more important is unity of religious background; and reasons of race and religion combine to make any large number of free-thinking Jews undesirable. There must be a proper balance between urban and rural, industrial and agricultural development. And a spirit of excessive tolerance is to be deprecated.

The notorious sentence is very like something which George Eliot has Mordecai say in *Daniel Deronda* (book VI, ch. 47):

> 'What is the citizenship of him who walks among a people he has no hearty

kindred and fellowship with, and has lost the sense of brotherhood with his own race? It is a charter of selfish ambition and rivalry in low greed. He is an alien in spirit, whatever he may be in form; he sucks the blood of mankind, he is not a man. Sharing in no love, sharing in no subjection of the soul, he mocks at all.'

His Jewish interlocutors don't altogether agree with Mordecai, and George Eliot doesn't altogether expect her readers to agree either. My point is this, that Eliot's sentence is not anti-semitic if you put it in George Eliot's context. Moreover, his own context is rather nearer to hers than to Hitler's *Mein Kampf.* Nevertheless, the remark coincided with the establishment of the dictatorship of Hitler and the Nazi party in Germany – this had been going on throughout 1933, and was completed well before the end of the year – and the persecution of the Jews in Germany had already been initiated with the proclamation of a national boycott of Jewish shops on 1 April 1933. Set in that context of political events Eliot's remark becomes dangerously like Nazi propaganda. There is no reason to suppose that he was thinking of Germany when he made it – but it is precisely that which makes the remark so wrong. Eliot himself realised this, and refused to allow *After Strange Gods* to be reprinted. The reason, as he told J. M. Cameron, according to the latter's letter to the *New Statesman* of 7 October 1966, was that 'he regretted the tone and content of the political remarks contained therein'. He might have seen his error even as the book was being published, for early in 1934 he drafted the scene which ends part 1 of *The Rock*, in which the totalitarian ideologies are satirised, and the Blackshirts chant anti-semitic abuse at the Chorus when it asks them: 'Are you obedient to the Law of GOD?/Are you with those who reverence the Temple?' In *Notes Towards the Definition of Culture* (1948) Eliot returned to the preoccupations of the passage from *After Strange Gods,* and attempted to clear his thought of the accidental taint of anti-semitism. To a paragraph on pages 69–70 he added the note:

Since the diaspora, and the scattering of Jews amongst peoples holding the Christian Faith, it may have been unfortunate both for these peoples and for the Jews themselves, that the culture-contact between them has had to be within those neutral zones of culture in which religion could be ignored: and the effect may have been to strengthen the illusion that there can be culture without religion.

In the 1962 edition the note was rewritten as follows:

It seems to me highly desirable that there should be close culture-contact between devout and practising Christians and devout and practising Jews. Much culture-contact in the past has been within those neutral zones of culture in which religion can be ignored, and between Jews and Gentiles both more or less emancipated from their religious traditions. The effect may have been to strengthen the illusion that there can be culture without religion. In this context I recommend to my readers two books by Professor Will Herberg published in New York: *Judaism and Modern Man* . . . and *Protestant-Catholic-Jew.*

The Preface to that edition speaks of changes in his view on social and political matters, or of 'the way in which I would express my views': the changes I have been observing would appear to be of the latter kind. Clearly he was convinced that the point he wanted to make was not anti-semitic, and he didn't mean to retract it; but the expression of it in *After Strange Gods* had been open to misunderstanding in the light of the Nazi persecution of the Jews, and that he tried to atone for, by not reprinting that book, and to correct in the more careful formulations of *Notes Towards the Definition of Culture.* It does seem to me that, whatever else is to be said about it, his thought cannot justly be associated with Hitler's anti-semitism.

19 *Criterion* III.10 (January 1925), p. 163.
20 Review of Wyndham Lewis' *The Lion and the Fox* (1927) in *Twentieth Century Verse* no. 6/7 (November/December 1937), pp. [6–9].
21 'Foreword' to new edition of Lewis' *One-Way Song* (1960), p. 10.
22 Cf. the allusion to Plato's *Republic* (book ix 592 A-B) in *W. L. Drafts*, p. 31 and editorial notes pp. 127–8: ' "you mean . . . the city whose home is in the ideal; for I think that it can be found nowhere on earth." "Well," said I, "perhaps there is a pattern of it laid up in heaven for him who wishes to contemplate it and so beholding to constitute himself its citizen . . . The politics of this city only will be his and of none other." '
23 *Criterion* II.7 (April 1924), p. 235.
24 *The Idea of a Christian Society* (1939), p. 20.
25 Broadcast talk 'The Church's Message to the World' (1937), as appended to *The Idea of a Christian Society*, p. 94.
26 *The Rock* (1934), p. 46.
27 *Criterion* XVIII.71 (January 1939), p. 272.
28 *New English Weekly* XV.22 (14 September 1939), p. 291.

Appendix D: The secret history of 'Four Quartets'

1 A review of Helen Gardner, *The Composition of 'Four Quartets'* (1978), from *Cambridge Quartely* VIII. ii (1978), pp. 164–79.
2 This point was taken by Helen Gardner and corrected in the 1980 edition.
3 The American publishers however collected all of Eliot's poems up to 1950 in *The Complete Poems and Plays 1909–1950* (New York, 1952).

Appendix E: Artful voices: Eliot's dramatic verse

1 Originally published in *Agenda* XVIII. 4 – XIX. 1 (1981), pp. 112–19.
2 'A Dialogue on Dramatic Poetry' (1928), *S.E.* p. 46.
3 *P.P.* p. 82.

Index

Index

Note: well-known works are indexed by author, not by title